ON PAEDOPHILIA

ON PAEDOPHILIA

Cosimo Schinaia

Translated by Antonella Sansone

KARNAC

Originally published as *Pedofilia Pedofilie* (Turin: Bollati Boringhieri, 2001)
English translation first published in 2010 by
Karnac Books Ltd
118 Finchley Road
London NW3 5HT

Copyright © 2010 by Cosimo Schinaia
Original text © Cosimo Schinaia
English translation © Antonella Sansone

The rights of Cosimo Schinaia and Antonella Sansone to be identified respectively as the authors and the translator of this work have been asserted in accordance with §§ 77 and 78 of the Copyright Design and Patents Act 1988.

All rights reserved. No part of this publication may be reproduced, stored in a retrieval system, or transmitted, in any form or by any means, electronic, mechanical, photocopying, recording, or otherwise, without the prior written permission of the publisher.

British Library Cataloguing in Publication Data

A C.I.P. for this book is available from the British Library

ISBN-13: 978-1-85575-589-5

Typeset by Vikatan Publishing Solutions (P) Ltd., Chennai, India

Printed in Great Britain

www.karnacbooks.com

To Manuela, Jacopo and Lorenzo

Then you will know the truth and the truth will set you free.

John 8: 32

Healthy mental growth seems to depend on truth as the living organism depends on food. If it is lacking or deficient the personality deteriorates.

W.R. Bion, *Transformations*

CONTENTS

ACKNOWLEDGEMENTS	ix
ABOUT THE AUTHOR AND CONTRIBUTORS	xi
FOREWORD Donald Campbell	xiii
INTRODUCTION TO THE ENGLISH EDITION	xxi
INTRODUCTION	xxxi
CHAPTER ONE Social and cultural aspects which foster paedophilic behaviour	1
CHAPTER TWO Myth and paedophilia *Clara Pitto and Cosimo Schinaia*	31

CHAPTER THREE
Fairy tales and paedophilic fantasies 57
Franca Pezzoni and Cosimo Schinaia

CHAPTER FOUR
Notes on the history of paedophilia 89

CHAPTER FIVE
Paedophilia in medical and psychiatric thought 115
Paolo F. Peloso and Cosimo Schinaia

CHAPTER SIX
Psychoanalysis and paedophilia 139

CHAPTER SEVEN
Contributions to the definition and typology of paedophilic personalities and behaviours through fiction 165
Paolo F. Peloso, Cosimo Schinaia and Giuseppina Tabò

CHAPTER EIGHT
The paedophilic relationship 189

CHAPTER NINE
A case of paedophilic perversion 219

CHAPTER TEN
A case of paedophilic perversity 235
Luisella Peretti and Cosimo Schinaia

CHAPTER ELEVEN
The working group 249
Luisella Peretti and Cosimo Schinaia

BIBLIOGRAPHY 265

INDEX 291

ACKNOWLEDGEMENTS

I am grateful to Antonella Mancini for her valuable suggestions on the history of childhood in the Middle Ages, Uliano Lucas for helping me in the search for photographic texts, Giovanna Terminiello Rotondi for her passionate discussions on artists, and Aristo Ciruzzi for his cinematographic advice.

I wish to acknowledge gratefully those who accurately read the original text of *Pedofilia Pedofilie* before it went to press: Anna Berardi, Stefano Bolognini, Franco De Masi, Marie Antoinette Ferroni, Costantino Gilardi, Gianni Guasto, and Alberto Lampignano. Special thanks to Francesco Barale for his beautiful preface to the Italian edition.

I should like to thank Luiz Meyer for his encouragement, and Carlos Fishman and Paola Franciosi for their active interest in the publication of this book in English.

I am especially grateful also to translator and author Antonella Sansone and editor Anna Nilsen for the patience, sagacity, competence and generosity with which they helped me achieve the project of publication of the English edition.

ABOUT THE AUTHOR AND CONTRIBUTORS

Cosimo Schinaia is a psychoanalyst and psychiatrist, Director of the Mental Health Centre of Central Genoa. He is an ordinary member of the Italian Psychoanalytical Society and a full member of the International Psychoanalytical Association. He is the author of several scientific articles published in both Italian and foreign journals: *Rivista di Psicoanalisi, Revista de Psicoanálisis* (Argentina), *Psiche, Psicoterapia e Scienze Umane, Gli Argonauti, L'Information Psychiatrique*. He is copy editor of *Psyche*, the journal of the Italian Psychoanalytical Society. His previous books are *Dal Manicomio alla Città: L'Altro Presepe di Cogoleto* (Bari: Laterza, 1997) and *Il Cantiere delle Idee*, (Genoa: La Clessidra, 1998). He deals predominantly with the psychoanalysis of serious pathologies, the relationship between psychoanalysis and psychiatry, and the communication between psychoanalysis and other disciplines.

Paolo F. Peloso is a psychiatrist and criminologist, and Director of Mental Health Centre district 9 of the Mental Health Department in the Genoa Azienda Sanitaria Locale 3.

Luisella Peretti is a psychoanalytically oriented group psychotherapist and psychiatrist in Mental Health Centre district 13, Mental Health Department, Genoa ASL3.

Franca Pezzoni is a psychoanalytically oriented psychotherapist and psychiatrist in Mental Health Centre district 11, Mental Health Department, Genoa ASL3.

Clara Pitto is a psychologist and psychoanalytically oriented psychotherapist in Mental Health Centre district 12, Mental Health Department, Genoa ASL3.

Giuseppina Tabò is a psychiatrist in Mental Health Centre district 12, Mental Health Department, Genoa ASL3. She is an associate member of the Italian Psychoanalytical Society.

FOREWORD

Donald Campbell

Introduction

The report of a paedophilic act may arouse at a conscious level profound pity for the victim, and disgust and violent retaliatory wishes towards the often demonised perpetrator. At a deeper, perhaps preconscious level, there may be a pang of guilt about the failure to protect the sexually vulnerable and immature child from the sexually mature adult. At an even deeper, unconscious level, there may be a hint of primal terror in response to the breach of a timeless foundation of society, namely the maintenance of the sexual boundary between the generations. The paedophilic act is difficult to think about because it disturbs our normal orientation to reality. It is not uncommon for us to defend against these strong, disturbing feelings and fantasies at a conscious, preconscious, and unconscious level by projection, denial and repression. Even psychoanalysts, with our special interest in the unconscious, have written relatively little about paedophilia. Cosimo Schinaia's book *On Paedophilia* is an exception. It is an impressive, scholarly, and much needed addition to psychoanalytic literature on this neglected subject.

In his Introduction, Cosimo Schinaia responds to the meagre psychoanalytic bibliography on paedophilia by asking: "Why have psychoanalysts not been interested in the issue of paedophilia, and specifically in the psychopathology of the paedophile?" He not only proceeds to address that question, but through the eleven chapters of his book Dr. Schinaia and his five colleagues Paolo F. Peloso, Luisella Peretti, Franca Pezzoni, Clara Pitto and Giuseppina Tabò proceed to deepen and broaden our knowledge of the psychopathology of the paedophile.

One source of the resistance to the study and understanding of paedophilia lies in the nature of the paedophilic act itself. The disturbing impact of the paedophilic act undermines our orientation to reality, and hence to thinking and writing about paedophilia. Psychoanalysts view resistance as a primary source of understanding. In response to Dr. Schinaia's initial question, I will focus on a particular type of paedophilic act, namely one that projects the paedophile's own infantile trauma into its child victim. For over 30 years I worked at the Portman Clinic, a National Health Service outpatient facility in London, where we assessed and treated those patients who were violent or delinquent, or who suffered from a perversion. During that time I treated paedophiles in individual psychoanalytic psychotherapy, usually on a once a week basis. I found that the exploration of the disturbing impact of the act of child abuse on my patients and on me in the countertransference led to progress in their treatment and deepened my understanding of paedophilia.

Paedophilia is distinguished from other perversions by virtue of the fact that the paedophile fundamentally attacks generational difference. Generational difference along with gender distinction, which it predates, are the bedrock of reality (Chassequet-Smirgel, 1985, pp. 1–12). I have found from my experience of treating different types of perversions that paedophilia often underpins other perversions. Early self-object differentiation, before the recognition and enforcement of an incest barrier, leads to a sense of a nurturing Breast and a protecting Other as having qualities and capacities that the infant does not possess. Acute or cumulative trauma may arise when parental intrusion or deprivation inflicts physical or psychological pain. It is not uncommon for the victim to reconstitute itself by identification with the perpetrator of the trauma, and then by inflicting pain on dependent and more vulnerable objects. When the aggression behind that identification is erotised, that is, when the aggression is converted into sadism, the foundations are laid for a paedophilic sexual orientation. However, the adult perpetrator's shame about being abused as a child (Campbell, 2008), or their guilt about sexually abusing children, often leads to repression, denial and dissociation.

Child abuse and doubt

While grooming his or her child victim the paedophile fosters the impression that they are the child's best friend or special companion. The child victim's expectation is radically contradicted in the sexual climax of the seduction. Reality was not what it appeared to be. When a child is sexually abused, this contradiction of expectation amounts to a global betrayal.

The first moment of doubt during seduction occurs when the child realises that the adult or parent it trusts will not keep it safe. It is a moment when the hope of parental love and trust, that they can be depended upon to ensure security and safety, is shattered. When generational and sexual barriers are breached and the child's physical integrity is violated by a paedophilic act, Oedipal relationships are turned upside down. The mind of the seducer becomes incomprehensible and the original, expectable object is destroyed. The victim is left without a trusting orientation to the mind of the other within which to find a representation of itself. This first betrayal shatters the "known" reflecting object; one of the building blocks upon which internal representations are built.

The mind of the other that inflicted pain is viewed as split between loving and hating parts, and the victim is left in a state of confusion and doubt. If the victim becomes a paedophile and seeks analytic treatment, he or she will project these contradictory parts into the transference, in such a way that the analyst will, in turn, feel confused and in doubt about what he hears. This affects the analyst's capacity to think about the patient and trust the veracity of what the patient says.

The second betrayal of trust occurs *after* the child was abused. If the parents ignore, minimise, or deny the physical and psychic reality of the child's abuse, the child feels that its parent has betrayed its trust that the parent will represent reality, and this reinforces the child's sense of utter aloneness and fear that it cannot be found by another's imagination or belief. Regardless of who abuses the child, the child feels that its trust in the parent has been betrayed. At a fundamental level, the child blames its parent for not protecting its body from pain and its mind from doubt and confusion. Lack of trust breeds more doubt. The child's experience of being abused shatters its trust in its parents to represent reality, and to provide meaning for experience. In order for trust to be re-established parents must "be able to represent to the child a deep, an almost somatic conviction that there is a meaning to what they are doing" (Erikson, 1977, p. 24). When the parents, or another caring adult, fail to provide meaning for the abuse, motivation to conceptualise an abusive experience by the victim is undermined and replaced by reliance upon action to resolve traumatic experiences.

The experience of being abused fundamentally challenges one's reliance upon internal perception of experience and sense of self. The victim must choose between what he or she "knows" as reality and a contradictory and false reality represented by those who minimise or deny reality. It is a choice between reality and psychosis based on a denial of reality. It is not uncommon for those who have been abused to preserve their orientation to reality outside their abusive experiences by disavowing abusive experiences and identifying with the aggressor. The self that was abused has to be denied and replaced by a false self that was not betrayed and abused. This process is similar to that in the hysterics described by Brenman (1985), who "change identities in order to destroy the intuitive knowledge of what is real and true" (p. 427). While I have focused on the interpersonal consequences of abuse in terms of the breakdown in trust, and the intrapsychic consequences in terms of the disturbance of the victim's orientation to reality and dissociated mental states, I now want to turn to another consequence of abuse that it less frequently written about, namely physical pain.

Child abuse, pain and the splitting of the ego

There are, of course, different types of childhood abuse. For instance, the child's visual exposure to parental intercourse may trigger an overwhelming sexual excitement and anxiety, but the child's body has not been directly involved in the seduction. However, abuse which painfully transgresses the child's sexual body barrier is of a different order because it alters the child's relationship to its body. As Blass and Simon (1994) remind us: "Seduction, the actual physical act of assault, reminds us that there is 'a body'; that over and beyond the construction of our mind, there is actuality. There is a history of experience registered in us in interaction with, but also beyond, our creative fantasies regarding it" (p. 692).

If, while walking barefoot in the dark, we step on an upturned drawing pin, we may feel the pin, but it is our body which is hurting us. The drawing pin causes our pain, but it is our body that is the source of pain (Scarry, 1993). For the person in pain there is nothing so vibrantly certain as their pain. However, in spite of the sufferer's certainty, the observer can never know the victim's pain. Pain cannot be objectively denied or confirmed (Scarry, 1993, p. 4). The sufferer is to some extent alone with their pain: they are dependent upon another's belief that they are *in* pain, and the other's willingness or capacity to *imagine* the nature of their pain.

Pain "to the individual experiencing it is overwhelmingly present, more emphatically real than any other human experience, and yet is almost invisible to anyone else, unfelt, and unknown" (*ibid.*, p. 51). Because the other can never know the victim's pain, there is always an element of doubt in the mind of the listener. Pain cannot be denied or confirmed (*ibid.*, p. 4). The victim may have the fantasy that he can overcome the other's doubt about the victim's pain by projecting pain via an action on the other. The original victim, now the perpetrator, may believe that the doubting other, now the victim, is experiencing the perpetrator's pain. This is, of course, a fallacy. The unknowability of another's pain means there is an inevitable isolation that leaves the sufferer alone and the observer in doubt. The experience of being doubted or disbelieved contributes to a network of expectations that what the victim/perpertrator says will not be believed by internal or external objects.

Pain also destroys language. Severe pain reduces us to presymbolic screams, cries and groans. Language, which enables us to communicate self experience to others, is replaced by sounds which predate speech. Although pain is history and may, more than any other experience, inform behaviour and procedural memory, pain also overwhelms the victim's attempts to conceptualise pain.

The core of the representational process, the capacity to represent bodily states, is undermined by our response to pain. We may mobilise splitting mechanisms to defend against pain. "When there is physical pain, a high degree of narcissistic cathexis of the painful place occurs", observes Freud (1926). He goes on: "This cathexis continues to increase and tends, as it were, to empty the ego" (p. 171). The narcissistic cathexis of pain occurs at the expense of the development of a cohesive sense of self and investment in the environment. When this process is excessive it creates a split between a hyper-cathected body on the one hand, and an "empty ego" and objects on the other hand. When pain during abuse is defended against by creating splits between the mind and body, the process of conceptualising sexually traumatic experience is undermined. This process is similar to that experienced by hysterics. The paedophile I just referred to said it was "not forgetting, just not there to forget".

Pain is often experienced as destroying a trustworthy, taken-for-granted, physically, sexually and narcissistically gratifying body and leaving us frightened, helpless and confused with an unpredictable, attacking, alien body. After a painful abuse, failure to mourn the loss of a secure internal representation of the body and physical damage consolidates the splitting which is first engendered by pain. As a result of this splitting process, we may also react to the pain by disavowing our body and viewing it as "not me" or "against me" (Scarry, 1993). In this way pain further undermines attempts to conceptualise experience. In order to avoid the remembrance of pain in abuse, the victim is likely to repress memories of seduction. A paedophile told me about his experience of being abused by saying: "I know something happened, but I don't know what happened." In his case, the splitting that resulted from this internal disavowal was reinforced by the perpetrator's disavowal of his pain.

A paedophile's narcissistic cathexis of his body is intensified by his anxiety about its vulnerability to pain. Paedophiles cathect objects (boys and young adolescents) insofar as they provide relief from anxiety. In order for an abused paedophile to feel safe and powerful, they are likely to sexualise the rage about their pain and sadistically seduce children. In this way, the original trauma is reversed by doing to a child what had been done to them.

Ferenczi observed splitting of the ego as a consequence of childhood rape when he maintained that "it seems likely that a *psychotic splitting off* of a part of the personality occurs under the influence of shock" (1930, p. 121). Freud himself never stopped considering the impact that actual seduction had on psychic development. In one of his last papers, "Splitting of the Ego in the Process of Defence" (1940b), Freud also identified splitting of the ego that occurs as a defence against the trauma of sexual abuse. Today the link between childhood sexual abuse and dissociative states is well documented (Davies & Frawley, 1994; Mollon, 1998).

A paedophile, who was my analytic patient, described his abusive behaviour as the terror and manic triumph of an omnipotent infant. "No one can stop my abuse. The abuse is out of control. I'm a baby." Ferenczi (1933) observed that in an effort to defend themselves against hurtful and dangerous adults, sexually abused children can develop instantaneously the emotional and intellectual maturity of an adult, which he referred to as *traumatic progression of a precocious maturity*. He linked this phenomenon to the typical dream of the wise baby in which a newly-born child talks wisely to the adults. "The fear of the uninhibited, almost mad adult changes the child, so to speak, into a psychiatrist and, in order to become one and to defend himself against dangers coming from people without self-control, he must know how to identify himself completely with them" (Ferenczi, 1933, p. 229). The wise baby, paradoxically, can't be a normal baby because it doesn't know what it thinks. And, without an alternative to the mad abusing adult to relate to, the wise baby becomes the object it fears—a paedophile.

In an analytic session with a paedophile the analyst is subject to the same projections as the child victim. The experience and understanding of those projections is a valuable source of information about the nature and function of the paedeophilic act for that paedophile patient. Cosimo Schinaia's book is another indispensable resource. As Dr. Schinaia shows, only a multidisciplinary approach can begin to address the complexity of paedophilia. The historical, sociological, mythical and psychoanalytical approach represented in *On Paedophilia* casts a welcome light into the darkness of paedophilia.

INTRODUCTION TO THE ENGLISH EDITION

When the devil strokes you, he wants your soul.

—Old Italian saying

In his erudite and flattering introduction to the Italian first edition of *Pedofilia Pedofilie*, Francesco Barale called it a treatise on paedophilia. Although I understand the reasons that led him to express himself in these terms (such as the attempt to fill a real scientific void on such an incandescent subject and the extent of the topics covered), I find it difficult to agree with this definition. On the contrary, I conceived *Pedofilia Pedofilie* as a proposed research route, a *work in progress*, a colourful text in motion, which is thus characterised by features that are far from the plainness and systematisation typical of a treatise, which can in some ways be a dangerous Procrustean bed tending to pigeon-hole unique and specific phenomena by levelling them off and flattening them.

An urgent need for deeper study of some of the topics touched on in the book has manifested itself in the different venues in which it has been presented and discussed. These topics include the psychopathological differences between paedophilia and incest, the characteristics that distinguish and differentiate female paedophilia from male paedophilia, as well as the differences existing between the paedophilic relationship of a boy child and an adolescent and that of a boy child and a girl child; and would certainly deserve to be sounded out. In relation to these topics, I refer the reader to future in-depth studies.

I have taken the opportunity to make the bibliographic studies more complete, and to give more depth to some concepts and reflections, having realised that since *Pedofilia Pedofilie* came out, interest has been growing in the social phenomenon called paedophilia as well as in the pathology of paedophilic behaviours. At the 2004 IPA congress in New Orleans a panel was created on the topic "Paedophilia: its Metapsychology and Place in Contemporary Culture", with contributions from Carlos Fishman, Luiz Meyer and Cosimo Schinaia. At the 2005 IPA congress in Rio de Janeiro, one of the leading introductory papers, given by Luiz Meyer, dealt with the topic "Trauma and Paedophilia", and the panel "Traumatic Violence and Sexualisation in Paedophilia" was created, with contributions from Franco De Masi, Alain Gibeault, Luiz Meyer and Cosimo Schinaia. In 2004 the volume *The Mind of the Paedophile: Psychoanalytic Perspectives* was published, edited by Charles W. Socarides and Loretta R. Loeb. Lastly, in 2007 an article by Franco De Masi, "The Paedophile and his Inner World: Theoretical and Clinical Considerations on the Analysis of a Patient" was published in the *International Journal of Psychoanalysis*.

Unfortunately when the first Italian edition came out, it was followed by sensationalist news items which demonstrated the confusion that still surrounds the phenomenon of paedophilia. This is why it appears to be even more necessary to face up to it with scientific attention and relational sensitivity, without being overwhelmed by easy emotional rejections, but also without assuming excessively and cynically detached attitudes.

In this new foreword I shall mainly dwell on three aspects which need more study in depth, although they have already been tackled.

The fear of paedophilia

In September 2001 the French Minister with responsibility for family affairs released a survey according to which paedophilia was the main source of concern for French people. This book consistently deepens the communicative dynamics by which even through the mass media the paedophile has become the plague-spreader or the werewolf of our days. The witch-hunt and the media's emphasis have led to a projective directing of the spotlight onto the phenomenon of paedophilia, allowing the denial of underlying micro-phenomena such as a lack of attention to and any sense of responsibility for children, a certain cultural "infantolatry" (idolatry of children), and non-acceptance of the passage of time and consequently of generational differences. Nevertheless, I believe that it might be useful to linger over some ethological aspects generating the fear of paedophilia, which necessarily come to swing with the defensive aspects already described.

Some eminent palaeontologists, such as Stephen J. Gould and Richard Leakey, have pointed out that the human being shows some evident neoteny, in other words, some morphologically functional features typical of youth which are still present in adulthood. For instance, due to the hypertrophy of its cranial volume and having to contend with a precise anatomical limitation—the diameter of the birth canal—our species undertakes premature birth. It follows that a human newborn's cranial volume is about 20% of its adult size, while in anthropomorphic primates such as chimpanzees and gorillas, it is 50%. With regard to human beings, we can talk about deferred encephalic development (Boncinelli, 2000).

In any case, whether we believe in the hypothesis of neoteny or consider it a theory far from being well grounded, it is certainly true that individuals of our species are more immature at birth and thus need a more articulated repertoire of parental care than other anthropomorphic species. Moreover, human individuals develop over a longer period of time, and consequently their period of socialisation is significantly longer. This would explain adults' tendency (desire) to care for the child, while we see in the child the disjunction between the possibility of desire and the impossibility of satisfying it. According to this hypothesis the human being would be virtuous in parental care, but this would have the inevitable consequence of being particularly sensitive to immature forms of such care, in other words vulnerable (passionate) to the baby's charm. (Marchesini, 2001, 2002).

Paedophilia would represent the perverse transformation of the parental competence to care for babies, so that according to these theories the feeling of repulsion for the paedophile and his behaviours would not simply be a cultural and moral attitude, but a kind of species-specific reflex designed to protect and preserve the human species. The "naturalness" of the anti-paedophile attitude and consequently the intrinsic "unnaturalness" of paedophile behaviours can make us understand—though certainly not justify—most analysts' tendency to refuse to treat paedophiles and the consequent rationalisation of such resistance.

Violence on television and violent attitudes

A study published in *Science* (Johnson et al., 2002) contradicts the cliché that violence on television has a significant influence only on children. The study highlights the negative effect on young adults as well. In addition, this research has built up the hypothesis that it is television that makes young people more likely to be aggressive, rather than aggressive young people being more likely to prefer watching violent television programmes. Citati (2002) wrote that television kills children's fast-developing analogical imagination, their whirling logical abstraction potential, the sense of fun, paradox, absurd, senselessness, the gift of looking from other worlds and of belonging to other worlds. Johnson and his colleagues from Columbia University and the Psychiatric Institute of New York State went beyond Citati's subjective comments and followed 707 children from adolescence to adulthood. They found that adolescents who were used to spending a hour or more a day in front of the TV screen in *prime time* at around the age of twenty more easily gave way to aggressive acts against other people (Johnson et al., 2002). The link between time spent watching TV and violent behaviour remains significant when considered in relation to other factors that encourage either behaviour, such as previous aggressive behaviour, low family income, poor parental care, and presence of psychiatric disturbance. The most common aggressive behaviour among boys was physical violence, while robbery and threats emerged among girls. Only 5.7% of young people who had watched television for less than an hour a day committed violent acts in the following years, as against 28.8% of those who had watched it for more than three hours a day.

Anderson and Bushman (2002) from Iowa Polytechnic, commenting on the findings of Johnson and his colleagues, make the point that people do not seem to fully perceive the danger represented by violence on television. They state that the link between television violence and young people's violence can be equated to the link between smoking and cancer: the correlation between cigarettes and cancer is still questioned now, a long time after the scientific community proved it beyond any reasonable doubt.

Another piece of research carried out at the University of Michigan (Huesmann et al., 2003) and published in *Developmental Psychology*, the journal of the American Psychological Association, re-tested 329 twenty-year-old boys and girls who had already been tested in 1977 between the ages of six and ten. The findings of the study of children showed that the fact of watching violent programmes on television, their identification with same-gender aggressive characters and their perception that violence on television is real are all factors linked to aggressive acts committed by adults, for both boys and girls. This correlation is independent of the initial level of aggressiveness, intellectual capacities, the family's social status—measured on the basis of the parents' education and occupation—and the parents' aggressiveness. In addition, this piece of research highlighted that if parents watch the programmes with their children and comment on them, this seems to reduce the effects of television violence on the child, probably because it reduces the child's identification with the person who commits the violent act.

These remarks strongly support the hypothesis repeatedly put forward in my book, but I think it is worth expanding the field of observations further. I would like to underline a specific risk that (in the same way as with violence) the media is also inducing a perverse scenario, though this simultaneously has a personal and individual origin related to the particular way an individual dramatises and maniacally "repairs" an original trauma.

At the launch of the book *Pedofilia Pedofilie* in Padua, Milella commented:

> An external image, a "landscape" proposed on an iconic level, or generally representative, may sometimes perform an organisational function towards drives of undifferentiated sexualisation ... As far as the boundary of sexualisation is concerned—as chaotic as the underlying personality and disorganised in islands of psychic aggregation—the large series of images shown by the

media, especially pornographic ones, widely disseminated by means of the Internet with a clear intention to attract, can play the role of a catalyst of a pseudo-integrative internal erotised scenario. The possible resulting attempt to compel the external reality to conform to the internal scenario can give rise to the perverse ritual, acting at the same time as a kind of dam retaining the extensive loss of reality itself, as would be the case in a psychotic lack of balance. In other words, the external reality could provide disorganised drives seeking a representative aggregation with specific representative tools. [Milella, 2001]

Milella's arguments seem to me quite convincing, and I believe that they must be applied to all those forms of television violence that may encourage emulative attitudes and behaviours, in which mere imitation cannot be enough to explain the intense identification process often present. However, these arguments have to be made dialectical, in other words accepted in their fluctuating relationship with an opposite phenomenon. Watching DVDs containing scenes of paedophilic sex could stem violence and keep possible switchovers to action at bay, through a voyeuristically passive use of virtual sex, which would saturate instinctual demands, thus weakening them. As often happens, we are dealing with complex phenomena which can only be understood by acknowledging the co-presence of opposite mechanisms that are in a fluctuating relationship with one another.

On paedophilic priests

After years of official concealment of the phenomenon of paedophilia within the Catholic Church (despite several criminal charges and some convictions, as may be learned from historical documents and news items), nowadays we can witness the opposite phenomenon, that of demonisation, with what amounts to journalistic scandalmongering, as is clear from the way reports on American paedophile priests have appeared in the press. The book *Predatory Priests, Silenced Victims: The Sexual Abuse Crisis and the Catholic Church*, a collection of ground-breaking articles edited by Mary Gail Frawley-O'Dea and Virginia Goldner (2007), explores the abuse situation in all its troubling complexity, as the contributors take into account the experiences, respectively, of the victim/survivor, the abuser/perpetrator, and the bystander (whether family member, professional/clergy, or the community at large).

In a letter to Catholic priests all over the world, Pope John Paul II stigmatised the offence of paedophilia with angry words, in reply to pressing accusations which could have undermined the ecclesiastical institution, especially in the United States. But he did not propose any reflection on the possible reasons for such a phenomenon, nor did he show any attempt to understand its specificity within religious institutions as against other educational and sporting institutions in which adults and children come into contact. The current Pope Benedict XVI seems to follow the same line as the previous Pope, despite his very hard opinion on paedophilic priests.

There are murmurs around the Catholic world that priests' celibacy must be by choice and not by necessity, as this rule is imposed by the Church only on its Latin component and not on the Eastern one. According to the New Testament there is no relation of compulsion between sacerdotal ministry and celibacy. Priests' celibacy would foster secrecy of sexual satisfaction and therefore (even if indirectly) the spread of paedophilic attitudes and behaviours.

Actually, a link has been highlighted between increased sexual liberty in adult relationships and reduced paedophilic behaviours, even though such a tendency cannot be read unequivocally, as the phenomenon of paedophilia also has to do with the consumerist degradation that has lately affected sexual liberty. However, I believe that the presence of paedophilic behaviours of various kinds in part of the clergy has its own peculiarity and must be related to the vicarious specific parental role played by priests and to a tendency to absolutism intrinsic to the Catholic religion itself.

Henry de Montherlant's play *La Ville dont le Prince est un Enfant* was first published in 1951. The theme of "special friendships" in religious boarding schools had already been dealt with, sometimes with complacence, sometimes with irony or, in contrast, with moralising fury. Montherlant chose to write the story of two adolescent boys aged sixteen and fourteen who fall in love with each other, and intertwined it with a priest's passionate attentions to the younger boy, putting him in competition with the older adolescent, and the intervention of the Father Superior, who on his own authority interrupts the impossible triangular relationship. The title of the play comes from Ecclesiastes 10:16: "Woe to you, O land, when your king is a child, and your princes feast in the morning". This verse on the one hand expresses a devaluation of the child's emotional world and revival of a dissolution intrinsic to human nature, and a contrasting overvaluation of adult rational control, as we shall find in the thinking of many Catholic theologians; on the other hand, the verse vehemently indicates the risk of "infantolatry", which means idolatry of the child in a world in which the adult is an eternal child.

When childcare is perversely transformed into passionate idolisation in the name of purity of attentions and absoluteness of the educational intent, the risk of moving into the paedophilic act is high. A priest and teacher says to the adolescent Sevrais: "When I thought of you I told myself that I understood you as if you were my son, or rather, judging from my experience of the father-son relationship, no doubt even better than if you were my son" (Montherlant, 1951, p. 29). Real fathers and their role are underestimated in the name of an educational capacity that is narcissistically idealised, as one can infer from the following line: "But God has created men more sensitive than fathers, so that they can look after children who are not theirs, who are not loved properly, and you must have come across one of these men" (*ibid*).

Kochansky and Cohen connect priestly narcissism to the self-selection of men who were drawn to the priesthood to neutralise feelings of inadequacy, impotence and inferiority through a social role that allowed them to feel superior, special, admired and powerful. They hypothesise in the histories of these men an "inordinately intense, not infrequently eroticised, maternal attachment combined with painful paternal deprivations involving emotional rejection through a father's distancing and/or devaluation of his son … this pattern of relationship between a boy and his parents often results in narcissistic vulnerabilities and defences involving unrealistic self-representations and an instability of self-esteem, with underlying feelings of inferiority, defect, and shame, and longings to achieve and maintain a sense of specialness and superiority" (2007, p. 54). The family universe and its earthly finiteness are contrasted with an educational passion having an aspect of absoluteness that distinguishes it from other teacher-pupil relationships, which also contain the risk of a sexual relationship.

There is space neither for fathers nor for mothers. There is no space for a third who can make the idealised educational relationship triangular: "It is better that you don't talk about these affairs to your mother. Parents and boarding school are very different worlds and we have no interest in mixing them up" (Montherlant, 1951, p. 44). At most, the world of paedophilic relationships can unfold in parallel to that of everyday life, but it cannot be undermined in its total purity by the family's social life.

This is the task, arduous but fascinating, which we set ourselves when we set up a working group on paedophilia. The group was composed of six members, including psychoanalytically orientated psychiatrists and psychologists, and was co-ordinated by me. We met fortnightly for a few years. Some of us followed in their private consulting room, through a psychoanalytical treatment, patients who had had paedophilic experiences; some treated institutionalised paedophiles (by which I mean they followed patients with paedophilic behaviours in the consulting rooms of the Mental Health Department); others made assessments in court and had the opportunity to follow in jail paedophiles who had been charged.

The paedophilic ideology is built through the match of infantile passion, uncontrolled and unlimited, with the authority represented by adult age and nourished by experiential competence, with which the other boy cannot compete as it is chronologically inaccessible to him. We are talking about a child's heart in an adult body and mind having all the prerogatives of power. This is exactly the way paedophiles tend to describe themselves even when they strongly emphasise their love of the child, and underestimate—and even deny—any evidence of a power gap.

The priest's morbid attraction for the boy, clearly expressed in his words: "I enjoy following your eyes, seeing if they will stop on mine. And they never look at me. Never at me" (*ibid.*, p. 33), is interrupted by the Father Superior's authoritarian intervention, but the deep reasons are not analysed or understood. Even this latter authoritarian and repressive decision is taken within the concentration-camp universe of the boarding school, deprived of any communication with the outside world. Galimberti (2001) comments: "The reserve walls are those of the institution which must not be profaned, as well as those of the individual's interiority, of the refusal to see clearly among one's own sexual fantasies, impulses and disconnected tendencies, at the same time being compelled to offer others, and perhaps oneself, an acceptable self-image."

We would be better advised to debate more openly on these topics, on the risk of seduction intrinsic in the educational attitude and in continuous contact with children and adolescents, including the special case of the religious world (Catholic in particular), and to avoid games of concealment and demonisation, as they are obstacles to understanding. More attention to the emotional education of teachers, to the identification and acknowledgement of one's own and thus of others' feelings, and to knowledge of the differences between children's and adults' sexuality, could represent a first opportunity to counteract that relational ignorance on which didactic relationships often feed and which can nourish that surrogate of emotions and affects which characterises paedophilic perverse relationships.

INTRODUCTION

> There is never sun without shade, and it is necessary to know the night.
>
> —Albert Camus

In the analytical index of Freud's works the term "paedophilia" never appears. Nor does it in the works of Melanie Klein, Winnicott or Bion. Moreover, a study I have carried out on the fifteen most popular English psychoanalytical journals reveals that very few articles have been written on this subject—and most of them are dated.[1] I shall quote the entry "Paedophilia" from Rycroft's *Critical Dictionary of Psychoanalysis*, which already reveals the absence of psychoanalytical studies on this subject:

> Lit., love of children, but in practice reserved for the tendency to commit sexual offences against them. No psychoanalytical studies of paedophilia exist, but the sociological evidence suggests (a) that it is only rarely associated with violence towards the victim, (b) that it is not a perversion in the sense of being

the subject's *preferred* form of sexual behaviour, and (c) that the 'victim' is not infrequently a willing one. [1968, p. 110]

French psychoanalysts have provided a greater number of studies of paedophilia: in 1993 the *Revue Française de Psychanalyse* published an entire issue on the subject, and in 1996 Claude Balier wrote the book *Psychanalyse des comportements Sexuels Violents*. Psychoanalytically orientated pieces of writing appeared in a monographic issue on paedophilia of *L'Evolution Psychiatrique* in 1998. In Italy Franco De Masi stands out for delving deeper into the subject of paedophilia and investigating the paedophile's internal world. However, basically the phenomenon of paedophilia has suddenly erupted in the scientific community, finding experts more or less unprepared (Camarca & Parsi, 2000).

In view of such a poor bibliography, the first question to ask ourselves is the following: why have psychoanalysts not been interested in the issue of paedophilia, and specifically in the psychopathology of the paedophile? I don't believe the fact that the paedophile tends not to seek analysis could be a satisfactory answer for two main reasons. First of all, many know about the presence of paedophilic experiences or paedophilic fantasies in analysed patients (Freud and Ferenczi already made extensive mention of them). Secondly, psychoanalysis has often had a lot to say about pathologies and social behaviours not immediately analysable on the couch (I am thinking, for example, of the abundance of bio-ethical elaborations).

Furthermore, if psychoanalysis explains phenomena in terms of fantasies, it should be interested, as Balier (1996) says, in what happens in the psychic reality when fantasies become concrete, when a father rapes his daughter or when the sexual spell goes as far as murder. The lack of interest, though not entirely proportional with the importance and the social significance of the phenomenon, also does not correspond to the sociological finding that increasing numbers of psychoanalysts, especially those from recent generations, who work within public psychiatric institutions are concerned with pathologies that they could hardly face in the analytical room.

I feel that the ethical and cultural aspects which play a major role in the relationship with the paedophile patient may significantly impact on someone's decision to keep themselves away from this kind of disturbance, although the DNA of psychoanalysis has never contained conformism or moralism. Nevertheless, Freud (1928) made mainly ethical comments on the criminality of Dostoevsky, whom he also reproached, among other things, for having had paedophilic experiences.

Freudian attitudes to child sexual abuse and more generally the psychoanalytical view of it have been extensively criticised. Alice Miller (1988) explicitly and polemically talked about repression and denial of the phenomenon of abuse by psychoanalysts, who are even unable to voice the child abuse to which they have been subjected.

Bowlby wrote: "Freud's famous about-turn of 1897 regarding the aetiology of hysteria had led to the view that anyone who places emphasis on what a child's *real experiences* may have been, and perhaps still are being, was regarded as pitifully naïve" (1988, p. 43). It was assumed almost by definition that whoever was interested in the external world was not interested in the internal world, which he even sought to escape.

Contrasting views also emerge in the current psychoanalytical debate. In most recent theorisations (Spence, 1982; Shafer, 1983) we can see a further decrease of interest in the real trauma present in the patient's history, in favour of the reconstruction of existential narratives that are perceived as more useful. Eagle writes (1992, pp. 29 ff.): "Whatever the relationship between this narrative and the person's real history (beyond the fact that it may or may not be possible to access it), and most importantly, whatever the relationship between this narrative and the actual real internal world of emotions, desires, memories etc., this narrative represents a very narrow pragmatic point of view." Although these remarks are ungenerous towards narratology, the foundation on which the theory of the bipersonal field rests, and which has made it possible to use new observational views of the psychoanalytic event, no doubt we see the pre-eminence of relational transformations. These transformations should then modify the relationship with the external reality, in some sense putting the patient's real history aside.

By contrast, in his last writings Rosenfeld (1987), radically modifying Klein's previous approaches, acknowledged the value of reality and the role of a good anamnesis in an analysis that cannot have the *hic et nunc* (here and now) as the only point of reference. Therefore, he began to attentively analyse the patient's relationships with his or her own past as well as his or her present environment to try to understand the role played by the analyst in the transference, and to avoid misunderstandings which might induce an overwhelming negative countertransference and mix up the sane parts and the insane parts.

While an essential lack of attention to the paedophile's world is a matter of record, we have to acknowledge that cognitive and therapeutic interest in the abused child has gradually increased with the increasing attention to children's rights, to safeguarding their development from trauma, and to the increasingly frequent emergence of real sexual trauma from their history. This recalls Freud's early intuitions. Citing *Coitus in Childhood* by Dr. Stekel in Vienna, Freud was the first to remind us that children are exposed to sexual offences far more often than we might expect, due to the poor precautions taken by parents (Freud, 1896b, p. 207). In his first writings, he shows a preventive-didactic concern and warns parents and paediatricians to look after children better in order to prevent situations which could increase the chances of sexual abuse. It is only later on, as we shall come to see, that the trauma was increasingly considered an artefact, a subsequent construction of the imagination, and a real aetiological-explicative myth. However, in Freud's early thinking the trauma plays an important role, which the latest findings about child abuse seem to validate.

The same denial, splitting and repression mechanisms that adults, parents and experts themselves use seem to be reflected in the history of psychoanalysis: "In their ordinary life adults do not show an irreducible denial mechanism, but tiring and painful swings which, through partial admission and minimisation, lead to acknowledging the abuse; we can observe the same phenomenon in psychoanalysis and in Freud's thinking in particular" (Vassalli, 1994, p. 8).

Therefore, if we ignore savagely exaggerated criticism, such as that of Masson and Miller, it is possible to note in psychoanalysis, since Freud's early thinking, a tendency to swing from the internal reality pole to the external reality pole. A similar swinging is also present in the current debate about the meaning which should be given to the trauma. Echoes of this debate appeared online in the discussion organised in 2000 by the Italian Psychoanalytical Society on the role played by the child's trauma in the genesis of mental disturbances.

In my opinion, our understanding and cure of the paedophile should go hand in hand with the cure of the abused victim. By this I certainly do not mean that we should put them on the same level and not acknowledge the abuser's huge responsibility for causing, through an asymmetrical relationship, serious—sometimes irreversible—damage to the victim's psycho-emotional development, or even for killing him or her (and thus having to answer the appropriate charges). I mean rather that we need to try not to nourish for the time being a mythicised picture of the paedophile, in order to understand who he is in reality, what he wants, what feelings overwhelm him, what emotions he experiences, and what the motives of his behaviour are. Like Augustine, who said that we should hate the sin but love the sinner, we also should show loathing for this kind of behaviour from an ethical and social point of view, while from a therapeutic perspective we should find a way to get closer to the paedophile's world respectfully, in order to help him modify his behaviour. It is necessary to verify whether we can talk about paedophilia in scientific terms or whether, as in many other cases, we can use an all-embracing term which is increasingly deprived of sense and does not really help us detect those differences which, once detected, would allow us to distinguish one case from another and therefore set up more targeted therapeutic interventions. These interventions have the long-term effect of preventing possible second offences, rather than accepting inevitable measures which are at best morally and socially questionable, such as chemical castration, even when this is deliberately accepted by the abuser.

One of the characters in Isaac B. Singer's novel *Shadows on the Hudson* wonders with dismay:

> What goes through people's minds when they shove a child into an oven? Some thoughts must occur to them; they must even find some justification. But what passes through their minds? Afterwards, what do they tell their wives, fiancées, parents? How does a man come home to his wife and children and say, Today I burned fifty infants? And what does his wife answer? What does such a person think about when he finally lays his head on his pillow? I simply want to know how the mind works in such fiends. [1998, p. 32]

Some of my colleagues have told me that they could never become analysts for paedophile patients because they are too horrified by them and would only hope that they would be subjected to highly punitive measures. These colleagues identify completely with the abused child, and avoid any possible understanding of the "reasons" and pathology of the abuser, whom indeed they feel to be just the monster of an aberrant sexual behaviour. With regard to paedophiles, some psychoanalysts talk about a "false request", an attempt to manipulate the psychoanalyst in order to obtain from him or her a sort of acquiescence, or authorisation, even tacit, of their sexual peculiarity. In this regard, André (1999) talks about denial, a form of deafness or unreasonable panic, a manifestation of what Lacan called "the passion for ignorance". On the reasons for this difficulty, Bouchet-Kervella wonders:

> Who are the paedophiles? Anybody thinks they are perverse people, as their sexual satisfaction is directed towards an aberrant choice of erotic object. They are considered particularly abhorrent, perverse people, because they are irresistibly compelled by their impulses to abduct innocent children in order to relieve their odd deviant desire on them, to use violence against them, and to murder them in order to prevent their accusation. Ultimately, they are probably considered incurably perverse people, because their perverse polymorphous child's drive potential seems to have resisted education and risks rebelling against any attempt at therapy. Not only does this apply to the mass media, but also to the spontaneous countertransference experience of any observer—whether psychiatrist or psychoanalyst—induced by the horrible cases of violence and rape against children which we hear regularly on radio and TV news. [1996, p. 56]

Although I greatly respect people's difficulty in dealing with such a subject, and am aware of the objective emotional risks of meeting a paedophile and of the negative ethical-cultural elements which interfere with the development of a countertransference used significantly in the relationship, I believe it is absolutely necessary to explore this complex field—one which is so beset with difficulties and sometimes relational impossibilities, so foreboding of identification anxieties—and to avoid a point of view based merely on punishment.

Psychoanalysis appears to me to be the only therapeutic tool able to free itself from the punishment-acceptance polarisation which seems to grip and impoverish the present debate on paedophilia. Understanding does not mean passively accepting this phenomenon in the name of an absurd exaltation of the legitimacy of paedophilic behaviours; nor, in contrast, does it mean accepting the punitive social attitude that the elimination of the paedophile would lead to the elimination of the problem—which only removes responsibility. It is indeed a difficult position to maintain, since the psychoanalyst is subjected to the social and cultural tensions of the historical period in which he or she lives, but any other solution would risk being just comforting and mystifying.

This is the task, arduous but fascinating, which we set ourselves when we set up a working group on paedophilia. The group is composed of six members, including psychoanalytically orientated psychiatrists and psychologists, and is co-ordinated by me. We have been meeting fortnightly for a few years. Some of us follow in their private consulting room, through a psychoanalytical treatment, patients who have had paedophilic experiences; some treat institutionalised paedophiles (by which I mean they follow patients with paedophilic behaviours in the consulting rooms of the Mental Health Department); others have made assessments in court and had the opportunity to follow in jail paedophiles who have been charged.

Starting from the intense emotional difficulties raised by the relationship with paedophiles, we set out to reflect in the group on the origin of these difficulties, and at the same time to study the phenomenon of paedophilia from different perspectives: sociological, historical, artistic, and literary. The group's fundamental hypothesis rested on the necessity to confront paedophilia by looking at it from several different points of view and observational perspectives, as we believed that the term *paedophilia* and the pathology to which we generally refer needs to go through a process of review and probably of conceptual reconstruction. In fact we felt that the formulations used up to now have been misused and confused, and are consequently basically incorrect, being hidden by the general term *paedophilia* and thus not really appropriate to represent the complexity and specificity of disturbances in psychopathological pictures that are aetiologically different.

This is a subject which has been at the centre of the mass media's attention for some years, and is almost always tackled in outraged and sensational tones—dominated by the journalistic rhetoric of the monster. We have decided to face it in scientific terms, with more moderate modalities, and with as much modesty as possible. This would be made possible by acknowledging the strong resistances used both by ordinary people and by experts when they come to deal with this particular aspect of human behaviour in cognitive and therapeutic terms. The account of this intense group experience—the diverse routes taken, the hitches encountered and the turbulences faced, the crises and recoveries, the emotional experiences and subsequent reflections—will be given in the last chapter of this book, written in collaboration with Luisella Peretti.

Clinical considerations (which we will examine later) are not the only factor in favour of abolishing the term *paedophilia*, which (like *ephebophilia*) should indicate love for children: love which, on a subliminal level, could transform itself into a pedagogic attitude. Our reflections when we discussed the developments in our group—on the group structuring and de-structuring experiences we had in relation to the diverse clinical pictures of paedophilic behaviours—also led us to the same conclusion. However, since the term *paedophilia* is the one in common use, even in scientific treatises, I will continue to use it in this book, though I am aware of it being inappropriate and confusing, and will try as far as possible to highlight the limits and overlapping between terms.[2]

The term *pederasty*, which is probably more appropriate to define a sexual relationship between an adult and a child, has acquired over time a meaning equivalent to *homosexuality* not only in ordinary usage but also in scientific language, as we read for example in Rycroft's *Critical Dictionary of Psychoanalysis* (1968, p. 110), where it is defined as *sodomy*, and in Longanesi's *Nuovo Dizionario di Sessuologia* (p. 920; quoted in Galimberti, 2000b), where it is defined as *immissio penis in anum*. In this book the word will refer specifically to sexual relationships between adults and adolescents in Ancient Greece.

It is not up to us to make judgements on social rigour, which is not necessarily directly proportional to clinical gravity, but I consider it necessary to talk about *paedophilias* and not *paedophilia*, and, as we will be able to go into more depth, to distinguish between the concepts of *paedophilic perversion* and *paedophilic perversity*.

In this book we will not deal with the subject of incest, the particular characteristics of which deserve a separate treatise. Television programmes as well as many newspaper articles fail to distinguish between paedophilia and incest, though they are situations and behaviours which are totally different. The psychology of the incestuous father has nothing to do with that of the paedophile, whatever its expressive modalities are, since in the former we find forms of sexual appropriation related to fantasies about replacement of the wife (with the daughter), and sometimes about symbiotic fusion (with the son), which do not belong to the paedophile's psychic world. The incestuous father, unlike the paedophile, cannot bear paternity; indeed, he feels the irresistible need to scoff at it and dissolve it. In contrast, paedophiles who have children not only do not abuse them, but are generally model fathers, or try hard to be so (André, 1999). The incestuous father's wife is often aware or unconsciously collusive (incest that is subjected to judgement rarely relapses), and the abuser has rarely had significant experiences of victimisation in his childhood, in that the incestuous act towards the child does not depend on his own incestuous experience. In addition to moral deficiencies on the superego level, the abuser often suffers from fluctuating alcoholism and mood swings; therefore we should talk about incestuous sexual abuse and distinguish it from paedophilia (Martorell & Coutanceau, 1998a).

The emotional consequences for the abused boy child or girl child vary radically depending on whether the abuser is a stranger or someone known to the child (statistically the latter is the more frequent situation), or even the child's parent. In the last case the pathology developing consequent to the sexual trauma is far more serious, causing extremely deep psychic devastation, as the parent is not only the adult who fails to understand and perverts the child's need for protection, but also the person whom the child has trusted completely. The parent is the person on whom the child depends totally from any viewpoint, and cannot therefore so licentiously undervalue the child's needs or betray his or her expectation of love and protection, as they are the primary source of necessary narcissism.

While from a psychoanalytical perspective the bibliography dealing specifically with paedophilia is certainly poor, the bibliography on perversion is abundant. A quick journey through this concept, a complete definition of which was formulated by Freud in successive stages, will help us understand what we are talking about. By this I mean that we will see whether paedophilia is a clinical picture belonging to the diagnostic category of perversions—like fetishism, sadism, masochism, etc.—or whether it is a clinical picture with its own characteristics, which requires us to attempt an approach able to go beyond that commonly used for perversions, as there is a huge discrepancy between fantasy and putting it into action in the external reality, in that there is no continuity between the two. We will realise that we should acknowledge the inadequacy of the term *paedophilia* to contain, from a diagnostic point of view, different clinical situations that are only partially ascribable to the group of perversions.

Chapter One deals with the subject of the cultural and social roots of paedophilia today, the emergence of the phenomenon and its current expressive features, and some of its possible causes. Alongside the parental qualities that in some cases may foster the paedophilic evolution of sexual attitudes, we shall take into consideration the role of television and advertising, and some hedonistic and selfish tendencies which risk putting the agreement between generations in a difficult position.

Chapter Two, written with the collaboration of Clara Pitto, takes us to the dawn of human history, going through mythology and its interrelationships with the human unconscious. Myths make it possible to represent universal phantasies—including those of the paedophile—which, without an appropriate narrative container, would risk transforming themselves into real events able to destroy the connective texture of human society.

Chapter Three, written with the collaboration of Franca Pezzoni, contains important theorisations about fairy tales and the relationships between psychoanalysis and fairy tales. Those with predominantly incorporative content will be distinguished from those with more direct sexual content, to conclude that the narration of fairy tales frees the sexual fantasies which adults develop about children and those which children develop about adults from moral unutterability and unacceptability. The function of fairy tales as a social prophylactic preventing progression to concrete paedophilic behaviours is quite evident.

Chapter Four presents some notes on the history of paedophilia. Without attempting to be comprehensive in our coverage, we shall examine the Greek Classical Age, the Middle Ages, the Renaissance and then the late nineteenth and early twentieth centuries. It will be made clear that ancient Greece was not an "El Dorado" for paedophiles, but that pederast practice was characterised by very intense individual and social conflicts. The history of childhood is outlined with the help of great historians such as Ariès and DeMause, who highlight its peculiar characteristics of submission and violence and its complex socio-cultural factors. We are not talking about a fresco, but a picture in which impressionist brushwork is predominant, as the objective is not to offer a thorough view, which is not and cannot be our task, but to underline the most important elements of its complexity.

Chapter Five, written with the collaboration of Paolo Peloso, outlines the evolution of the concept of paedophilia in the history of medicine and psychiatry up to the latest formulations of DSM-IV, and examines critically the most frequent therapeutic measures, acknowledging the difficulties—still present today—of arriving at an unequivocal and comprehensive definition of paedophilia which is not intended to be moralistic.

Chapter Six describes the journey of the concept of paedophilic perversion through the history of psychoanalysis, from Freud to the latest formulations by the psychologists of the Self, to an ultimate definition. Despite its ancient origins, the concept of paedophilic perversion, once re-elaborated and updated, can be used to distinguish between different paedophilic pictures.

Chapter Seven, written with the collaboration of Paolo Peloso and Giuseppina Tabò, lingers over some novels and stories that describe diverse paedophilic attitudes and behaviours. These can provide a rich phenomenology of paedophilias and help us in our attempt to differentiate between them.

Chapter Eight considers the specificity of paedophilic relationships and describes the complex texture of interactions developing within the therapeutic relationship with the paedophile. The topic of "paedophilic watching" and the construction of a reality in which the incorporative and projective aspects take over are dealt with in a brief journey through some artistic paintings and photographs.

Chapter Nine presents a peculiar case of paedophilic perversion, in which the outstanding "benignity" and thus the therapeutic potentialities are detected.

Chapter Ten, written with the collaboration of Luisella Peretti, presents a case of paedophilic perversion considered paradigmatic, which brings us closer to the relational deadlocks, to the countertransference *enactments* characterising the difficult therapeutic route of these meetings.

The patients' accounts, the intense and anxious transference and countertransference experiences induced by the therapeutic relationship, and the resistances and transformations within the therapeutic journey enable us to get to know these people and their worlds more closely.

This book cannot and does not intend to be a treatise on paedophilia, but, more modestly, attempts to make some points on the subject, starting from the psychoanalytic foundation and culture, yet without disdaining various scientific contributions and forays into other cultural territories. Moreover, it is an attempt to underline that only an integrative approach can give an appropriate answer to the clinical complexity characterising paedophilic pictures.

This difficult journey through paedophilic emotions and behaviours allows me to endorse Hannah Arendt's view, in *The Origins of Totalitarianism* (1951), that understanding means tackling reality open-mindedly and attentively, whatever reality is.

Notes

1. A similar study by Galimberti (2000b) reveals that the terms *paedophilia* and *pederasty* are completely ignored by the *Dizionario di Psicologia* published by Laterza and by Cesare Musatti's *Trattato di Psicoanalisi*. De Martis gives very little space to this subject in the *Trattato di Psicoanalisi* edited by Alberto Semi, and even less space is given in the *Dizionario di Psicologia* by Dalla Volta and in the *Dizionario di Psicologia* by Galimberti himself. A little more space, but still too little, is given to paedophilia in the *Nuovo Dizionario di Sessuologia* published by Longanesi. I would add that Fenichel hardly mentions the subject of paedophilia in the chapter on male homosexuality in his *Psychoanalytic Theory of Neurosis*. Likewise, Rycroft writes seven lines on this subject in *A Critical Dictionary of Psychoanalysis*, and it is not mentioned at all in *The Language of Psychoanalysis* by Laplanche

and Pontalis, in the *Encyclopedia of Psychoanalysis* by Eidelberg, or in the *Trattato di Psicologia Analitica* by Carotenuto. Only Thomä and Kächele's *Lehrbuch der Psychoanalytischen Therapie* and Gabbard's *Psychodynamic Psychiatry in Clinical Practice* present and extensively discuss cases of paedophilia which have been followed in psychoanalytical psychotherapy and also in a hospital setting.
2. Maria Rita Parsi would like to replace *paedophilia* with *paedophobia*, while Sergio Angeletti suggests that we talk about *Herod syndrome*.

CHAPTER ONE

Social and cultural aspects which foster paedophilic behaviour

> The world is a dangerous place, not because of those who do evil, but because of those who look on and do nothing.
>
> —Albert Einstein

A variety of reasons have been provided over time to account for the emergence and spread of paedophilia. Two of the main reasons are a lack of respect for children and the failure to recognise the value of the specific emotional and affective language of the child, which, indeed, is often reduced to the predominating adult standard, namely the language of production, of the market place, of a lack of imagination—a language whose gratuitousness reflects the fact that our induced needs are mass-produced. We can add to these two factors the ever-increasing indifference which governs our social relationships, and the perverse mechanism of advertising, which—in the name of the god of profit—is eager and willing to sacrifice children and their own special needs on the altar of consumerism. Others speak of an absence of restrictions, others still of a weakening of social bonds with micro-social groups defending micro-social interests, often with a totally egoistical attitude which bears no relationship to the larger social body; quite the contrary: they are often in opposition to wider society. In this chapter I will deal only with those points that seem to me to be central to my argument, and even when I speak of social and cultural themes, I will do so predominantly from a psychoanalytical standpoint.

It has now become commonplace to note that in many families the television is left on all day. It is watched randomly and distractedly. Its real function is to act as the soundtrack of incommunicability, as the filler of an existential void and a cover for the lack of affective exchanges within the family.

The direct repercussions of the communicative void fall increasingly on the woman, who may often be depicted as the dissatisfied housewife, who remains at home for long periods performing role-related tasks which are experienced as frustrating and repetitive. Not only does housework deny her any gratification, but together with the isolation it produces it may also lead to depression.

With regard to television messages, the absence of two-way communication and the passivity which this type of message fosters may also indirectly impose themselves as a model of interrelationships—or rather of the lack of interrelationships, that is to say of unilateral transactions in which the receiver absorbs everything without giving anything in return. Children immediately learn to live with this third party—the extraneous and pacifying entity represented by television—and this may seriously compromise their attention span and their ability to concentrate.

In the course of infant and baby observation discussion groups in which I have taken part, the observer reported noting strong correlations between depression in the mother, the television being on and the passivity of the child. Depression in the mother was often connoted by untidiness (still in pyjamas, curlers in her hair, not wearing makeup), boredom, apathy, and continuous (almost compulsive) recourse to food, while the TV was kept at a high volume for the entire length of the visit, even though no one was watching the pictures and even less listening to the sounds it produced. For his part, the child went from unsuccessful attempts to attract his mother's attention in any way possible to attitudes apparently conveying self-care, basically autistic in nature, such as shifting his attention to repetitive and monotonous games, probably employed as kinds of precursors to television, in an attempt to alleviate the solitude and disappointment caused by the lack of maternal response to his requests, no matter whether these responses were positive or negative.

Even children begin to sit in front of the television for hours as though hypnotised, often cluttering up their minds with the gestures and the screams of those violent Japanese animated cartoons. Worse still, this already happens when they are in the early stages of growing up. (The fact that television has a hypnotic effect on people had already been pointed out by one of the all-time great film directors, Sergei Eisenstein.)

What more can one expect? For when dinner is ready and all the family are sitting at the table, even father wants to "enjoy the evening news in peace and quiet", and thus bestows on the event the sacredness of a ritual which is repeated every day. In this way the fact of the family being together for dinner is deprived of any ritual and communicative value it could have. The pleasure of conviviality is relinquished and the satisfaction of the child's need for attention is denied. Thus, driven by paternal rejection, the child is virtually obliged to direct his attention and curiosity to that all-powerful device, the television. With regard to children expectantly and trustingly addressing requests to their parents, Freud (1890)[1] had this to say: "It may be remarked … that outside hypnosis and in real life, credulity such as the subject has in relation to his hypnotist is shown only by a child towards his beloved parents" (p. 296).

At dinner time, the television presents the most horrific images of atrocities: exterminations, murders, traffic accidents and capital punishments, garnished with women virtually in the nude, newscasters screaming obscenities, stupid quiz shows, and heads of state who have just decided our futures. Statistics show that the number of crimes our children witness on television each and every day of their lives is incredibly high.

More recently, television has started rendering the contradictions and conflicts present in interpersonal relationships with increasingly intrusive and vulgar modalities, thereby depriving them of the privacy and fragile intimacy they rightfully require, and consequently of any communicative power whatsoever. The result is a depressing series of psychological striptease acts, in which all sentiment, all emotions lose their original connotations and are transmuted into a funereal and disgusting exhibition of a state of intimacy whose delicate language should not be totally distorted but faithfully protected and defended against any intrusion by the media.

The border between animate and inanimate, which was once identifiable by the ancient concept of piety, has been demolished. Pain is no longer perceived in its essence, death is no longer sacred and terrible, for it belongs only to the realm of pornography.

The epoch of the macabre develops in the midst of pathos and cynicism. The discourse is circular and irrelevant; everything has the same value as everything else, and remains indifferent in the presence of a continuous, interminable flow of stimuli which are senseless, or at the very least interchangeable. A very special form of violence is thus created: the indifference which comes from habituation. Think of the union between the screen (the Italian playwright and actor Eduardo De Filippo defined it as a household appliance like the refrigerator and the washing machine) and a science-fiction scenario, such as the Gulf War: the almost comic-like technological abstraction of this tragedy might well have made it appear like a video game to some adults, but this is certainly the way it was perceived by all children. Hence a game, one in which a human being can destroy and kill without feeling any emotion, where the absence of borders or differentiation between fact and fiction is internalised with increasing indifference, which in time may be transformed into a lack of compassion and the non-existence of a sense of responsibility.

The more recent images of the war in Serbia lend weight to my previous observations. To these a large dose of technological disenchantment must be added: everyone knows that intelligent bombs, capable of hitting the strategic objective with surgical precision and without inflicting casualties, do not exist, that the technical term "integrated defence" is in actual fact a diplomatically devious and deceitful way to define an attack, that civilian casualties are unfortunately the most realistic aspect of warfare, and yet the sensation of having become accustomed to the sanitised images presented on television has become prevalent, if not ubiquitous (Schinaia, 1999).

Roccato (1998) speaks of emotional illiteracy and of an inadequate perception of the self in many patients today who require psychoanalytical treatment. He describes them as "ex-children detached from everything, because they are detached from themselves ... frightened by real encounters ... where others really do risk existing" (p. 227).

Joyce McDougall (1982) introduced the term *alexithymia* into psychoanalysis. This term was coined by Peter Sifneos in 1972. Etymologically, it means "the absence of words to describe emotions"; it characterises the difficulty people find in detecting and describing their own feelings and emotions, in discriminating between them, differentiating one from another, and in communicating them. Speziale-Bagliacca (1997) points out that this difficulty also affects the ability to describe, comprehend and distinguish the sentiments and emotions of others.

Magris (1999), recalling the work of the philosopher Gianni Vattimo, describes the constitution of a new Ego, one which is no longer compact and unified, but is made up of a multiplicity of psychic nuclei, and the drives of which are no longer imprisoned within the rigid armour of individuality and consciousness.

Barale and Ferruta speak of "hyperbolic masks of an unstable and scattered subjectivity, within which there no longer exists a recognisable 'nucleus', hence no distinction can be made between the real Self and the false Self. Only open Selves exist; these take shape and organise themselves and undo that organisation in relation to each act they execute. Provisional identities" (1997, p. 375). A society in which the figures of Postmodernity (such as a constitutional void and the deconstructability of every identity) make an excellent match with the absence of constraints (the latter being strongly determined by the virtual nature of communicative events) obliges us to radically reconsider our theoretical models of psychosexual development, since these models are dominated by "obligatory linear sequences instead of networks of multiple movements consisting of 'comings and goings' in which organisations prone to continual reorganisations take shape and then de- or recompose" (ibid). Magris adds: "Today reality is increasingly virtual, consisting as it does of this possible mutation of the Ego" (1999, p. 8).

Rolling a bowling ball and throwing a stone from a bridge over a motorway have become equivalent gestures for some adolescents.[2] It would appear that no difference is discerned between the falling ninepins and the car containing people in all their flesh and blood. Thus, despite the fact that television is a powerful tool for the acquisition of knowledge and for entertainment, it risks taking the process of de-animation of human beings and de-symbolisation of events which it shows on the screen to extreme consequences, by procedures of symbolic equation which tend to coincide with those practices which Hanna Segal (1957) regards as characterising psychotic thought. Over the last years of his life, the philosopher Karl Popper dealt extensively with television violence, particularly in his book *Cattiva Maestra Televisione* [Television: A Bad Teacher] (1994).

The difficulty of distinguishing animate from inanimate and real from virtual, severely impaired communication in the family, the domination of the computer and video games which act as training in the control of others (who are seen as devitalised, that is incapable of experiencing emotions and sentiments other than those which are narcissistically attributed to them) can constitute elements heralding a withdrawal into oneself which is autistically omnipotent. This explains why speaking of juvenile suicide on television, and especially showing their lifeless bodies, risks being counterproductive, and increasing rather than decreasing this social phenomenon, because television may drive adolescents to imitate what they see. In a similar vein, continuing to speak of the bravado of stone throwers or the actions of the latest monstrous paedophile may induce imitation instead of carrying out the functions of education and prevention.

Note, however, that this is by no means a plea for censorship, one important reason being that I am convinced it would be of no avail. Instead, this is a plea for reflection on the part of the entire community on the risks we run of making such massive and often distorted use of television. These include impeding the development of the capacity (a) to discriminate between infantile fantasies and elements pertaining to present reality, between animate and inanimate, and (b) to distinguish what is real from what is virtual. It is a problem which all social institutions involved in education—the family, the school, religious bodies, cultural associations—should set themselves, without branding a given phenomenon as evil for anti-historical reasons pertaining to their own ideology, but at the same time without making concessions to a fashionable pseudo-modern stance.

In "Delusions and Dreams in Jensen's 'Gradiva'" (1906), Freud discusses a well-known etching by Félicien Rops (a Belgian painter and engraver who scandalised the nineteenth century with his irony) in relation to repression. Petrella describes this work, entitled "The Temptation of St Anthony", as being

> ... finely etched and humorously blasphemous. An ascetic monk takes refuge at the feet of an image of the Saviour on the cross, most probably to escape from the temptations of the world. But this cross disappears like a shadow, and in its place there emerges, instead, the radiant image of a naked and voluptuous woman in the same crucified attitude. [1981]

Freud comments on the work as follows:

> Other artists with less psychological insight have, in similar representations of temptation, shown Sin, insolent and triumphant, in some position alongside of the Saviour on the cross. Only Rops has placed Sin in the very place of the Saviour on the cross. He seems to have known that when what has been repressed returns, it emerges from the repressing force itself. [1906, p. 35]

The shock provoked by of Rops's etching produces a smile today when we think of the front pages of many weekly magazines with high sales figures, but I believe it still expresses perfectly the fantasies which perturb the unconscious of even the most virtuous of men. We must come to terms with these by seeking their origins in order to remove their potential for damage instead of denying their existence or repressing them.

Taking Plato as his starting point, the American forensic psychiatrist Robert J. Simon comes to the conclusion that evil women and men do what good people simply dream of doing. To support his thesis, he quotes an interview in which His Holiness Tenzin Gyatso, the fourteenth Dalai Lama and the winner of the 1989 Nobel Peace Prize, spoke about the dark side of his dreams:

> In my dreams, sometimes women approach me, and I immediately realise, "I'm *bhikshu*, I'm a monk"—so you see, this is sort of sexual ... Similarly, I have dreams where someone is beating me, and I want to respond. Then I immediately remember, "I am a monk and I should not kill". [Simon, 1999, p. 4]

If one had to judge people by their behaviour when they are part of a crowd, for example when they start looting in the wake of serious incidents, or when they steal with nonchalance in a supermarket or in a bookshop without ever having indulged in delinquent behaviour before, then one would definitely have to recognise that in every human being there is a dark, unfathomable side that can emerge on certain occasions.

At the same time, however, one must ask oneself: Why does the exhibitionist solve his problem of inadequacy by showing his genitals to a woman? And why should this act be so shocking to her that it leads to an expression of surprise and bewilderment which reverses the man's sense of fear, thereby transferring it into her? And finally, why does the impotent man go to the sexologist and the one who suffers from *ejaculatio praecox* go the psychoanalyst?

We know that a certain measure of aggressiveness which is generally kept under control is often present in normal sexual intercourse. Cesare Musatti spoke of the sweet violence of penetration, and was heavily criticised by the feminist movement for this (unjustly, in my opinion), but his statement does not lead to the conclusion that we are faced with potential rapists, or that even the strongest sexual fantasies can come close to the real-life experience of degradation and violence which characterise rape.

The sense of incapacity and inadequacy which is typical of the child when his sense of narcissism is contradicted by external reality may develop into a variety of different modes of existence, in various personality structures, and in various pathological organisations. Whether the result is depression, or a sense of persecutory guilt, or aggressiveness which is acted out in perversions, also depends on the mother's specific potential for containment, on the presence or absence of qualities such as elasticity and flexibility, on the ability to mediate between the extremes of tolerance and imposition, on the fluctuation between reverie and concentration.

One of the therapeutic objectives of psychoanalysis (and probably the main objective) is to enable the analysand to live and communicate his fantasies within the framework of the therapeutic relationship. No matter how violent and terrifying they may be, through the work of emotional, affective and interpretative containment by the analyst, the patient will come to realise that infantile fantasies are just that: infantile fantasies, and that desiring to kill and imagining killing someone are not the same as actually killing them. When the patient experiences the fact that the analyst manages to survive the destructive attacks launched against him by the patient, and that the analyst manages to contain within himself, both in his mind and in his body, the patient's infantile anxieties and projective identifications which are at times extremely violent, then the foundations are laid for working through and co-operating which leads to the patient learning to discriminate between reality and fantasy, that is, between present-day experiences and infantile fantasies. This is an extremely important victory, since the latter may overdetermine the former and weigh them down, thereby making them more difficult to tolerate and more frustrating (Schinaia, 1999).

While this therapeutic operation is possible with a neurotic patient, it is far less so with a perverse patient. A fully-blown perverse person is hardly likely to lie down on the psychoanalyst's couch, for the moment he decides to embark upon a course of treatment, he must cease committing the acts he commits as a paedophile and must thus forgo the beneficial secondary effects such acts procure him in the form of triumphant pleasure.

In the majority of cases, a paedophile and rapist who is found out and subjected, for instance, to psychiatric examination will appear in the report to be a person who is nondescript, not very intelligent, boring. He will give the impression that everything that he says at the level of information is exact, whereas in actual fact none of it is authentically true. The reports on his questioning by the police will show nothing that is complex, and his answers will be predictable and hackneyed, and will exhibit no empathy or emotion whatsoever. It is as if one were faced with an emotional paralysis with regard to the victim, and at a general level the patient exhibits a limited emotional repertoire. It is not by chance that one symmetrical defensive response provoked in the paedophile's analyst is that of apathy and boredom. If this type of response does break into the relationship then it may compromise the possibility of providing effective help.

The act of rape is not a seeking after authentic pleasure but a seeking after power: to reassure himself that his power does exist and that consequently he exists. The rapist seeks the power to frighten, to humiliate, to degrade the object, through a process of dehumanisation which is indispensable if he is to arouse his own excitement, just as he himself was probably frightened, humiliated and degraded when he was a child. He seeks the power to dominate, to gain possession of the other's body like a predator, to inflict pain and employ violence, just as probably happened to him as a child at the hands of violent parents who hit him and who failed to respect the integrity of the child's body in the framework of pathological family relationships.

Until a man of this kind is discovered, it is hardly likely that he will be able to stop his actions by himself and give up enjoying the sensation of triumph that comes from his criminal deeds. Were he to do so, he would experience the void to which he is prey as intolerable and banal. It must, however, be added that sometimes it is the paedophile himself who deliberately leaves clues behind in order to give the police the opportunity to discover and catch him, inasmuch as his sense of guilt works at subterranean levels. As Freud (1916) pointed out in "Criminals from a Sense of Guilt", in this case the guilt precedes and triggers the criminal act.

In *The Compulsion to Confess* (1925), Theodor Reik describes the need the criminal feels to confess and expiate. He considers the compulsion to confess a peculiar characteristic of the tendency to communicate, of the impulsive and unconscious need to make others participate in the most important aspects of his intrapsychic life.

In those rare cases in which a rapist or a paedophile turns to the analyst, their decision to do so is virtually never motivated by the desire to be cured, but often by their fear of the social consequences of the impulse which drives them to sexual contacts which society judges reprehensible or illegal. They live their drama in a non-conflictual and egosyntonic manner.

Thus, the compulsory therapies which some nations enact as an alternative to imprisonment are virtually never transformed into requests for help on the part of the delinquent. In this sense, Italy in recent years is no different from other countries: magistrates have been increasingly asking in a disorderly and disorganised fashion for state psychiatric help for paedophiles in lieu of prison sentences. Two important reasons why the therapeutic results appear to be poor are firstly the nature of the secondary motives for the patient's request for treatment (defence counsel pleads for a lighter sentence because the patient has asked for treatment); and secondly the magistrate's confusion of therapy with social control, which causes the paedophile to experience rejection of the therapy. Both factors reduce the paedophile's "consciousness of being ill", which is already weak to start with—a disastrous effect, for it is this type

of consciousness that is the necessary precondition of an authentic request for treatment.
The mother's affective, structuring containment may fail for a wide variety of reasons: from maternal depression, which diverts her attention away from filial requests, to the father's absenteeism and the lack or insufficiency of role models available to the child, to socioeconomic conditions, which may reduce the quantity and impair the quality of the contact the child has with his parents, to the cultural environment, which may help or hinder the child's encounter with the environment. All these factors may increase the possibility that the child's fantasies may become a strong, armour-plated shield, that the child may lose his integrity and thus become subject to an uneven process of psycho-emotional development.

> The various contexts with which the growing subject will interact will have the power both to enable him to integrate his natural violence into sentiments and activities, which will be increasingly oriented to a relationship of trust and tenderness with the other, and to impede such a harmonious development. The latter case will produce a tendency to depression which may lead the subject to turn the violence inward against himself; or, worse still, this depression may intensify and the subject may be incapable of finding a way out. The initial violence will then turn into individual aggressiveness, and sometimes into collective aggressiveness, and the extremely negative consequences this has in modern life are only too well known. [Bergeret, 1998, p. 92]

In rationalising paedophilia, often with the aim of causing a public stir, some intellectuals idealise free pleasure and reject any limit whatsoever, any borderline, any crime or nefarious act, any law, as Dogliani (1997) points out in his introductory essay to the Italian translation of Thomas Mann's *Das Gesetz*. For example, Aldo Busi (1997) exalts the search for a different type of childhood, one which is totally emancipated, one where sexual polymorphism is not suffocated by social hypocrisy. This stance is publicised as a categorical imperative in the name of the right to satisfy one's desires. Such people proclaim themselves to be mentors of the sexual development of the child and, in assigning themselves the role of initiating children into paedophilia, they claim that paedophilia is lawful and express the desire that society recognise a genital component in infantile sexuality.

Bonnetaud (1998) claims that argumentation is a multi-layered discourse which may be interpreted at a multiplicity of levels. It varies from the discourse of salvation in Gide's *Corydon* to Foucault's vindication of the right of the child to live his sexuality in the utmost freedom. In André Gide's novel *Corydon* (1924), the eponymous protagonist falls in love with an adolescent who returns his love. However, Corydon firmly rejects the boy's advances. Nevertheless, unrequited love leads the boy to commit suicide. This sad event obliges Corydon to give free rein to his paedophilia in order to avoid endangering the life of another adolescent. Hence Corydon does not take advantage of the boy—on the contrary, he saves the boy.

Michel Foucault has fought strenuously to make "soft" paedophilia (namely cases of paedophilia between a consenting child and an adult) legal. Indeed, the transcript of his broadcast discussion with Guy Hocquenghem and Jean Danet (1979) may be considered to be the manifesto of the pride of the paedophile. Furthermore, the French philosopher speaks with compassion of the poor peasant who was tried in Lorraine in 1867 because "at the border of a field he had obtained a few caresses from a little girl, just as he had done before and seen done by the village urchins round about him". The peasant was reported to the mayor by the girl's parents. Here is Foucault's comment on the case:

> What is the significant thing about this story? The pettiness of it all; the fact that this everyday occurrence in the life of village sexuality, these inconsequential bucolic pleasures, could become, from a certain time, the object not only of a collective intolerance but of a judicial action, a medical intervention, a careful clinical examination, and an entire theoretical elaboration. [1978, p. 31]

Here is Foti and Roccia's harsh rejection of Foucault's position:

> Despite the fact that Foucault normally pays great attention to the "microphysics of power", he yet fails to perceive the potential conflict between the sexuality of adults and that of minors as

well as the fact that adults tend to appropriate and manipulate children ... Foucault identifying with the "village simpleton" might be a good thing if it went together with identifying with the little girl, which, however, is completely missing. What should the parents have done: not report the incident to the mayor to avoid a society motivated by a "will to know" falling upon the poor peasant to satisfy their own needs for novel discourses and analyses of perversion? Foucault underlines the negative aspects of the "will to know" inherent in the social reaction, while he is not interested in underscoring the positive aspects of the—albeit partial and contradictory—emergence of a "will to protect" inherent in the social reaction. [1994a, p. 20]

Bonnetaud (1998) also reminds us of the repercussions for the child: increased aggressiveness, the presence of antisocial behaviour, a confused sexual identity, and an increase in the risk that he too may become a paedophile. Freud (1905) had already warned us of the danger of seduction in setting the child on the road to all possible abuses.

Denial of the need to set limits and of the assumption that those limits should be respected in individual and social development (despite the fact that the limits are continually being shifted forward by scientific and technological progress) is strictly connected to the cultural models imposed by a market economy, their basic value being quite simply that if you have enough money to pay, then anything is possible. "The categories of risk and uncertainty together with that of the amount of time one has to wait are placed second to those of unlimited certainty and immediacy, inasmuch as the latter are improperly and incorrectly promised by our social environment in an implicit fashion" (Lebrun, 1997, p. 153).

The prevailing ideals of health and beauty tend to play down the aspects of the decomposition and decay of the body, the treatment of which becomes an absolute value. That body, which has been emptied of all value by idealistic discourses, martyred and destroyed by the Catholic religion, comes to occupy a central position in present-day culture by a reversal in perspective.

Those societies that base their conduct excessively on values exalting technology, information and the mass media, as has happened in this era of scientific progress, are essentially narcissistic. Here seduction thrives on its features of hegemony, dictatorship and avidity for domination, which render it capable only of favouring a flattening of values and a levelling of needs. [Racalbuto, 1999, p. 51]

Often, in order to defend the ethno-historical relativity of paedophilic taste, sexual rites of initiation engaged in by certain cultures are cited: for example, the Sambia people of New Guinea define those "bachelors" who do not allow pre-pubertal youths to suck their penises as aberrant (Herdt, 1981). What is forgotten, however, is that those rites are inscribed in culture and, consequently, in the register of symbols and not in that of transgressions (Lopez, 1997). Luther Blissett (the name of an English football player, adopted as a collective pseudonym by artists and activists disseminating counter-information) holds that we must distinguish between love for children on the one hand and infantile prostitution and sexual violence on the other (1997). Jones (1990) would like to replace the term "sexual abuse" with "intergenerational intimacy", arguing that sexual contact does not necessarily produce negative effects on the child. Thorstad (1990) considers the fight against the criminalisation of paedophilia to be an integral part of the fight in defence of the rights of homosexuals.

Those intellectuals who support such theses and who speak of the emancipation and the sexual freedom of the child (as well as of the adult paedophile) fail to admit that their own emancipation is, in actual fact, from those prohibitions which impede the deployment of the power an adult has to seduce a child. This power comes into being in an asymmetrical and narcissistic relationship which is not equally innocuous to both parties.

Paedophilia can count on the complicity and support which is implicit in the entire social body: we are referring not only and not principally to elitist ideological sympathies (for instance, those of certain intellectuals who identify in what is perverse the representative of a persecuted sexuality, seen as antithetical to the order constituted by the family and the system of production), but rather to widespread attitudes of emotive identification with paedophilia, which are more implicit and immediate …

Paedophilia is not a wholly isolated perverse reaction, but has wide-ranging adherents and sympathisers whose stance is often not clear-cut. The deeply-rooted tendency in the collective erotic imagination (especially in that of the male) to prefer "fresh meat", the young body, is encouraged by modern society, which favours the differentiation of erotic stimuli and of sexual supply (in such a way as to involve pre-adolescence and infancy), viewing it as one way of escaping the anxieties and the problems created by adult heterosexual relationships. Indeed, some scholars have connected the development of paedophilia with the spread of AIDS and the consequent concerns with impotence and with the death of the male. These worries can, when one's aim is self-defence, be more easily overcome in a relationship with a child partner, who presents less risk of contagion and can be more easily manipulated. [Foti & Roccia, 1994a, p. 25 ff]

Sexual identity, especially male sexual identity, may suffer profound damage; sometimes such damage is irreparable. This is why many men are incapable of relationships involving real exchange between partners. "When we are incapable of relating to others, hence of having sentimental and sexual relationships which are satisfactory to both parties, we activate a need for power which for some people becomes omnipotence" (Baldaro Verde, 1997, p. 103).

Paedophilia which occurs without violent physical acts and without apparent constraints is based on the force of narcissistic seduction. The destructive power of this variant is as great as that of the violent one. In the final analysis, for a child it is easier to believe that he is an active partner in determining the abuse rather than the innocent victim, because the latter would cause his idealisation of the adult (which he has constructed with great effort) to collapse, and would bring back to the surface of his memory the angst-ridden passivity with which the traumatic event was experienced. This may help account for precocious sexual experiences being described in positive terms by many paedophiles as an important source of gratification.

The paedophile feels powerful only with partners whom he deems inferior and seducible. Love is thus also a defence against a relationship with an object that is perceived as being independent.

> The defensive line of argument is very often a projection. The subject attributes to the other the sentiments and the desires which he refuses to see in himself. He believes that he has been provoked, that he is a passive victim of a game of seduction in which the only part he played was that of succumbing. [Dubret, 1996, p. 144]

The intensity and the warmth of the child are perceived as an invitation to participate in a feast of sex. Time cannot wait for the process of physical and mental maturation to run its course. The paedophile's pleasure consists of tasting the potential of the unripe fruit. But in the paedophile's imagination, the child cannot wait either; he must immediately give genital concreteness to his sexuality, otherwise he will appear as a child who has repressed his capacity and desire for pleasure.

> Given the fact that the paedophile confuses sexual promiscuity with sexuality, sexual love loses its characteristic of belonging to the world of personal intimacy and becomes a public encounter between bodies. The child and the adolescent become sexualised and the fantasy is lived that they enjoy being used. [De Masi, 1998, p. 25]

It is one thing for a child to dream, devoting such dreams to sexual play with himself or with his peers; it is quite another to find himself faced with the reality of an adult's orgasm (Bonnetaud, 1998).

> Certain pre-pubertal girls undergoing analysis may exhibit attitudes of vanity, sensuality and seduction. Generally, this type of behaviour is stereotypical and without any foundation in reality. It may be classified as a form of defence which can be labelled "false self", which seeks to cover up internal conflicts and difficulty in acquiring new models of identification. [Machado, 1996, p. 1169]

To claim that satisfying drives is an affirmation of joy is an invention of the fantasy of a person who is motivated by a strong denial, according to Green (1997). Children who seem relatively well-disposed towards an intimate relationship with an adult generally come from economically or socially poor backgrounds where the family is unable to guarantee protection and valid affective ties. These children, more than any others, allow strangers to approach them, and the stranger can take advantage of the child's excessive willingness to talk to him, of the child's highly vulnerable defences, and also of a certain degree of confused and confusing promiscuity and desire to seduce:

> He trusts him. As if he already knew him. As if the adult's behaviour was the embodiment of a model which the child had acquired to perfection. Almost as if the encounter with the paedophile was a possible event within the child's scheme of life. [Camarca & Parsi, 2000, p. 15]

A precocious process of "adultification" and an explicit manifestation of the use of sexuality are often employed as defences against the perception of the pain caused by neglect and by affective deprivation (De Masi, 1999).

In her novel *What We Don't Know About Children* (1997), Simona Vinci provides an effective portrait of how the erotic games of a group of small children, whose behaviour is at once ambiguous and innocent, are transformed into forbidden games which become increasingly transgressive through the perverse contamination of the adult gaze. The presence of adults through the introduction of magazines which are gradually more and more pornographic (the aim being to stimulate the imitative tendencies of the children) changes the meaning of the games and corrupts the aura of ambiguous curiosity which envelops them, transforming them into degradation and death.

There are people and movements who are fighting against the criminalisation of all forms of paedophilia. Sapir (1997) speaks of an ignoble campaign carried on in the political arena and by the mass media branding all paedophiles as brutal murderers. I too believe that we must distinguish between simple perversion, inciting, aiding and/or abetting the prostitution of minors, and violent sexual behaviour. However, we must do so in order to intervene with greater efficacy in manifestations which are aetiologically different but which are all pathological, not to create an artificial distinction between "good" and "bad" forms of paedophilia. This is what Luther Blissett does in the book *Lasciate che i Bimbi* (1997), where the cry of "witch hunt" is shouted to the heavens in order to justify a sexual pseudo-liberty which lies at the root of paedophilia.

Magris states: "In order to tackle seriously the web of evil in which we are entangled and which each one of us weaves like a poisonous silkworm, a public avowal of one's good intentions, no matter how sincere these intentions may be, is not enough, nor is the wild apotheosis of transgression, which often involves a warm and reassuring sentimental pathos" (1999, p. 40).

Herbert Marcuse (1963) and Reimut Reiche (1968), two of the last *adepti* of the Frankfurt School, speak of "repressive desublimation" when describing the permissiveness which in late capitalist society replaces the old sex-phobic morality. Excessive emphasis is given to *deregulation*, by which is meant the rejection of all normative systems as well as a demand for a drastic reduction in the number of rules, which are held to be excessively numerous and stifling. "The dangers of repressive desublimation, which increase with every widening of the bounds of what is socially permitted in terms of gratification, cannot be done away with by a programme of political asceticism" (Reiche, 1968, p. 140).

Paedophilia is a complex theme, because it involves from the very outset extremely strong and deeply rooted feelings, such as the child's love of the adults on whom he is dependent, and an adult's love for a child onto whom he often projects his own childhood, his own fantasies of omnipotence. "Paedophilia inhabits that no-man's-land where transgressive gestures are so entangled with gestures expressing tenderness, care and love for the child that it is truly extremely difficult to distinguish from the outside, and perhaps even from the inside, where a gesture signifying favourable reception ends and where a gesture signifying transgression begins" (Galimberti, 2000b, p. 15).

Ernest Beaumont Schoedsack and Merian Creelman Cooper's film *King Kong* (1933) and its successive remakes successfully portray the ambiguity of paedophilic sentiments in the scene in which the monster holds the hand of the frightened girl who is exceedingly small compared to him, and cries tears of love while bullets of all types from all imaginable kinds of weapons try to annihilate him in order to prevent the town from being destroyed.

In addition, giving undue weight to paedophilic behaviour may contribute to the onset and entrenchment of behaviour of a paedophilic nature. Society already exhibits tendencies to reduce sexual contacts for fear of contagion from AIDS, and there is a general move to privileging virtual relationships, a phenomenon which is facilitated by the expansion of the Internet. To these tendencies must be added reduced contact time between working mothers and their children, the frequent abandonment or significant reduction of breastfeeding, and the important loss of the cultural value of forms of physical contact between mother and child, such as kissing the child all over after having washed and powdered him. The fear of accusations of paedophilia, whether these be internal or external, may further reinforce the development of anti-paedophile tendencies by triggering what may properly be called a reaction, whereas such a reaction should be curbed in the name of sane physical contacts which can enhance the development of the child. While we are on this point, it is worth noting that there has been a considerable increase in the number of accusations of infantile sexual abuse which spouses level at each other in divorce cases. Often many of these are unfounded, but they risk seriously compromising the accused parent's relationship with the child. There is also an increased tendency for many fathers to reduce the amount of time they spend in naked contact with their children, especially with their daughters. "Every hand stretched out to touch a child's head in an instinctive movement betokening tenderness risks, even in the street or in a public garden, being mistaken for an act of paedophilia" (Mafai, 2000, p. 15). "It is counterproductive to create an atmosphere of suspicion around all those normal and spontaneous emotional outpourings, or around those harmless games alluding to private parts of the body which can be played between adults and children" (Oliverio Ferraris & Graziosi, 2001, p. viii).

Sohn (1989) points out that in some legal cases, mostly prior to 1900, politics and sexuality were closely intertwined (which is not dissimilar to what happens nowadays), for when disputes arose, mayors, but also teachers and clerics, were infamously attacked by their political opponents with accusations of being paedophiles.

Finally, it must be borne in mind that placing unjustifiable stress on encounters with paedophiles, when communicating with children in an unbalanced fashion, may result in children's trust in adults being undermined. There is then a risk that adults are seen as the enemy against whom children must protect themselves. Many associations which provide help to abused children have reported cases of young children, influenced by information gleaned from television, having invented purely fictional stories of assaults, transforming fantasies of seduction into reality. Often these fantasies are substitutes for the care and attention they have not received from their parents. Virginie Dumont wrote the fairy tale *J'ai Peur du Monsieur* for the very reason that she wished to highlight the risk of providing too much information. To do so, she makes an eight-year-old child interviewed by a journalist say:

> "We should indeed be informed in order to be protected. But at the age of eight and older we are not yet adults. We need to dream, we still need to tell ourselves that adults are good and happy people. Otherwise, if we know too many things, we will no longer wish to grow up; growing up is too sad then. So be very careful about what you say to us, about the scenes we see on television, about what we hear." [1997, p. 46]

We do not know for certain whether paedophilia is on the increase today, but what cannot be doubted is that the phenomenon is given much fuller coverage than previously. Alice Miller writes: "Dr Elisabeth Trube-Becker, a specialist in forensic medicine, maintains that, based on the most recent studies, for every reported case of sexual abuse of children there are fifty unreported cases to be assumed" (1988, p. 61). Miller also reports that in the vast majority of cases paedophiles are people children know and not strangers.

The crisis in the sex-phobic visions of the past has brought about a radical change in the way the problem of paedophilia is presented: from being taboo, something which is not mentioned (the term "paedophilia" does not appear in the ANSA archives until 1987, as Iaria et al. [1996] point out), to being a scandal, something which is mentioned too much as well as being heavily criticised, and finally from an attitude of indifference to one of sometimes hysterical prejudice. Lately we have witnessed a proliferation of films and novels whose subject is paedophilia. This induces us to think that there has been a deliberate choice of a topic which is "marketable" rather than one which is motivated by authentic artistic and social considerations. Since the cinema and literature exaggerate the extent of the problem in this particular case, they end up depicting it as an epidemic, thereby aggravating the situation (Schinaia, 1999).

> There is a continuous oscillation between the two extremes of silence and the "I couldn't care less" attitude at one pole and the clamour for repression which could have devastating negative effects on the perpetrators of abuses at the other pole. Indeed there is mental and behavioural continuity between the two positions, since both are founded on the common need to stave off the perception of violence and "evil" and to maintain an idealised image of the adult world at all costs; on the common incapacity to perceive the phenomenon of the sexual abuse of children in an adequate and responsible manner; and on the common refusal to recognise and elaborate the adult's emotional ambivalence towards the world of the child, which is present, in various forms, in all components of adult society, not only in paedophiles. [Foti, 1998, p. 13]

The spasmodic attention paid to the theme of the abuse of minors aggravates the shock and the scandal provoked by individual cases, but this in actual fact justifies the failure to take notice of our daily behaviour (Resta, 1999).

Calandra, Monteleone and Di Rosa (1998) collected a series of articles published in the national (Italian) and the local (Sicilian) daily papers concerning cases of child ill-treatment over about a year (1994–1995). These included cases of sexual abuse. What they underlined was the lack of reflection on the information conveyed in the news from an educational and preventive standpoint.

A sensationalist approach to the topic of sexual violence perpetrated on minors may stimulate aggressiveness in the reader. Furthermore, the younger the reader, the more he will be stimulated, thereby moving him further and further away from the possibility of understanding his own limits and the principles which govern social relationships. The reader is increasingly induced into isolation and into grasping only decontextualised fragments of a phenomenon whose dynamics are complex, thus increasing the probability that he will not only passively accept violence, but even act it out (Calandra, Monteleone & Di Rosa, 1998).

In research carried out by Marchiori, Simioni and Colombo (2000) on articles concerning sexual violence which appeared in three complete years a decade apart (1977, 1987, 1997) in three Italian national dailies (*La Repubblica*, *L'Unità* and *Il Gazzettino*), the authors stress the fact that the information appears to be redundant, confused and stereotyped: "Instead of increasing readers' sensitivity to sexual crime, the news and the images pertaining to the various forms of sexual abuse, exploited to satisfy the needs of news-making and sales, efficiency and marketability, progressively decontextualised and impoverished, seem rather to have created a cultural climate which is emotionally anaesthetised, or, to put it another way, a climate of impotence and resignation" (Marchiori, Simioni & Colombo, 2000, p. 191).

One of the features of the news items concerning abuse which remains substantially unchanged in the two decades scrutinised in the aforementioned study is that while the dailies provide a plethora of information about the perpetrator of the act and the act which was actually carried out, the information they furnish regarding the psychology of the victim is scarce (obviously bearing in mind the protection of the victim's privacy). "This method of news reporting contributes to creating an atmosphere of suspense, counting on the novelised aspect of the crime which thus induces the reader to lose sight of the gravity of the fact with regard to the emotional effect on the victim" (*ibid.*, p. 198). The result of these newspaper operations may also be an increase in the fear and mistrust of people and social institutions, with a consequent growth in pessimism and aggressiveness.

> Convicts deem ensnaring and damaging minors to be such infamous acts that those who are accused of deeds of that nature need to be placed in isolation as a preventive measure. Such a call to man the bastions suggests the presence of unexpressed conflicts which secretly characterise all moralistic and intransigent attitudes. Indignation generally constitutes the attempt to control a disposition to let oneself go and commit those shameful acts. [Brandi, 1998, p. 111]

The theme of the monster in Fritz Lang's film *The Monster of Düsseldorf* deals with the problem of the adult's ambivalent attitude towards the child, which is then transformed into a collective fear of the monster and from there into a projective search for the scapegoat, represented by the eloquent sequence of images of the lynching of an innocent person by an infuriated mob. Paradoxically, such images are in actual fact reassuring because of their Manichean character, which opens and maintains the gap between what is monstrous and what is normal. The brutally headlined monster on the front page is a caricature of the real monster, and the reductionism and the simplification which support this superficial journalistic sketch enable readers to avoid both coming to terms with daily examples of abuses against children and identifying paedophilic attitudes frequently present in people who are "apparently normal", a stereotype which is supported and fed by the equally "normal" propaganda of the media. D'Avanzo quotes the British journalist Decca Aitkenhead, who wrote the following in *The Guardian* in 1998:

> There are now very few groups of people that the general public may continue hating while continuing to feel virtuous. Paedophiles fit the bill perfectly. When the paedophile Sidney Cooke was released from prison and sent home, a crowd of grandmothers, adolescents and businesswomen besieged the Somerset County Police Headquarters without even knowing for certain that Cooke was there in hiding or under protection. The ignorance of those women was second only to their determination to do something: "Kill the bastard!" They did not know what Cooke looked like, whether he really was a paedophile, if he was really guilty, what he had done and what he was accused of having done. They knew he existed, they knew that he had the reputation of being a paedophile, and that was more than enough. So, "Kill that paedophile!" [D'Avanzo, 2000, p. 1]

D'Avanzo comments: "Everyone can leave the prison of their own private life, free themselves—for one afternoon of their uncertain destiny—of their provisional life, and breathe beyond that ubiquitous fog of anxiety, fear and insecurity which renders each shadow a danger and each day uneasy" (*ibid.*, p. 16).

Bryan Appleyard writes (2000) that paedophiles are the new witches, and that faced with a paedophile, citizens can lose their usual self-control. Another phenomenon which manifests itself when a victim reports to the police a paedophile who up to that moment had been believed to be "above suspicion" is a crisis of identity both in the community to which the victim belongs and in the one of which the paedophile is a member. Reactions may be triggered which stigmatise the victim more than the person committing the abuse. Foti and Roccia, basing their work on Girard's theory of the sacrificial victim as the foundation stone of the cultural order of the primitive community, comment:

> The confusing abolition of the differences, produced by the paedophile through the sexual initiative he has taken, has thus spread in circular fashion to the attitude of the entire community, which ends up banding together the responsibilities of the adult with those of the child ... The circularity of hate and the spiral of vengeance risk infecting anyone who is involved in an explosion of violence, placing perpetrator and victim on the same plane regardless of their differing responsibilities at the onset of the episode of violence, for both participate in the same threat levelled at the social order. The community must therefore take steps to distance itself from both parties and do everything it can to exorcise the risk of being overwhelmed by the destructive escalation sparked off by the act of violence. To this end, the community decides to unleash a "founding act of violence" through a ritual which has the community's consensus: this act is the revenge of many upon one member of the community who is transformed into a sacrificial victim, a scapegoat. This is the only way to put an end to the spiral of individual vendettas and re-establish the equilibrium of peace within the community. [1994b, pp. 51–52]

I wish to stress the point that when a phenomenon like paedophilia (or perversions in general) leaves the individuality and secrecy of the terrain of the hidden personality, and instead of being limited to private psychoanalytical treatment takes on forms which are almost collective, then at least two important consequences ensue. First, justification of its existence is achieved through the assertion of a necessary quota of aggressiveness, which is propagandised as a visible component of individual liberty; and second, it becomes a market phenomenon, it is offered on the Internet and it generates a certain form of pornography which is not even particularly clandestine. This should constitute a great cause for concern, for the phenomenon risks acquiring the proportions of a social epidemic, one in which "the search for others with common interests also represents an attempt to avoid individual guilt through shared responsibility" (De Masi, 1998, p. 22).

SOCIAL AND CULTURAL ASPECTS   25

If paedophilia is ennobled into a way of life, requiring the same social recognition as other ways of life, if it becomes a philosophy, and if this operation creates a justification for such a mode of conduct which eludes a sense of guilt, making it inaccessible, then we may possibly reach the point where this type of behaviour is evaluated positively and might even confer a sort of universal superiority on its practitioners. The creation of a neo-morality, the construction of an individual's personal philosophy in which the subject may find a location for his deviance, is often done with the aim of keeping at bay any possible emergence of a sense of guilt. The frequent references paedophiles make to the customs of Ancient Greece are a manifestation of the same defence mechanism (Dubret, 1996).

> Rigid ideological attitudes, with no possibility of contemplating alternatives, tend to take root in groups which have emerged from splitting operations. Group thought becomes obsessive and monothematic. The situations which have been excluded from group interests become issues which are extraneous to the group ... The ultimate consequences are impotence and impoverishment. [Di Chiara, 1999, p. 24]

Di Chiara further points out that members of subgroups produced by mental splitting operations exhibit a loss of the sense of community. "Attachment to the part overwhelms the sense of belonging to the whole" (*ibid.*, p. 26).

The encounter between the rich Western world and the poverty of the Third World has given rise to the young of the weak being systematically violated on a world-wide scale through the phenomenon of sexual tourism, as is brutally narrated by Claudio Camarca in his essay *I Santi Innocenti* (1998). Even worse, this is done in the name of a sort of decontamination achieved through a relationship with the natural purity of the little ones, where the poorer the little ones, the greater the purity. He describes the silence that accompanies the abuses perpetrated on minors, shown on certain Internet sites which appear to be inhabited by anorexic models of twelve, going from images of young naked children running after one another to advertise a new line of bathroom tiles, to those of a little girl in a cage imitating a canary rocking on a swing. Such behaviour can only call to mind the grave responsibilities of the consumer society for creating organised paedophilia, for transforming children not only into new consumers, but also into new objects of consumption. "Paedophilia is the exact reproduction of a society based on power. Absolutely hierarchical and absolutely consumerist" (Camarca & Parsi, 2000, p. 22).

Kevin Bales (1999) stresses the fact that even juvenile prostitution in the poorer countries has changed. In Thailand, for example, daughters were originally sold when the family was faced with an extremely serious financial crisis, whereas today in Bangkok a little girl is sold for a television set: one consumer object in exchange for another consumer object. Casilli ironically states that "unlike the long claws of the tiger that abducted Indian children and the *vulkodlak* (werewolf) of the Bulgarian tradition, the modern *raptor* is overly human, it imitates the daily rituals of normal production, and in no case whatsoever does it aspire to abnormality" (1998, p. 37).

> The barrage of information, of publicity, of new and increasingly sophisticated technology can produce stimuli that obfuscate individual capacities to reason and reflect, and interfere with the capacity for autonomous choice, diminishing it ... The stimuli produced by narcissistic seduction tend not to favour individual life stories; instead they tend to unify the various options available in the name of a "product" which ensures wellbeing and peace of mind and which caters for people's needs with ever-increasing effectiveness and range. But the subtle and underhand violence in this type of "social order" brings with it a sort of traumatism which produces too strong a homogenising effect, and leads to the appreciation of violence and of ambiguity, so that the human being finds he is no longer able to make authentic choices ... The seductive value behind the concrete reality of instantaneous possession lies in a drift in which everything is the same as everything else, homogenised into the sole need that must be satisfied: that of grabbing, dominating, possessing, of *having* rather than of *being*. We no longer recognise that it is only by accepting the finite that we can open the horizons of infinity, thereby resolving the opposition between subject and object, internal and external, nature and culture. [Racalbuto, 1999]

Who is not struck by the realisation that the model of our ideal city is offered to us in two versions, two standardised images which couple like an operatic duo: Disneyland and Las Vegas? One represents the child's world imagined as a miniaturised adult; the other represents the adult's world imagined as an eternal child. We have entered, without realising it, a real idolatry of the child, a "childolatry". [André, 1999, p. 5]

Advertising fosters immediate gratification and generates the illusion that total gratification is possible.

> Once the world of the child is viewed as goods, as a product, as a raw material (which is, of course, the view the market favours), then the child, who should be the receiver of *cultural transmission* in the human community (which is not the case in the animal world), acquires exactly the same status as all other goods, namely that of a link in the chain of *material production*, and through this process of the "materialisation of childhood" the human community loses its *cultural* trait, which, ultimately, is the feature that distinguishes it from the animal world. [Galimberti, 2000a, p. 17]

In this case, perversion, which is constantly seeking social confirmation which will render it presentable inasmuch as it is accepted as a variant of normal present-day sexuality, is an indication of the degradation of social life, where necessary and mature tolerance has been replaced by licentiousness, by a refusal to recognise limits and the demarcation lines of those limits, and above all by indifference—by which I mean lack of differentiation—and by the pseudo-normalisation of perversion and of civil and ethical disorder in a population or a collective which can be classified as large (Petrella, 1997). All this is deeply rooted in the family and in society.

> If for Lombroso and Freud socialisation brought with it the effect of preventing the individual from enacting behaviours towards which his instincts and drives impelled him, we may ask ourselves if the processes of socialisation that are enacted today do not produce the opposite result, namely a facilitating effect which arouses rather than inhibits possible initiations of acting out: the role of images, the trade in human bodies. [Arveiller, 1998]

There exists an idea of sexuality in contemporary culture which overturns the logic which had made of it an absolutely negative experience, intended to produce feelings of guilt and therefore to be criticised and repressed; instead, it is represented as a domain which is absolutely devoid of problems and conflicts. Sexuality is purportedly an area which is intrinsically and globally pleasurable or, at the extreme end of the argument, as easy as drinking a glass of water. Sexuality as an intrinsically positive reality is also contrasted with culture as a repressive and suffocating reality, forgetting that those mental operations and those interpersonal relationships which are a source of suffering and destructiveness can condition sexuality just as much as they condition culture, in the same way that constructive mental operations and interpersonal relationships can salvage both the former and the latter realities. [Foti & Roccia, 1994b, p. 28]

If the slogan "make love, not war", with its Marcusian allusions, indicates on the one hand a non-destructive way to channel the libido, on the other hand it runs the risk of making sexuality appear to be free of any conflict, purged even of the aggression necessary to undertake the standard wars involved in interpersonal relationships and existence in general. Even Freud, in "Beyond the Pleasure Principle" (1920), had stressed the negative effects inherent in the tendency to dwell on pure pleasure, judging such a mental attitude to be non-developmental and non-constructive.

"When Luchino Visconti wanted to represent the signs of the ethical decadence of the German bourgeois family between the two World Wars in his film *The Damned*, what he presented was a symptomatic episode of paedophilia as a symbol of that tragic confusion and degradation that was to lead inexorably to Nazism" (Petrella, 1997). Michel Tournier is another writer who has associated paedophilia with Nazism. If Fascism had overestimated youth, making a value out of it, an end in itself, an obsession in advertising, then "Nazism, which was rooted in this 'youthophilia', aggravated the situation with maniacal attitudes … causing 'youthophilia' to incline to paedophilia … If fresh meat is to be good, it must be blond, blue and dolichocephalic, its opposite being bad brown meat, black and brachycephalic" (1977, p. 77). Sexual violence on a child who will later commit suicide is portrayed in Roberto Rossellini's film

Germany Year Zero as the metaphor of the degradation of human relationships brought about by the devastating brutality of the war, which—as Mosse (1985) points out—encourages reactions of violence and domination, including in the field of sexual behaviour.

This history of sexual appropriation continues today in forms which are new and less obvious, though it must be stated that the older and more brutal forms have not ceased to make their tragic appearance on the stage of modern history (Foti & Roccia, 1994b). This is borne out by the recent cases of rape in Bosnia, perpetrated, moreover, on an extremely high number of minors, and committed with the total indifference of the international community (Doni & Valentini, 1993; Oberti, 1999; Unità di Crisi "Luciana Nissim", 2000). "In this barbaric order, even the special status of women and children is not only denied, but inverted, to allow the persecutors the pleasure of dominating through killing and raping" (Oberti, 1999, p. 819).

The novelty in our epoch of the social organisation of paedophilia and the call for visibility (in contrast to the anonymity and secrecy to which perversions were relegated until a short time ago), the sinister intertwining of the personal and the social which is at stake here, are too complex even to be understood by the limited resources of a psychiatrist or a psychoanalyst. What is required, therefore, is a joint effort by many scholars in the various fields involved: together with the psychiatrist and the psychoanalyst, the participants must definitely include the sociologist, the educationalist, but above all the politician and the legislator. In interpreting new social phenomena and proposing new laws, it is the task of the latter two categories to protect the individual and the community, dynamically harmonising individual needs with those of community life.

A law was passed recently against the merchants and clients of children, which establishes harsher sanctions for those who exploit young children, with powers to prosecute extended to include those who commit sexual crimes abroad and the clients of minors under the age of sixteen. Fines and money confiscated from the paedophile market will be put aside in a special fund to finance programmes of prevention, and of aid and recovery for the child victims.

Building a culture of respect for the integrity of the child is not an easy task in today's world, and pro-paedophile propaganda risks finding easy terrain when—in order to protect itself against accusations of commercialising the child and his sentiments—it brings into play an attention to the child's desires, including his sexual desires, defining them as natural and hence not to be repressed. The answer to the paedophiles' argument must be a clear enunciation of the nature of infantile desire, its gratuitousness, its specific language, its autonomous nature as play. It must not be short-circuited into a sexual relationship with an adult, which would result in the devitalisation of infantile desire and the death of the child's faith in the adult who is incapable of understanding and translating the language of the child's senses and sentiments, flattening them into his or her own language of passions (Ferenczi, 1933). For the paedophile, the sexual encounter is the repetition of a rite constructed through his own imagination, built with a precision which has nothing to do with the spontaneity and liberty which characterise infantile omnipotence, which is the kingdom of potential and creativity.

Notes

1. Freud wrote his paper entitled "Psychical (or Mental) Treatment" in 1890; the date was incorrectly given as 1905 in the Standard Edition.
2. In the last few years Italian newspapers have written at length about adolescents throwing stones. These adolescents lie in wait on motorway bridges to play the game of hitting passing cars travelling on the motorway below, causing death and injuries.

CHAPTER TWO

Myth and paedophilia

Clara Pitto and Cosimo Schinaia

> What is this about? Whence come those offensive fables? From which continents, which distant journeys do such horrors arise? For everyone to be so excited and to say that all those tales are so shocking and embarrassing there must be a reason, a motive, or at least a pretext.
>
> —Marcel Detienne

> A child asks his father, "Daddy, what does myth mean?" and the father replies, "What a stupid child you are, what a stupid child not to know what myth means!"
>
> —Cesare Musatti

In the strict sense of the term, a myth is commonly held to be a story which refers to a world order existing prior to the present order, whose aim is to explain not local and limited situations in detail but an organic law of the nature of things (Grimal, 1951). Myths may also be defined as prodigious stories which have been handed down over the centuries, replete with profound revelations on the human condition (Grant & Hazel, 1973). Myth is thus "something choral in which many take part: a race, a population, or even the whole of humanity. Hence, even though it is an imagined account, it appears to be an integral part of that race, that population, or humanity considered as a whole" (Musatti, 1987, p. 34). The narration of myths gave rise to mythology.

> On the one hand, [mythology] is a combination of discursive statements, of matter-of-fact narratives or even, as the saying goes, of narratives and stories … But at the same time mythology is represented as a dissertation *concerning* myths, a scholasticism that understands myths in general, their origin, their nature, their essence; a scholasticism that lays claim to being transformed into science, today as of yore, through customary usage; that lays claim to structuring some of its subjects, systematising different scholastic pronouncements as it designates, and formalising concepts and schemes. Intuitively, mythology is for us a semantic crossroads of two discourses, the second of which speaks of the first and springs from the interpretation of it. [Detienne, 1981, p. 1]

By dint of being a cultural product of the world of the Greeks, from its very beginnings mythology engages in interpretation which transforms it into a discourse:

> The meaning of myth may be found (a) in myth itself: this is the philosophy of tautegory adopted by Schelling and going through to Lévi-Strauss; (b) outside myth: through allegory, which seeks one or more hidden meanings underlying the immediate, surface meaning, which is deemed unacceptable, as do the Pythagoreans and the Stoics; (c) through myth: mythology contains something that cannot be expressed, that rational argument cannot put into words. It is the symbolism of the Neo-Platonists and, in more recent times, of Kerényi and of Ricoeur. [Detienne, 1980, p. 360]

Psychoanalysis and mythology have many points in common. Freud wrote: "The theory of the instincts is so to say our mythology. Instincts are mythical entities, magnificent in their indefiniteness" (1933, p. 95). According to Freud, mythopoetic effects may be "an attempt to give (in play, as it were) a disguised representation to universally familiar, though also extremely interesting, mental processes" (1932, p. 191). In "On Dreams" he states that "dream-symbolism extends far beyond dreams; it is not peculiar to dreams, but exercises a similar dominating influence on representation in fairy-tales, myths and legends, in jokes and in folklore" (1901, p. 685). And again, Freud writes: "myths … are distorted vestiges of the wishful phantasies of whole nations, the *secular dreams* of youthful humanity" (1908, p. 152). "People's 'childhood memories' are only consolidated at a later period … this involves a complicated process of remodelling, analogous in every way to the process by which a nation constructs legends about its early history" (1909, p. 206). Freud explains that "myths contain the same psychical 'complexes', the same emotional trends, which have been discovered at the base of dreams and symptoms" (1913, p. 183).

The highly dramatic nature of mythological images, their indecency, their extremely direct and explicit mode of communication, their resistance to any form of censorship bear a great similarity with both drives and dreams, the difference being that they belong to the sphere of the collective rather than that of the individual. Myths, like dreams, are recognised as such by all readers, in every part of the world (Lévi-Strauss, 1958).

But it was a writer, Thomas Mann to be precise, who was the first to provide an effective description of the parallels between myth and psychology:

> The mythical interest is as native to psychoanalysis as the psychological interest is to all creative writing. Its penetration into the childhood of the individual soul is at the same time a penetration into the childhood of mankind, into the primitive and mythical. Freud has told us that for him all natural science, medicine, and psychotherapy were a lifelong journey round and back to the early passion of his youth for the history of mankind, for the origins of religion and morality … The word *Tiefenpsychologie* ("depth" psychology) has a temporal significance; the primitive foundations of the human soul are likewise primitive time, they are those profound time-sources where the myth has its home and shapes the primeval norms and forms of life. For the myth is the foundation of life; it is the timeless schema, the

pious formula into which life flows when it reproduces its traits out of the unconscious. [Mann, 1956, p. 112]

Musatti writes: "How could a psychoanalyst interpret the dreams of every single patient, if there were no common basis in many groups of dreams experienced by various individuals? All oneirology (both the original strand which was slightly fantastic and approximate and the brand practised by modern psychoanalysts) is based on the presupposition that there exists a pool of shared motives which manifest themselves in the various dreams experienced by different individuals" (1987, p. 40). Starting from these considerations, Musatti affirms that psychoanalysis has re-evaluated myth, transforming it into an object of scientific enquiry and, taking up Freud, has defined the unconscious with all its products as the world of myths. Speaking ironically of psychoanalysis, the protagonist of *Zeno's Conscience* states: "It was a sickness that elevated me to the highest noble company. An illustrious sickness, whose ancestors dated back to the mythological era" (Svevo, 1923, p. 403).

Jung also investigated myths. He considered them to be the expression of the collective unconscious. In Jung's view, in the innumerable variants that may be found in the various populations, a mythological theme is the expression of a unitary and atemporal structure of the human unconscious. Myths are therefore the expression of the basic mechanisms of the human psyche.

Kerényi, a historian who has applied Jungian concepts, considers myth to be the direct expression of one's cultural vision of the world and of the existence which characterises a culture. Myths are often similar in many parts of the world because it is of their very essence to express world views and fundamental aspects of life: people reflect the universal drama of life in myths.

According to Kerényi, images presupposed neither questions nor thought. In fact, those images always appeared to have "depth", but from the Greek thinkers onwards people made the mistake of believing that those images stood for something else, a concept which was hidden behind them; that is to say, they were taken for allegories. This stance goes not only against the theory of allegory but also against structuralism, both of which aim at writing a grammar of the mythical world. Kerényi compares mythology with music or any true work of art. He writes:

> Just as music has a meaning that is satisfying in the sense that every meaningful whole is satisfying, so every true mythologem (mythological picture) has its satisfying meaning. This meaning is so hard to translate into the language of science because it can be fully expressed only in mythological terms … From this combined pictorial, significant, and musical aspects of mythology there follows the right attitude towards it: to let the mythologems speak for themselves and simply to listen. Any explanation has to be along the same lines as the explanation of a musical or poetic work of art. [Jung & Kerényi, 1940, p. 5]

Green (1992) considers myth to be "a transitional, collective object". Myth functions as representation: not the translation of current desires, but a production of the spirit, which is created starting from the derivates of drives.

In Chabert's view (1993) myths constitute an attempt to answer the great questions concerning human origin. The comparison with our origins, with the unexplainable, gives rise to the creation of the ghost phantasy in the individual and of myth in the community.

Graves (1955) takes a different stance. In his view Greek myths are not the blind manifestation of the collective unconscious, but are to be interpreted in historical and sociological terms. He stresses the fact that the study of myths must start from a comparative study of archaeology, history and religions. Many myths are an almost faithful reproduction of the political and religious history of a country. In this sense, the myth of Zeus and Ganymede, which was extremely popular in Greece and Rome, furnished a religious justification for the practice of an adult male loving a young boy, rendering that practice not only legitimate but also desirable.

According to Graves, Ancient Greek mythology mirrors the social changes beginning with the annual sacrifice of the king and ending, at the time of the *Iliad*, with the decline of matriarchy. Each year the tribal nymph chose a lover, a boy, who became the king and who was sacrificed at the end of the year. His flesh was devoured raw by the queen and her priestesses, and his blood was scattered over the fields to guarantee fertility. The sacrifice of the adolescent lover was connected with the life cycle of plants. Fertility rites including human sacrifice were common throughout the world. Later the king was allowed to live longer, but the fields still had to be fertilised, the ceremony had to take place, so the king entrusted his kingdom for only one day to a young boy, who was sacrificed in his place. At a later stage, the adolescents were replaced on the sacrificial altar by animals.

The matrilineal tradition weakened over time. According to Graves, the establishment of patrilineal descent, which was reflected in myth with the shattering of the Olympian equilibrium in which there were as many goddesses as there were gods, discouraged the creators of myths. Historical legend was born at this point, which in its turn declined to give way to history proper. Neumann (1949) also takes the view that the confrontation between the patriarchal world and the matriarchal world is depicted as epic history and is personalised as family history in the myths of the gods and heroes. Lopez has this to say:

> The history of the gods, of the heroes, of the ancestors and of mythical Greek castes is a history of incestuous relationships, of parricides, matricides, fratricides, infanticides, in which the overriding theme, the deep-seated plot, the primary driving force, is not so much Oedipal hate of the parent of the opposite sex as the mortal battle for domination and supremacy between two religious universes, two cultural worlds, namely matriarchy and patriarchy, a deadly struggle between the two sexes, where the destiny of the offspring, the choices they made, and incest itself, were a function of the alliance made with one or the other parent in the struggle for power. [1985b, p. 165]

In Lopez's view, the grand themes of myth embody the deep plot of vital libidinal-emotional conflicts. Lopez takes up the theory of the passage from matriarchy to patriarchy and endows this theory with the psychic significance that "there is no solution to the problem of generation, there are no prospects for the creation of a great civilisation … if the manner of surmounting the maternal symbiotic world is not thought out and achieved" (*ibid.*, p. 169).

While Graves considers that myths reflect and dramatise what happens in the real world, the other scholars quoted hold that myths depict in numerous ways the transgressions of the gods and of heroes, transgressions which are prohibited to mortal humans. Arfouilloux expresses the view that "in functioning as illustrations of genealogical bases of society, myths defy prohibitions, while those to whom the myths refer remain subjected to those prohibitions" (1993, p. 497). Every time a strong emotion affected them, Greek heroes attributed the responsibility to a god. This diminished their responsibility, for it was a god who guided their actions. There was no guilty party. There was only guilt, an immense guilt which was experienced by the victim as much as by the guilty person himself (Calasso, 1988).

In his theories, Freud often refers to the myth of Oedipus. But as Arfouilloux points out, in the genealogy of Oedipus cursed lines intersect, mixing incest, infanticide, parricide and homosexuality. These acts brand lineal descent forever and they cannot be cancelled out by the expiatory sacrifices which mark their history.

In Brenman's view, myth has two fundamental features: firstly, "the powerful omnipotent gods are determined to triumph over human compassion and understanding, and this in itself prompts counter-cruelty"; and secondly, "the omnipotent cruel and relentless gods are actually worshipped and revered and given a higher status than human love ... they are in fact 'loved' (as well as feared) more than humanity" (1988, p. 257).

In more general terms, myth may also illustrate the common features shared by death and paedophilia. The word *ogre* is derived from *Orcus*, in Roman mythology the divinity that reigns in the hereafter, and equivalent to the Greek *Hades*. By extension Ogre means death, and metonymically it stands for the kingdom of death, hence the devourer par excellence; *sarcophagus* means *flesh eater* (Brandi, 1998).

Post-Kleinian psychoanalysts believe that the plot of myths could contain material which is important in helping to comprehend the unconscious fantasies which the analysand relives in his transference relationship with the analyst. Hence, myths and mythology may be employed not only to attempt to explain intrapsychic phenomena, but also to investigate the complex relational intertwining (as well as complex domain interweaving, one might add) which may be witnessed in the consulting room.

Grinberg (1981) believes that the myths of Eden and of Babel help in enabling a better comprehension of the phenomena pertaining to that part of the personality which actively opposes the acquisition of knowledge and the functions of the Ego assigned to establishing and maintaining contact with reality. However, it is above all the myth of the death of Palinurus[1], described in Book V of Virgil's

Aeneid and quoted by Bion, which is most suitable to serve as a model contributing to the understanding of the psychotic part of the personality, of its effects on the neurotic part, and of the situation that comes about in the transference-countertransference relationship, when the psychotic part of the patient produces its effects on the analyst through pathological projective identifications. A young child overcome with envy and greed feels his distress as an injustice inflicted on him by the "gods", just as Palinurus rages against the unjust sacrifice ordained by Venus (Bion, 1977).

> We could compare Palinurus with the vicissitudes of an analyst, who is carrying out his psychoanalytical treatment in the peace and quiet of his consulting room (with the calm that the familiar and comfortable surroundings give him), when suddenly he sees himself in danger of being thrown violently from the analytical situation by the elements that appear as a model in Virgil's story. The effects produced by the "psychotic personality" affect both members of the analytical couple. It is possible to see in the myth the relationship between the analyst and his patient, or between the psychotic and the non-psychotic parts of the personality, between the ego allied to phantasy and the ego in contact with reality, between dreams and hallucinations, lethargy and psychic death, and so on. We can see the fate of the analyst if he does not guard himself adequately against the effects of the "psychotic personality" of his patient and/or his own. [Grinberg, 1981, p. 251]

In order to illustrate the use of his well-known grid, Bion (1977) referred to the excavations of the royal cemetery of Ur, an ancient Sumerian town. He represented the environment in which psychoanalysis is normally practised by resorting to two visual components: burial and pillage.

> Myths have a richness peculiar to them. They transmit certain ideas in constant conjunction in such a way that on occasions they do it better than technical terms that refer specifically to the idea they are trying to describe ... Myths can be compared to a mobile polyhedron, which, according to the angle we

see it from, demonstrates different faces, vertices, and edges. [Grinberg, 1981, pp. 245, 244]

Myth and fairy tale

The problem of the relationship between myth and fairy tale has interested scholars of various disciplines: folklore, anthropology, psychoanalysis and mythology. Widely differing relationships have been hypothesised between myth and fairy tale: one holds that fairy tale is a derivation, or rather a degeneration, of myth (Propp, 1928); an opposing view sees myths as deriving from folk tales, and—more radically—the more the myth resembles the folk tale, the older it is (Kirk, 1974); and finally, myth and fairy tale co-exist contemporaneously in the same culture and are no different in nature (Lévi-Strauss, 1967). In many of these stances we may discern an implicit, underlying evolutionary scheme in the sense that one phenomenon is seen as deriving from another, with the idea that the more "fantastic" it is, the more primitive it is, and in any case the more it is destined to disappear, to be replaced by forms which are more highly developed (Propp, 1928). In von Franz's view (1970), myths are closer to conscience and to history, and compared to fairy tales, myths are easier to interpret because they are less fragmentary.

With regard to the topic of this book, it is significant to note that both myth and fairy tale are *traditional stories*, that is to say they are handed down orally from one generation to the next. Most importantly, they have managed to achieve the status of being "traditional" because of some lasting qualities which have become important to the individual and to society, both at a narrative level and a functional level (Kirk, 1974). Another common feature is that both have a problematical nature. Both present one or more aspects of a conflict, of an existential problem. Theirs is the language of debate, not of a harmonic chorus (Leach, 1954).

According to Kirk, however (1974), the fairy tale differs from the myth because it is realistic and impersonal, its basic subject matter is life, people's problems and aspirations; it does not deal—as myths do—with gods or cosmological and religious issues, and above all with the family environment. Bettelheim (1975) comes to similar conclusions about the distinction between myths and fairy tales, working along totally different lines. Myths present grandiose, unique events inspiring sacred wonders, while fairy tales present unusual and improbable events which, notwithstanding these features, are ordinary and accessible to common mortals.

In myths the finale is often tragic, while the fairy tale always comes to a happy ending. The myth is pessimistic, the fairy tale is optimistic. Mythical heroes have lofty and unrealisable ideals and do not need to be emulated in real life, whereas the fairy tale is populated by ordinary human beings who are anonymous, or who have generic names which facilitate projection and identification, and manage to fulfil their human destiny, handling conflicts with means which can adequately solve those conflicts.

Even though both forms are narratives which have been traditionally handed down, another important difference between myth and fairy tale is that the fairy tale explicitly denies any claim to speak of religious or historical truths which must in some way be believed or made the object of faith or rational conviction. Opening formulae such as "Once upon a time", which have been employed since Ancient times (in Latin: *erant in quadam civitate rex et regina*), act as signals which convey to the reader the message that an imaginary tale is about to be recounted, one which differs from a legend or from *ordinary conversation*. Propp aptly reminds us that at the end of the fairy tale Russian narrators would say: "And now we will stop lying".

Fairy tales cannot be situated in time and space, their language is not very explicit, and they do not make many allusions to truths; the truth they do refer to is emotive. Furthermore, through the direct contact which comes about between narrator and listener, who often belong to different generations, fairy tales enable people to talk about contents and conflicts which are *transgenerational* and which would be unbearable if expressed directly.

Myths of origin

To judge by the myths which have survived, in all of Neolithic Europe there was a homogeneity of religious beliefs. These beliefs were based on the cult of an omnipotent and immortal Great Goddess, who was also venerated in Syria and Libya. This Goddess Mother went under many names: Gea; Gaia or Gaea; Eurynome. In

Olympic mythology she was known as Mother Earth and was considered to be the origin of all things. The concept of paternity had not yet been introduced into religious thought (Graves, 1955).

The gods were to appear later. In the various theogonies (mythological narratives describing the origins of the gods), three generations of divinities are generally seen as succeeding one another. The first generation is made up of Uranus and Gaia, the sky and the earth, and their children. The second consists of the generation of Cronus and his descendants. The last is that of Zeus and his stock. All the gods of Classical mythology descend from these divinities, and mythical heroes are born from the union of these gods with mortal beings.

Mother Earth had many offspring, including Uranus, who became her spouse. From this union Gaia gave birth to the sea, the mountains, the Giants, the Cyclopes, and the Titans. The Cyclopes were rebellious offspring forced to leave by their father and driven into Tartar, the hereafter, which was as far from the earth as the earth was from the sky. To avenge herself, Mother Earth persuaded the Titans to assassinate their father Uranus. In other versions, Gaia's desire for vengeance stemmed from the fact that Uranus did not allow her to give birth and obliged her to keep her babies in her womb. As in the primordial ordeal (Freud: 1912–13), the Titans, led by Cronus, the youngest of them, assaulted Uranus in his sleep and castrated him. It would seem that Aphrodite, the goddess of love, was fertilised by Uranus's genitals after they had been thrown into the sea.

In Davide Lopez's view (1985b), Cronus's act represents an abortive attempt to break the symbiosis with and dependence on the archaic mother. The myth of Uranus who never detaches himself from his mother-wife is, in Lopez's opinion, a magnificent representation of the symbiosis of man with woman-mother: Uranus was in perpetual erotic contact with Mother Earth, to the point that there was neither time nor room for childbirth.

Cronus seized power and married his sister Rhea. However, both Uranus, who was on his deathbed, and Mother Earth prophesied that Cronus would be dethroned by one of his children. Hence, in an attempt to avoid this fate, each year Cronus devoured the children generated by Rhea. Rhea was furious, and when she gave birth to Zeus, her third male child, she threw him into the river Neda, entrusting him to Mother Earth. Thus Zeus was brought up in Crete by the nymph Adrasteia and her sister Io, and was weaned by the goat Amalthea.

Once Zeus had reached adulthood, he ensured that his mother Rhea assigned him the position of cupbearer to Cronus, and poured an emetic into his father's cup. The father proceeded to vomit up all the children he had devoured. This gave rise to a long war between Zeus and his brothers on the one hand, and the Titans led by Cronus on the other hand; Zeus emerged as the winner and married his sister Hera, and the mythological Olympian cycle began.

The child in myths

The abandoned child running extraordinary risks, such as that of being killed or of being cut to pieces and devoured, is a recurring figure in mythological stories. The child's enemy is frequently his own father, who kills the child in order to avoid being usurped; or at times the father is simply absent (Jung & Kerényi, 1940).

The child in myths is a child alone. Zeus himself is abandoned by his mother at birth in order to save him from his father, who wanted to eat him. Dionysus loses his mother before he is even born, and his father Zeus is not present to defend him when he is attacked and cut to shreds by the Titans. Nor must we forget the terrible end of Astyanax, the son of the Hector the Trojan: Pyrrhus threw him down from the walls of Troy in order to prevent the city from having a new generation of sovereigns.

Another persistent theme is that of the child abandoned and exposed to the elements, generally because an oracle had greeted his birth with inauspicious presages for him or for his family (Rank, 1909; Ferrari, 1999). Even Oedipus was abandoned in swaddling clothes on Mount Cithaeron. In Kerényi's view, this very sad situation from a human standpoint takes on a different meaning in mythology. The abandoned child represents the solitude of the primordial element: it is the world at its birth, and through the image of the child the world is speaking of its own infancy.

At times, children are barbarically sacrificed, as in the story of Thyestes, who is invited at a macabre banquet to eat the flesh of his own children. The same fate awaits the young Pelops, killed and offered to the gods by his father Tantalus. Equally dramatic is the story of the young Demophon, thrown into the fire by Demeter in order to destroy his mortal parts and thereby ensure his immortality (Ferrari, 1999). The divine infant who is subjected to exceptionally cruel dangers and events often survives, as did Zeus and even Oedipus himself, or rises again, as did Dionysus: the abandoned child alone in the world becomes a hero.

According to Neumann (1949), these myths reflect the view of the world held by primitive man, who necessarily perceived existence as constituting a continuous danger. The situation of the abandoned and persecuted child is destined to be a recurring theme in many fairy tales.

Paedophilia in myths

Stories may be found in classical mythology recounting the practice of pederasty. Here we will discuss the myths of Zeus and Ganymede, and of Laius and Chrysippus, though it must be added that there are many myths which have paedophilic love as a substratum, even though they are less renowned.

We may recall Abderus, son of Hermes and young lover of Heracles, son of Zeus; and young Hylas, who was also loved by Heracles; or young Ampelus, lusted after by Apollo (Biondetti, 1997). Apollo had many lovers, both female and male. In addition to his relationship with Ampelus, Apollo also loved Hyacinthus and Cyparissus. After their deaths, the former was transmuted into the homonymous flower and the latter into a cypress tree. With regard to Apollo, Colli (1977) establishes a relationship between his attributes, the bow and the lyre, and his deceitfulness. On the one hand art, beauty, persuasive music and a gratifying appearance reflected in the lyre; on the other hand a killer arrow which contrasts starkly with the illusoriness of beauty. "Herein lies Apollo's duplicity: the gentle and pleasing face next to the terrible, devastating visage" (Colli, 1977, p. 26). Apollo also killed his young friend Hyacinthus—though by accident—when a discus he threw struck Hyacinthus during a game.

Another divinity who fell in love with Hyacinthus was Thamyris, son of Philammon and of the nymph Argiope. Some scholars consider Thamyris to be the first homosexual. Another story that can be recalled is that of Agamemnon falling in love with the handsome youth Argennus. In order to escape Agamemnon's pursuit, Argennus threw himself into the river and drowned.

It is said of Orpheus that after the death of Eurydice he no longer wished to have relationships with women, so he devoted himself to pederasty (Ferrari, 1999). Aristophanes cites Falete, a friend of Bacchus and a lover of young boys. Ovid narrates the story of Phyllius, who fell in love with the very handsome divinity Cycnus, son of Apollo and Thyria (Biondetti, 1997).

Minos, son of Zeus and Europa, is also said to have practised pederasty. Certain versions of the myths have him, and not Zeus, abducting Ganymede. Minos is also said to have been the lover of Theseus (Biondetti, 1997). Theseus established the cult of Aphrodite Pandemos, an epithet meaning "popular, common". In *Symposium*, Plato claims that Aphrodite, the goddess of love, is actually two goddesses. One is the "common" Aphrodite, and belongs to the poor and miserable in spirit; the other is Aphrodite Urania, who does not possess feminine features, was conceived and born without a mother, and represents love for youth, considered to be a nobler form of love (Biondetti, 1997).

As Sergent (1986) has pointed out, those myths which more or less explicitly conceal paedophilic love all exhibit the trait of having the structure of the myth of initiation. Within the framework of these myths, the homosexual relationship is nested within a tale representing the transformation of a young male into an adult through the performance of a heroic deed, or (frequently) through death explicitly or implicitly followed by the resurrection of a new individual, destined to take the place of the adolescent—who has ceased to be a member of that class—in the category of adulthood.

Zeus and Ganymede

Ganymede was an extremely handsome young man, a descendant of Dardanus and the son of Tros and Callirhoe. The myth recounts that Zeus, disguised in eagle feathers, abducted Ganymede and made him his cupbearer and lover. In exchange for this, Ganymede received the gift of immortality: he was transformed into the constellation of Aquarius. When it came to Ganymede's father, Zeus gave him his two immortal horses and a branch of a golden vine.

The myth deals with the issue of the status of infancy and eternal youth: where passivity arouses the love of a father god, it staves off death. As is often the case, this myth also comes in two versions. In the first version, since Zeus desired Ganymede as a bed companion as well as his cupbearer, he kidnapped him. In the second version Ganymede was first abducted by the goddess Eos, who had fallen in love with him, and was subsequently abducted from the goddess by Zeus in order to make him his cupbearer. Hera considered the abduction an insult to herself and to her daughter Hebe, who had been cupbearer to the gods until then.

This second version takes us back to Graves's theory (1955). Graves posits that the custom of youthful love emphasised the victory of patriarchy over matriarchy, and transformed Greek philosophy into an intellectual game which the men played without the help of the women. As we will see shortly, for the Greeks, love with young men was also a means of transmitting metaphysical knowledge: the beloved gives himself because he desires education and wisdom.

In other myths love for youth is intertwined with violence and death. Unlike the myth of Zeus and Ganymede, that of Laius and Chrysippus is set on a mythical stage which is one of high drama. Greek historical myths may be subdivided according to a geographic criterion: north or south of the Gulf of Corinth. To the north we find the killers of monsters coexisting with civilising impulses (Apollo, Cadmus). To the south lies the Peloponnese, with the story of Pelops and years of violence, family tragedy, revenge and death which follow one another inexorably. It is in this story of extreme ferocity that the roots of the myth of Laius and Chrysippus lie.

The story of Pelops

Pelops was the son of Tantalus, one of the kings of Lydia who entertained relationships with the gods. According to some myths, Tantalus was the son of Zeus and Pluto. When Pelops was a child, Tantalus wished to thank the gods for having invited him to their table and offered him nectar and ambrosia by returning their invitation. But the dish he offered the gods contained the flesh of his son Pelops, who had been cut to pieces and cooked for them. When the gods realised this, they were horrified by this banquet in which they had been offered the flesh of a child massacred by his father. No one touched the food, with the exception of Demeter, who was so hungry that she ate a shoulder. The gods were furious, and Tantalus, who up to that point had been their favourite, was cursed and condemned to eternal hunger and thirst. Some have advanced the explanation that Tantalus's gesture constituted an act of devotion; others have interpreted it as a challenge to the gods to test their omniscience.

Pindar recounts that Pelops was brought back to life and the shoulder eaten by Demeter was replaced with an ivory shoulder. His beauty at rebirth was so great that Poseidon fell in love with him, carried him away to Olympus in a chariot drawn by golden horses, and made him his cupbearer and lover. Pelops later returned to Earth, remaining under the protection of the gods, and became a highly venerated and powerful man, but also a man who was capable of killing Stymphalus, King of Arcadia, after having lured him into a trap by inviting him to take part in a friendly discussion. Pelops killed Stymphalus and cut him to pieces, thereby reproducing the same violent act perpetrated on him by his father. The consequence was a famine that affected the whole of Greece. This story contains violence endured turned into violence perpetrated, which is what appears to happen in young children who suffer sexual abuse: in adulthood such people often become child sexual abusers themselves.

The story continues with the children borne by Pelops and Hippodamia, and it is a story of repeated family vendettas, curses and violence, such as the fratricidal struggle between Thyestes and Atreus, who fought to the death over the kingdom of Mycenae. The merciless fight between Atreus and Thyestes is stained by the monstrous act committed by their grandfather Tantalus. Atreus massacred Thyestes's children and offered them to their father as food. On the advice of the Oracle at Delphi, and in order to achieve vengeance, Thyestes copulated with his daughter, and from this union was born Aegisthus, the avenger, who was later to kill Atreus. The repetition of violence to be found in myths may be superimposed on the repetitiveness of the paedophilic act, which is always subject to recidivism and to transgenerational repetition.

Pelops's youngest son, Chrysippus, was not born of Hippodamia, but from Pelops's union with the nymph Axioche. He was Pelops's twenty-third son and he was really beautiful.

Laius and Chrysippus

The crime committed by Laius, father of Oedipus, is generally hidden. And yet the myth quite clearly states that Laius was a paedophile and that he seduced Chrysippus, the adolescent child of his host Pelops. Just as the myth of Zeus and Ganymede offered a religious justification for the love between an adult male and a young male, the same may be said of the myth of Laius and Chrysippus, which is claimed to offer a justification for Theban pederasty (Graves, 1955).

When Laius, son of Labdacus and King of Thebes, was forced to flee his kingdom, he took refuge with Pelops, and there he fell in love with Pelops's son, Chrysippus. Taking advantage of the boy's interest in driving chariots, Laius kidnapped Chrysippus and, according to most mythological accounts, raped him. In seducing Chrysippus, Laius violated the sacred laws of hospitality and committed a double crime: he imposed a homosexual relationship on a young boy and he was responsible for the boy's death. Devereux (1935) reminds us that what is at stake is not the moral value of paedophilia, substantially accepted by Greek culture, but the values of convention and hospitality which have been brutally erased.

Here too, the myth has more than one version. One of these states that Chrysippus took his own life out of shame. In another version, Chrysippus was killed by Hippodamia, wife of Pelops, with the aim of preventing Pelops from appointing Chrysippus as his heir, to the detriment of her own sons. Here we find yet another mother who does not wish to be cast aside intervening because her son has become an object of love (Graves, 1955). But in Chabert's view (1993), the ambiguity of the identity of the murderer—man or woman, father or mother—is an indicator of the ambiguity of the object of desire: boy-son, child-adult.

According to Graves (1955), in one version of the myth Pelops is first driven by a desire for vengeance, and then decides to forgive Laius, having recognised the fact that only an irresistible love could have made him violate the rules of hospitality. On the other hand, in the dominant version of the myth Pelops was avenged by the gods. At the temple of Apollo in Delphi, the oracle pronounced that Laius was destined to produce a son who would kill him. Laius would be punished by his adolescent son, just as he had brought about the death of Pelops's son. What is punished is paedophilic behaviour which is taken to excess and becomes violent. It is criminal love and violent seduction which arouse the wrath of the gods and the curse of the oracle.

Laius abandons Oedipus in order to avoid his destiny and evade death, but this only hastens his end. "His egocentrism and his brutality make of his son, who is potentially a loving and respectful child, a stranger and an enemy, so that the prophecy comes true" (Durieux, 1993, p. 554).

Denis and Ribas speak of the "Laius complex" as the incestuous desire of the father for the son, and endow this complex with the status of a founding phantasm of psychic life. When this phantasm breaks into reality, when the father decides to take action, to the point of committing murder, the chorus clamours for the death of Laius, as it does in Antiquity (Denis & Ribas, 1993). Devereux (1953) believes that the fulcrum of the tragedy is not Oedipus's crime but the recognition of the tendency and of the deeply rooted need in every adult to attribute the entire blame to the child, ignoring his own responsibility for the act in question. There is no hope for Oedipus, with a father like Laius, who in turn had a father like Labdacus, who had been deprived of power by his mother and, according to Apollodorus (quoted in Biondetti, 1997), was killed and cut to pieces by the Bacchantes: Oedipus is doomed before he even starts. Durieux (1993) claims that Laius is the prototype of the bad father: ignorant, weak, and above all a homosexual. Laius likes boys but he tries to kill his son. Calasso (1988) calls Oedipus "the unhappiest of heroes".

In the genealogy of Oedipus, fathers are absent, often in concrete terms: Labdacus, father of Laius, is orphaned at an early age; Labdacus too dies when Laius is still very young. In both cases there is no father to guide the son up to adolescence and help him until he reaches sexual maturity. Even Oedipus is abandoned by his father when he is still in swaddling clothes. In the story of Oedipus fathers and sons cannot meet. Confrontation is avoided, and when the encounter does take place, as is destined to happen in the case of Oedipus, the results are fatal. Raskovsky (1973) highlights the enormous efforts that have been made to deny the tendencies to filicide in man's history which provoke, through identification, parricidal impulses.

Paedophilia and anthropophagy

Two persistent scenarios may be observed in Greek mythology. On the one hand there is the god who abducts a youth because he is strongly attracted by him and makes him his lover and cupbearer (Zeus and Ganymede, Poseidon and Pelops). The other scenario is more violent and consists of the sacrificial banquet in which the body of the child is cut to pieces and offered to the gods as an act of love, as if it were an extreme attempt to deny hate. The image of the sacrificial banquet in which the father offers his guests his own son as food (and hence the figure of the monstrous father) is common to other Greek myths (Lycaon and Nyctimus, Dionysus, Zagreus).

Lycaon, son of Pelasgus, who some scholars believe was a wise man and others declare was bloodthirsty and violent, civilised Arcadia and instituted the cult of Zeus Lycaeus. But it was to Zeus himself, disguised as an unknown labourer, that Lycaon's arrogant and evil children offered soup containing the flesh of their brother Nyctimus. Zeus was not deceived; he overturned the table and transformed everyone into wolves, except Nyctimus, whom he brought back to life. Incensed, Zeus subsequently unleashed a flood. Calasso (1988) points out that after this banquet Zeus hardly ever presents himself again as an unknown guest: from that point on, the act he most frequently engages in publicly is rape.

In Ferrari's opinion (1999), the tale of Lycaon lies at the origin of the numerous legends that have werewolves or lycanthropes as their protagonists, that is men who turn into wolves on nights when there is a full moon. In Ancient Greece it was believed that a fate such as this awaited those who, during the sacrifices in honour of Zeus Lycaeus, ate the flesh of the sacrificial victim. According to popular tradition whoever met the wolf lost his voice.

Dionysus was the son of Zeus and Semele, daughter of Cadmus of Thebes. Out of jealousy, Hera, wife of Zeus, first tried to kill Semele when she was pregnant, but Hermes saved the child and sewed him into Zeus's thigh. Zeus thus completed the pregnancy. Hera therefore ordered the Titans to seize Dionysus, cut him to pieces and boil him, but Dionysus was saved by his grandmother Rhea. In another version, when Dionysus descends to the Underworld to meet his dead mother Semele, he encounters Prosymnus, an infernal being who promises to show him the ways of the Underworld provided Dionysus agrees to have a homosexual relationship with him. Dionysus agrees to do so after meeting his mother, but by the time he returns Prosymnus has died, so Dionysus carves a branch of a fig tree into the shape of a phallus and uses it to keep his promise symbolically. "Dionysus cut to pieces and eaten, but also a homosexual in a passive position, evokes the idea of a dismembered child who is the object of sexual violence" (Brandi, 1998, p. 111).

Zagreus was the son of Zeus and Persephone. Zeus decided to make him his successor as dominator of the world and this aroused the wrath of his wife Hera. So Hera turned to the Titans, who were Zeus's enemies. After whitening their faces with chalk in order to avoid being recognised, the Titans lured Zagreus into a trap, offering him toys. Then they assailed him. Zagreus began to change into various animal forms, but the Titans managed to stop him by grabbing hold of his horns when he had taken on the form of a bull, and they devoured him alive. Athena recovered his heart and enclosed it in a chalk figure. In this way Zagreus became immortal.

In another version of the myth Zagreus's heart was consigned to Athena by Zeus. Or else it is Semele who eats Zagreus's heart and conceives Dionysus. To punish the Titans, Zeus struck them with lightning. A number of myths recount that the human race was born from the ashes of the Titans, thus starting its existence already branded with a sort of original sin. Zagreus was often identified with Dionysus. In actual fact the stories of the sacrifice and the resurrection of Dionysus and Zagreus are identical, the only difference being that Dionysus's flesh is eaten cooked instead of raw.

According to Graves (1955), at the time to which these myths refer, sacrifices of children really did take place; in particular, in Ancient Crete sacred kings could extend their reign by sacrificing a young child each year in their stead. Orphic philosophers continued the tradition of sacrifice, but replaced the child with a calf.

Ferrari (1999) also believes that sacrifices of children might actually have occurred in Ancient Greece, and as evidence in support of this hypothesis he quotes the finding of children's bones at Knossos bearing clear signs of blows inflicted with knives. Ferrari also cites references in Homer's *Iliad* to funeral games in honour of Patroclus, on whose body twelve young Trojans are offered in sacrifice; and by Pausanias to the Spartans' custom of offering human sacrifices to Artemis. Children were later replaced with goats or calves, but in the remotest recesses of Arcadia children were still sacrificed at the time of Christ (Graves, 1955).

Nicolaidis and Nicolaidis (1993) draw attention to a temporal sequence in which, in the transition from Titanic to Olympian mythology, paedophilia replaces anthropophagic desire. Pindar rejects the anthropophagic myth of Tantalus offering the gods the flesh of his son Pelops, and advances the thesis that the gods are not cannibals:

> I cannot say, not I,
> That any Blessed God has a gluttonous belly—
> I stand aside.
> Those who speak evil have troubles thick upon them:
> And if the watchers on Olympos
> Ever showed honour to a mortal man,
> Tantalos was he. [Olympian I, vv. 43–55]

Pindar thus proposes a different version of the myth, one which is more acceptable and not as strong: Pelops is not eaten by Poseidon but simply abducted:

> Son of Tantalos, in my tale of you
> I shall counter the poets before me.
> When your father called his companions
> To his most innocent banquet, and to Sipylos—his home
> Making the Gods his guests, who had made him theirs,
> Then the bright Trident's God
> Lost his heart for love of you, and seized you.
> [*ibid.*, vv. 35–40]

Pindar does not want to call the gods anthropophagic; he prefers to think they are pederasts (Nicolaidis & Nicolaidis, 1993).

We may also recall the story of Minos, king of Crete, who imposed on the population of Athens a periodic levy of young men to be fed to the Minotaur. The sacrifices came to an end when Theseus killed the Minotaur, but it should not be forgotten that Theseus was actually one of Minos's lovers. With regard to young children being sacrificed, Aristotle denied that this really did occur and advanced the hypothesis that the young people were not eaten but remained in Crete at the service of Minos (Biondetti, 1997).

Another reference to the complex relationship between human sacrifice and paedophilia is to be found in the history of the sacrifices offered by the Spartans to Artemis. Later such sanguinary practices were replaced by the offer of blood obtained through the whipping of ephebes (Ferrari, 1999).

Thus, according to Nicolaidis and Nicolaidis (1993) there exists a phagic desire, a real cannibalistic desire for incorporation. Anthropophagy, paedophilia and incest have a common denominator: the desire to incorporate. The most archaic part of the desire to return to a state of fusion which annuls the differences between the sexes and between generations is expressed through the phagic impulse.

In numerous myths children are killed and devoured. In addition to the renowned banquet which Atreus offered to Thyestes, various stories may be cited. First there is the example of Tantalus, who cut his son Pelops to pieces. Then there is Harpalyce. Wishing to take revenge on her father who had raped her, Harpalyce killed the son who had been born of their incestuous relationship and offered him as food to her father. Thirdly, we have the account of Procne, another mother who, seeking revenge, killed her own son Itys and offered him as food to her husband Tereus.

From a symmetrical perspective, Freud (1926) speaks of the infantile fantasy of being devoured by the father and states that this idea is a "regressive degradation, to a passive, tender impulse to be loved by him in a genital-erotic sense" (p. 105).

In pre-Olympian Greek mythology anthropophagy is frequent. We may recall Cronus eating his children to defend his power, and the Titans, who cut Dionysus to shreds and then eat him. With the advent of the Olympian gods things gradually change. We still find Zeus swallowing wise Metis, but from his forehead is born Athena, the goddess of wisdom. Or Zeus again, this time incorporating the embryo of Dionysus into his calf. In the opinion of Davide Lopez (1985b), Zeus temporarily appropriates the procreative function in an attempt to avoid the repetition of the model of the mother allying herself with her son in order to castrate the father. Once the Olympian order has been established, phagic acts gradually disappear, whereas paedophilic acts which are clearly sexual in nature become increasingly frequent.

Chervet (1993) speaks of a transition from a pre-Olympian conception of "keeping children inside oneself" to an Olympian conception of "keeping the children for oneself". Hence, the Olympian cycle renounces paedophagy and paedophoria in favour of paedophilia. Cronus eats his children, and his paedophagy is evidence of his tendency to absorption. His investment in children does not go beyond the level of "fruit of my own flesh": paedophoria. The child is devoured in order to be kept. Cronus is eternally "pregnant" with his children inside him, and this "pregnancy" keeps at bay his incestuous desires. With Zeus, on the other hand, appropriation and possession to achieve symbiosis dominate his relationship with his children (Chervet, 1993). For Apollo and Dionysus, children of Zeus, possession is the highest form of knowledge and of power (Calasso, 1988).

In Olympian space, paedophilia is organised by the original ghost fantasy of the seduction of the child by the adult, and is translated into the theme of abduction: Ganymede and Hyacinthus are kidnapped by Zeus, Pelops by Poseidon, and Chrsyppus by Laius. At the opposite pole to the events of the anthropophagic act and the sacrificial banquet, in the Olympian world abducted children receive from the gods the gift of immortality. They become stars, like Ganymede; or plants, like Ampelus; or flowers, like Hyacinthus, who was kidnapped and killed by Apollo.

The ghost of anthropophagy lives on in the fantasies of children and in fairy tales, where the ogre and the wolf are representations of the father who devours his children (Arfouilloux, 1993). Devereux (1966) declares that parents have extremely strong cannibalistic impulses towards their children.

I will now deal with a myth which comes from the north of Senegal, in which the paedophile is a female. The myth is quoted by Denis (1993). A woman was living with her husband and two children, only one of whom was hers. One day, when the children were seven years old, the mother realised that she could not tell who was who, which of the two was her child. So she went to the village soothsayer who said to her, "Have a silver bracelet made, lie down on the doorstep of your house and uncover your intimate parts, then you will discover which of the two is your son." When the first son arrived at the door, he suddenly took a step back. His brother asked him what was happening. "Something has hit my eyes," he replied, rubbing them. The second brother approached his mother and shouted, "Mummy, you're undressed!" and covered her up with her robe. The mother slid the bracelet over him saying, "This is my son!"

In Denis's view, the mother, the first seducer, must to some extent be a paedophile. She must consider the child an erotic object if she is to love him; she must obtain pleasure from breastfeeding him if she is to nourish him. All mothers, Denis argues, must one day face the problem of their son being a stranger: the traumatic effect on mothers of their children's puberty is constant, and the taboo on incest comes to their aid to defend them from a paedophilic desire which has been active up to that point. The opposite is true, argues Denis, for sexual contact with the father, for that act leads to a curse. When Noah was drunk, he took off all his clothes in his tent. Ham saw the private parts of his father exposed, derided him and told his brothers. Shem and Japheth took a cloak and, walking backwards to avoid seeing him, covered their father up. The descendents of Ham were cursed, while the two brothers who had protected themselves from sexual contact with their father, even if it was only visual contact, were saved.

Freud discusses the puberty rites of primitive communities. The function of these rites is to undo the knot of the incestuous relationship with the mother and to reconcile the son with the father (1915–17, p. 335). However, on another occasion Freud states: "It is our suspicion that during the family's primeval period castration used actually to be carried out by a jealous and cruel father upon growing boys, and that circumcision, which so frequently plays a part in puberty rites among primitive peoples, is a clearly recognisable relic of it" (1932–36, p. 86).

Seduction, bodily contact with the mother, actually did occur, while fatherly seduction is only a fantasy, and it had to remain in order to allow the son to develop his mental faculties (Denis, 1993). In the myth of Tantalus and Pelops, the only one to eat the flesh of Pelops is a goddess (Demeter), and Pelops received an ivory shoulder in remembrance of this incorporation. When the act of seduction is carried out by a god, the consequences are more dramatic. Thus, once he has been seduced by Laius, Chrysippus takes his own life.

Hyacinthus, one of the lovers of Apollo, dies at the hand of Apollo himself.

Balier (1993) writes that seduction is an act of violence, both in its essence and even more so in its roots, even though the meaning of the word with which we are more familiar today is connected to attraction. Seduction, Calasso (1988) reminds us, also means destruction in Greek: *phtherein*. Where does this violence come from? If we go back over our journey through mythology, at the beginning of the road we meet Uranus, son and husband to Gaia, Mother Earth. Uranus is the first god to appear on the Olympian scene, and he is the first god to perpetrate violence on children, when he prevents them from being born since he wishes to remain in a perpetual erotic relationship with the woman-mother.

When children are killed and devoured in mythical accounts, many motives come into play, though the myths themselves never mention them. According to some scholars, there is an archaic desire for incorporation. Another reason is the wish to avoid confrontation with the other, with someone who is different, due to fear of defeat. This is the case with Cronus, who devours his children in order to avoid them usurping his throne. On other occasions, it is the anger and jealousy of a woman who has been excluded that triggers the violence, as happens to Dionysus, who is cut to shreds by the Titans on the orders of Hera. On yet other occasions the driving force of violence is shame, as in the case of Chrysippus, who kills himself after being seduced by Laius. We may find accidental homicide in myths, as in the case of Apollo accidentally killing his lover Hyacinthus during a game. But we may also find ferocious, cold-blooded murder, which is the case in the story of Tantalus offering the gods the flesh of his son, perhaps out of devotion, perhaps as a challenge.

Kidnapping for reasons of love seem to be a different case. These events appear to be motivated by the desire to appropriate the beauty of youth, the myth of eternal beauty. In these cases, the abducted youth cannot grow or the spell will be broken, hence he receives the gift of immortality and is transformed into a constellation, as was Ganymede; or into a flower, as was Hyacinthus; or into a vine, as was Ampelus.

Whether the child is torn to pieces and devoured, in the grimmest and the most primitive scenario, or whether the desire of the adult is manifested in abduction, in a framework which appears to be a little less violent, the fate of the young victim is decided: he must either die or become immortal; whatever the outcome, he must stop growing. In the same way, even when they do not appear to have experienced violence, children who are victims of paedophiles today exhibit a block in their psychic development.

Note

1. The legend as told in the twelve books of *The Aeneid*, Virgil's quasi-historical epic poem on the origins of Rome, identifies Palinurus as the helmsman of Aeneas's ship. In the fifth book the fleet sets sail from Sicily to Italy, and Venus promises her son Aeneas a safe journey. Only one of his crew will be drowned, a sacrifice which will guarantee the lives of the others. Palinurus, alone on deck, falls prey to the god of sleep, and while he is trying to keep a steady gaze on the stars in order to navigate, he begins to fall asleep. He clings fast to the helm, but a sudden movement of the ship pushes him overboard. Nobody hears his cries as he falls, and he is drowned. [Bléandonu, 1990, p. 285]

CHAPTER THREE

Fairy tales and paedophilic fantasies

Franca Pezzoni and Cosimo Schinaia

> "And you, my dear," said the little man, turning in a flattering manner to Pinocchio, "What do you intend to do? Are you coming with us, or are you going to stay behind?"
>
> —Carlo Collodi

Two main approaches have been employed in the study of fairy tales. The first approach sees them as a literary genre aimed at children, to be found in a special set of books, whose basic function is pedagogical, and whose main feature is supposedly to stage a world of fantasy which stands in stark contrast to daily life (Corno, 1979). The second approach sees the fairy tale as belonging to the traditions of folklore, hence not as a "high" literary genre but as a product of popular poetic creation; it is claimed to be a belated, hence a "positioned" historical commentary (Picard, 1951).

The two approaches which thus emerge are contradictory. One expresses benevolent condescension towards—if not outright belittling of—the fairy tale, while the other idealises the fairy tale as the depository of profound truths (in Carloni's opinion [1987a], fairy tales are the fount of the endless flow of culture, constituting the essence of each and every narration) and national values, which at times are proclaimed as standard bearers against invasion by foreign cultures (as is the case with the Brothers Grimm).

The definition of the fairy tale thus hinges on two theses. The first regards it as a relic of ancient rites and myths which have now disappeared, while the second considers it to be a narrative which has its own autonomous laws of composition and its own social function: that of a vehicle for the transmission of mental and emotional knowledge to the following generation.

Perhaps the best definition provided so far is that of Lüthi (1947), who posits that the fairy tale is an adventure story which, thanks to its specific abstract style, is capable of dealing with *universal content*. This definition is significant because it highlights the extraordinary capacity the fairy tale has, as a specific and autonomous literary genre, to act as a container in which the most varied of human experiences and fantasies can be elaborated—including, as we shall see shortly, paedophilic fantasies.

Theories of the fairy tale

Vladimir Propp was the first scholar to develop a theory of the fairy tale as an autonomous genre. His book *Morphology of the Folktale*, which appeared in 1928, remained unknown in the West until 1958. When comparing different texts, Propp notes that in a fairy tale the same action may be attributed to a variety of characters. What is important for a structural analysis is *what* is done, not *who* does it or *how*. If there are an extraordinarily large number of characters, then the number of functions they carry out will be extraordinarily small, and this factor accounts for both the variety and the uniformity of the fairy tale.

The actions the characters perform, which Propp calls functions, are the constant components of the fairy tale. There are only a limited number of such functions, and the sequence of these functions is always the same. The only function hypothesised as being obligatory is "lack", a situation of absence, insufficiency or harm provoked by the villain, which is followed by departure, that is to say the hero or heroine leaves home in order to find a remedy for the initial lack which was the starting point of the story.

With regard to the study of paedophilic fantasies, it is important to emphasise some of the aspects of the list of functions identified by

Propp. First of all, the fairy tale almost always begins with an antagonist who tries to deceive the victim in order to take possession of his/her person or his/her goods. This he does by changing his/her appearance, imitating the victim's parents, deploying persuasion, employing magic, deceit or violence. The victim often violates some interdiction, thus getting him/herself into trouble, or else he/she falls into the trap set by the antagonist, thereby furnishing him with information or abetting the antagonist's plans in some way. In addition to attempting to deceive, the antagonist often actually does do harm to one of the members of the family. The forms of harm include kidnapping, disappearance, mutilation of eyes, arms, legs or heart, exile, putting the evil eye on someone, drowning, killing, imprisonment, forced marriage, incest, cannibalism (even amongst relatives), torture during the night, or war. The hero/heroine is then begged or allowed to go, or sent, to find a solution to the misfortune or lack, and must travel to distant parts and overcome difficult tasks or a series of tests in order to obtain magic with which to defeat the antagonist. The antagonist can only trigger the disaster when the hero/heroine or the victim has been brought to a point of impotence: in the majority of cases they must have been separated from their parents, their elders and their protectors. This situation can be achieved either by making them infringe a ban (such as not leaving the house), or quite simply by having them go out for a walk and allowing them to fall into the antagonist's trap (such as accepting an invitation to go into the woods, and so forth).

In the second place, Propp's functions always appear in pairs. In the fairy tale lack is always complemented by the elimination of lack; prohibition is always followed by transgression; deceit is always accompanied by allowing oneself to be deceived (as a result of which the victim may in some way become an accomplice to the antagonist). The difficult task is followed by the acquisition of magic; killing by resuscitation; struggle by victory. In this sense it may be said that for Propp the fairy tale has the same nature as for Bettelheim (1975): it is optimistic even though, as an examination of the various functions Propp identifies clearly shows, it does speak openly of the most serious forms of harm that adults may cause children, without any form of mitigation, and he affirms that the insufficiency or the mischief comes about in part also because the victim plays a part in bringing it about, and the harm can only be defeated successfully by a demanding working through.

Propp believes that the functions (the actions carried out by the characters) are fixed, whereas the attributes of the characters are variable. It is the richness of this variability that endows the fairy tale with its liveliness, its beauty and its fascination. This amalgamation of rules and freedom allows the fairy tale to produce an infinite number of variations on a theme and infinite repetitions, as in music. And it is precisely its specific structure that allows the fairy tale more easily than other art forms to contain uncontainable emotions and fantasies, such as paedophilic fantasies, and to speak the unspeakable.

Lüthi (1947) also studied the fairy tale as an autonomous literary genre, trying, like Propp, to identify its specific style, and independently reaching similar conclusions. A fairy tale cannot be classified as such because of its contents or because of its components, which are neither exclusive to nor characteristic of the genre, but because of the rules which govern the way content and features are amalgamated. The abstract style of the fairy tale is obtained through the use of rigid formulae, repetitions, simple names bearing no attributes, pure colours, clear contours, and journeys taking the character away from the places he/she habitually frequents. This abstract style enables the fairy tale to achieve a specific *isolation* of both the objects and the characters of which it is constituted. Its one-dimensional perspective does not spring from poverty or incapacity, but from great skill and from a stringent formalism. Lüthi describes the fairy tale as pure and clear, with joyous and light agility, and states that it conforms to extremely strict rules.

Thanks to its specific structure and its specific style, the fairy tale can not only accommodate any component, but it also manages to faithfully reflect all the essential elements of human existence: family life and social life, the acquisition of knowledge and abilities, power, fights, good and bad actions, and comparisons with totally different worlds.

Lüthi has worked out a complex position on the theme of optimism and pessimism in the fairy tale. The hero/heroine is naturally a wanderer by constitution, who strays from home for a variety of reasons, almost always by him/herself, faces well-defined hurdles, almost always connected with extreme prizes or punishments (life or death), and knows exactly what must be known at a given point in an event thanks to the intervention of magic helpers.

The fairy tale is not a story of unrestrained magic, where everyone can do what he or she wants or likes. Supernatural intervention does not satisfy all desires indiscriminately, but occurs only when it is essential in finding the solution to the difficult task which determines the hero/heroine's fate. The real miracle is that the magical gift should be received precisely when the situation is critical. According to Lüthi, the hero/heroine is isolated, but not alone. He/she is capable of establishing universal relationships—he/she is not held in thrall by superior forces, but is capable of making the necessary contact with the essential existential forces when the need arises. Rather than optimism and pessimism, it would be more appropriate to speak of two different, albeit complementary perspectives on the human being's condition in the world and his or her relationship with reality.

Marie-Louise von Franz, a Jungian psychologist, writes: "Fairy tales are the purest and simplest expression of collective unconscious psychic processes … In this pure form, the archetypal images afford us the best clues to the understanding of the processes going on in the collective psyche" (1970, p. 1). She sternly criticises the structuralists who, in the wake of Lévi-Strauss, attempted to discover "the basic structures" of the fairy tale, and states: "The fairy tale itself is its own best explanation; that is, its meaning is contained in the totality of its motifs connected by the thread of the story" (*ibid*).

Italo Calvino (1973) has dealt with the fairy tale as a writer and not, as he himself declares, as a specialist: perhaps it is precisely for this reason that he seems to have identified some of the salient features of the genre through his acute intuition. First of all, he highlights the shrewdness of the characters, of the narrator, and of the narrative style itself. The narrator eludes the tradition with a kind of instinctive cunning: perhaps he believes he is simply producing a few variations when in actual fact he ends up talking about what really interests him. The *fascination* of the fairy tale, in Calvino's view, depends on its *truth*. The fairy tale presents us with the catalogue of destinies, with special reference to youth—which is, of course, the time in life when destinies are forged. Birth is often already loaded with auspices or condemnations (or with transgenerational fantasies, as psychoanalysis would put it in less elegant terms). The hero/heroine must leave home, face ordeals to become an adult, submit to spells, experience being determined by complex and unknown forces, and must free him/herself and determine his/her own future, maintaining his/her integrity and being faithful to his/her own true self.

In Calvino's opinion, the fairy tale migrates not only between peoples but also between folklore and literature, in both directions. Migration also occurs between the fairy tale and history, in the sense that historical customs enter the fairy tale, but also in the sense that the fairy tale configures events that are still to come, as in the case of the fairy tale of Bluebeard, which appears long before the real-life episode of Gilles de Rais.

The *moral* of the story is not so much in the content as in the very fact of telling the story. The moral is always implicit, never sententious or pedagogical. Above all, the moral is the very institution of narrating and listening. In the story to be found at the beginning of a collection of fairy tales, the central character saves herself by telling her husband an endless sequence of stories. Scheherazade saves herself and brings her cruel husband back to humanity by recounting thousands of stories. "She had collected a thousand books of chronicles of past people and bygone poets. Moreover, she had read books of science and medicine; her memory was stored with verses and stories and folklore and the sayings of kings and sages, and she was wise, witty, prudent and well-bred" (Bettelheim, 1975, p. 88).

The story of Scheherazade appears to be not so much an expedient providing a framework for her tales as an expression of the deep meaning of the narration of fairy stories: achieving reconciliation after experiencing serious physical and psychic threats to one's survival. It is a kind of summary of the tale of Beauty and the Beast, in which the Beast, who the story tells us is a cruel character because he has suffered a betrayal which has made him lose all faith, is transformed thanks to Beauty's patient storytelling. "The Frog King", the first story in the Grimm collection, introduces Iron Henry, who is also freed from the iron bands that suffering had tightened around his heart.

Calvino also notes the intrinsic *co-operation* that characterises the fairy tale. Co-operation takes place at many levels: (i) within the story itself, (ii) between narrator and listener, (iii) between narrators, and (iv) between narrators and collectors of fairy tales. Co-operation within the story is manifested, as we have already seen, not only in the more or less involuntary complicity between the antagonist and the victim, but also in the suggestions and help offered by the hero/heroine to the magic benefactor/benefactress who subsequently comes to his/her aid. This point may obviously also refer to paedophilic fantasies, in both a positive and a negative sense, so to speak. The fairy tale expresses the fact that there is some form of sharing between the adult and the child both of the fantasy of violence and seduction and of the means to face it and handle it in a non-destructive fashion.

Co-operation between narrator and audience is present at many levels. In his introduction to *Tales and Stories of the Past with Morals: Tales of Mother Goose,* Perrault[1] speaks of the empathy with children's emotions from which the narratives seem to stem, describing the dejection and sadness, or the joy and rapture that appear on children's faces when they hear the misfortunes or the good luck of their heroes and heroines as the story progresses. Literary criticism has not yet ascertained whether the tales were written by Perrault himself or by his adolescent son, or whether they are the product of collaboration between the two. Questions of reality aside, this may indicate how, on an emotional level, the tales may have originated from some form of close interaction between the two generations. Another example is that of Pinocchio,[2] when young readers wrote many letters to Collodi asking him not to have the story end with puppet's hanging but make it go on to a happy ending, as actually happened. The Brothers Grimm, who worked closely together, deliberately entitled their collection *Fireside Fairy Tales* to indicate the shared family space in which the generations met and transmitted their traditions.

Naturally, a concomitant factor existing in parallel with collaboration is *antagonism*. The Grimms' fireside reminds us of the oven which provides the final and definitive solution for the witch who ends up as ashes in "Hansel and Gretel". As compared to the narrators of these stories, the collectors exhibit what might be called a structural infidelity, even when they are guided by methods informed by the highest science. The *violence* perpetrated on the fairy tale, in the sense of producing arbitrary versions and interpretations, seems to accompany the violence contained within the fairy tale. As Lüthi states, the fairy tale itself invites interpretation, but on the other hand any unilateral interpretation is arbitrary. On the one hand the listener free, in that he or she can fill out the characters in the story with his or her own personal contents; but on the other hand he or she is subjected to violence because these personal contents must be inserted into the closed form prescribed by the tale genre itself. The spell or enchantment of the fairy tale is actually a kind of seduction. Again, it is Lüthi who states that it is magical not in the sense that it talks about magical events, but in the sense that it has a magical effect by virtue of its own nature.

The fairy tale, that domestic and innocuous entity, thus discloses disturbing aspects, not so much with regard to its contents, as with regard to its very nature. It is necessary that many people through the generations are involved in narrating stories in order to be able to share and bear the responsibilities, the weight and also the cruelty of their own fantasies and those of others.

In conclusion, the fairy tale is far, far more than simple amusement or fulfilment of desires regarding our daily lives. As a traditional story, in other words one that has been collectively elaborated and that has constructed personal and direct contact between generations, and as a literary form with its own specific structure, it appears to be a container which is highly qualified to convey a wide variety of human emotions and experiences, even those which are especially difficult to imagine and to express, such as paedophilic fantasies. These fantasies are not only expressed, but also somehow organised and communicated, and hypotheses are advanced for the handling and solving of those fantasies.

The fairy tale and psychoanalysis

Hans Christian Andersen appears in "Studies on Hysteria" (Freud, 1893–95) as the first reference to fairy tale material in the psychoanalytic literature. Perhaps this is not fortuitous. In her "absences" Anna O begins to tell stories on the model of Andersen's *Picture Book Without Pictures*,[3] and when she completes her narration she achieves a momentary state of calm. In addition to writing about fairy tales as a screen memory, and identifying in ancient legends convincing examples of family romance, Freud devotes an essay to the reason for the choice of the jewel-case, and on various occasions quotes "Little Red Riding Hood", "Snow White and the Seven Dwarfs", "The Wolf and the Seven Young Kids", "Green Henry", "The Emperor's New Clothes", "The Story of the Severed Hand" and "Rumpelstiltskin" (Carloni, 1987b).

Freud ironically subtitles his first formulation of the neuroses of defence in 1986 "A Christmas Fairy Tale". The origin of neuroses lies in a traumatic premature first sexual experience. This is followed by a successful defensive phase and then by the return of the repressed ideas after puberty, together with the creation of the symptoms of the illness. It is the first of his papers in which the return of repressed ideas appears, a concept which will play an important part in the development of the uncanny, with its literary references. Furthermore, the entire theory of neurosis, which Freud calls a fairy tale perhaps because he presents it as an imaginary and daring form of narration, deals with material normally contained in fairy tales: the origin of traumas and conflicts (first and foremost paedophilic conflicts), and the path taken to deal with and try to overcome them, with the risk of succumbing. In the end, fairy tales guarantee a return of what is repressed in a manner which is gradual and vague, so that their handling of the phenomenon is less harmful than the neurotic symptoms. Freud often returns to the fairy tale, dealing above all with its symbolism, its contents, its function and its origins.

Before embarking on our analysis, it is interesting to note that Freud makes metaphorical and analogical use of fairy tales in order to illustrate psychoanalytic concepts. The fairy tale "The Three Wishes", for instance, exemplifies the reciprocal action of the conscious and the unconscious, of repressed material and the Ego, and of the Id and the Superego, which results in the requests made by the other member of the pair being distorted and negated. In another metaphor he equates of the work done by a dream with the content of the fairy tale "The Brave Little Tailor". The dream work manages to bring together multiple meanings in a single expressive form (overdetermination), just as the little tailor manages to kill seven flies in one swat, and just as the interpreter in his turn skilfully manages to explain the multiple meanings. This story shows how the fairy tale functions as an explanatory model, as a cognitive structure deployed to solve theoretical problems. Both at an emotional and at an intellectual level, the fairy tale thus seems to possess the capacity (one which has not been openly and officially recognised) to function as a container and as an organiser of thoughts.

Generally, what interests Freud most is to show that fairy tales, like myths and legends, use the same mode of symbolism employed in dreams, that they represent a masked form of wish-fulfilment, and that they employ an archaic form of primary thought in which omnipotence prevails. For example, "The Emperor's New Clothes" by Hans Christian Andersen represents the hidden fulfilment of the forbidden desire to show oneself off, as does the dream of nudity.

According to this view, the function of the fairy tale, and of art in general, thus represents temporary escape from hash reality, momentary consolation which does not, however, have any real effect on people's lives. The fairy tale as a genre does not have any specific properties of its own.

However, in his discussion of the uncanny, Freud notes that many elements, such as the magical fulfilment of desires, inanimate subjects coming to life, and the resurrection of the dead, which would otherwise have an extremely disquieting effect, do not produce this result in fairy tales. According to Freud, from its very beginning, the fairy tale "quite frankly" (1919b, p. 246) establishes the narrative as one of imagination, thereby excluding the uncertainty which is the source of the uncanny: the omnipotence of thoughts and desires and the return of what has been repressed come about at the level of animism. "I cannot think of any genuine fairy story which has anything uncanny about it" (*ibid*).

With regard to the origins of the fairy tale, Freud believes that it may derive from children's theories of sexuality (for instance, childbirth through a cut in the belly is the basis of the fairy tale "Little Red Riding Hood"). A fully-fledged theory of the genesis of the fairy tale appears in "Group Psychology and the Analysis of the Ego" (1921). The hero has a difficult task to fulfil; often he is the youngest child or stupid; and in his task he is sometimes helped by a large number of small animals. According to Freud, citing Reik, in actual fact the hero is the killer of his father in the primal horde; the small animals represent the brothers who help him; and each of the difficult tasks is a substitute for the heroic deed of assassinating the father. The poet who relates the fairy tale manages on the one hand to free himself from the bounds of group psychology, and on the other hand to return to the path that leads back to the masses, wandering around to recount the myth. "Thus he lowers himself to the level of reality, and raises his hearers to the level of imagination. But his hearers understand the poet, and, in virtue of their having the same relation of longing towards the primal father, they can identify themselves with the hero" (1921, pp. 136–137).

Like Propp and Bettelheim, Freud notes the constant presence of a difficult task, which in the case that appears in "Totem and Taboo" (1912–1913) is the killing of the father. Co-operation is also evident, consisting in this case of association to commit a crime: between the hero and his brothers and between the poet and his audience. On this occasion, Freud does not see this fantastic tale as being one of mere evasion of reality, but also as a kind of passage, if not a way of escape, which enables the poet to "break away from group psychology" (1921, p. 136) in order to then engage with emotional realities which are much cruder in a more direct fashion (a father who is a paedophile and a castrator who must be killed), making his audience experience the oscillation between fantasy and reality.

Jung and the school of analytical psychology took a greater interest in fairy tales than did Freud, who had himself already taken much interest in that genre. Of Freud's disciples, Géza Róheim (1945) was the one who devoted the greatest attention to fairy tales, both from a general standpoint and from the standpoint of ethnology, by comparing the products of our society with those of primitive cultures.

Bettelheim delves deeply into one significant aspect of fairy tales. He regards them as something which enables the child to structure his fantasising without, however, diminishing the importance of his internal difficulties, without demanding or advising; thus they allow him to find his own personal solutions to his emotional problems. Optimism, which in fairy tales is represented by the happy ending, is not a means of evading reality but a way of taking stock of the fact that internal and external difficulties are an inevitable constituent of life, which can be overcome by fighting against them. The internal and external enemies who try to conquer or seduce us are strong indeed, but they can be defeated by the use of astuteness and through perseverance.

On a cognitive level too, fairy tales are easier for children to understand, for they do not oblige children to make a precocious attempt to deploy logical and rational thought. Furthermore, unlike edifying or religious tales of the kind that can be found in the Bible, they accommodate sentiments of rivalry, jealousy and aggressiveness without demanding repression. Hence, faithfulness to an ethical or confessional system is not called for.

In Bettelheim's view (1975), the function of the difficult task described in the fairy tale is first and foremost to achieve autonomy and personal integration, and this is achieved through going away from home and overcoming difficult trials. The fairy tale achieves its results by deploying a number of devices. The events are situated elsewhere; they are distant both geographically and historically; they do not pertain to concrete reality. These features indicate that what is being described is internal, emotional reality. The number of characters in each single fairy tale and the large number of different tales enable internal pressures to be externalised, but more fundamentally, they help the child to avoid being overcome by the externalisations themselves, by giving a hierarchy and order to the contents which are externalised. The fact that fairy tales belong to a cultural heritage helps the child to understand that he is not the only one to have certain fantasies—others have had them in the past and in the present. Finally, the fact that the person who wishes to kill or imprison the hero has at his side another person who hopes the hero will win out (i.e. a person who helps the hero even when the hero is in a condition of utter despair) helps the child to understand that there exists a parent (or at the very least an adult) who has confidence in the child, who is certain that the child will gain his independence in the future and accepts the consequence that the child will detach himself from the adult.

If Freud and his followers believe that the main themes of the fairy tale are sexual and prevalently oedipal, with Melanie Klein and the post-Kleinians oral, pre-oedipal conflicts acquire central importance: the dramatic events of early infancy, the first intense and complex object relationships. "It will come as no surprise to meet more frequently not only protagonists of both sexes with features which are decidedly childlike, but also a variety of anthropophagic characters—witches, ogresses, step-mothers and wicked mothers—in the part of the antagonist and, less frequently, fairies: magical assistants with angelic features evoked to help fight the antagonist, according to that dichotomy with which Klein has made us familiar" (Carloni, 1987b, p. 29).

Székács reminds us that fairy tales help the child to solve intrapsychic conflicts. Furthermore, "while they listen to fairy tales, children gain the understanding that they are not alone in the world when they face those dark internal forces; terrifying experiences can be shared and even communicated under the guise of these symbolic forms" (1987, p. 729). In addition, the same story may represent different conflicts of the unconscious for the same child at different ages, inasmuch as fairy tales express different aspects of the development of psychic integration.

In Carloni's opinion, fairy tales are extroversions of our internal world and of the fantasies which populate it. "Those events which are recounted by fairy tales and which are sublimated by legends and myths take place precisely between the different parts of our minds and the various characters we have internalised in the course of our lives" (1987a, p. 738).

Ferro (1985) takes up a number of points made by Bettelheim, such as the classification of the fairy tale elsewhere and its cultural transmission. The latter enables us to share and to give a name, a plot, a meaning to our anxieties by demonstrating that they have already been experienced by others in the past. However, he underlines the function of the symbols of fairy tales as an *unsaturated container*, since they do not represent a complete and completed meaning but are rather proposed symbolisations which may be employed in different ways.

Ferro hypothesises that fairy tales are born from the child-parent relationship. From the circuit of projected identification and reverie, from the "I'll eat you, I'll eat you" spoken by mothers. It is thus possible to hypothesise that there exists in this circuit a two-way movement, an implicit conversation in which the generations exchange experiences which are fundamental to them. The relationship between parent and child is no less important in the genesis of the fairy tales. Indeed Bettelheim had already mentioned, albeit briefly, the fact that fairy tales contained not only the oedipal fantasies of children, but also the fantasies adults had towards children.

Fairy tales and paedophilic fantasies

As we have already seen while examining the various theoretical stances, claiming that fairy tales also express paedophilic fantasies in addition to their other contents is not saying very much. Fairy tales not only describe fantasies and emotions but also illustrate them in detail, and above all they implicitly suggest ways in which those fantasies and emotions can be handled. Fairy tales differ from entertainment literature and from ideological or religious literature inasmuch as they present all emotions, whether licit or illicit, pleasurable or painful, as existing and even inevitable, without censuring them *a priori*. They also differ from the literature of myths because they offer a way out which is not necessarily tragic. In this sense, it may well be claimed that this is one of the most realistic and least "fairy tale-like" literary genres. As Bettelheim argues, fairy tales are not moralistic stories about the world which induce compassion for the oppressed. "What the child who feels downtrodden needs is not compassion for others who are in the same predicament, but rather the conviction that he can escape this fate" (1975, p. 105).

Paedophilic fantasies appearing in fairy tales may be schematically classified into either openly sexual or more or less oral fantasies of incorporation. Fairy tales also exhibit the feature that the violence present in perversion, though sometimes masked by a seemingly narcissistic idealisation of the object or by forms of pseudo-protection and tenderness, is not integrated and always gains the upper hand, leading to brutal and repetitive destructiveness, that is into perversity.

As Nicolaïdis and Nicolaïdis (1993) and Arfouilloux (1993) affirm, deep-seated ties exist between incest and paedophilia on the one hand and cannibalistic incorporation on the other. Ingesting the other means allowing oneself to be penetrated, gaining pleasure from his flesh, mutual penetration and fusion in a reciprocal act of seduction which is intrinsically deadly. Paedophilia seems to replace the pre-existing anthropophagic desire (a desire on the part of parents for their children long before its opposite), but it maintains the feature of oral identification through incorporation. On the basis of anthropological and mythological data, these scholars ask themselves whether paedophilia is a primitive fantasy and whether it precedes the fantasy of the adult seducing the child. They also remind us that in a letter to Marie Bonaparte (1932), Freud had considered cannibalism and incest to be the two fundamental taboos.

Sexual paedophilic fantasies

> I love you, your beauty has wakened my lust;
> Little boy, I'll take you by force if I must. [Goethe, "Erlkönig"]

The first written fairy tale appears in Ancient Egypt, and it is the story of a woman's attempts to seduce a young male. He rejects her advances, and she complains to her husband, accusing the young man of sexual molestation. The husband, driven mad by jealousy, tries to kill his rival. The young man flees. The gods intervene to re-establish the truth, but in the meantime the youth dies. The drinks in the husband's house go off, making him realise that the young man has died. He repents, departs to save him, and manages to bring him back to life.

The event is famous, for it appears repeatedly in the Bible and in mythology. As Bettelheim (1975) says, there exist at least 770 versions of the story. Here the maze of reciprocal accusations begins: the woman accuses the youth whom she wanted to seduce of having seduced her. However, might it not be the youth who projected his desires onto another man's wife, accusing her of a deed which he himself did not dare to carry out?

The fairy tale, venerable for its antiquity, does not take long to establish the exact point of departure for the fantasies at issue. Above all, however, it admirably highlights various aspects of paedophilia. First of all, it presents the fact that an adult might seek to seduce someone who belongs to the younger generation not only as possible, but as a common occurrence. In the second place, it shows that the adult tries to cast all the blame onto the minor, attributing to the latter desires and initiatives which are actually the adult's. The fairy tale does not deny that the younger person might possess such desires, but it points out that the desires are explicitly translated into concrete reality by the older woman. Acting in bad faith and projection are presented as components of human relationships: far from being idealised at the outset, adults are described as what they are.

In this and in numerous other fairy tales, the character who attempts to seduce is a woman and not a man—which is not normally what we imagine when we think of paedophilic behaviour. We should, however, remember the numerous cases of seduction concerning nurses and governesses reported by Freud. Other points that emerge from an event which is apparently so brief are:

1. The force of a lie, which manages at first to hold sway, thanks also to the husband's inclination to believe a version which is easier for him to accept and which causes less disturbance to the family order.
2. The deadly character of the lie itself, which causes the death of the young man and the poisoning of the entire environment, represented by the deterioration of the beverages.

3. The existence of a higher order (represented by the gods) above that of the individual, which guarantees the truth at a conceptual level, which does not admit lies and violence, and which (at least ideally) seeks to reinstate the truth. Here, what Jolles (1930) calls the ingenuous moral of the fable makes its appearance. This could actually be defined as the moral full stop, in the sense that the events which take place in our lives are compared with an ethical order which is outside the family and acts as the standard reference point against which those events are judged as acceptable or unacceptable independently of the affirmations and the actions of the individual characters. Furthermore, the fairy tale always witnesses the repair of injustice, which is always vigorously declared as such and never accepted with resignation as inevitable or even legitimate.
4. The strong component of violence and retaliation present in the event, unleashed by the female character through manipulation, and perpetrated by her husband. One of the aspects of the situation is denying the existence of one's emotions and responsibility for one's actions, not acting them out oneself but attributing them to others, to the point of attacking thought and creating a confusion which is similar to psychotic confusion.
5. The need to leave the family, which in this case is forced upon the character. Departure, which Propp and Bettelheim consider one of the most characteristic features of the fairy tale, seems to express in this case the need to escape from the environment of one's origin in order to survive physically and psychically, a priority which comes well before the need to achieve independence and autonomy.
6. The need to counter the temptation represented by paedophilic seduction, in order to maintain one's personal identity before one can even think about retaining one's moral integrity, and also the inevitable danger of the situation (the boy risks dying and actually does die, even if death in the fairy tale means above all leaving one state in order to enter a successive state).
7. The situation of having impossible alternatives or of finding oneself in a situation with no apparent way out: either he accepts being seduced or he risks not being believed, and even being accused, discredited and killed, i.e. psychically rejected and cancelled out by the family (as sometimes happens to young

people who report cases of incest to the police). Being abandoned by adults emotionally, if not physically, means death for a child who is dependent on them for his affects, self-esteem and identity.
8. The need, as Bettelheim notes, for an internal transformation in order to reach a happy ending in the story. In this, as in all fairy stories, magic and the intervention of supernatural forces are far less important than the personal changes which take place within an individual. In this case it is the husband, the other adult figure in the story, who undergoes transformation through repentance, recognition of the truth, and his attempt to save the youth, which actually does have the power to bring him back to life. What seems to be required in order to guarantee survival is the presence of an adult who recognises the truthfulness of the youth's account and, above all, who will bear the weight of the emotional difficulties the truth entails for himself as much as for the youth. This withdrawal also requires a great effort, for it requires one to detach oneself from one's previous convictions and to revise one's entire mental setting and attitudes to the individual and family setting.

In actual fact, breaking with the past is the main feature of this fairy tale, both as a violation of the barrier between generations and as the need for an almost total inversion in order to achieve a positive ending to the story. On the other hand, the fairy tale does not envisage a total and definitive detachment from the original environment, but renders reconciliation possible through the processing and elaborating of one's emotions. Detaching oneself completely from one's family roots and the past leads to catastrophe, that is to death, just as remaining pathologically tied to one's place of origin leads to death. The two attitudes are embodied by the two male characters, as Bettelheim notes, and the positive outcome is seen as an integration of the two attitudes, though the process of achieving integration is a dramatic and costly one.

It may also be thought that the wife and the husband in their turn represent the two aspects present in the adult and in the parent. The wife expresses the tendency to keep the youth tied to herself through seduction, the promise of an easy life in which all the conquests of maturity are achieved effortlessly, bestowed by the adult, provided that this is based on the lie of a relationship without separation and without transformations. The husband expresses the effort to recognise the child's individuality and to resist the temptations of reciprocal seduction and falsity.

In fairy tales the characters are virtually never perfect: even the husband is seen as a person who at first gives credence to the lie, yields to temptation, and only later realises that things around him are going badly and seeks to remedy the situation. As we have already pointed out, this tale too contains a character who hopes for the well-being of the other, who supports him in his escape from a situation of entrapment and his search for autonomy.

Although fairy tales begin with the classic opening "Once upon a time" and talk a great deal about the past, they also talk about the future. As we have seen, the dimension of hope is given space, even in moments of maximum despair or even death. Additionally, from his very infancy the child is presented with the conflicts that he will have to face in later life, when he enters adolescence. This Egyptian fairy story narrates a dramatic situation which occurs after a period of relative tranquillity for the family. The hearer somehow perceives that the tale concerns not only the period of infancy, when the child exits the period of symbiosis and dependency, but also the conflicts the child will have to face in adolescence, with the tensions unleashed by new psychological developments. We are dealing with the transition from one mental state to another, and this requires the loosening of old ties before new ones can be created, with all the anxiety this process entails. After the boy has gone away from home, he ends up in an emotional void. However, he must pass the test on his own, without an adult trying to make a move which will allow the boy to avoid having to face the test, or trying to take the test in the boy's stead.

Another fairy tale which openly and explicitly deals with a paedophilic fantasy is "Donkey Skin". I will refer to two quite different versions of the story, one by Perrualt and the other by the Brothers Grimm entitled "Allerleirauh" [All kinds of fur].

Naturally, the folk tale long precedes Perrault's version written in 1697, so much so that the expression "stories of donkey skin" was already an independent expression which in its own time indicated fairy stories, "Donkey Skin" being almost the fairy tale *par excellence*. The Egyptian story with openly paedophilic content is the first written fairy tale known to us, while "Donkey Skin" was the fairy tale *par excellence* in France. Although this proves nothing, it suggests at least the great importance of this type of content in fairy tales, constituting in one sense the raw material of the genre.

Perrault recounts that there was once a King and a Queen who were very happy, delighted by the birth of a daughter and reigning over a prosperous kingdom. The Queen falls seriously ill, and on her deathbed she begs the King not to remarry unless he finds a woman who is wiser and more beautiful than her. She hopes that this will be impossible, and hence obtains from him in practice a promise that he will not marry again.

The King promises, and a better woman indeed cannot easily be found—until his daughter grows up. The King falls in love with her, and manages to find a casuist theologian who deems the marriage possible. The Princess turns to her fairy godmother, who suggests that she ask the King to obtain for her a dress the colour of the sky, another the colour of the moon, and a third the colour of the sun, in the hope that he will be unable to have them made. The King, however, manages to secure the required garments. So the godmother asks him to procure the skin of the donkey which lays gold coins every day (thereby constituting the source of the kingdom's wealth). The King agrees to carry out this request too.

Then the godmother tells the Princess to flee hidden under the donkey's hide, taking the three gowns with her. The girl walks and walks, and is eventually taken on to do the most menial work on a farm. There a Prince sees her when she tries on her dresses in secret, and falls in love with her. The girl places a ring in the cake she bakes for the Prince. Of all the women in the kingdom, that ring will fit only her. The Prince recognises her under the donkey skin, marries her and invites her father, who in the meantime has repented having fallen in love with his daughter. The moral, according to Perrault, is that it is better to expose oneself to severe suffering than fail to fulfil one's duties, and that even though morally correct behaviour may at first give rise to enormous difficulties, in the end it is rewarded.

In the version by the Brothers Grimm the beginning is the same, but when the King proposes marriage to his daughter, he meets with the disapproval of his Councillors. They are shocked by the proposal and declare that such a marriage would bring the country to rack and ruin.

The girl does not turn to her godmother for help but invents the test of the three dresses herself. She flees from the royal household wearing a cloak made from the hides of every kind of animal in the kingdom, which the King has managed to provide for her. In this story too, the Princess is taken on to do the most humble tasks, and she lives in the dark space under the stairs. She goes to the Prince's ball on three evenings, wearing each of her three dresses in turn; she places three gold objects in his soup, and in the end she manages to make him recognise her.

It has been pointed out (Foti & Roccia, 1994b) that the premise of the story lies in the promise obtained by the Queen. In practice, she asks to be replaced by a woman identical to herself. In this way she will continue to possess her husband even after her death. Thus the two main features characterising the whole of family life that seem to emerge from this tale are possessiveness and control. It is interesting to note that the story begins with a bereavement, which represents a situation of absence for the daughter. For a long time the father seems preoccupied by grief.

In the Grimm version, the King, after a long period in which he had ignored her, looked at his daughter and suddenly saw her. The daughter seems to awaken his interest only when she grows up and becomes sexually attractive. The interest she arouses, however, is not in herself as a person, but only as a substitute for her mother. The situation of paedophilic temptation also appears in other stories after a lengthy period in which the parents have abandoned or neglected their children because of a death in the family, or a long journey, or personal worries such as starvation or poverty, or having been forced to leave their homes by reasons of this nature.

Both versions of the fairy tale show the daughter at first not wanting to acknowledge reality: she hopes that she will be able to make the father forgo her by making impossible demands of him. Only as a last resort does she decide to leave home. The fairy godmother in Perrault probably represents, as we stated earlier, a benevolent adult figure or the good side of the mother (Maffeo, 1994). She is also the other voice in an intimate dialogue, a voice which sometimes supports the girl in her fight against the paedophilic requests made of her, while at other times she seems to minimise those requests or even accept them. Initially, the fairy godmother sought a compromise:

> "In your heart there is a great sadness. But I am here to help you and nothing can harm you if you follow any advice. You must not disobey your father, but first tell him that you must have a dress which has the colour of the sun. Certainly he will never be able to meet that request." [*Perrault's Fairy Tales*, p. 84]

But the expedient actually has the effect of underscoring the extent to which the father can really satisfy all the daughter's desires, lavishing gifts on her, exalting her beauty and giving her the impression that she can effortlessly play the adult role of the mother at his side. Looking at the beautiful dress, the princess almost decides to consent. Her father's gifts have the effect of confounding her. Bewilderment, as Perrault notes with great acumen, is the goal of and the effect achieved by paedophilic promises. This brings to mind Ferenczi's observation (1933) on the confusion of languages when discussing the relationship between adult and child.

The adult's proposals seem to promise the child that he can keep the omnipotence of his desires and thoughts for ever, while in actual fact the child must relinquish them to have access to adult life and thought. What this shows is that the paedophilic situation involves not only the emotional sphere but also the cognitive sphere to a significant extent: the child and the adolescent witness the adult magically confirming the fantasies that should instead be tackled fairly and negotiated with the external environment. The test of reality is in some way implied, and the consequences are disturbing rather than gratifying. Freud emphasises the fact that it is sinister to see one's desires turn into reality, and to see the return of what was repressed, the reappearance of what one believed to have been confined to the past and to the unconscious. The highly disruptive effect of a paedophilic experience is attributable not only to breaking the limitations imposed by the generation gap but also to crossing the boundary between reality and fantasy.

The fairy tale realistically shows that the paedophilic offer constitutes an extremely strong temptation for the girl, for it is based on the realisation (which in this case is a real act of magic) of all her desires to take her mother's place and to take on the role of an adult without experiencing any conflicts, while achieving her own aspirations exclusively at a narcissistic level and at the cost of real autonomy and of her own personal identity. Her hesitations and her second thoughts cogently illustrate the force of the temptation she undergoes: the fairy tale avoids any simple black-and-white moralistic message, showing instead how both characters are involved in the conflict. When she obtained the three dresses,

> The Princess did not know how to thank the king, but once again her godmother whispered in her ear: "Ask him for the skin of the donkey in the royal stable. The King will not consider your request seriously. You will not receive it, or I am badly mistaken." But she did not understand how extraordinary was the King's desire to please his daughter. Almost immediately the donkey's skin was brought to the princess … Once again she was frightened and once again her godmother came to her assistance. "Pretend," she said, "to give in to the king. Promise him anything he wishes, but at the same time, prepare to escape to some far country." [*Perrault's Fairy Tales*, pp. 85–86]

On the one hand it would appear that the King really is prepared to ruin his country in order to satisfy each and every wish his daughter expresses; on the other hand the hide of the sacrificed animal contrasts bloodily with the beauty of her clothes, thus seeming to reveal a different reality behind the previous appearances, one which is instead degraded and revolting. The fairy tale, with its usual insight, shows the other side of paedophilia, which is closely and immediately linked to the first side: narcissistic exaltation goes hand in hand with destructive sadism and, in a specific and characteristic fashion, with the fall into a degrading subjection.[4]

At this point the princess flees in disguise from the palace. In both versions of the fairy story the situation in which the princess finds herself appears to be the exact opposite of the preceding state of affairs: where she had been highly revered, respected, praised and exalted, protected from any form of toil and conflict, now she was ill-treated and disparaged, and forced to do the most menial tasks. Leaving home appears here, as it does in the Egyptian fairy tale, as the logical conclusion of her adventure, representing the need to relinquish the relationship with the adult figure since she is unable to modify it.

The dark space under the staircase, which never sees the light of day, where the girl now has to live, metaphorically recalls the condition of death, of the extreme abandonment to be found in the

Egyptian fairy story. In the biblical story, Joseph undergoes a similar experience when he is thrown into a prison-tomb. The Grimm version of "Donkey Skin" clearly embodies this emotional situation following the abandonment of the family environment. "I am a poor child, deserted by father and mother; have pity on me, and take me with you" (Grimm, *Complete Fairy Tales*, p. 285).

Another analogy with the Egyptian story is the presence of a supra-individual moral law which is external to the family and whose function it is to disapprove of the situation and declare its illegitimacy, as the reaction of the councillors in "Allerleirauh" shows: "When the councillors heard that, they were shocked, and said: '... no good can come from such a crime, and the kingdom will be involved in the ruin'" (*ibid.*, p. 284). It is also true, as well as extremely realistic from both a moral and a concrete standpoint, that such instances of morality may be corrupted. Perrault comments that the King found a casuist who judged the situation tenable.

Here we come face to face with a feature which seems to be characteristic of paedophilia in particular: the capacity to contaminate and manipulate arguments, reasoning and what is right and wrong, to make the paedophilic relationship out to be a privilege or an advantage, not only on a personal level but also at an ideological level, almost at the level of propaganda. As in the Egyptian tale, lying seems to be pervasive, it seems to affect all of reality, supported by an absolute and tyrannical power such as that of the father King, who threatens the craftsmen with death if they do not finish their work in time, and who seems to be able to count both on unlimited resources and on the ability to modify moral doctrines to his own advantage.

The continuation of "Donkey Skin" shows the Princess becoming brutish for some time, facing a life which is less protected in order to free herself from her dependence on her father, and hiding her beauty, which has become a possible cause of danger to her. The situation described in the fairy tale, i.e. a denial of one's gender identity, may frequently be observed in little girls who have been abused. The story shows the girl now taking on a more active role, gradually revealing her identity and developing the ability to look after herself and after others too. Two features should be noted:

(a) the gradual way in which the relationship with the Prince (and with the new King in "Donkey Skin") is established, contrasting

starkly with the excessive speed with which the paedophilic relationship would apparently have rocketed ahead in the developmental process, whereas in actual fact the process is not faced at all; and
(b) the fact that the three dresses that belong to the preceding life are also used in the new life; they are not repudiated but integrated as tools of seduction, but this time the seduction is deliberate and handled in an active fashion.

The Princess seems to have learnt from experience and has learnt to make her own use of the means the King deployed to affirm his power over her. The theme of the difficult task, which is omnipresent in fairy tales, appears twice in "Donkey Skin": first it is the father who must satisfy the increasingly demanding requests made by his daughter; then it is the daughter who must leave home, earn her living using only her own abilities, and win the Prince, a new partner outside the family. The difficult task faced by the Princess seems to be not repudiation pure and simple, but the integration of her previous experiences and their deployment in her new life.

As Foti and Roccia (1994b) observe, the ending of "Donkey Skin" presents us with a reconciliation between King and daughter when the latter marries: however difficult the past has been, it is not rejected or cancelled out, but their respective roles within the family are re-established. It should be remembered that the king seemed to be seeking in his daughter a substitute for his dead wife (in other words for a lost idealised figure), with whom he had a relationship that in his mind was conflict-less and should have been never-ending.

This starting point of the paedophilic situation has analogies with the events described in *Gilles et Jeanne* by Michel Tournier (1983). The book is a kind of *summa* of paedophilia: the protagonist is constantly and insatiably seeking young men, whom he proceeds to kill in horrendous ways. His behaviour seems to start from needing (but finding it impossible) to replace Joan of Arc, who was burnt at the stake, whom he experienced as an androgynous figure and the depository of all perfection, and whom he lost in a highly traumatic manner after a period of total harmony. This kind of insatiable collecting tries to fix the desired being in the immobility of death, and intrinsically requires more and more new victims, since the desire can never be placated. It constitutes the salient feature of fairy stories which present paedophilic fantasies of the oral-incorporative type.

Oral-incorporative paedophilic fantasies

> His mouth uplifted from his grim repast,
> That sinner, wiping it upon the hair
> Of the same head that he behind had wasted.
>
> —Dante's *Inferno*, XXXIII (Longfellow)

Nicolaïdis and Nicolaïdis (1993) recall a letter written by Freud to Marie Bonaparte in 1932 in which he identified incest and cannibalism as the two original prohibitions of mankind. In Freud's view, the son's desire for incest and parricide is the original fantasy, while the adult seducing the child is only a secondary fantasy compared to the former, and is almost always simply a projection on the part of the child without there being any real action on the part of the adult. In the opinion of Nicolaidis and Nicolaidis, it is above all the mother who may, during pregnancy and during the breast-feeding period, experience particularly intense feelings of incorporation with regard to the child. However, the father may also have defensive paedophilic fantasies by projecting onto his son his own former desires for parricide and incest.

These themes have also been dealt with by Arfouilloux (1993). Oral incorporation by means of cannibalism is, as Freud has argued, the metapsychological model of the work of mourning. Moreover, oral incorporation also has a sexual aspect since, through having the body of the other enter one's own body, it involves possessing and being possessed.

Incest and cannibalism both involve enjoying flesh which is one's own. They, and the paedophilic relationship in general, present a desire which is simultaneously also a fear: the return to the same, a relationship of mutual penetration and fusion with one's like. As Freud points out in the case of the feral man (1914c), the ogre and the wolf in fairy tales are images of the father, and the fear-desire to be devoured experienced by the child corresponds to the fantasy of being incorporated by the father, of returning to a state of fusion within the father's body. Arfouilloux (1993) poses the question of whether these fantasies start in the adult or in the child. The child has a natural disposition to seduce and be seduced, expressed through modalities which are proper to childhood, i.e. basically oral.

According to Devereux (1966), who bases his conclusions on ethno-cultural data, cannibalistic drives and paedophilic attitudes are primary in adults and only secondary in children. Arfouilloux is less categorical. Above all, he sees the fantasies of the adult and those of the child as being complementary. However, as we have already seen, he emphasises that the seductive attitude of the child should not be employed as a pretext to take the next step forward and actually commit the act, for it would be seriously traumatic for the child, and extremely difficult for him to work through, if the real behaviour of the adult superimposes itself on the fantasies of the child.

I will now speak in detail about "Little Red Riding Hood". Two different versions are known in which oral themes overlap with more explicitly paedophilic themes. As we know, Perrault presents a story of Little Red Riding Hood which has a sad ending. In fact, it is the only story in his collection which does not have a happy ending. He concludes with a moral which is more than crystal clear:

> Children, especially young lasses, pretty, courteous and well-bred, do very wrong to listen to strangers, and it is not an unheard thing if the Wolf is thereby provided with his dinner. I say Wolf, for all wolves are not of the same sort; there is one kind with an amenable disposition: neither noisy, nor hateful, nor hungry, but tame, obliging and gentle, following the young maids in the streets, even into their homes. Alas! Who does not know that these gentle wolves are of all such creatures the most dangerous? [*Perraiult's Fairy Tales*, p. 69]

The wolf is an extremely transparent metaphor for the adult paedophile who seduces little girls.

Lang (1888) and Bettelheim (1975) have criticised Perrault's version. Bettelheim in particular stresses the fact that the sexual aspect is presented in far too explicit a manner, leaving nothing to the individual imagination and limiting the content of the fairy tale to only one level. Furthermore, there is no character who warns the protagonist not to stray from the straight and narrow path—which does happen in the Grimm version. This, as is well-known, ends well thanks to a hunter opening the wolf's belly with his knife, enabling Little Red Riding Hood and her grandmother, whom the wolf had just swallowed, to emerge still alive.

In both versions the central theme is the fear of being devoured. Premature sexual experience is presented as "the experience of being swallowed", with highly destructive connotations, since it generates arousal and anxieties which are uncontrollable. In the Grimm fairy story the sexual implications remain at a pre-conscious level, as is only right, and the mother's exhortations to keep to the straight and narrow express the fact that the mother is aware that her daughter tends to succumb to temptation, and of her ambivalence towards the figure of the wolf.

As in "Donkey Skin", the child expresses the fact that she is attracted by the wolf by giving him detailed instructions on how to get to her grandmother's house. As Bettelheim states, if there were not something in us that is attracted by the wolf, he would have no power over us. This situation, with its deep truth, is typical and recurs in many fairy tales. For instance, in the story of the seven kids, it is to all practical intents and purposes the goats themselves who suggest to the wolf first that he should disguise his voice and then that he should paint his paw white so that it can be mistaken for that of their mother and thus he can gain access to the house. In "Hansel and Gretel" the children rush to eat the sweets decorating the house of the witch who wishes to eat them.

The theme of temptation is complementary to that of seduction. In "Little Red Riding Hood" the wolf presents himself first under his real guise and then disguised as the grandmother. On seeing a grandmother whose features are radically different from those she was acquainted with, the child asks questions which clearly and effectively denote excitement, attraction, but also the mental and perceptual confusion felt by the minor who has come into contact with a figure who presents himself as reassuring and familiar, but who is in actual fact threatening and, above all, overwhelming.

The two sides of the paedophilic personality—the fierce ogre and the adult who apparently comes to succour the child—are the most frequent and the most important in the various fairy tales. The seducer-devourer presents himself either as an ogre, explicitly in his most ferocious aspect, ravenous for fresh flesh, or else as a false substitute, equal if not superior to the child's parents. For example, an ogress appears in Perrault's version of "Sleeping Beauty" (a not uncommon example of a female figure related to the ogre, i.e. to all-devouring death); the ogress must make a strenuous effort not to throw herself upon children and eat them. Furthermore, notwithstanding the fact that her husband the king and her son the prince are fully cognisant of her proclivity, which constitutes a family secret, they leave nephews in her "care", thus exposing them to the risk of being devoured.

Quite correctly, Bettelheim notes that in "Little Red Riding Hood" the ferocity of the wolf has its counterpart in the weakness of the adult figures, mother and grandmother, who seem to have abdicated their roles and transferred their seductive powers onto the little girl. This situation brings to mind clinical cases in which the mother knowingly allows or supports incest in order to keep the husband tied to the family in some way; otherwise he might abandon the home.

The seducer seems to occupy a void, a weakness, or to act with the tacit consent of the family, promising either progress which comes about through the operation of magic or indefinite permanence in an idealised infantile state. Everything changes, but to tell the truth, nothing changes: the paedophile seems to find it extremely difficult to accept separation and change, even more so than his victim. This difficulty poses some questions. It has often been noted that the personal history of the paedophile is characterised by traumatic experiences. In particular, as is well illustrated by Tournier's work (*Gemini; The Wind Spirit*), the child undergoes a premature and traumatic separation from contact with the mother, from experiences of physical closeness in bed and in the bath. This is justified by "common decency", that is by the child's respect for external rules, and not by the need for growth and development. It is important to study which factors determine the surmounting of the condition which renders children vulnerable to a paedophilic relationship, intended in the widest sense of the term as a mental condition of submission and a blind alley. Writing about "Little Red Riding Hood", Bettelheim states: "With its violence, including that which saves the two females and destroys the wolf by cutting open its belly and then putting stones into it, the fairy tale does not show the world in a rosy light" (1975, p. 182).

The situation is resolved both by the intervention of the external helper (the hunter, who represents the protective father defending the child both from the external world and from her own temptations) and directly by Little Red Riding Hood herself, who decides what to do with the wolf and puts her plan into action, filling his belly with stones. If the adult had done it for her, she would never have gained the impression that she had really prevailed over the situation. Achieving freedom thus involves a death, that is, a clear severance, an interior change which enables one to move to a higher level of emotional awareness. The story finishes with Little Red Riding Hood talking to herself: "As long as you live, you won't run off the path into the woods all by yourself when mother has forbidden you to do so" (*ibid.*, p. 181). The solution is the internalisation of protection and the values of one's parents, not the obeying of external rules. It should also be noted that in saving herself, the child also saves her grandmother, which is exactly what happens in psychotherapeutic treatment. One is reconciled with one's parents and recovers the positive aspects of one's relationship with them.

Overcoming the obstacle thus seems connected first to entering a timeless paradise and then leaving it behind. Hansel and Gretel, who are abandoned by their parents during a famine, find a witch who at first offers them unconditional and boundless hospitality:

> Then good food was set before them, milk and pancakes, with sugar, apples, and nuts. Afterwards two pretty little beds were covered with clean white linen, and Hansel and Gretel lay down in them, and thought they were in heaven. [Grimm, *Complete Fairy Tales*, p. 91]

Only later will they discover that being possessed and alienated, i.e. devoured, is the other side of the coin to this hospitality.

In *The Erl-King* (1970), Michel Tournier quotes Collodi (1883) and Toyland as an example of what might be defined a paedophile's paradise. The quotation encourages us to re-examine the entire episode with great care. In actual fact it furnishes an excellent summary of the themes of paedophilia, from temptation to liberation.

Pinocchio is enticed by his friend Lampwick, who assures him that in Toyland children do not study, there are no schools, and it is holiday time all year round (i.e. no development is required). The way the author presents the coach which will take the children to their destination is indeed quite sinister:

> At last the coach arrived; and it arrived without making the slightest noise, for its wheels were bound with tow and rags.
>
> It was drawn by twelve pairs of donkeys … [which,] instead of being shod like other beasts of burden, had on their feet men's boots made of white kid.
>
> And the coachman?

> Picture to yourself a little man broader than he was long, flabby and greasy like a lump of butter, with a small round face like an orange, a little mouth that was always laughing, and a soft caressing voice … All the boys as soon as they saw him lost their hearts to him, and vied with each other in taking places in his coach to be conducted to the true land of Plenty, known on the geographical map by the attractive name of Toyland. [Collodi, *Pinocchio*, pp. 127–128]

Using very simple but highly effective means, what is highlighted is the man's power to attract: note also that he possesses both infantile and feminine traits, and seems to have no rough edges. In particular, he seems to be offering the children the promise of avoiding all those anxieties and conflicts which are connected with the transformations brought about by puberty. The picture drawn by the author of the boys on the wagon is no less striking:

> The coach was in fact quite full of boys between eight and twelve years old, heaped one upon another like herrings in a barrel. They were uncomfortable, packed close together, and could hardly breathe: but nobody said Oh!— nobody grumbled. The consolation of knowing that in a few hours they would reach a country where there were no books, no schools, and no teachers, made them so happy and resigned that they felt neither fatigue nor inconvenience, neither hunger, nor thirst, nor want of sleep. [*ibid.*, p. 128]

The trip seems to all intents and purposes to be a deportation. However, as the next utterances in the conversation show, it is presented to the children as a real privilege, constituting access to a special relationship conceded by the adult. A further aspect is what might be termed the paedophilic collector syndrome, namely the pressing need not to stop at one relationship but to collect a group of children, to create an entire environment, a kind of universe.

> The little man turned to Candlewick, and smirking and smiling said to him:
> "Tell me, my fine boy, would you also like to go to that fortunate country?" [*ibid*]

Lampwick and Pinocchio accepted the invitation, even though they had been warned by a brief episode in which one of the donkeys rebelled and was punished by the man, who bit one of his ears off. The image is one of castrating violence, and anthropophagia to boot.

Toyland corresponds perfectly to the children's expectations: the only things to be heard are children shouting, running and playing, children intent on all sorts of entertainment, with a final effect whose commotion and immutability recall a hellish bedlam rather than a paradise.

As is well-known, the two friends soon realised that they were changing into donkeys: in other words, that this total absence of rules was beginning to reveal the other side of the situation: degradation, exploitation, even the loss of human identity. After suffering privations and humiliations, Pinocchio managed to free himself from his new identity of a beast of burden, but Candlewick died. In this case too, the death of one of the characters may represent the need for separation and for a definitive loss if one is to free oneself from a condition of alienation and submission.

It would seem that one leaves inside one a part of oneself which perhaps is connected with infantile omnipotence. The paedophilic character—whether it be the father of the primal horde, or the absolute monarch of the era of the Roi Soleil or of the Nazi regime depicted in *The Erl-King*—in actual fact always seems to be greedy, craving new flesh to sacrifice on the altar of his own power, in order to maintain a raving omnipotence which, however, is always precarious and needs continual refurbishing.

Notes

1. Like Bluebeard, Perrault had at the age of 44 married a young woman of 19, only to be keft a widower with four children after seven years of marriage. He decided to take care of their education himself instead of sending them to a boarding school, at an age when he could actually have been their grandfather rather than their father.
2. Before it appeared in book form, "Pinocchio" came out in instalments in the *Children's Newspaper* published in Rome (1881–83).
3. *Picture Book Without Pictures* was first published in 1839. It does not appear in Freud's works, either in the German edition or in

the Italian edition. It has been translated into German with the title *Bilderbuch ohne Bilder*, published by Inselbucherei.
4. This theme emerges in *Pinocchio* in the episode of Toyland, where Pinocchio, to his great astonishment, grows a pair of donkey's ears, and he becomes a little donkey, tail and all, who is pitilessly exploited and then skinned.

CHAPTER FOUR

Notes on the history of paedophilia

The European history of childhood was a tremendous history of tyranny, suffering, exploitation, and all kinds of violence—sexual abuse was "normal" as much as it has always been part of the history of all oppressed people, women and slaves. Since sex was the primary form of possession, domination through sex has always been an aspect of the relationship between slave and master, dominator and dominated, winner and vanquished, and the powerful and the subject person.

—Ida Magli

Sexually abusive behaviours towards children have always existed in any human group, so they cannot be considered as historical incidents, yet they have to be inscribed and interpreted within social and cultural relationships, with different meanings depending on the historical period considered and on the predominant culture. "In the features of this abuse—malediction of beauty, youth and weakness—we can see the configuration of social relationships, the images of sex, the accumulation of frustrations, the nature of anxieties" (Corbin, 1989).

We shall see that the different meanings and the historical relativity the paedophilic relationship acquires go beyond the observation that there is constantly present a lowest common denominator consisting of the asymmetry within the relationship between adult and child or adolescent. This asymmetry in any case becomes the cornerstone of an abusive relationship, one in which a power gap builds up which cannot be eliminated or reduced by any passive acquiescence exchanged or smuggled by consensus. "The idea of a benign paedophilia does not justify millennial silence over its malignant degenerations" (Brandi, 1998, p. 117).

I shall look at three historical periods, the Classical Age, the Middle Ages, and the late nineteenth and early twentieth centuries to see how, although the attitude towards children and their world varies, sexual abuse has never gained the full, convinced and unequivocal approval of society, even when it has been subject to norms or informally (if not legally) accepted.

The pederast relationship in Classical Greece

Generally the first significant paedophile relationship dates back to Classical Athens, although Plutarch describes how in Sparta twelve-year-old boys were left in the care of lovers chosen from the best adult men, from whom they learnt to be real Spartiates[1] (Cantarella, 1995). The term *paedophilia* never appears in documents of that period, while the verb *paidofilein* and the substantive *paidofilis* are constantly used.

Pederasty, which became widespread mainly between the sixth and fourth centuries BC, consisted of a sexual relationship between male adults and adolescents, often within a spiritual and pedagogic experience through which the adult lover passed on the citizen's virtues. Sodomy was considered part of the developmental process leading to adult manhood, probably because it was believed that the virile virtues were transmitted through the lover's sperm; or perhaps because, being a humiliating act, it symbolised the adolescent's submission to the adult in order to become eligible to join the dominant group. The involvement of a large number of spiritual masters in pederasty in those days makes it possible to gain information on pederasty from a considerable number of documents. Those masters were the very "shapers" of culture, becoming real *opinion formers*—in this respect Socrates and Plato are cited, as well as the poetry of Alcaeus, Anacreon and Theognis. The transmission of knowledge certainly required competence, but also art as well as technique. Plato had already described *eros* as an essential condition of any kind of teaching, apart from simultaneously being desire, pleasure and love. Eros made it possible to keep power-related pleasure at bay to the advantage of gift-related pleasure (Morin, 1999).

These are the philosophical assumptions from which the sexual concretisation of Eros originates in the teacher-pupil relationship, in the absence of a working through of the risk of seduction. Camarca and Parsi write: "Moulding and teaching are two of the dogmas of paedophilia. The paedophile wants to feel that he is a master—the guide who leads to unexplored territories" (2000, p. 8). As Weitbrecht points out, "Between the *eros paidagogos*—the adult's psychic and spiritual love of the young disciple he is educating—and the gradual sliding into a sensual paedophilic relationship the step is small" (1963, p. 175).

In this relationship the *erastes* was the lover, the one who would take the initiative and arrange courting. He was subject to a proper etiquette, with a series of rights, such as the enjoyment of a quick pleasure, and duties, such as providing protection and sometimes support for the boy. He would wander the gymnasia with a feigned air of inattention and set his gaze on the youngsters who were training in the dust. In contrast, the *eromenos* was the loved and courted one, though he had to resist giving in too easily, in order not to appear too compliant and thus of little value as prey. Sexual pleasure was prohibited to the *eromenos*, who had to give himself reluctantly and enjoy the other's pleasure, which is in some ways what middle class wives were advised to do in the nineteenth century (Calasso, 1988). According to Pausanias (Plato, *Symposium*), on the one hand the *nomos* encouraged the lover to court the loved one, but on the other he wanted the loved one to resist courting.

The loved one's role in the sexual relationship was passive, and adults who let themselves be sodomised by boys were held in the lowest repute by the public opinion (Ames & Houston, 1990). The passivity of the loved one, who was just a container of the lover's love, emerges clearly from this passage in *Symposium*: "But the love of young boys should be forbidden by law, because their future is uncertain; they may turn out good or bad, either in body or soul, and much noble enthusiasm may be thrown away upon them."

The presence of detailed rituals of courting illuminates two relevant and contradictory aspects of the pederast relationship. The first aspect is that having a love relationship with a boy was not only permitted by law, but it was in fact a custom accepted by public opinion. It was punished only in Ionia and in the regions dominated by barbarians. "The ill-repute into which these attachments have fallen is to be ascribed to the evil condition of those who make them to be ill-reputed; that is to say, to the self-seeking of the governors and the cowardice of the governed" (*ibid*). The practice of having love relationships with boys was in fact strongly supported by the authorities within some important social classes, such as military and educational institutions. It was religiously celebrated through rituals and feasts and was culturally valued, with literature and thinking celebrating its excellence.

The second aspect of the pederast relationship is its controversial nature. For instance, Pausanias was unable to say whether such a form of love, which was commonplace in Athens, aroused indulgence or hostility. A sexual relationship between a man and a boy was neither easy nor taken for granted, yet it had to be subject to very precise rules.

> According to Plutarch men's relationship with boys lacks the harmonious blend of Eros and Aphrodite which would nourish a spiritual bond associated with physical pleasure. On the basis of this statement, he certainly described love of boys as *acharistos*, lacking that consensus (*charis*), tenderness, and mutuality which exclude violence, deception or vile condescendence. [Fornari, 1999, p. 157]

In Athenian law, pederasty was,

> depending on the case, highly formative or extremely dangerous for young people. Athens was concerned, as far as it could be, with guaranteeing that the life of *paides* unfolded according to rules aimed at prohibiting non-educational and vulgar relationships. [Cantarella, 1995, p. 58]

There was a quite precise time in a boy's life when he was ready for loving relationships. The boy had to be pubescent, so that sexual relationships with children before their puberty were severely punished by law. The age of the *eromenoi*, the loved ones, was to be no less than twelve years.

> Loving a child who was too young was considered much more reprehensible than loving one who was too old. In short, loving a child whose age was over the upper limit was at most a matter of taste. Ignoring the lower age limit, on the contrary, was a sin. [*ibid.*, p. 62]

However, Plutarch confirms that sexual abuse concerned not just boys who had turned eleven or twelve years, but that despite the norms, sexual abuse of younger children by pedagogues and teachers must have been a common thing. According to Cantarella, although indulging in sexual relationships with children below twelve years was considered disgraceful, the person responsible for this was not given any criminal sanction.

The earliest appearance of the beard represented the definitive sign of transition from adolescence to adulthood, and the cutting razor would cut the thread of the loving relationships (Foucault, 1984).

> Then the boys, like having a break, come out of the storm of the male loving relationships. But shortly afterwards they return into that storm, and in a new fashion. Rather than being spied naked in the gymnasiums, they themselves wander around others boys in the same places, sniffing for prey. [Calasso, 1988, p. 104]

> From the age of twelve to seventeen or eighteen years a boy was the passive partner in a relationship that bound him to an adult. Once he had reached his majority, when he became *neaniskos* (approximately from the age of twenty-five), he began to play an active role, first with the *paides* (until marriage) and then both with the *paides* and with women. [Cantarella, 1995, p. 65]

Girls' sexual life began quite early as well. They got married around the age of twelve or thirteen years. In Lesbos and Sparta, female adults often had adolescent lovers, and it was common to have a relationship with girls before marriage, in a similar fashion to the initiation ceremonies of boys.

In the communities of young women, called *thiasoi*, girls lived an overall life experience, received education and were taught a variety of subjects. Sappho, who was the head of a *thiasos*, besides being a teacher of intellect, was a teacher of the body and its representation in a global sense. In fact, girls learnt from her all the bodily expressions from singing to dance, beauty, charm, seduction, and sex. They loved each other intensively and passionately.

The introductory marriage lessons that Sappho taught her girlfriends included homoerotic relationships between teacher and pupils, as well as the male pedagogic system (Bambino, 1995). Since love between women was not yet an educational tool for the citizens, it was not of interest to them; therefore it had no space in the thinking of philosophers and was not considered in the legislation (Cantarella, 1995).

These annotations on the history of sexual relationships between adults and adolescents might give us the impression that in Ancient Greece there was complete sexual freedom and social acceptance of paedophilia. In fact a large number of intellectuals who justify or even practise paedophilia describe that historical period as a mythical golden age of paedophilic relationships, in contrast to the barbarian repressive fury of modern legislative culture.

Some have thought of defining paedophilia not as a form of perversion but as "social corruption" (Scardaccione & Baldry, 1997), as it is considered a perversion only in certain societies or historical periods, whereas in others it is an absolutely natural behaviour. This distinction seems to be inconsistent with the historical facts and is in actual fact merely a justification.

Foucalt (1984) reminds us that actually the use of pleasure in a relationship with children was a very disturbing subject. Alongside an apparent social acceptance there was a diversity of attitudes including contempt for either too-easy or too-interested youngsters and a low opinion of feminine men. Moreover, pornographic or mercenary homosexuality was punished: "On the one hand philosophical works, or at least some of them, and legal logography sometimes exalted paedophilia; on the other hand comedy considered it heavily ridiculous" (Cantarella, 1995, p. 9).

Although it was widespread, pederast practice seemed to be surrounded by an intricate game of appreciation and depreciation, to such an extent that both morality and norms were difficult to interpret. If on the one hand it was encouraged, on the other we can see the fathers' concern with protecting their children from love affairs or requiring pedagogues to prohibit them. And so peers and friends could be heard blaming each other "if they see something similar happening", as Plato says in *Symposium*.

A vigorous hostility against paedophilia emerged, though with difficulty, from some details we can find in Plato's works. On the one hand paedophilic practice was idealised as an educational tool of knowledge and culture, on the other hand it was feared to be a source of tyranny, even if often covered with knowledge and education.

> The erotic surveyor Plato describes with the most detailed accuracy the admirable dissymmetry on which Athenian love for children is based. The whole metaphysics of love is focused on the gesture with which the loved one donates his grace (*charis*) to the lover … Plato considers the intertwining of a body to conquer as a fortress and the metaphysical flight to be the image itself of Eros. In fact the loved one will give himself because he has a desire for "education and knowledge of all kinds". [Calasso, 1988, pp. 95–96]

Knowledge becomes introjected as it goes through physical denial, passivity, and "proper submission" (Plato, *Symposium*), and the exchange of knowledge and pleasure. The loved one lived for the lover: he could not have his own psychological autonomy, his own will, but was a source and object of pleasure, willing to pay with his body for the knowledge and culture offered by the teacher or the military commander.

There is no trace of the reciprocity that Vattimo, citing Kierkegaard, sees at the base of any educational relationship, which should only be symmetrical. He wrote: "The disciple is a tool for the teacher to understand himself, and vice versa: the teacher is a tool for the disciple to understand himself" (1995, p. 6). As we will see later on, these topics will be dealt with again in regard to the teacher-disciple relationships within artists' workshops from the Middle Ages onwards.

Pederasty continued to be practised among the Romans, but in some sense it lost its philosophical investment. The free ephebe was replaced by the slave and the slave's child, and sometimes by the defeated enemy. As Foucault reminds us, this resulted in the loss of the heritage of the great Greek speculation on loving relationships with children, replaced with the tendency to brutality and abuse.

> The young Roman was taught from infancy to be a conqueror: *tu regere imperio populos, romane, memento*, wrote Virgil. The Romans' rule of life was to impose their will, subjugate everybody, and dominate the world. Their sexual ethic was nothing but an aspect of their political ethic.
> In his moralistic invectives, Cicero did not condemn homosexuality as such. He only condemned the particular form of homosexuality that was pederasty in the Hellenic sense, which was love for available adolescents. [Cantarella, 1995, p. 10, 129]

Homosexuality had one only limitation, which was that it should never involve free adolescents, who as adults had to learn to impose themselves and not to be the object of others' desires. "Plutarch narrates that Romans used to put a golden *bulla* around their children's necks, so that while playing naked, they could not be mistaken for the slaves and made the object of attempts at seduction" (*ibid.*, p. 132).

The problem was not the fact of going out with a slave, "joining a life model which was not in accordance with the strict and rigorous model that the Romans continued to exalt and disseminate, even when the increase of wealth brought a new luxury into the town" (*ibid.*, p. 136). Nor was the problem having a relationship with other people's slaves, as this would have implied a decrease in the work done by the slave. The *lex Scatinia* only punished *stuprum cum puero* (i.e. involving a free-born boy) with fines. However, in the Augustan Age, pederast relationships were no longer an expression of social and sexual abuse, but of romantic love for available adolescents, in accordance with the Greek model that had influenced Roman culture. The Christian Emperor Justinian outlawed any form of homosexuality, since it was in any case an offence to God.

The total asymmetry of power within the pederast relationship and the complete neglect of the child's emotional world were a valuable source for Freud's notes on this subject. In a footnote added in 1910 to his "Three Essays on the Theory of Sexuality", Freud emphasised that "the most striking distinction between the erotic life of antiquity and our own no doubt lies in the fact that the ancients laid the stress upon the instinct itself, whereas we emphasise its object. The ancients glorified the instinct and were prepared on its account to honour even an inferior object, while we despise the instinctual activity in itself, and find excuses for it only in the merits of the object" (Freud, 1905).

Paedophilia in the Middle Ages

Although Judaeo-Christian tradition condemned homosexual paedophilia, as it considered heterosexual relationships natural and homosexual relationships (in both the active and the passive position) to be "against nature", it was less incisive in defending girls. In fact, throughout the Middle Ages marriage between a ten-year-old girl and a much older man was not exceptional, even though twelve years was by law the minimum age for marriage (Aguglia & Riolo, 1999).

Although the ethical-religious beliefs of those days forbade even talking about paedophilia, the discovery of a large number of thirteenth-century contracts by which children were hired by masters proves how common it was to be trained as an apprentice in a stranger's house. Here a sort of relational promiscuity usually developed. This apprenticeship began at the age of eight or ten, when children left their parents' house to follow their own fate. The training finished at the age of twelve or fourteen.

> Looking at these contracts without first of all ridding ourselves of our modern habits of thought, we find it difficult to decide whether the child has been placed as an apprentice (in the modern meaning of the word), or as a boarder, or as a servant. We would be foolish to press the point: our distinctions are anachronistic, and a man of the Middle Ages would see nothing in them but slight variations on a basic idea—that of service. [Ariès, 1960, p. 366]

The child could learn the manners of a gentleman, or a profession, or could study with a priest as an altar server, or be a servant in monasteries, private houses, or among soldiers and sailors. The training unfolded through practice, which was not limited to the profession but also involved private life. It is within this socio-educational dimension that we have to set the child's life in the workshop, where the artist played more than one role at the same time: putative father, teacher, master.

> Apprentices (known as "errand boys" or "disciples") were usually younger than fourteen years and sometimes were only seven years old. Normally they learned the profession by making copies of the drawings from the workshop collection … They also used to do casual jobs, such as grinding the colours, until they became ready to assist the older man in more difficult undertakings. [Burke, 1979, p. 88]

Apprenticeship away from the family was a form of learning that was to disappear with the subsequent establishment of boarding schools and state schools. The promiscuous environment in which the child was treated both as a servant and as a son had made sexual contacts between adults and children more accessible. The apprentices' apparent submissiveness to their masters reveals the difficulties of that age, the condition of total dependency in which the population lived, but also

> the internalisation of a relationship model of ancestral production, based on acquiescence and submission … It is not difficult to imagine the condition of these adolescents, who felt that they were at the same time the object of desire and of contempt, and who had to accept what all of society considered the most shameful and demeaning thing. [Carrasco, 1989, p. 60]

Gargani (1995) sees the teacher-pupil relationship within the more general topic of the authentic and inauthentic living condition of human beings. According to Magris,

> a teacher is such because although he asserts his beliefs, he does not want to impose them on his disciple. He does not look for followers, and wants to mould not copies of himself but independent, intelligent adults who are able to go their own way.

Indeed, he is a teacher just because he is able to understand what the right track is for his pupil, and in order to help him find it and walk along it without betraying the essence of his being. (1999, p. 35).

However, the relationship between the teacher and the disciple, beyond idealisation, continuously swings between the opposite poles of authenticity and inauthenticity, of creativity and repetitiveness, of dialogism and authority, of seduction and self-discovery, of acting humanly or inhumanly (Lampignano, 2000). A shift to any of these polarities leads to an unbalanced, sometimes perverted relationship, which is transformed and deformed by the new features. We cannot deny or repress asymmetry related to experiences, knowledge and authority, as this is one of the features of the teaching relationship. It fluctuates towards a tendency to symmetry, being concordant, magical mutual understanding by which one satisfies the other's desire by meeting his expectations. Only by considering the wholeness of the relational universes in which the relationship is structured (and is also damaged) can we provide a thorough description of it (*ibid*).

Any teacher-pupil relationship contains the risk of narcissistic investment on the one hand and uncritical idealisation on the other. The teacher, comforted by the pure potentiality of the infantile gesture, sees his idealised self in the disciple, and tends to invest in him any hope of going beyond his own limits by projecting every personal compensating experience onto the pupil. The relationships may become symbiotic, lacking any dialogic space—the child exists only as a projection of the teacher's idealised self or of an extreme extension of it. On the other hand, the teacher represents for the pupil an object of identification, a safe harbour, the omnipotent father provider of good and evil, the opposite of the nasty father who sent him away from home and thus deprived him of his protection and of his mother's care.

The peculiar and subtle aesthetic quality which characterises moods, emotions and feelings within the relationships that develop in art workshops must be taken into consideration as a further element that increases the chances of a love relationship (sometimes openly sexual) being established between adult and adolescents. The child and adolescent body's beauty, its smoothness, the pure potentiality which precedes the appearance of the secondary sexual characteristics, so often represented in art works, nourish sensuality within relationships and the desire to possess Beauty even physically. This was the artist's greatest and inaccessible aspiration.

Leonardo's workshop, in which one could breathe wonder, charm and admiration for the art works as well as for the great scientific discoveries, and the intense and passionate relationship between Pontormo and Bronzino, are clear examples of a teaching relationship sliding into a paedophilic homosexual one.

Paedophilic relationships, however, cannot be limited to the apparently subtle, sometimes stuffy and sordid space of the workshops, places essentially governed by a sort of ethical extraterritoriality, like many aspects of the artists' life. There are forms of paedophilia which are less sublime, less culturally invested, of which it is difficult to find evidence.

Le Roy Ladurie (1978), writing the history of an Occitan village in the fourteenth century, reconstructs the initiation to "homophilia" of a twelve-year-old child who has gone to study grammar with a priest. The abused child would later become an active pederast who seduced adolescents and young men. These naïve pupils remained possessed by the former pupil who once was seduced at school: a cultural reproduction (p. 144 ff). Le Roy Ladurie underlined that sodomy and pederasty were practised in the cities, although the seduced pupils were born in the countryside: they came from rather well-to-do families who had good reasons to send their children to study in the city. The premature separation from the family, however it may take place, is obviously an event that increases the child's vulnerability, weakens his capacity for self-defence against the seductive attacks of adults, and means that he is poorly protected.

Jean-Pierre Leguay describes an event which scandalised the peaceful town of Rennes in 1466: "Jehannico Darbieto, a young Spanish merchant who had been resident here for a long time, and two Breton friends of his, sons of well-to-do, esteemed and well-respected parents, came to be accused of an offence against the law of public morals: the rape of a twelve-year-old girl, Margot Simmonet, a whitewasher's daughter." The child was raped and deflowered against her will. Despite the large number of witnesses, the whole thing was hushed up and Jehan Simmonet sold his daughter's heart and reputation cheaply. "The rape cost thirty

Breton gold shields … the equivalent of tree Anjou wine casks or a year's wages for a skilled worker" (1989, p. 20).

Such stories of immoral behaviour are relatively rare in the archives of the Middle Ages, since they are economically reconstructed before a possible complaint, unless they are particularly monstrous or despicable. According to Leguay, the causes of child rape are to be seen in the boredom affecting the children of well-to-do families and in the lack of youth associations able to entertain and educate adolescents. Moreover, citing Duby and Le Goff among others, Leguay mentions the weight of moral constraints, sexual segregation, social frustration, and misogyny in those days.

One of the differences between paedophilic behaviours in the Middle Ages and in later times resides in the increasing value of money, which characterises the socio-economic reality of the increasingly wealthy and industrialised West (Aguglia & Riolo, 1999). The literature shows some evidence that the streets in fourteenth-century Florence were full of boys and girls selling their bodies (Goodrich, 1976). Carrasco (1989) mentions that Valencia market was throughout the eighteenth century a centre and meeting place for social outcasts and young prostitutes.

Child sexual abuse was not subject to significant social disapproval because, as Ariès underlined, it is the perception of childhood itself that (if it existed at all) was poor in that historical period. The invention of childhood as a world in itself, a conceptual category, a social problem and a life stage, not a mere transitional phase, began to acquire historical evidence from the 16th century. The first perception of children by adults is to be found in modern age with the establishment of the middle-class family. The little we know about non-adults in the past generally refers to upper-class children, but it does mainly concern the mass condition—though anonymous—or exceptional single stories which are not representative of the infantile condition (Becchi, 1994).

Ariès notes that through Middle Ages, until around the seventeenth century, there is no artistic representation of childhood. "This suggests too that in the realm of real life, and not simply in that of aesthetic transposition, childhood was a period of transition which passed quickly and which was just as quickly forgotten" (Ariès, 1960, p. 34). The first representations of childhood appeared after the fourteenth century and consisted of the Angel with adolescent features, and of the infant Jesus (or infant Jesus with the Virgin Mary), progenitor of all children in art history. In the Gothic period, the naked and often asexual baby appears as an allegorical representation of the soul that escapes from the dying person's mouth. In the fifteenth century, two new kinds of child representation appear: the portrait and the *putto*. However, until the sixteenth century, all these representations have little to do with the real child as belonging to history. "The historical child, however tiny he/she was, had no imaginative space in the nudity of the mythological and decorative child" (*ibid.*, p. 46).

In the writings of the Church Fathers the word "child" designated the place of imperfection. "The weakness of the child was proof of the existence of original sin and of the defectiveness of human nature. Augustine described as 'sins' all those actions of children that revealed vulnerability and malice: greed, arrogance, rebellion, jealousy, and selfishness" (Becchi, 1994, p. 45). Childhood, especially early childhood, meant deficiency, not being, deprivation, abnormality, and infirmity. It is only in the Renaissance that the discovery of human beings in their naturalness would lead to the acknowledgement of the child's potentialities and an increased sense of tenderness.

The innocence-guilt dualism—a central issue in Christianity from the first centuries—was the basis of the medieval pedagogical ethic, divided between conceiving childhood as asexual and considering it inclined to any sort of vice. Given these contradictory aspects, preventive norms were proclaimed and restrictive measures were taken, which taught from birth a certain detachment from the body, and forbade parents, teachers, and adults in general to show any loving gesture towards children. Children themselves were also forbidden to show affection to one another. DeMause (1974) writes that unfortunately conceiving a child as innocent and incorruptible is the most common defensive attitude assumed by those who molest children, in order to deny that their abuse has harmed them.

The Church council recommended teachers to approach pupils with the utmost caution. Songs against corrupted teachers sung by youngsters since the tenth century document homosexual practice in religious environments and the "incredible crime" that occurred between spiritual fathers and spiritual sons. The *Carmina Burana* also mention the teacher's relationships *"cum pueris"*.

In outlining the family environment in this historical period, Ariès cites Père de Dainville, the historian of the Society of Jesus (the Jesuits):

> The respect due to children was then [in the sixteenth century] completely unknown. Everything was permitted in their presence: coarse language, scabrous actions and situations; they heard everything and saw everything ... This lack of reserve with regard to children surprises us: we raise our eyebrows at the outspoken talk but even more at the bold gestures, the physical contacts, about which it is easy to imagine what a modern psychoanalyst would say. The psychoanalyst would be wrong. The attitude to sex, and doubtless sex itself, varies according to environment, and consequently according to period and mentality. [Ariès, 1960, p. 103]

Ariès also describes a 1511 engraving by Hans Baldung Grien, a representation of the Holy Family in which St Anne appears to open the child's thighs as if she wanted to grab and tickle the genitals. He warns, though, that it would be a mistake to see a licentious allusion in it, since the gesture was set in the normal relationships of that period. In underlining the necessity to avoid any interpretation that does not consider the common expressions of communication of those days, Ariès disputes the psycho-historical ideas of DeMause, who claimed that traces of a feeling of childhood date back to the Middle Ages.

The interpretation of identical historical phenomena varies according to the observational perspective. According to Ariès, since a feeling of childhood does not exist, paedophilic behaviour or sexual abuse quite simply cannot exist either. In contrast, DeMause conceives the history of childhood as a nightmare from which we have only recently begun to wake up. The further back we go in history, the less consideration is given to the child, and the more frequently the child is murdered, abandoned, beaten, terrified, and subjected to sexual abuse.

According to DeMause (2000), the central mechanism of the whole historical evolution is *psychogenesis*, a spontaneous drive existing within any adult-child relationship, which allows adults to re-experience their own childhood trauma through their children and to satisfy their childhood needs and the related independence anxieties in better conditions than those of their childhood. DeMause disputes Ariès's contention that a specific concept of childhood remained unknown in the late Middle Ages. According to his psycho-historical theories, three possible reactions are available to an adult relating to a child's needs: (a) he can use the child as an object of projections that satisfy his own unconscious (projection reaction); (b) he can use the child as a substitute for an adult figure who has been important in his childhood (reversion reaction); or (c) he can empathise with the child's needs and try to meet them (empathy reaction). We must distinguish between projection and real empathy: the former constantly entails the preliminary projection of the adult's unconscious onto the child and, unlike the latter, is inappropriate or unsatisfactory for the child's actual needs. It is not that medieval parents were incapable of love, but they did not have the emotional maturity necessary to see the child as an individual person.

It is enormously difficult to collect evidence on children's sexual life: the source's reticence and repressive attitude adds to the difficulty of tracing books, manuscripts, and objects that are fundamental for historical research. However, when the archives are open, they give us an image of a game with death, dominated by shame, money and violence.

DeMause (1974) stated that child sexual abuse was quite frequent and that the child was essentially only a random victim, according to the role he played in the adult's defensive apparatus. In a later work (2000) he explained that the exploitation of children as scapegoats to alleviate individual internal conflict was a tool to maintain our mass psychological homeostasis. Those who dare to oppose this mass fantasy run the risk of being declared sacrilegious and of being regarded as undermining world peace. The main psychological mechanism working in child abuse is the same as that working in infanticide. According to DeMause, this mechanism entails the use of the child as if it were what he calls a *poison container*: a receptacle into which adults project all their own unacceptable feelings, so that these dangerous feelings can be manipulated and controlled in the child rather than being related to themselves. "It is obvious that severe measures must be taken to keep this dangerous 'toilet-child' under control once the swaddling bands are outgrown" (2000, p. 11). "It is this condition of being used as a vehicle for projections which was usual for children in the past" (*ibid.*, p. 7). But DeMause suggested that Klein's term *projective identification* is replaced with *injection*, represented by the image of a syringe injecting poison.

The interpretations the two theories make of paedophilic behaviours in the Middle Ages are certainly important. However, both leave us with the feeling of a child who is helpless, whose individuality and specific needs are not acknowledged, who is transformed into a passive ephemeral object, sometimes the victim, but also the protagonist of a diffuse violence (Niccoli, 1995). This feeling is also reinforced by the violence against children that spread across Europe in some historical periods. Some children, considered to be possessed by the devil, were tortured and often burned alive in order to expiate their guilt. They were sacrificed on the altar of a cruel and aberrant inquisitorial mechanism.

Eveline Hasler (1997) cleared many hurdles to trace the sources that document two such episodes, which took place in Lucerne in 1652 and in Upper Swabia in 1658, and wrote a remarkably suggestive novel, *Die Vogelmacherin* [The Bird-Maker]. The first case concerns an eleven-year-old child burned at the stake because she had boasted about being able to "make birds". The second concerns two young brothers accused of witchcraft and trading with the devil, who were looked after in a convent for four years until puberty (that is to say until they acquired the "capacity" to pay the penalty for their alleged actions), and only then were they killed. In a period of religious obscurantism, imagination and flights of fantasy (which are typical of childhood in all times and places) became a crime liable to capital punishment. Those children were simply the scapegoats on whom adults vented their lust, authoritarianism, political-religious resentment, superstitions and fears. In her novel the author creates an appropriate confrontation between the child's uncorrupted mind and the world of Nature, one exposed to the aggression of perversions, the other to economical exploitation by adults.

However, law does not apply equally to everybody. Carrasco (1989) highlights a case in which complaints to the Supreme Inquisition about the paedophilic behaviour of a teacher of novices, who exerted in his monastery endless and successful sexual pressures on the children who had been left in his care, do not come to a happy conclusion. The clergyman is secretly arrested, but the trial ends at the judicial inquiry. "The council thought that the cure—fatally scandalous—would be worse than the illness" (p. 59).

Between the guilty child and the innocent child

In the nineteenth century it is possible to detect two distinct social representations of the child. The guilty child of the Christian doctrine of original sin, and childhood as the place of imperfection in Augustine's and Martin Luther's thinking, are in contrast with the innocent child and childhood meant as a synonym for good quality in Rousseau's *Emile* (1762): a blend of primitivism and irrationalism.

The child's unintentional and non-conscious faults are proof of the existence of original sin and of the dissolution intrinsic to human nature. The predominant belief that the child's nature was more prone to evil than to good entailed the necessity for him or her to be subjected to continuous disciplinary measures, sometimes even violent, to develop character and reason. This belief fostered the establishment of an educational system focused on the necessity to repress, inhibit and correct the child's natural inclination to evil. In contrast, according to Rousseau's theories (which, incidentally, were condemned by both Catholic and Protestant Churches), children had to be left free and independent. Re-interpreting the original doctrine of sin, Rousseau placed emphasis on the human natural dimension and its essential importance in forming human beings (Giallongo, 1990).

This, then, is the contradictory cultural setting for an explosion of sexual offences against young girls in the nineteenth century. Anne-Marie Sohn (1989) reports that from 1826 to 1830 in France the annual rates of rape or indecent exposure against adults and children were 137 and 136 respectively. From 1856 to 1860 sexual offences against adults almost doubled (203 cases), while child sexual abuse increased fivefold (684 cases). The highest rates were between 1876 and 1880, with 791 trials a year, followed by a multi-stage regression with a gradual decrease (600 cases in 1885 and 1886, and 345 between 1910 and 1914). Between the two world wars there were "only" 150–180 documented cases. Sohn asked herself the following questions, which are indeed still topical: Is this explosion of crimes against children a consequence of new charges being brought for crimes long tolerated but now condemned? Or is it rooted in a weakening of social prohibitions that allows people to put into action things they have long held at the level of imagination? The two explanations can certainly coexist. In inverse terms, would these crimes document a "moralisation" of society or, by contrast, a new form of laxity?

Of the young girls who were seduced, 86% were below the age of fifteen years, 75% were aged no more than thirteen years, and 25% were younger than ten years. The two youngest were three years old. Overall, we can say that young age, physical weakness, low social class and ignorance of sexuality explain why childhood represents an easy hunting ground for abusers.

Sohn describes the nineteenth century abuser's typical traits: rather than an old satyr, he is a man in the flower of youth—he is almost always a poor man who exploited other poor people. He may be an agricultural worker, farm hand, servant, trader, craftsman, market trader, coach driver or cab driver. In the higher social classes the abuser may be an official, a teacher or a clergyman. Although many employers and publicists deplore the immorality of the workers, this is only seldom mentioned in offences against one's sense of decency.

The abusers give the following reasons to justify their sexual offences and relieve their responsibility: (a) the safety of having sex with someone who has never had sexual contacts before; (b) the substitutive sexuality of many paid farm workers, of disabled, mentally ill, impotent and alcoholic people; and (c) "libertine" and "dissolute" people claim that it is impossible to inhibit their paedophilic instincts. These are the individuals whom medicine will term "paedophiles". Paedophilia is defined as "inclination" or "passion"—which explains the irrepressible feature of this peculiar taste. "The second offences or outrages committed by an accused against several young girls represent a presumption of paedophilia" (Sohn, 1989, p. 85).

The shame that affected the girl and her family could be faced in two ways: by hiding the scandal or by demanding public compensation. The first attitude was far more common.

> Rapes become indecent exposure and indecent exposure is punished with no more than a fine. The legal ambiguity of the texts, which leaves judges totally free to define sexual offences, clears the way for specious interpretations. If physical or moral violence

is not sensational, the charges can be dropped. It is therefore important to investigate the victims' (and their families') morality to prove, as a general rule, the absence of consensus, or to blame the young girls and redeem the accused. [*ibid.*, p. 102]

The decreasing number of crimes shown in twentieth-century accounts can be related to the increased protection of young girls, the reduction of child labour, and the liberalisation of sexual customs—which, by facilitating sexual relationships between adults, has paradoxically perhaps contributed to protecting children. If this is true in the first part of the twentieth century, is not so in the following period, when easy access to sexual contacts, Marcuse's and Reiche's "repressive desublimation", the lack of depth and complexity in meetings advertised by the media fostered a new sexual access to children.

The dichotomy between the angelic child and the wicked child persisted throughout the twentieth century[2] (it was indeed the satanic and delinquent image which prevailed in the scientific world), although photographs, advertisements, and copious literature tended to favour the image of the angelic, innocent child. The child appeared in photos of those times dressed up as a miniature adult, with all the features of elegance and aloofness, or as a playfully impertinent Cupid, or as a sweet fairy. Innocence is absent in the history of child photography, and the history of "well-educated" photography is rich in alien children, foreign and transfigured beings, masks and transvestites.

According to Cesare Lombroso, innocence as a synonym for the child was nonsense, since the human being is born an absolute criminal. Education therefore consists essentially of getting the child adjusted to society, teaching him that harming individuals of his own species and environment is harmful to everybody.

> Children certainly lack a moral sense in their first months and first year of life. For them, good and bad are what is allowed or forbidden by Papa or Mama, but they never feel by themselves when something is wrong … Children share this lack of far-sightedness with savages and criminals; a non-immediate future has no influence on their imagination. Experiencing pleasure eight days or a year later is for them the same thing. [1884, p. 551]

If in Lombroso's notes there seems to be a certain affinity with Freudian theories according to which a child cannot delay pleasure, his conclusions that "the child's criminal tendencies are general" (p. 553), and that only good education can explain "the normal metamorphosis occurring in most cases" (*ibid.*), are different. Rather than detecting the act itself, Lombroso tries to identify it with its author, who is classified as being a criminal from birth, originally the product of biological taints and subsequently of an altered psychic process that can be circumscribed within precise pathological categories.

> Anyone attentively observing the wilful and bizarre, ferocious and playful behaviour, like the jerky movements of the monsters that have appeared in our films ever since, could easily recognise their secret model: the child. Even *The Turn of the Screw*, by Henry James, is full of wild horror of the children Miles and Flora, whom the governess sees as closely linked to filthy ghosts. The monster created by Baron Frankenstein with parts of dead bodies is a sort of artificial child endowed with uncontrollable and dangerous instinctual drives. [Scaraffia, 1987, p. 41]

It is the image of the nasty child who needs to be disciplined and redeemed, therefore, that prevails in the culture of those days and, is adopted not only by pedagogic theories but also by psychological theories and psychoanalysis itself.

Freud's theories reveal some non-linearity, dissymmetry, and even contradictions which provide evidence of the intense work invested in developing a coherent psychoanalytical system. The Freudian child gains his own grandiosity when he dwells inside the adult, moves inside the folds of his unconscious and becomes representative of it—in other words, when he is created as a psychoanalytical child and becomes the protagonist of scientific examination. By contrast, the child becomes an object of little importance and consideration when he is observed in his personal data, daily concrete needs and limits, and in the relationship with the adult. The child's sexuality is seen in an adultmorphic sense (Imbasciati, 1994).

Anna Freud used to remind her colleagues that analysts love images of childhood emerging from their theories more than children in their "complex realities", which interpretations should help face (1964). However, if Dora's treatment clearly reveals authoritarian and imposing attitudes, these would weaken and be replaced with a new sensitivity that Freud shows towards little Hans and his individual characteristics and needs. This remarkable changed attitude is related to Freud's concomitant self-analysis, which allows him to go through his own childhood (Bergeret, 1987; Geissmann & Geissmann, 1997; Borgogno, 1999). The child emerging from the subsequent notes is a healthy child endowed with intelligent and curious answers, addressed to reality and relationships and open to life and novelty; a child often compelled to shrink from confrontation with adults because they do not listen, they are unreliable and sometimes obviously harmful, with consequent serious damage to his development (Borgogno, 1999).

If in his earliest writings (1896) Freud intended to be preventive and educational when he explicitly reproached parents for not acknowledging enough the risk their children ran of being subject to sexual abuse from adults, in "Three Essays on the Theory of Sexuality" (1905) the child is defined as polymorphously perverse. He indicated in polymorphous perversity a sort of early development of sexuality, and in "A Child is Being Beaten" (1919a) he described the child as being attracted and taken by the perverse fantasy. This intuition was fruitful, as it allowed an understanding of perversion free from social condemnation instead of being considered merely a pathological phenomenon. However, it has brought an element of strong ambiguity (De Masi, 1999).

Likewise, we should remember that in the "Introductory Lectures on Psychoanalysis" (1915–1917), Freud relativised the child's instinctual set-up, taking the adult's into consideration too: "We must not omit to add that the parents themselves often exercise a determining influence on the awakening of a child's Oedipus attitude by themselves obeying the pull of sexual attraction" (p. 333).

Caper (1998) highlighted that it is a mistake to equate the primitive with the pathological. Perversion does concern sexuality, but unlike polymorphism, it contains a non-sexual destructive element. Meltzer (1973) had already distinguished polymorphous sexuality from perverse sexuality. While perverse sexuality relates to a destructive attack on the symbolisation of the parental couple, polymorphous sexuality belongs to the realm of undifferentiated sexuality.

In "Civilization and its Discontents" (Freud, 1930) the natural way in which the human condition expresses itself is described as a pile of violence and aggression: fantasised, yet never completely controlled by the superego. Aggressive instincts and primitive passion which drive an individual to rape, incest or murder constitute an unconscious of an immoral nature, and are imperfectly governed by social institutions and a sense of guilt. Human unhappiness is consequent to civilisation, which compels an individual to adhere to a system that is in conflict with the primitive one. Neurosis and perversion would then result from the eternal conflict between nature and nurture, and the socially necessary censure of primitive sexual instincts.

The child described by Melanie Klein is also constitutionally inhabited by scary, aggressive fantasies, fantasies of destructive hatred and sadomasochistic domain, even though Klein describes a tendency to repair the damaged internal parents. "By placing the love object in a position of ideal goodness, Klein's perspective overlooks the offences coming from the object and tends to underestimate defensive and vital hatred" (De Masi, 2000, p. 145).

It is only with Winnicott and Bion that the child described above loses the negative characteristics which are partly linked to the dominant "guilt" view and partly a reaction to the anti-sexual bigotry of those days. A new child is created between the angelic child and the perverse child: the relational child, who will be observed in a developmental dimension that unfolds in the relationship with his mother. With the transition from the "linear achievement" of the instinct to "reflective and symbolic competence", the "competent" child and the "explorer" child replace the "instinctual" child (De Simone, 2002).

One of the most significant achievements of psychoanalysis is the increasing importance given to the acknowledgement and preservation of the child's integrity and relational capacity. Winnicott's concept of *holding* and Bion's concept of maternal *reverie*, though different from each other, indicate how the presence of the mother—representative and mediator of the outside world—allows the transition from incapacity to think to the appearance of thinkable elements, from which the capacity for representation and symbolisation will later develop. The mother has contained the third, the Lacanian father, since the beginning of the relationship with her child, so that when she is *good enough*, her emotional containment is also structuring.

Green (1997) refers to the *reverie* of the bonding between parents and between child and father, a *reverie* of the triangular union of which the mother is the mutual object. The child then assumes the characteristics of a whole person, though still in the process of development, and integrated with the maternal unity.

The lack of a sufficiently welcoming environment facilitates the child's regression to narcissistic survival mechanisms, characterised by illusory experiences and a swing away from contact with reality. According to Masud Khan (1979), when the depressed mother is not able to adequately stimulate the child's libidinal potential, the child is compelled to use his body and orifices as surrogates, and erotisation takes over the development process.

The natural perversion described in Freud's early formulations is replaced with the child's natural integrity, which can be damaged by the mother's incapacity to contain. The failure of *alpha function*, determined by maternal incapacity for *reverie*, can lead to the reintroduction of *beta elements* that were previously projected onto the mother and violently rejected by her as she was unable to contain them. Children who cannot benefit from an appropriate supply of alpha elements are bound to use projective mechanisms in their persistent and frustrating search for a container able to satisfy their fundamental needs. "When approaching parenting, those who were frustrated in their attempts to deliver their bad experiences to their mother, and be released and rewarded, will not be able to use their internal space to contain their child's projections; this results in the formation of a vicious cycle able to harm future generations" (Guasto, 2001).

Guasto supposes that when it comes to child sexual abuse, the consequence of the alpha flow inversion resulting from the adults' projection of their paedophilic desires onto the child is the occurrence of clinical phenomena similar to those identified by Williams (1997) in some *eating disorders*. In other words, the indiscriminate invasion of projective elements from which the child is unable to protect himself results in his mental apparatus becoming an *inert receptacle*. This situation, called *omega function*, produces evidently poisonous effects and serious clinical conditions in which the child is unable to build appropriate defensive systems, such as *no entry syndrome* or the encapsulation of the traumatic experience as a foreign object.

If the cultural roots of psychoanalysis and positivist medicine are the same, since the child is in any case a savage, polymorphously perverse and delinquent from birth, who needs to be disciplined, educated and rescued, psychiatric and psychoanalytic thinking will evolve differently and nowadays come to different conclusions. We shall attempt to see how the clinical picture of paedophilia originates: its cultural context and its theoretical assumptions and links with current morals, and then examine how it differentiates over the evolution of psychoanalytic and psychiatric thinking.

Notes

1. The Spartiates were the most powerful caste in Spartan society, consisting of males with full citizenship who formed an elite warrior class.
2. Laura Albert dealt creatively with the theme of the fluctuation between sanctification and degradation of the child in her novel *Sarah* (2000), purportedly written by the teenager Jeremiah "Terminator" LeRoy. The novel tells the story of a twelve-year-old boy, the son of a prostitute who became a mother at the age of fourteen, who through identification with his mother begins to work as a prostitute, dressed as a girl. From a little prostitute he is transformed into Saint Sarah who performs miracles. When his sexual identity is unveiled, he becomes a demonised and degraded prostitute, a slave in a Wonderland inhabited by unreal and grotesque figures; an alienated, archaic humanity imbued with the impoverished remains of pagan rites, in which the protagonist Sarah seeks solidarity, acknowledgement and affection.

CHAPTER FIVE

Paedophilia in medical and psychiatric thought

Paolo F. Peloso and Cosimo Schinaia

> What point can there be in comparing pain and punishment?
> Do we know what scars they bear, what dreams wake them?
>
> —Chaim Potock

Lantéri-Laura (1966) argues that medical science began to take an interest in the subject of perverse behaviours and the carriers of "odd instincts" only from the mid-nineteenth century, with exhibitionism in France, which was dealt with by Lasègue and Magnan, implicated by magistrates. Doctors, psychiatrists and warders published scientific works based on a methodology of anamnesis and clinical-nosographic observation, presenting a description and specification of a number of sexual anomalies classified according to their external manifestations (Forel, 1905).

Krafft-Ebing's monograph on sexual psychopathy dates back approximately to the same period in Germany. From 1886 he began to deal with a group of perversions characterised by an erotic inclination for childhood, which he named erotic paedophilia. The central objective of this piece of work was to regard sexual perversions (homosexuality in first place) as pathological, moving them from the area of criminal justice to that of cure (Arveiller, 1998).

Krafft-Ebing described a phenomenon whose spread was often overlooked: brothels which offered male youths and adults to satisfy the sexual appetite of "normal" adult paedophiles existed in many European cities.[1] For example, Dostoevsky sadly mentions child prostitution on the streets of big capitalist cities, recalling his visit to London in a famous section of *Winter Notes on Summer Impressions* (1863). We can see the same situation flourishing in degenerate suburbs and slums of big cities in the nineteenth century and in the misery of European cities in the period following the Second World War. The latter is brilliantly illustrated by Curzio Malaparte in *The Skin* (1949), in which American soldiers' sordid illicit trade in a young girl's virginity unfolds in degenerate Naples. The girl was exhibited as an original and appetising phenomenon, and was, in return for payment, subjected to adults touching her hymen in order to verify her virginity.

The same subject is dealt with from a sociological perspective by Lino Ferriani (1902), a King's attorney at the court of Como, who took a decisive stand in support of the magazine *Nuova Antologia* [New Anthology] and others who spoke out against the "trade in children". Ferriani identified the main forms of this trade as parents or children's homes selling children to exploiters and hoarders who travelled abroad, or children being conveyed to tramps for begging, to craftsmen ostensibly in order to be trained as apprentices but in reality to satisfy their masters' "obscene purposes", to factory owners to do work requiring skills and strength beyond their capabilities, to chimney sweeps or farmers. He then got to the heart of child prostitution, which he believed was often fostered by parents, noting: "Some ironing, milliner's and hairdresser's shops sometimes hide, under the mask of honest trade, a trade in juvenile innocence that is infamous and as lucrative as the other" (p. 133).

Ferriani listed twenty-seven cases he knew, six boys and twenty-one girls involved in this particular kind of trade, whose families had accepted a monetary arrangement between 50 and 350 lire. Then he added twenty-six more cases of Italian girls taken to Greece and involved in public or clandestine prostitution after having been sold, between the ages of eight and thirteen, as apprentices in Italian workshops.

The cases reported by Krafft-Ebing in 1886 were just four, all concerning men. The first case was a paranoid attracted only by young girls but not by adult women, a hair fetishist (the assonance with the protagonist of Süskind's *Perfume* is evident) whose love of young girls never manifested itself through concrete acts. The second case was a man described as affected by a hereditary defect, who was sexually aroused by five- to ten-year-old girls from the onset of his puberty at the age of twenty-four. The mere sight of them induced ejaculation, and the slightest physical contact with them made him fall into excessive sexual hyper-affectivity, the length of which he could remember only faintly. Barely satisfied by conjugal sex, he managed to control his sexual impulse towards young girls until he gave in to it due to the worsening of his neurasthenia as a possible consequence, as Krafft-Ebing explains, of the practice of *coitus interruptus*, or of the lessening of moral resistances, or increased sexual excitement. The third case was a man affected by "constitutional neurasthenia" and a hereditary defect, whose cranium was anomalous and who had no real inclination for adult women, although during intercourse he behaved like a rutting animal. This man, who became a paedophile at the age of twenty-five, would become aroused by libidinous fingering of young girls' bodies. The fourth case was another man described as affected by a hereditary defect, who was always sexually excited by pre-pubescent girls, whilst having a very weak inclination for adult women. At some point, affected by impotence perhaps caused by *tabes dorsalis*, and by the onset of paralytic dementia, he became unable to resist the stimulus. Krafft-Ebing identified the following features of erotic paedophilia:

- it concerns individuals affected by a hereditary defect;
- there is inclination for pre-pubescent individuals of the other gender, which appears in the first place (as is not the case with libertines), with representations characterised by abnormal and intense feelings of pleasure;
- the criminal acts of these individuals (who were all potent, except for one) simply consist of libidinously fingering and masturbating the victims, from which they gain satisfaction even without ejaculation;

- paedophiles are not excited by the sexual allure of adults, with whom they have intercourse only when pre-pubescent individuals are unavailable, and without psychic satisfaction.

A fifth case was presented by Krafft-Ebing in *Friedrich's Blätter* (cited in Ferrante Capetti, 1910), with the most scabrous sections written in Latin (Krafft-Ebing intended his work to be a serious reference source and wished to discourage lay readers):

> P, forty-nine years old, married, and admitted to a sanatorium, is charged with the following horrendous indecent behaviours towards ten-year-old D and nine-year-old G, which took place in his workshop on 25th May.
>
> D reports: "I was in a meadow with my three-year-old sister I. P invited us to his workshop and locked the door. Tum nos exosculabatur, linguam in os meum demittere tentabat, facemque mihi lambebat, sustulit me in gremium, bracas aperuit, vestes meas sublevavit, digitis me in genitalibus titillabat et membro femina mea fricabat; it ut umida fierem."
>
> G reports: "P nates et genitalia D(...)ae exosculatus iisdem me conatibus agressus est. Deinde filiolum quoque tres annos natum, in manus acceptum, osculatus et nudatumque parti suae virili appressit. Postea quae nobis essent nomina interrogavit at censuit, genitalia D(...)ae meis multo esse maiora. Quia etiam nos impulit ut membrum suum intueremur, minibus comprehenderemus et videremus, quantopere id esset erectum."
>
> P does not remember anything during questioning. He comes from a psychopathic family; one of his brothers is epileptic. He used to be an alcoholic, and since suffering a head trauma he has gone through mental disturbances that began with sadness, irritability, tendency to drink, anxiety, persecution delirium and even violent impulses, acoustic hyperaesthesia, vertigo, headache, cerebral congestion and consequent disturbances of consciousness and amnesia lasting throughout the admission to the sanatorium, sometimes even for weeks.
>
> He intermittently suffered from headache spreading from the site of the trauma he had suffered, and when this pain worsened, he became irritated, sad, even affected by *taedium vitae* and loss of consciousness, like one who is drunk.
>
> He was judged to be epileptic and discharged. [pp. 109 ff.]

"For all the keenness of some of his intuitions, Krafft-Ebing did not succeed in formulating an appropriate theory of perversion; unlike Freud, he lacked a conceptual apparatus that could draw a line of demarcation between mental health and illness and distinguish between constitutional factors and early environmental experiences" (De Masi, 1999, p. 10). Nevertheless, Freud acknowledged the importance of Krafft-Ebing's thought, as evidenced by a note at the bottom of the first page of "Three Essays on the Theory of Sexuality" (1905), in which he quoted Moll, Moebius, Ellis, Schrenck-Notzing, Lowenfeld, Eulenburg, Bloch, and Hirschfeld. Besides, it seems that Krafft-Ebing sent Freud a copy of each edition of his treatise, as a token of his esteem (Sulloway, 1979).

Psychiatry had already dealt with paedophilia before Krafft-Ebing, though in a non-systematic way. Arveiller (1998) opens his historical notes on paedophilia with the case of a paedophile assessed in 1842 by Guillaume Ferrus, Achille Foville senior and Alexandre Bjerre de Boismont, three of the most illustrious French psychiatrists of the time. In 1857 the forensic expert Ambroise Tardieu reported that 50% of the 400 cases of indecent exposure he had collected involved girls younger than eleven years old. The same author went on to formulate the so-called "law of Tardieu", according to which in sexual abuse the age of the abuser is in inverse proportion to that of the abused. The French psychiatrist Victor Magnan, known as one of the first theorists of degenerationism, mentioned erotic paedophilia in his lessons on psychiatry, and that it was also present in women. His first case concerned a twenty-nine-year-old woman affected by a hereditary defect and by phobias and compulsive ideas. She had felt for eight years a violent need to have intercourse with all her nephews, first with the oldest when he was five, and then with each brother as he turned the same age. The sight of the child was enough to induce an orgasm in her. The patient was able to resist her impulse, which she found inexplicable. The second case was that of a thirty-two-year-old woman with two children, severely affected by a hereditary defect, and separated from her husband as a result of his brutality. She had neglected her children for some months, and used to visit some friends of hers every day at the time their son returned from school. She used to stroke and kiss him and once declared that she was in love with him and willing to marry him. One day she told the boy's mother that her son was ill and unhappy and that she wanted to have intercourse with him in order to heal him. When she was shown the door, she besieged her little beloved's house, until one day she was taken to the mental hospital for manifesting violent behaviour. There she continued to be enthused about that child.

The subject of sexual abuse had begun to be of interest to the courts in the mid-nineteenth century, as a consequence of childhood coming under the trusteeship of the government; previously it had been the family's prerogative. This transition implied that the first attempts to examine this phenomenon saw the emergence of the slippery and complex knots of the capacity for consent, of seduction, the trap represented by myth of the perverse and dissolute child and issues related to simulation, whether conscious and deliberate or unconscious.

Among the interpretative models, the first to become established were those of satyriasis and phrenological abnormality, which is a constitutional pathology of the genital organs and brain. They gradually fell, with all the other complex interpretation and classification problems of paedophilia, into the mishmash of Esquirol's *monomania*, hovering between illness and nastiness, and responsibility and irresponsibility. From this point paedophilia would not change its position significantly, being grouped with other weak and omnivorous diagnostic categories—from degeneration, a subject introduced by Morel and Magnan in the mid-nineteenth century and reconsidered and further generalised by Lombroso on his decline, to Prichard's moral insanity, and all the way to perversion.

According to Krafft-Ebing, paedophiles remain uninterested in masturbation during their psychosexual development, since they are attracted by individuals who are not yet pubescent. He considers that the lack of exclusive interest in adults of the opposite sex would be a consequence of the absence of masturbation. Besides, it happens more frequently that individuals originally driven by a sexual instinct only for adults may become paedophiles as a consequence of impotence which is not accompanied by a simultaneous reduction of sexual appetite (concupiscence).

August Forel would express his disagreement with Krafft-Ebing in his volume *The Sexual Question: A Scientific, Psychological, Hygienic and Sociological Study for the Cultured Classes* (1905). In the chapter on sexual appetite for children, Forel argued that paedophilic behaviour is a consequence of senile dementia or an episode within the picture of a sexual life which is otherwise normal, sometimes in conjunction with homosexuality or sadism. However, in some cases children have represented the special and exclusive object of sexual appetite since youth, which would contradict an inherited disposition. Forel explained that Krafft-Ebing, who did not believe in the existence of hereditary pederosis, defined depraved individuals' extreme behaviour towards children as erotic paedophilia. Krafft-Ebing actually wrote:

> It is psychologically incomprehensible that an adult of full virility and mentally sound should indulge in sexual abuses with children ... Unfortunately we have to acknowledge that most of these horrendous libidinous offences are committed by mentally healthy people, who, overwhelmingly sated with filthy and lascivious pleasure, sometimes drunk, forget human dignity. However, a large number of these offences concern morbid causes, especially in the cases of old seducers of girls. [Ferrante Capetti, 1910, p. 108]

Forel also presented a case study, starting with an artist endowed with fine and high moral sentiments who from his youth had been interested only in five- to ten-year-old girls, whose short dresses and young legs made him aroused. When the girls grew older, even before puberty (so from the age of twelve), they lost any sexual attractiveness for him. He had absolutely no sexual interest in adults, either men or women, throughout his life, and never practised *coitus*.

Having long acknowledged the anomaly of his appetite, he could manage to control it throughout his life, yet sometimes he allowed himself to stroke girls without making himself conspicuous. He sat them on his lap and pressed them against him in order to induce some erections and ejaculations under his clothes, of which the child had no idea. His moral sentiments and principles were strong enough, according to Forel, to prevent him going further—he masturbated to calm and restrain himself, which, incidentally, he did not need. This state caused him an increasing nervous irritability and a melancholic depression which was very close to desperation. In another educated yet very irritable individual, sexual appetite had also been perverted since its appearance, and its object was represented exclusively by twelve- to sixteen-year-old boys (except for a short time when he had been excited by girls of the same age), while men and women left him uninterested. Ferrante Capetti (1910) wrote about the following case:

> I remember, to my personal knowledge, about a peasant who was caught being masturbated by his master's seven-year-old daughter, whose hand he was holding under his clothes. He was sacked and later admitted to hospital, after being taken on the street seized by a paroxysm, and was diagnosed as being epileptic. [p. 111]

Ferrante Capetti, showing a bright long-range perspective of things, recommended extreme caution in handling these kinds of offences, and thought it is wise to ask for the doctor's enlightened opinion, as life in prison "enrages the longing, can be the determining cause of many kinds of perversion and drive these poor sick people towards aberration" (*ibid*).

Krafft-Ebing's work introduces a rich variety of clinical cases which clearly show the diversity of paedophilic behaviours. One example is the case of a fifteen-year-old youngster who was sent to prison for the attempted rape of a five-year-old girl. He is described as affected by a hereditary defect, the son of a mentally ill mother and a formerly alcoholic father, with relatives on his mother's side including an eccentric uncle, a great-uncle who died in a psychiatric hospital, and an idiot great-aunt. This is a typical example of how close positivism is to paedophilia (and, indeed, to many other psychiatric and criminological problems), and recalls the way psychiatrists in the second half of the nineteenth century approached criminals in general (De Paoli, 1878, quoted in Maura & Peloso, 1999).

> X is a natural son, but his father should be precisely his mother's husband, as he looks extraordinarily like his younger brother, and both suffer sometimes from severe cephalalgia, which starts from the base of the nose and spreads over the supraorbital edge, depriving the two boys of the capacity to work and concentrate ... X is physically well developed. He is 1.55 m tall, with a 78 cm wide thorax, normal tendon reflexes (no Babinski), and slow cremasteric reflexes. He does not show any particular abnormality in cranial dimensions: 14.75 cm wide, 17.75 cm

long, index 83, perimeter 53 cm. His muscular strength is very low, only 8 on Coburgh dynamometer … He shows no genital abnormality. The testicles are well placed in the scrotum and firm at palpation, the penis is normal, and the glands are almost completely capped by the prepuce. During his custody no sign of onanism was found, although the prison guards' attention was given to it. A careful examination of his linen reveals no traces of stains—which would indicate that X is sexually insensitive. He had a seventeen-year-old school teacher to whom he was very attached. She was good with that poor boy, and from time to time gave him a pencil or some dainty. X was passionately fond of her and was happy whenever he could be close to her, go for a walk with her, or be touched by her. In these situations he did not have an erection and did not feel the need to have intercourse with her. What did he feel then? He does not know how to describe it. A kiss from her would have given him celestial happiness. Looking at her with lewd thoughts or sexual ideas about her would have felt like a profanation. He felt roughly the same admiration for a twelve-year-old girl he went to school with. Touching her, helping her whenever he could, picking up a dropped pencil or book for her, were for X a pleasure and a joy. He emphatically states that no sexual thoughts ever mixed with his sentiments. He states that this would have rather upset him and made him ashamed—he thought that he would have contaminated those girls if his love had been accompanied by ideas of that kind. But the girl against whom he committed the offences for which he was sent to jail inspired him in a quite different way. When he met her, he suddenly felt the desire to have intercourse with her. After promising her a coin, he dragged her into a bush and made her rub his penis. There is in the town another girl, aged almost fifteen, with whom he had had intercourse several times, but he declares that he did not feel the slightest desire to be together and go out with her, and instead felt disgust for her after intercourse. Some weeks before being arrested he had gone off into a corner with a five-year-old girl, and after laying her down, he had folded her petticoat over her head and urinated on her. In so doing, he had had no sign of erection, which is quite understandable, as urination during erection is difficult, if not impossible. [Krafft-Ebing, 1886/Moll, 1923, p. 584[2]]

According to Krafft-Ebing, in many cases the paedophile gains satisfaction simply from masturbation, since it is impossible for him to commit indecent acts on pre-pubescent individuals for reasons of morality or penalty, thus because of lack of opportunities.

Krafft-Ebing then described other cases. One is concerned with what we can describe as a borderline situation in terms of the ages of both the protagonist and the objects of his desire. A twenty-five-year-old man, whose parents are healthy (though his mother is very irritable), has been addicted to masturbation for seven years, having sometimes practised it without ejaculation at the age of approximately nine years. In certain periods the young man has refrained from onanism for months, but there are times when he is so aroused that he can masturbate several times a week and even more than once a day. He has twice been to a brothel, but his erection was not strong enough. He has erections in the morning or at night, and nocturnal emissions, usually while dreaming of kissing a girl or having intercourse. In a waking state, he is sexually aroused only by the thought of thirteen- or fourteen-year-old girls. Just this thought has sometimes given him an erection, and he could almost always masturbate with this mental representation. He believes he has noticed a slight change recently, as sometimes he is also aroused by the thought of mature women.

The cases mentioned include a fifty-year-old trader and a fifty-three-year-old artist. In another case, a teacher gave up his job because, more for moral reasons than for fear of the law, he wanted to fight his paedophilic instinct, which only manifested in the presence of children (see avoidance strategies as an aspect of the cognitive-behavioural therapy of paedophilia mentioned by Dettore, 1999b). His new profession allowed him to get rid of his disturbance, which consisted of a fairly keen desire to know how far the genital development of certain twelve- to fourteen-year-olds had progressed, and even a desire to touch their genitals, whilst in girls' schools he was attracted by the pupils' little breasts.

In other cases we note having been abused as a risk factor of abuse. A twenty-one-year-old man was aroused by the thought of everything related to the baby's suckling or by the sight of the objects necessary for his care, such as the baby's suckling linen, the pram, rubber objects, and by imagining that the baby under the care of these was an eight-year-old, and felt them as an outrage. Another image he found arousing was that of a child smacked on the bottom by a man or a woman (see the case of Stavrogin in Chapter Seven). Krafft-Ebing goes on in his case studies to note the presence of paedophilia also among women, when they become aroused by the handling of a child—this picture is particularly frequent among childminders and cleaners.

After these extensively documented descriptions, psychiatric knowledge seemed to lose interest in paedophilia. It became the object of study in criminology and forensic science, and psychoanalysis began to deal with it within the category of perversions. We can see between the 1950s and 1960s the gradual emergence of interpretative and therapeutic models related to the phenomenological and psychoanalytical culture, alongside the persistence of attitudes still related to a large extent to degenerationism (see Capri, 1999). An extremely restrictive classifying attitude is that of Fritzlaer (1969, quoted in Capri, 1999), who considers perverse only those individuals in whom paedophilia represents the only expression of sexuality, or is complicated by other kinds of perversion such as sadism, or manifests itself through actions harmful to the child. For Fritzlaer a normal male or female individual can be violently aroused even by the very immature genitals of the opposite sex.

Capri also reports the findings of an interesting piece of research on the morbidity of 156 paedophiles (of whom six were women), carried out by Iaria in 1968 at the Mental Forensic Hospital of Castiglione delle Stiviere. Of these cases, 42.29% were classified as feeble-minded, 12.17% as schizophrenic, 11.53% as chronic alcoholics, 10.25% as affected by age-related involutional psychosis, and a smaller number as affected by progressive paralysis, epilepsy and other psychotic conditions, while 14.1% were classified as psychopathic personalities. Although it is not easy to re-interpret these findings using modern classificatory models, this piece of research seems to be interesting as it helps us to bear in mind that paedophilia can be a behavioural epiphenomenon to be considered a possible element of the process of a number of psychiatric illnesses where a definition of their identity (especially sexual) is unsatisfactory.

The extensive psychiatric literature gives very little space to paedophilic behaviour, which is restricted to the group of perversions, steeped in moral judgements. There is a lack of any real desire for knowledge in order effectively to overcome the theories of degenerationism and heredity, which have been set up as a sort of instinctive imaginary teratology.

Kraepelin explains in *Clinical Psychiatry* (1902) that within the borderline between the normal and the pathological psychic states we find cases in which an individual gains satisfaction from indecent acts against children. We can find this aspect mainly in an epileptic twilight state, but also in subjects with whom physical contact has become difficult, therefore in old or "feeble-minded" people. This topic is limited to the few psychiatric cases described, while the bulk of paedophilia seems to be considered not of psychiatric but of criminological interest.

Meanwhile, in Bleuler's *Textbook of Psychiatry* (1916) we read: "Another form of displacement in the object is paedophilia, or the desire for relations with children of the opposite sex, which occurs perhaps most frequently as an acquired anomaly in senile dementia (it is not rare also among imbeciles *faute de mieux*)" (p. 574). Bleuler explains that paedophilia frequently occurs among childish individuals and oligophrenics, and that these individuals are afraid of sexual relationships with adults, and perceive children as *partners* as old as themselves. Nor do they find other opportunities, as they are also rejected by mature women. Some people with senile dementia can also commit indecent acts against children—their sexuality appears undifferentiated, and during sexual excitement they lose any inhibition. Like Kraepelin, Bleurer also limits paedophilia to the sexually abnormal behaviour of oligophrenics or weak-minded people, or those with senile dementia.

The description of paedophilia in Leonardo Bianchi's *Trattato di psichiatria* is more complex and in accordance with the moral judgements of Italian culture at the time. Bianchi writes:

> Wherever human societies are unable to satisfy sexual impulses, when they are not used to dominating instincts—in military camps, holiday camps, prisons, colleges, seafarers, etc.—they deliver strong individuals who impose their will, and weak individuals who give in to the will of others. Most of them return to normality once that particular condition of existence ceases. Those who are predisposed may become active or passive perverts. Pederasts show a preference for youngsters who look like females, and can also have sexual relationships

with women. They are often brutal, impulsive individuals. Sometimes these individuals idealise their abnormal tendency. We have to distinguish these cases from those in which there is consciousness of the inversion, with an intense struggle to avoid the shame related to the acts to which these individuals are violently attracted. The illness has the semblance of a fixed idea or compulsory impulse. Essentially, these subjects are evolved inverts, or perverts. [1924, pp. 504 ff.]

Paedophilia is in some ways justified if it is a substitute for an absent adult object and if, once the environmental difficulties fade, "normal tendencies" are restored. It is the excessive that is to be considered pathological. It is important, therefore, to distinguish between idealised paedophilia, elevated to a philosophy of life, and paedophilia felt to be shameful and egodystonic. In his *Manuale di Psichiatria*, Moglie states:

> Rape is not always a sign of ethical fault, but rather the violent expression of a transcendent eroticism, of an uncurbed sexual impulse, such as we frequently see in epileptic people. But we cannot ascribe the same benevolent meaning to violence against children, so-called "paedophilia", which is in any circumstances the sign of a serious perversion of the genesic sense and the ethical sense in general, and not infrequently a kind of sadism. [1940, p. 232]

Therefore Moglie seems to justify violence against women to some degree, whilst expressing a firm opinion on violence against children, whose defence thus acquires far more social importance than that of women.

In *Sex and Character*, Weininger disputes the degenerationist theories on the one hand, while on the other hand disagreeing with those who consider sexual perversion a quality acquired during life. With regard to paedophilia, he relates it to old age:

> Sexual inversion is no more *inherited* from parents or grandparents than it is acquired … *sexual inversion is not an exception from the natural law, but only a special case of the same* … A phenomenon analogous to juvenile sexual friendship is perhaps the

reappearance in older men of latent amphisexuality alongside the senile atrophy of the sexual characteristics that developed unidirectionally in their prime. This may be the reason why so many men aged 50 and upward are prosecuted for committing "indecent acts". [1903, pp. 42, 44]

Many other treatises of that period, such as Tanzi's *Malattie Mentali* (1905), Lugaro's *I Problemi Odierni della Psichiatria* (1906), Arturo Morselli's *Manuale di Psichiatria* (1915), Tanzi and Lugaro's *Malattie Mentali* (1916), and Bumke's *Lehrbuch der Geisteskrankheiten* (1924) make no mention at all of paedophilia.

Among the most popular treatises of the period following the Second World War was Biondi's *Manuale di Psichiatria* (1950). Biondi notes that paedophilia (love of children), which he regards as mirroring gerontophilia (love of old people), is often an aspect of homosexuality (p. 161). He differentiates it from incest, which is defined as a psychological perversion, thus avoiding the mistake that would be made by DSM-IV of grouping incest with paedophilia. Porot's *Manuel Alphabetique de Psychiatrie* describes paedophilia as an erotic attraction for children, and aims to provide a sociological view of the period, in which he sets out the diverse paedophile behaviours:

> Male homosexual paedophilia seems to benefit from long-lasting tolerance in rural areas, where it often contributes to the erotic initiation of following generations by an educator who is subsequently removed: a neurotic craftsman, or a weak-minded man. In heterosexual paedophilia, a male's choice of a pre-pubescent girl depends on different factors according to the seducer's age. Below the age of twenty, the major factors are intellectual backwardness or perversity; between twenty and forty a major element is represented by frustration, the likelihood of which varies, but a certain amount of emotional immaturity is indicated by the general behaviour; between forty and sixty alcohol seems to play the most important part; and in old people we can stress the presence of a mistaken conviction of being assured of erotic survival.[3] In any case, choice is not privileged as it manifests itself vicariously, while it is a feeling of virile inferiority or guilt about an adult woman that is in conflict with having normal relationships. We must also

take into consideration the situation in which "dissolute" girls make themselves available for paedophilic relationships with interested and vain compliance. [1960, p. 409]

We can see in this French manual a rough attempt to insert a psychodynamically orientated observation within the traditional social prejudices.

In *Psychiatrie im Grundriss*, Weitbrecht describes paedophilia as being

> … similar to exhibitionism, in very similar circumstances of immaturity or personality defect, with paraphilic tendencies … The fact of arousing sexual curiosity in others seems to have wide appeal for instinctually insecure people, usually no longer or not yet able to conquer a girl of a suitable age. We have frequently seen girls of school age, still far from pubescence, "seducing" by the rule book people well advanced in years in order to receive money or chocolate. Usually the seduced satisfies his desire by watching, touching or kissing the child's genitals, sometimes with simultaneous masturbation, sometimes even inviting the girl to satisfy him manually or orally. While it is not so unusual for homosexual paedophiles to become dramatically infatuated with an adolescent (remember Thomas Mann's brilliant novel *Death in Venice*), real infatuation for a young girl before her puberty (like Lolita in Nabokov's novel) is rare, but certainly possible. [1963, p. 175]

Weitbrecht finally describes the case of a paedophile, showing how a cerebral-organic disease (encephalitis) can cause "on the one hand a regression towards early phases of pubescent libido and thus towards strong primitive erotic shaping, on the other hand the disinhibition of instincts, which are felt with lucidity and experienced as inexplicable internal change, so much so that the patient is led to seek medical help" (p. 176). Weitbrecht concludes by saying that two kinds of therapy—somatic and psychotherapeutic—bring about a good outcome, with remission of the paedophile desires. This text seems to indicate a transitional phase, in which the old organicistic ideas and attempts at psychotherapeutic intervention coexist without excluding each other.

In contrast, paedophilia is not mentioned at all in Henderson and Gillespie's *Texbook of Psychiatry for Students and Practitioners* (1927), Baruk's *Traité de Psychiatrie* (1959), Mayer-Gross, Slater and Roth's *Clinical Psychiatry* (1954), Arieti's *American Handbook of Psychiatry* (1959–66), Torre's *Psichiatria* (1969), Gozzano's *Compendio di Psichiatria* (1970), Hanus and Le Guillou-Eliet's *Psychiatrie Intégrée de l'Etudiant* (1971), Scoppa's *Trattato di Psichiatria Clinica Moderna* (1972), or Campailla's *Manuale di Psichiatria* (1975). The fact that many psychiatric treatises make no mention at all of paedophilia is probably related not just to a lack of interest in and undervaluation of paedophilic behaviours, nor to simply regarding it as something for criminologists to study. We believe instead that there has been systematic moralistic censorship, at least in Italian texts, of a subject considered taboo by a culture that is steeped in a priggish Catholic mentality.

The very limited psychoanalytical mention of paedophilia is superficial and academic, more a response to trends in classification than an attempt to disseminate real knowledge. Psychoanalysis and psychoanalysts are only quoted to be put aside and judged outdated, as we can see in Bini and Bazzi's *Psicologia Medica* (1954). In their later *Trattato di Psichiatria* (1967), Bini and Bazzi include paedophiles (to the limited extent of a few lines) in the chapter on psychically abnormal people. Hinsie and Campbell's *Psychiatric Dictionary* (1970) also offers a few lines on paedophilia, as does Disertori and Piazza's *Trattato di Psichiatria e Sociopsichiatria* (1970). Rossini's *Trattato di Psichiatria* (1971) terms those cases in which a young boy or girl becomes the object of sexual urges *paidofilia*, and reminds us that "this kind of perversion seems to be a male prerogative" (Rossini, 1971, p. 369). In Reda's *Trattato di Psichiatria* (1982, p. 195) Giordano and De Silvestri describe paedophilia as a deviant behaviour against a child, and therefore in relation to the object identity.

In Ey, Bernard and Brisset's *Manuel de Psychiatrie* (1967, p. 334) we find the definition "deformation of the image of the partner". This treatise represents an exception among the traditional treatises in that it is the first successful attempt to synthesise the different theories, including the psychoanalytical one, which is given significant space.

More recently, after the next editions of the DSM, psychiatric texts have been divided into two categories. In the first, which includes for instance Sarteschi and Maggini's *Manuale di Psichiatria* (1982) and more recently Piccione's *Manuale di Psichiatria* (1995), the subject of paedophilia does not appear at all. In the second category, including Giberti and Rossi's *Trattato di Psichiatria* (1996), Kaplan and Sadock's *Comprehensive Textbook of Psychiatry* (1989) and the *Trattato Italiano di Psichiatria* edited by Pancheri, Cassano and others (1999, vol. 2, pp. 2446 ff), the latest DSM international classifications are taken into consideration again.

The space given to paedophilia increases hand in hand with the interest the mass media take in this subject. We can therefore see a revival of interest in paedophilia with the publication of the DSM and the later addition of paraphilias to the diagnostic category. As with homosexuality, which was later to be excluded from psychiatric diagnosis, this addition was intended to keep away the moralistic prejudice linked to the term perversion, although this inevitably implied making the picture too psychiatrised.

The positive aspect of the abandonment of a dominant ethical view has as a consequence the limitation of "depriving paedophilia of its psychiatric centrality, to the advantage, once again, of the deficit related to the person's social functioning" (Aguglia & Riolo, 1999, p. 10). Stoller (1985), on the other hand, considers that changing the official term "perversion" into "paraphilia" is a misleading attempt to "reclaim" perversion. The term "perversion" needs to be kept, as a sense of sin is a prerequisite for a perverse activity to induce sexual excitement.

In the American Psychiatric Association's first *Diagnostic and Statistical Manual of Mental Disorders* (DSM) paedophilia was categorised as "pathological sexuality", and in DSM-II it was considered a "sexual deviation". According to DSM-III (1980) and its revised edition DSM-III-R (1987), paedophilia belongs to the group of paraphilias and is characterised by recurring and intense sex drive arousing fantasies about sexual activity with one or more pre-pubescent children. This definition, as we can see in Dettore (1999a), gives far more importance to psychic contents than behaviours, and thus allows for the tagging of people who have paedophilic fantasies but do not manifest them through action, while excluding those who commit paedophilic acts without being tormented by desires and drives of this kind.

We need to note that the term paraphilia is too generic and dull, and not only refers to presumed love elements (De Masi, 1999) but also seems to ascribe the disturbance purely to a problem of drive orientation. As a consequence, this implies a reductionism that short-circuits the whole psychic complexity (Balier, 1996).

> Therefore, including paedophilia in the group of paraphilias seems to be reductive, if we do not try hard to investigate the dimensional psychopathology which resides underneath fantasy, drive, or recurrent behaviour, and which reveals to us the phenomenological sense of paedophilia. We also need to realise from now on that doing "that thing" with children is a source of pleasure for the paedophile. [Aguglia & Riolo, 1999, p. 11]

DSM-IV (1994) adds the presence of "recurrent behaviours" to the definition and sets a maximum age for the partner of thirteen years. As for the paedophile, he has to be older than sixteen years and involved in some social work or any significant area; the age gap between them must be at least five years. DSM-IV invites us to make further distinctions: between subjects who are attracted by young boys, by young girls, or by both; whether the behaviours concerned are limited to incest; and whether the behaviour is exclusive or there are alternative sexual purposes. In order to consider a continuum between fantasy and action, DSM-IV has elaborated a gravity spectrum.

> In "mild" forms, patients are quite disturbed about their paraphilic sexual drives but do not act on them. In "moderate" degrees of severity, patients translate their urges into action, but only occasionally. In "severe" cases, patients repeatedly act on their paraphilic urges. [Gabbard, 1994, p. 329]

The DSM-IV diagnosis is basically similar to that of the World Health Organisation's ICD-10 (1992), which refers to a sexual preference for children, generally pre-pubescent or in early puberty, either boys or girls. Dettore (1999a) underlines that although it solves some problems, the DSM-IV diagnosis remains ambiguous about the definition of those who show "non-recurrent" paedophilic behaviours, that is to say limited to one or two episodes, who could not then be considered paedophiles by this definition. It also remains ambiguous about those who have no significant *impairment* in their social life, like those who lack a sense of guilt or remain uncaught.

This latter point seems particularly relevant to some pieces of research which tend to indicate cognitive distortions in a large number of paedophiles, with prevailing denial effects playing a protective role towards their sense of guilt. These denial mechanisms would express themselves through denial of harm, switching of the paedophiles' own responsibilities onto others or onto the situation, or convincing themselves of the positive effects of paedophilia on the child. This definition excludes sexual behaviours having older adolescents as objects.

Capri (1999) makes quite convincing objections, which seem to put the entire nosographic system of paedophilia into question. He makes the point that paedophilia does not represent a nosographic entity itself, but rather a symptom related increasingly to personality traits or to actual psychopathological disturbances, which therefore should guide the diagnostic setting of the paedophilic condition, to which the subject and the therapeutic set-up can never be reduced.

From an aetiological viewpoint, the current belief that paedophilia is frequently associated with the fact of subjects having themselves been the victims of child sexual abuse is still very important. Dhawan and Marshall (1996), for instance, have found a higher frequency of victims of sexual abuse among sex criminals than non-sex criminals. Another factor implicated is the number of older brothers.

However, neither of these hypotheses is sufficient to explain paedophilic behaviour, while multi-factorial models such as that proposed by Finkelor (1984) appear more convincing. Finkelor distinguishes between:

- reasons for which the abuser considers the child a source of sexual satisfaction: because he satisfies emotional needs, such as the need to exert control; because the child is a source of sexual pleasure in relation to conditioning or the fact of having been a victim of abuse; because the ability to use alternative sources of sexual pleasure is inhibited;
- the presence of internal factors which enable one to overcome inhibitions of a clinical nature—substance abuse or cognitive deficits of involutional or psychotic nature, or related to a distorted perception of the child's desires—or a socio-cultural nature;
- factors able to demolish external inhibitions, such as the mother's absence or inadequate regulatory function or promiscuous home life; and

- factors able to overcome the victims' resistances (compulsion, use of gifts, the child's insecurity or depression, exceptionally high trust between the abuser and the child).

Finkelor then comes to the conclusion that it is not possible to ascribe the aetiopathogenesis of paedophilia with certainty to one class of events (intrapsychic as well as external), but it is necessary to take several factors into consideration, also because paedophiles do not show just one typology.

The theorists of conditioning highlight factors that orientate a sexual preference for children, which is a hypothesis that for Dettore (1999a) can only explain some, but not all aspects of paedophilic behaviours, since this orientation does not concern a large number of paedophiles significantly. Other authors (Dorr, 1998), on the other hand, stress the high frequency of co-morbidity of paedophilia and psychopathy, and the several defining elements present in both disturbances. However, Dettore (1999a) reckons that aetiological research aimed at giving importance to this concomitance seems on the one hand misleading, as in a large number of paedophiles it is not possible to find psychopathic traits; while on the other hand it seems tautological, as even if paedophilia represented a subcategory of psychopathy, there would be still the problem of explaining why a small number of psychopathies evolve towards paedophilic behaviour. Moreover, the acknowledgement of this co-morbidity loses any real heuristic value when we think of the serious problems of definition which already concern the term "psychopathy" itself. This is a concept that Jervis correctly defined some years ago (1975) as a "diagnostic rubbish dump" due to the levels of confusion and the risks of non-understanding which characterise it.

Alongside the problems of defining paedophilia, we also have to tackle those concerning a possible distinction between several subcategories of paedophiles. These take into consideration the following aspects one at a time:

- the "strength" with which the realisation of the desire is pursued and its "exclusivity", i.e. to what degree the individual's sexuality is directed at children;

- the level of fixation and social competence, and the quantitative aspects of the contact with children (significance of the context, severity of physical harm, meaning of the assault for the abuser);
- homo- or heterosexual orientation in choosing the child; and
- the relationship between gender identity, gender role, and sexual orientation (Dettore, 1999a).

As far as the aetiological hypotheses are concerned, a lot of research has been done on possible biological alterations in paedophilia, implicating in some cases serotonin, in others dopamine, testosterone or prolactin concentrations in the blood. In other cases, blood flow alterations in specific cerebral areas or in the electroencephalogram picture have been taken into consideration.

As regards biological treatment, we have to bear in mind that surgical castration, as well as being fairly controversial from an ethical viewpoint because it is mutilating and irreversible (Bonafiglia, 1999; Dettore, 1999b), has been shown by some studies to be ineffective (Aguglia & Riolo, 1999). The first therapeutic castration dates back to 1892; in the first half of the 20th century this technique was widely used in Switzerland, Holland, Germany, Finland, Iceland and Denmark. The relapse rate before castration varied from 50% to 84%, while after castration it dropped to 1.1–7.4%.

Chemical castration, on the other hand, is reversible and therefore more widely accepted.[4] In the 1960s neuroleptics such as thioridazine, fluphenazine and benperidol were often used. This was later followed by the use of anti-androgen drugs, which inhibit the secretion of or block the receptors of androgenic hormones (Bonafiglia, 1999), and more recently by the use of inhibitory selective anti-depressants controlling serotonin, whose efficacy might be related to the emotional involvement in the co-determinism of paedophilia (as suggested in an attractive, yet poorly researched thesis by Aguglia and Riolo in 1999), and of LHRH agonists. In general, anti-androgens can be effective, but their use is controversial due to severe side effects.

> There is not enough research on the long-term efficacy of these therapies. It should also be borne in mind that paedophiles and *sex offenders* in general often commit their crimes led by motivations that are beyond mere sexual gratification. The fact of

having their libido reduced does not necessarily reduce the risk of a second offence. Furthermore, this kind of treatment implies the consideration of ethical issues that are not easy to resolve: it is in fact of the utmost importance that the patient consciously accepts this kind of intervention, in order to avoid those tragicomic aspects which the use of bromide for recruits had for decades. [Berti et al., 1999, p. 234]

We linger more attentively over cognitive-behavioural therapy,[5] which, whether or not it is associated with biological therapies, has proved rather effective, at least in some cases. Going beyond the primitive behavioural therapies, Dettore (1999b) focuses particularly on *relapse prevention*, a model deriving from the area of substance addiction and aimed at encouraging the possibility of self-control as well as external control exerted by social workers and community members. This model, of which we shall introduce just the fundamental aspects, assumes that relapse occurs in two phases: from a high-risk situation to the initial loss of control (*lapse*), and from this to the actual *relapse*, determined mainly by the level on which the subject is able to justify the *lapse* on the basis of a complex emotional reaction. In the case of sexual abuse, the high-risk behaviour may consist of a fantasy, or of an "apparently irrelevant decision", the *lapse* of an action such as buying pornographic material, and the *relapse* of the accomplished abuse. Dettore also examines the several possible paths towards paedophilia, together related to three typologies:

- powerful negative emotional states have a direct disinhibiting effect or lead to behaviours which themselves induce a loss of control due to deficiency of standards, inappropriate monitoring, or lack of sufficient cognitive resources;
- attempts to control deviant thoughts or fantasies or emotional states may paradoxically lead to a loss of control (e.g. use of alcohol or sexual fantasies to modulate a negative mood) and facilitate deviant behaviours;
- deviant goals, where the problem is not self-regulation processes, which paradoxically are highly efficient, but the choice of goals (such as regarding having sex with children as absolutely legitimate): the abuser tries to pursue his goals and does not believe that his lifestyle is particularly problematic.

The choice of goals and the associated forms of self-regulation would depend, according to this model, on the personality's pre-existing structure (which for instance recalls what Capri [1999] has hypothesised), and on developmental variables. Dettore believes that the cognitive-behavioural method is able to suggest specific treatments for each aetiological factor of paedophilia. However, in the *relapse prevention* intervention it is fundamental to avoid at all costs the development of the undesirable attitude that any possible new abuse should be considered not a relapse but simply a new crime. The *relapse prevention* intervention therefore needs to be preceded by or integrated with the use of techniques to increase the subject's motivation for the treatment.

It is not difficult to guess that these methods are unfortunately difficult to apply to those abusers who deny having committed a crime, or who have no intention of voluntarily facing a treatment aimed at re-organising their attitude towards both their sexuality and their aggressiveness. This implies the necessity to "take account of paedophilia's function of resolving internal conflicts, so that intervening with a specific treatment means facing a shift from a situation of apparent balance—in which the symptom is advantageous for the perverted individual—to a fluctuating psychic condition in which the symptom is present again, unresolved, and inevitably distressing" (Berti et al., 1999, p. 227).

> We can come to the conclusion that so far research has not clearly determined to what extent treatment strategies in general, and the relapse prevention concepts in particular, are factors that efficiently contribute to the therapeutic improvement of sex offenders. We believe, though, that these aspects are worthy of serious consideration, especially in Italy, where there is a limited number of precedents concerning the treatment of these subjects. [Dettore, 1999b, p. 352]

As far as we are concerned, we have come to the belief that biological interventions and cognitive-behavioural techniques—when they are applied with enough attention to each paedophile's wholeness and complexity and to the emotional aspects that come into play in the relationship with this difficult patient—may prove useful in providing a paedophile who at least to some degree accepts the treatment, and the whole of society, with tools aimed at solving problems that would otherwise be hard to tackle.

Notes

1. Suffice to mention Vienna, where the earliest records of prostitution show that between 1873 and 1883 most prostitutes appeared to be minors (Gilman, 1985).
2. The sixteenth German edition of Krafft-Ebing's *Psychopathia Sexualis* (1886) was entirely re-elaborated by Albert Moll, a Berlin professor regarded as one of the pioneers of modern sexuology. Moll inserted, apart from several personal annotations, his own rich clinical case study into Krafft-Ebing's text. The Italian translation edited by Pietro Giolla (Milan: Manfredi, 1952) is of this re-elaboration by Moll.
3. Remember the episode in Bertolucci's film *Novecento*, in which the old farm owner asks a young peasant girl to masturbate him in a cattle shed. The child replies that only cows can be milked, not bulls. After this event, the old man committed suicide, probably because he could not accept his innocence and realised that a full erotic experience was illusory. Another remarkable episode is the meeting between Zeno and Teresina, the farmer's little daughter, with whom he tries to get aroused to test his state of illness. Zeno offers her ten crowns, which Teresina accepts, but does not comply with the old man's advances. "If I get a man, he will certainly be younger than you," the girl shouts while riding off on the back of a donkey. "When are you going to devote yourself to old men, Teresina?" Zeno shouts back. "When I am old too," she shouts, laughing with delight, and without stopping. "But then old men won't be interested in you any more. Listen to me! I know them!" The old man's tragic death in *Novecento* contrasts with the bitter irony of Zeno, who concludes: "When you are old, you remain in the shade though your spirit is still alive" (Svevo, 1938, pp. 464–5).
4. In Italy in 2003 the National Committee of Bioethics came out against the use of clinical castration for paedophiles, citing the intangibility of the human body even in the case of a citizen charged with very serious offences.
5. Behavioural psychologists base their theoretical model, tested on laboratory animals, on the automatic reflex induced by a stimulus. For example, the image of a boy stimulates the beginning of an erection in the patient. The treatment consists of associating that image with a painful sensation, so a painful electric shock on the penis is associated systematically with the display of that image.

CHAPTER SIX

Psychoanalysis and paedophilia

> We would often be ashamed of our most beautiful actions if everyone saw the motives that produced them.
>
> —François de la Rochefoucauld

The theories of perversion, to which we have to refer in order to introduce the subject of paedophilia, are numerous and diverse, and, as we shall see, variously interlinked. They concern unresolved conflicts, delay in emotional development, repetitiveness in an attempt to overcome the trauma suffered, the narcissistic quality of object relations, and the sadistic evolution of destructive aggressiveness. They go from Freudian classic formulations which consider perversion to be in continuity with the individual's "normal" development, anxieties and basic conflicts, up to De Masi's (1999, 2000) recent theories, according to which sadomasochistic perversion belongs to the domain of pure evil.

Moreover, there are different contexts in which the paedophilic act can mature and take root, as well as different mental structures and pathological pictures which can lead to paedophilia. A first major distinction can be made between a neurotic and a psychotic picture.

A study by Glueck (1956), in which thirty jailed paedophiles were assessed, found that 76% were psychotics suffering from a schizophrenic disturbance. Their criminal act had been unpredictable and random, for the psychotic behaviour might have taken other directions, or the object of the sex offence might also have been an adult. Paedophilia, as the severe symptom of an undifferentiated and generically narcissistic sexuality, can also be detected in the sexual behaviours of some mentally retarded adults, who thus show a gap between mental age and physical development.

Kernberg (1992) identifies three groups related to the level of personality organisation that sustains perversion. The first group is the neurotic one; the second, of medium severity, includes the borderline and narcissistic personality; and the third group is represented by malignant narcissism, antisocial personality (in which aggressiveness knows no bounds and the functions of the superego deteriorate) and psychosis. Kernberg reckons that perversion within a neurotic picture depends on drive distortion and libidinous conflict. The cases of borderline personality show a condensation of pre-oedipal and oedipal conflicts with an excess of pre-oedipal aggressiveness. Only those cases involving perversion of the narcissistic structures show the dynamic constellation of the regressive anal universe. In these cases there is intolerance of reality and denial of gender and generational diversity (De Masi, 1999).

Bouchet-Kervella (1996) also distinguishes between forms of paedophilic behaviour that belong to neurosis, psychosis, and sexual perversion. Gabbard underlines that "the psychodynamic understanding of an individual patient involved in a perverse sexual activity implies a thoroughgoing comprehension of how the perversion interacts with the patient's underlying character structure" (1994, p. 332). As an example, patients with a neurotic structure can use perverse practices to facilitate sexual potency, while patients with psychotic traits can use the same activity to defend themselves from a sense of disintegration of the Self (Person, 1985). According to Barale,

> ... De Masi denies any continuity between "normal" and "perverse" sexuality. Instead, he emphasises the substantial clinical difference between the sadomasochistic perversion "proper" (perversion as "structure") and the variegated field of perverse acting out, of more or less episodic and defensive or

compulsive behaviour, or perverse manifestations symptomatic of depressive states or underlying dissolution anxieties (as often encountered in borderline pathologies)—or between the sadomasochistic perversion and the more or less sadomasochistic dynamics of hate, aggression and control of objects that appear in a complex range of relational scenarios or clinical situations (for example, typically in melancholia) ... Whereas Freud saw perversion in continuity with "normal" development with its conflicts, anxieties and vicissitudes (whether positive or negative), thereby ..."depathologising" it as an intrinsic possibility and irremediable nucleus of the human condition, Dr De Masi *pathologises* it as the expression of a destructive nucleus by no means in continuity either with the vicissitudes of psychosexual development and relationality or with the "normal" organisation of mental life ... It is therefore a thoroughly pathological phenomenon, which cannot be seen in terms of defence or conflict. [1999, p. 15]

The term *paedophilia* can also be regarded as relating to a large number of different clinical situations, which range from occasional acting out to the formation of a paedophilic personality, up to violent and criminal paedophilia, which shows clinical and symptomatic features that are completely different from the pictures described above. The psychodynamic constellations therefore cover virtually the whole spectrum of "normal" and "pathological" functioning (Arveiller, 1998). Nevertheless, it is necessary to highlight the polymorphism of paedophilic behaviours and the diversity of the mental organisations that sustain them.

Obviously, it is not always easy to make clear distinctions at a clinical level; in fact we more frequently observe heterogeneous pictures and varying clinical behaviours, clinical situations which transform from one picture to another. For instance we see occasional and disorganised pictures from which clear and stable perverse situations develop, situations apparently masked by tenderness and curiosity, which because of their remarkable plasticity are transformed into violent and sadistic paedophilic pictures, either occasional or permanently structured.

We shall see that some authors refer to Glover's (1933, 1955, 1964) and Bergler's (1938, 1949, 1958) theories, in which perversion assumes a defensive function of control and avoidance of more serious and unbearable hidden psychotic anxieties. Other authors refer to Masud Khan's theory of cumulative trauma; he in turn refers to Ferenczi and Winnicott; and some others, such as Goldberg and Storolow, refer to Kohut, regarding perversion as a strategy aimed at re-establishing and preserving the Self.

We can find at different moments of the pervert's clinical life different strategies and modalities, in which either the defensive or the restorative ones prevail, according to "neo-sexual" modalities (McDougall, 1990) which would relate to an invaded or abused, or insufficiently protected, nourished and supported Self. It is a Self whose drastic wounds would give rise, through diverse and complex mechanisms, to perverse strategy or destructive dynamics, as a desperate attempt at self-cure and objective reality (Barale, 1999).

De Zulueta (1993) notes that the perverse manifestations of sexually abused patients can have a real defensive function of protecting the Self from unbearable pain and loss of control. He reminds us that Freud himself seemed to be aware of the defensive function of perversions when he wrote about a young man whose severely perverse father got sexually aroused by licking his sexual partners' feet; he had done the same thing to his son, who in turn did it to his sister. Now this young man "abhors any kind of perversity, and consequently must suffer from disturbances". Freud adds that if he could be perverse, he would be sane, just like his father (Masson, 1984).

In "Three Essays on the Theory of Sexuality" (1905) Freud writes about paedophilia more as an occasional act than an actual perversion. He seldom describes the child as an exclusive and all-absorbing sexual object, more frequently considering him or her a surrogate object for those who cannot have sexual relationships with other partners, or when a sexual impulse cannot be released in any other way. In his clinical accounts there are several cases of children initiated to sexuality by adult partners (governesses, tutors, domestics, or impotent uncles). "Sexually Immature Persons and Animals as Sexual Objects" is the title of the brief chapter that Freud wrote on paedophilia. This, his only piece of writing specifically on paedophilia, tries to highlight that often "the nature and importance of the sexual object recedes into the background" (1905, p. 149) and that these represent a non-essential element of sexual urge[1] (Schinaia, 2000). According to Green,

Paedophilia came into the domain of psychoanalytic investigation by indirect means, through Freud's study of Leonardo. There, Freud presents a remarkably intricate analysis: the love for the mother, powerfully repressed, persists only in vestigial traces (the search for versions of the mother's smile in other women who aroused the artist's interest, transposed into painting); while it is replaced by an identification which compels him to rediscover maternal seduction by acting in her name, behaving like her towards young boys who now take the place of the child he was. [1997, p. 173]

In any case, we can say that paedophilia eludes Freud's early framework of 1905, which describes perversion as a fixation on the early stages of sexuality, in which situations of domination and aggression prevail, with the aggression turning into sadism and love made passive into masochism. Therefore, it is not about a pathological emphasis of some infantile instinctual components.[2] Nor is it about *acting out*, acting as generally meant by psychoanalysis, but "acting" that is understandable only in the light of a splitting reaction. According to Green, "there is indeed something mad in the thinking of the paedophile delving into his unconscious, to the roots of his own miserable childhood, to inflict such pain, to repeat the traumas of the past by making another suffer them" (1997, p. 175).

It is in the Introduction to "On Narcissism" (Freud, 1914a) that perversion becomes a form of the individual's strong structuring, and this evolution would reach a fundamental milestone in "Beyond the Pleasure Principle" (1920), in which Freud states that erotic and death instincts normally co-exist in human beings in the form of mixtures or fusions, yet defusions can occur. According to the dual theory of instincts the perverse individual loves nobody but himself. His perversion excludes love, and is considered an expression of the death instinct, though tempered by sexuality.

Although Freud did not write specifically about paedophilia in these terms, we can state by extension that love for children is basically no more or less than a mask for narcissistic love, and not the substitution of an easily available object for another in a relationship that is at present impossible. Fenichel (1945) would draw on paedophilia as a narcissistic object choice.

Reminiscences of the constitutionalist ideas which were highly influential in the scientific debate of those days also emerged from Freud's thinking. In the "Three Essays", concerning the great importance of seduction in initiating a child to perversion, we read:

> It is an instructive fact that under the influence of seduction children can become polymorphously perverse, and can be led into all possible kinds of sexual irregularities. This shows that an aptitude for them is innately present in their disposition. There is consequently little resistance towards carrying them out, since the mental dams against sexual excesses—shame, disgust and morality—have either not yet been constructed at all or are only in course of construction, according to the age of the child … It becomes impossible not to recognise that this same disposition to perversions of every kind is a general and fundamental human characteristic. [Freud, 1905, p. 191]

Besides, Freud had already written to Fliess: "… the factor of a hereditary disposition regains a sphere of influence from which I had made it my task to dislodge it—in the interest of illuminating neurosis" (Masson, 1985, p. 265). In his "Introductory Lectures on Psychoanalysis" Freud wrote:

> … These people, in consequence of the singular development of their libido, would have fallen ill in any case, whatever they had experienced and however carefully their lives had been sheltered … In the anamnesis of perverts a very early impression of an abnormal instinctual trend or choice of object was quite often found, to which the subject's libido remained attached all through life. [1915–17, pp. 347, 348]

The minor importance of paedophilia in the thinking of Freud, who nevertheless gave extensive space to perversions, can be explained by two factors:

1. The decreasing attention Freud paid, as time went by, to the real child compared to the psychoanalytic child, the child inside the adult. This historic inattention represented one of the reasons that probably led him later to modify the value and sense given to the

real sexual traumas experienced by children. Alice Miller (1979) reckons that the theory of the Oedipus complex has created a sort of scientific alibi for psychoanalysts, in that it has legitimised the desire not to acknowledge how widespread sexual violence against children is, and what devastating consequences it has on its little victims (Schinaia, 2000).

2. Theoretical conditioning determined by the model of instincts. In the primitive psyche good corresponds to what gives pleasure and evil to what causes sorrow. Freud wrote: "It seems probable that the sexual instinct is in the first instance independent of its object" (1905, p. 148). Roccia and Foti comment: "If sexuality is not examined in its relational dimension, if the defensive resort to the 'libido surge' resulting from narcissistic problems is theoretically underestimated, if ultimately the sexual urge is seen as structurally asocial and necessarily indifferent to the object, this might even result in an implicit justification of paedophilia or the paedophile, who after all would only seek the most advantageous conditions for his instinctual satisfaction" (1994, p. 194).

The treatment of Dora and the report of her case, even taking into account the socio-cultural background of the time, highlight the fact that it is the young girl who is to be considered in need of treatment, whilst the possible links between pathology and the sexual attentions the mature Mr K paid to a fourteen-year-old are not mentioned at all.

On the same line of thought, Abraham wrote: "In a great number of cases the trauma was desired by the child unconsciously … and we have to recognise it as a form of infantile sexual activity" (1907, p. 48). But even if he stressed the role of the trauma as a catalyst for the mental sexuality already present in the child ("there are children who will hardly oppose any resistance to the invitation of an unknown person to follow him"), Abraham seemed to consider that the child and his sexuality were responsible for any abuse he suffered, having encouraged it through seduction: "there are children who quite definitely provoke adults in a sexual manner" (*ibid*). In contrast, Ferenczi had this to say about paedophilia:

> The immediate explanation—that these are only sexual fantasies of the child, a kind of hysterical living—is unfortunately

made invalid by the number of such confessions, e.g. of assaults upon children, committed by patients actually in analysis ... [Adults] mistake the play of children for the desires of a sexually mature person or even allow themselves—irrespective of any consequences—to be carried away. [1933, p. 161].

Ferenczi reminds us that in cases of sexual abuse children tend to identify with the abuser.

> Through the identification, or let us say, introjection of the aggressor, he disappears as part of the external reality ... In any case the attack as a rigid external reality ceases to exist and in the traumatic trance the child succeeds in maintaining the previous situation of tenderness. The most important change, produced in the mind of the child by the anxiety-fear-ridden identification with the adult partner, is *the introjection of the guilt feelings of the adult* which makes hitherto harmless play appear as a punishable offence. [*ibid*, p. 162]

Ferenczi's view seems to refer to Freud's early thinking of 1896, prior the "Three Essays", which is often overlooked.

> In his last paper "Confusion of Tongues between the Adult and the Child", he makes it quite clear that trauma—and particularly sexual trauma—is a pathogenic agent, and that sexual abuse in children is commonplace. When he delivered his paper to the assembled gathering of psychoanalysts in Wiesbaden in 1932, their response was very similar to that which Freud had encountered 36 years before when addressing Krafft-Ebing and his colleagues: Ferenczi's paper was not published in English until 1949. [De Zulueta, 1993, p. 159]

The concept of identification with the aggressor enables us to see the relationship between the trauma suffered by the child and the paedophile behaviour he subsequently acquires in a new light, not simply in the mechanical terms of cause and effect, or of an automatic repetition against other children of the seductive acts to which he has been subjected.

In defining perversion as an erotic form of hatred, Stoller (1975) thinks of a revival of the trauma with inverted characters, so that the child's trauma is converted into an adult triumph. Revenge for the trauma suffered consists of dehumanising and humiliating the partner through fantasy or perverse acts. This theoretical stance does not seem completely tenable and shareable, since a strong emotion—hatred—is introduced. It is difficult to imagine a revenge which consists of dehumanising and humiliating the partner being part of a picture in which being unemotional seems to prevail over passion. Later, Stoller acknowledges the presence of some hostility and desire for humiliation in sexual arousal, and comes to the conclusion that intimacy is a certain critical factor of differentiation. An individual can be considered perverse only when the erotic act is used to avoid an emotionally intimate and stable relationship with another person.

The transition from the theory of the actual seduction to the traumatic ghost in Freudian thinking has been faced by a number of authors (among others Masson, 1984; Bowlby, 1888; Kluzer, 1996; Bonfiglio, 1996, 1997; Speziale-Bagliacca, 1997). While Freud is constantly concerned with preserving the importance of aspects related both to the subject and to the environment, Ferenczi at some point privileges the environmental factors (Bonfiglio, 1997).

When Freud listened to the accounts of sexual abuse, incestuous abuse in particular, committed by his patients, he first believed that those events really happened. This was a tribute to the teaching of Paul Brouardel, whose work he had come across during his stay in Paris in 1885–86 (Arveiller, 1998).

In April 1896 the young Freud submitted his paper "The Aetiology of Hysteria" to the Psychiatric and Neurological Society of Vienna, whose president was Krafft-Ebing, an emeritus professor in the Department of Psychiatry. Later Freud wrote to his friend Fliess: "A lecture on the aetiology of hysteria at the psychiatric society was given an icy reception by the asses and a strange evaluation by Krafft-Ebing: 'It sounds like a scientific fairy tale'. And this after one has demonstrated to them the solution of a more than thousand-year-old problem, a Caput Nili [source of the Nile]. They can go to hell, euphemistically expressed" (Masson, 1985, p. 184). Freud states: "Sexual experiences in childhood consisting of stimulation of the genitals, coitus-like acts, and so on, must therefore be recognised, in the last analysis, as being the traumas which lead to a hysterical reaction to events at puberty and to the development of hysterical symptoms" (1896b, p. 206–207). Therefore, among the aetiological factors of hysteria Freud detects a first group including assaults:

> In the first group it is a question of assaults—of single, or at any rate isolated, instances of abuse, mostly practised on female children, by adults who were strangers, and who, incidentally, knew how to avoid inflicting gross, mechanical injury. In these assaults, there was no question of the child's consent, and the first effect of the experience was preponderantly one of fright. The second group consists of the much more numerous cases in which some adult looking after the child—a nursery maid or governess or tutor, or, unhappily all too often, a close relative—has initiated the child into sexual intercourse and has maintained a regular love relationship with it—a love relationship, moreover, with its mental side developed—which has often lasted for years. [*ibid.*, p. 208]

Freud is remarkably refined when he faces the topic of vulnerability to traumatic actions: "Injuries sustained by an organ which is as yet immature, or by a function which is in process of developing, often cause more severe and lasting effects than they could do in mature years" (*ibid.*, p. 202).

Abraham distinguished "sexual traumas which take the child unawares from those which it has itself provoked or which are due to temptation or seduction, or which it could at any rate have foreseen and avoided. In the first group there are no grounds for assuming a compliance on the part of the child; in the second we cannot avoid assuming that there was a compliance of this sort" (1907, p. 49).

In "The Aetiology of Hysteria" Freud writes: "It is now no longer a question of sexual topics having been aroused by some sense impression or other, but of sexual experiences affecting the subject's own body—of *sexual intercourse* (in the wider sense)" (1896, p. 203). Abraham, in contrast, considers that "infantile sexual traumas play no role in hysteria and dementia praecox. The experiencing of such traumas indicates rather that the child already has a disposition to neurosis or psychosis in later life" (1907, p. 62). By 1897, however, Freud had already corrected his "theory of seduction", as emerges from the letter, full of disappointment, which he wrote to Fliess on

21 September. Freud nevertheless did not completely abandon his original theory, proceeding towards an interpretation of his patients' accounts which saw them as fantasies or projections of desires which were as violent as they were unacceptable.

The same original theory, on the other hand, had already been mitigated and limited in its economic aspects by the concept of *a posteriori* (*Nachträglichkeit*): traumas act at the moment they happen, but the psychic trauma may also manifest itself later on, starting from childhood memories which assume traumatic power only after a long time and in connection with new events. This idea, which we find first in the term *proton-pseudos* in "Project for a Scientific Psychology" (1895) and later in the case of the "Wolf man" (1918), highlights how the trauma unfolds through two stages. Berti reminds us that "even in the case of a single act of child seduction, the trace of this event, though it remains in the psyche, does not act as a trauma itself, that is to say it does not produce pathogenic effects until maturation conditions or later events retroactively convert the first event into a trauma" (1999, p. 189). It is only in this case that the pathogenic consequences of the trauma manifest themselves (see Baranger, Baranger & Mom, 1988).

In the "Introductory Lectures on Psychoanalysis" Freud wrote: "You must not suppose, however, that sexual abuse of a child by its nearest male relatives belongs entirely to the realm of fantasy. Most analysts will have treated cases in which such events were real and could be unimpeachably established; but even so they related to the later years of childhood and had been transposed into earlier times" (1915–17, p. 370). It was only later that Freud would stress the need for balance between the fundamental instincts— sexual on the one hand, destructive on the other—and draw a line of continuity between sexuality and aggressiveness. "A surplus of sexual aggressiveness will turn a lover into a sex-murderer, while a sharp diminution in the aggressive factor will make him bashful and impotent" (1940a, p. 149).

Unlike Masson (1984), I do not believe that Freud swiftly threw aside his first theory in an act of passive and cowardly compliance with the conformism of the times, in other words because of the social turmoil it would have generated. Nor do I believe that he altered the truth of things in a way that compromised the scientific reliability of the entire psychoanalytic journey, or that he led psychoanalysts to put themselves in a position of defending abusers and considering the victims of their violence "unreliable narrators of fairy tales" (Lopez, 1985a). One of the reasons why Freud abandoned the theory of seduction does seem to be his disappointment at the poor academic acknowledgement of his work on hysteria, as emerges from his letter to Fliess dated 21 September 1897:

> The expectation of eternal fame was so beautiful, as was that of certain wealth, complete independence, travels, and lifting the children above the severe worries that robbed me of my youth. Everything depended upon whether or not hysteria would come out right. Now I can once again remain quiet and modest, go on worrying and saving. A little story from my collection occurs to me: "Rebecca, take off your gown, you are no longer a bride." [Masson, 1985, p. 266]

I believe instead that we can think of a process on the part of Freud which is at the same time (and paradoxically) defensive and farsighted, tending to distinguish between reality and fantasy in order to not run the risk that the psychoanalyst becomes a police inspector searching at any price for the forgotten and repressed trauma. Lopez (1985a) underlines that both Masson's view and the psychoanalytic view—the latter expressing itself through absolute ostracism of the former's theories—are biased, and reveal the emotional involvement of those who sustain either view.

> Lopez considers that the Oedipus complex, a pulsating crossroads determining the child's development and thus the future of society, unfolds on two sides, through the reciprocal influences exerted by both parts. It is necessary to take into account the libidinal forces—which are indeed true, real and not sham—exerted by both parts, and which constitute, so to speak, the raw material that, through its transformation, fosters a healthy sexual maturity. [Todisco, 1985, p. 85]

In any case, Freud continued to give importance to the environment as an aetiological factor. Martin-Cabré (1997) stresses that Freud talks in "Analysis Terminable and Interminable" about "the strength of the instincts *at the time*" reinforced by new traumas and frustrations, and no longer just about "*constitutional strength of the instincts*" (p. 224).

Freud gave importance to new traumas and new frustrations, which could produce a reinforcement, therefore lessening the importance of the biological, the constitutional, the innate (Goretti, 1997).

It is nevertheless important to highlight that the theory of trauma was never abandoned, but coexisted conflictingly, yet also effectively, with the later theories. Indeed, Freud quite often acknowledged in his work the risk of overlooking the reality of child sexual abuse and its importance in the development of psychic disturbances (1915–17, 1931, 1940a).

The detection of an increasing number of paedophiles, and consequently of sexual traumas often experienced by children at home, raises an issue that the law considered of minor importance until recently: the value to ascribe to childhood memories. Recent sentences, in which account was taken of memories dating back twenty or thirty years, have provoked heated debate, especially in the United States. Parents and relatives who claim to have been wrongly accused of abuse have even set up the False Memory Syndrome Foundation. The fact that many people recovering memories of sexual abuse from their childhood are in analysis is a reason for believing that analysts can unduly influence patients with explicit or implicit suggestions; patients duly reward their analysts with dramatic revelations about having been abused in childhood.[3] Freud wrote the following in "The Aetiology of Hysteria", concluding his remarks with a hint of irony:

> It is less easy to refute the idea that the doctor forces reminiscences of this sort on the patient, that he influences him by suggestion to imagine and reproduce them. Nevertheless it appears to me equally untenable. I have never yet succeeded in forcing on a patient a scene I was expecting to find, in such a way that he seemed to be living through it with all the appropriate feelings. Perhaps others may be more successful in this. [1896b, pp. 204–205]

Psychoanalysis, one among many human sciences, can express its own view about humans, but cannot replace any other discipline. This means that the legal apparatus has to do its job, which consists not of being the perverse patient's analyst, but of defining a society's conditions for relationships at a certain historical time, and of assessing (as far as the criminal law is concerned) what can impair these relationships. In Lingiardi's view,

The objective of analytic therapy is certainly not to dig events out of the "archive of memories"; more importantly, the analyst has to avoid playing the role of "truth referee". In therapy, the aim of recalling is not to distinguish between truth and falsehood, to undertake an investigation, or to get an authorised version of what really happened; it is to re-construct the coherent and continuous personal history of an autobiographic memory, which, through the re-construction of the past, gives a new sense to present events too. Therapy and law have different needs. [2001, p. 105]

Ferenczi continued to insist on the historical feature of the trauma, and nowadays we can still evenly state that any destructive behaviour has its own roots in childhood traumatic experiences, although De Masi (1999) states that often the trauma cannot be traced, or the direct link with perversion cannot be proved.

Even if we avoid making any statement that could have a justificatory meaning, or theorising a sort of innate tendency to absolute evil (as De Masi seems to do when he talks about psychically "understandable" evil and illness that is far from any possible understanding [2000, p. 153]), we have to acknowledge that the trauma is not necessarily an occasional macroscopic event which, due to its severity, can definitely scar for life. It can be the result of subtle and insidious attitudes that can act in the individual even over long periods of time. Masud Khan (1979) described childhood micro-traumas which can cumulatively contribute to form the narcissistic traits that belong to a perverse picture. Balint (1969) also acknowledged the relational aspects of the real trauma when he shed light on the importance of environmental aspects alongside those related to the subjective phantasmic world, and stressed that the child's significant emotional environment is represented by the parental figures. Zerbi Schwarz (2000) reminds us that we need to conceive the trauma in relational terms in order to give specific importance to the impact of real events, yet at the same time we need to highlight the central role played by the intrapsychic mediation of the external events in the resulting pathology. Some authors (Cooper, 1986; Kramer & Akhtar, 1991; Krystal, 1978) relate the primary impact of the trauma to the intrapsychic organisation, mediated by the patient's fantasy, and they incorporate not only the unconscious meaning of the traumatic event but also the levels of excitement and stimulation, because when these are excessively high, they overwhelm the ego and hinder its functioning.

According to De Masi, "the abuse can be traumatic on the psychological level, as it impairs the sense of 'self confidence in the world', in other words that potential area which enables one to feel in harmony with others, to have desires, to project oneself into the future through an imaginary and personal space full of passions and emotions" (1999, p. 123). But Kluzer explains that with Freud, "the basis of the possible traumatic conditions had already expanded from the single event to more general and paradigmatic situations of the child's psycho-emotional development, such as the Oedipus complex, castration, the parents' sexual life—which from 1915 would be grouped with the term primal ghosts" (1996, p. 407).

The real trauma, and not the traumatic fantasy, can be present not necessarily in strict sexual terms, as shown in the following account by Michel Tournier, in which the terrible traumatic effects caused by an invasive medical procedure are evident:

> One morning two strangers in white uniform and with a flaming laryngoscope on their forehead burst into my room. It was an image typical of science fiction or horror films. They hurtled down onto me, wrapped me into one of the two sheets, and then started to break up my jaws with a dilator. Then the pliers came into action, as tonsils are not cut, but taken off like teeth. I was left drowning in my own blood. I wonder how possible it was to resuscitate the breathless wet rag that that vile aggression had made me. But almost half a century later those marks are still with me and I am still unable to recall that scene in cold blood. [1983, p. 101]

"The traumatic experience can be estimated on the basis not of the 'objective' consistency of adult behaviour, but of the diverse repercussions that such behaviour can have on the child's subjectivity, of the particular effects of disorientation, guilt, pain and solitude which it can induce according to the particular case" (Foti & Roccia, 1994b, p. 191).

McDougall comments: "The leading theme of the neosexual plot is invariably castration … But the triumph of the neosexual scenario lies in the fact that the castrative aim is only playfully carried out …

These [perversions] are all substitute acts of castration and thus serve to master castration anxiety in illusionary fashion, at every conceivable level" (1982, p. 252–253). In 1990, referring to Freud's essay on fetishism, McDougall detected in the perverse individual the failed internalisation of the phallus, which leads to a compulsive search in the outside world for a fetish, through repeated acts. The object of fetishism is in his or her lost freedom nothing but an extension of the subject's frustrated narcissism.

De Masi (1999), apparently referring to Abraham's theoretical views of the child's predisposition to trauma, declared that the real perverse structure is totally independent of the primal narcissistic wounds. According to De Masi "the trauma-perversion sequence may be reversed: in children secretly given to sadomasochistic pleasure, traumatic experiences may stimulate sexualisation. In these cases trauma, rather than being seen as a source of anxiety, may rekindle the sadistic pleasure and mobilise the masochistic fantasy" (Barale, 1999, p. xxiv). Barale puts forward the hypothesis that the fragility of the Self (and/or particular vulnerability to trauma) and the tendency to develop perversions are two aspects of one basic structure, which can only partially (though fruitfully) be investigated from the psychoanalytical point of view.

This reasoning could explain, not just in sociological terms, both why paedophiles search for problematic children, and why sometimes it is possible to note a certain gratified compliance with the abuse in the accounts of paedophiles who were themselves abused in their childhood. However, it could also encourage a sort of observational blindness regarding the role played by the real trauma in the patient's history, as Alice Miller has consistently underlined. De Zulueta comments:

> The human mind, including the psychiatrist's mind, tends to deny the powerful effects of trauma so as to avoid being a witness to the contortions of our psyche when it is overcome by a sense of overwhelming helplessness … As with psychoanalysts, both in medicine and in psychiatry the theoretical underpinnings of the current psychopathological models need to be revised to take into account the long-term consequences of post-traumatic stress disorder, not only in the adult but especially in the developing human being whose trauma becomes

manifest in both somatic and psychological symptoms. [1993, pp. 190, 272]

Freud was the first to underline the central part played by castration anxiety in perversions, whose function would be to deny castration (Fenichel, 1945). In fact "the fear of castration would explain, at least partially, the behaviour of the paedophile, who is frightened by a relationship with a woman of his generation and so prefers a relationship with a young girl, which allows him to have an orgasm without facing up to genital penetration; or, if he does face up to it, to do it in a position of superiority and 'competence'" (Foti & Roccia, 1994b, p. 195). As we can see, the little psychoanalytical work on paedophilia mostly refers to castration anxiety.

In 1927 Cassity reviewed the contributions of Krafft-Ebing, Havelock Ellis, Magnan, Bleuler, Stekel and Hadley, and presented four cases he had treated. He highlighted two aetiological factors: firstly, the premature loss of the breast (weaning trauma) stirs strong vindictive tendencies which are alleviated by attempts to compel the love object to gratify insatiable oral needs and at the same time by attempts to dominate and control her (the mother); and secondly, the subject avoids castration anxiety by choosing a love object identical to himself.

Karpman (1950) described a case in which the basic conflict seemed to be focused upon a fear of female pubic hair. This represented a traumatic experience in the patient's childhood, which the patient tended to avoid by choosing harmless pre-pubescent girls. In Karpman's report the incorporative aspects are just mentioned and the defensive mechanisms are not clearly described.

In a case report, Socarides (1959) emphasised that the Ego and object split are necessary conditions for the paedophile act. Perversion is able to interrupt the progression towards psychosis, acting as a preventive measure, in line with Glover's theories. He considered that premature serious libidinal frustrations and a consequent arrogant aggressiveness play a crucial role in the genesis of paedophile perversion. The primitive introjection and projection mechanisms—normal processes in the early phases of Ego development—were used to attain the satisfaction that vital love needs and to neutralise the aggressive instincts. In addition, these mechanisms allowed a good remission of anxiety.

Socarides (1988) described another case of paedophilia in which the patient resisted incorporation into his mother through his paedophilic activity. He sought to escape his unconscious female identification by incorporating a pre-pubescent boy's masculinity. Sexual relationships with a young boy made him feel as if he were part of the child. On a deeper level, the union with the child reflected the desire to incorporate his mother's breast and therefore to make up for the real lack of maternal care he suffered in his early childhood.

Starting from Freud's statement in "A Child is Being Beaten" (1919a) that perversion represents the opposite of neurosis, Chabert writes:

> The fantasy of the paedophilic father, which is the opposite of the primal scene and of castration, no longer places the child behind the door listening—the impotent child coming face to face with the adults' enigmatic enjoyment. Instead, this fantasy puts the child in a central position, rendering him an object of fascination and desire, master (passively) of the father's love, who removes not just the mother … but the other, that is the woman. The origin of the emergence of desires no longer resides in the difference between the sexes but in the difference between the generations. [1993, p. 336]

Castration anxiety seems to be a feature of all clinical pictures which variously show the constellation of paedophilic symptoms, and can be described as a necessary condition (but not sufficient in itself) for the emergence of a paedophilic mental organisation. Sexualisation seems to be a more primitive mechanism, and in some cases more specific, which together with castration anxiety can better define the picture.

Sexualisation

The term "sexualisation" has been used by Betty Joseph to indicate a very close relationship of futile tie, which prevents one from seeing reality, as it compels one to see only what has already been seen. According to Joseph, sexualisation overwhelms the creative vision present in sexuality. The sexualisation of the relationship might be a means of inhibiting the creativity of the psychoanalytic mind (since creativity is feared as a third presence that prevents a fusing collusion), and therefore of avoiding, through individuation, the thought of a state of suffering.

> These patients as infants, because of their pathology, have not just turned away from frustrations or jealousies or envies into a withdrawn state, nor have they have been able to rage and yell at their objects. I think they have withdrawn into a secret world of violence, where part of the self has been turned against another part, parts of the body being identified with parts of the offending object, and that this violence has been highly sexualised, masturbatory in nature, and often physically expressed ... It seems to me that instead of moving forward and using real relationships, contact with people or bodies or infants, they retreated apparently into themselves and lived out their relationships in this sexualised way, in phantasy or phantasy expressed in violent bodily activity. [1982, p. 137]

Meltzer (1973) also talks about sexual states of the mind, which, based on the sexualised distortion of perceptions, sustain the pictures of perversion. He distinguishes between:

1. *Habitual perversion*. This contains all the elements of the narcissistic picture of drug addiction: the attack on truth, the splitting of the object to form the fetishistic toy, the autoerotic sensuality, the defence against depressive pain, the transformation of the relationship with pain into masochism through the trick of projective identification with the victim of the sadistic fantasy. Yet the passivity deriving from defence against fear is absent.
2. *Drug addictive perversion*. While the adult part of the personality can continue to control behaviour concerning relatively non-traumatic and non-emotional areas, these are experienced as meaningless, as a frame for the drug addictive perversion. Behind this screen, desperation, with its suicidal component, leads the individual towards far more dangerous forms of perverse relationship, with the tendency to be killed by the destructive part of the Self as an extreme reparation-joke, that is to say an eye for an eye.
3. *Criminal perversion*. This is the product of spitting and projective identification of the personality's good infantile part into a

person from the external world—especially, in childhood, into a younger brother. If the typically fluctuating performance of the sadomasochistic game gives way to a coherent sadistic and masochistic behavioural model, the active partner may find himself more and more overwhelmed by the activity. When this happens, the game begins to vanish and violence is no longer very far away. Instead of violence against the old partner there can be a turning to seduction and debasement of younger "innocent" people, leading them to drug addictive perversions, like turning to an overwhelming passion. This is essentially psychopathy, a category of psychosis in which intellectual capacity is unaltered and moral capacity non-existent.

Goldberg linked sexualisation with narcissistic rage and dehumanisation: "Although one could say that the rage threatened a tenuous relation with the selfobject and necessitated a sexualisation to retain a tie and forestall further regression and possible fragmentation, one could also say that the sexualisation became so shameful and frightening that an angry reaction was needed to right the self and to correct the humiliation suffered by the unresponsive selfobject" (1995, p. 152). Goldberg reckons that the meaning of sexualisation would be that of filling a structural deficit in the Self.

Any therapeutic attempt with the paedophile must begin from the "terrible primal anxiety of non-existence" (Balier, 1993) that lies behind sexualisation. Sexualisation subsequently comes to disguise emptiness with fullness, more precisely with fake fullness. Balier places himself in the wake of Glover and Bergler, but also refers to the theories of neo-sexuality proposed by McDougall, whom he criticises for replacing the term "perversion" with "neo-sexuality". This terminological replacement on the one hand frees perversion from any moralistic connotation, and on the other hand encourages the thought that perverse behaviour could relate to new forms of sexuality, which—once they have been deprived of their pathological connotation—can gain some form of legitimacy.

Chasseguet-Smirgel (1985) conceived sexualisation as an obsessive operation, a real attack on mind and relationships in the service of the radical denial of diversities, of the oedipal articulation of experience and sexuality, and aimed at producing an idealised world of "oral confusion".

De Masi (1994) detected in sexualisation a mental structure developing in abandoned, deficient and isolated children during their early childhood. These children escape into an imaginary sexualised world, in which the sexual fantasies represent a continuous source of stimulation, excitement and support, and survive through mechanisms of mental sensual pleasure of a masturbatory nature. Once the perverse fantasy has asserted itself, it remains a closed world, which prevents any evolution towards other forms of love and sexual relationships. Sexualisation, therefore, is a withdrawal of the mind, a psychic retreat (Steiner, 1993), an element of a psycho-pathological structure, and not a defensive operation against anxiety, pain or Self-control (De Masi, 1999).

While De Masi, in the wake of Joseph and Meltzer, depicts sexualisation as a pure state, a syndrome which characterises sadomasochism, Balier reconsiders Masud Khan's and thus Goldberg's intuitions and basically talks about a very severe particular defensive modality—in this sense he distinguishes between perversion and perversity.

Perversion and perversity

Perversity was defined by Ey (1950), from a phenomenological perspective that does not neglect the psychoanalytic lesson, as evil attraction and desire, will to harm, and pleasure in overpowering. Nowadays the term has acquired a more civilised meaning and could be defined as a deliberate tendency to commit cruel and aggressive acts merely aimed at causing harm (Dubret, 1996).

If Meltzer had distinguished perversion, as an organised aspect of psychic life, from perversity, which can take the features of perversion but can also remain as such, Balier (1996) gave a new definition to the terms perversion and perversity, and clearly distinguished perverse behaviours from violent sexual behaviours. He creatively introduced the concept of sexual perversity, in which the criminal is totally absorbed by the resultant play-acting in order to be acted and vanish as a subject. Sexual perversity is very close to psychosis and must be considered a form of pure violence, which leads to the annihilation of the other to the benefit of a narcissistic appropriation.

In the perverse organisation, on the other hand, defined as a modality of defence against castration anxiety or object loss anxiety, the subject is capable of elaborating and diversifying. The perverse moments of fetishists, masochists, exhibitionists and voyeurs allow them to integrate the primal violence as such, to limit it, to prevent it from overflowing further. Pornography, often surrounded by sadistic images, can have a function of defence against putting homicidal fantasies into practice.

In serious cases the opposite happens: not only does the perverse scenario not facilitate the integration of a certain destructive violence, but it even serves violence. We can say that there is a perversion of sexual perversion in the Freudian sense of the term, which is inversion of the corresponding psychic organisation: a setback, in any case, of what seems to work from time to time in the perverts we see on our couches.

In order for us to understand how this evolution malfunctions, it is necessary to step back to the metapsychology of the partial instinct. In any instinct there is a sexual and an aggressive aim. As long as the two aims articulate themselves under genital primacy, damage is limited. Only when the destructive aim prevails so far as to make sexual satisfaction relative is there a perversion of perversion, leading to sexual perversity, with associated violent recourse to action, which implies a deficit in (or even lack of) the capacity to symbolise. In order to get closer to this topic, Balier referred to the concept of the *pictogram* (Aulagnier, 1975), which he described as

> ... what is most primal, above any representation of the primal scene. This model would be represented by the mouth-breast match in which the object would not be distinguished from the erogenous area. We are talking about a sort of bodily experience which animates the most primitive emotions where displeasure and pleasure, and representative and represented, merge into each other. However, it is all about a "representative bottom", which is to take shape in the course of the following processes, in which the primal scene can be represented through the parental relationships in an *après coup*. The act that unfolds in the reality breaks up with the thought and becomes a crazy act. [Balier, 1996, p. 8]

Nevertheless, Balier wonders whether, in its function of mirror of pictogram, the crazy act could preserve an organisational adjustment to this "representative bottom". In this case we should reserve for it the same positive potential that Winnicott ascribed to the antisocial reaction, which attempts to make up for something "good enough" that has been lost. "Sexual perversity calls upon a process which denies the object and the subjective nature of the other, which makes it possible for the patient to escape a psychotic disaster, yet reducing his or her existence—for a relatively long period—to the sex urge itself and to its manifestation in the surrounding world, even to its homicidal extreme" (*ibid.*, p. 205).

Kernberg also distinguishes perversion from perversity, and defines perversity as "the conscious or unconscious transformation of something good into something bad: love into hatred, meaning into meaninglessness, cooperation into exploitation, food into faeces" (1992, p. 255). Perversity, as Kernberg sees it, is at the service of malignant narcissism:

> If perversity is based on polymorphous perverse fantasies and activities that disregard the distinctions between the sexes and the generations and unconsciously equate not only all sexual activity but all object relations with faecal matter, and if the mad worlds of de Sade's *120 Days of Sodom* (1785), a fantasy, and of Auschwitz, a reality, represent the rock bottom condensation of aggression and perversion, then "ordinary perversions" that maintain a rigid, obligatory sexual scenario in the context of preserving ordinary genital relations and the capacity for maintaining differentiated object relations represent a truly "innocent" side of perversion. [*ibid.*, p. 257]

In Gabbard's view, "when paedophilic activity occurs in conjunction with a narcissistic personality disorder with severe antisocial features, as part of an outright psychopathic character structure, the unconscious determinants of the behaviour may be closely linked to the dynamics of sadism" (1994, p. 336).

I have considerable experience of extremely compound and varying clinical pictures, which subsequently stabilise, and in which it is possible to note the coexistence of both painful attempts at communication and a basic destructive narcissism that simultaneously makes the desperate attempts to form a relationship fail. Thus I believe it is useful and appropriate to distinguish situations with communicative and object aspects from those characterised by pure Thanatos, primal destructiveness—therefore to distinguish perversion from perversity.

The distinction between perversion and perversity seems to me extremely convincing and useful from a clinical point of view, since it enables us to prevent the term perversion from comprising clinical pictures which refer to different forms of mental functioning. However, this distinction is not considered significant by De Masi, who tends to underline instead the independence of the sadomasochistic syndrome not only from perversity but also from occasional perverse behaviours and from pictures in which the perversion element is just a symptom of a constellation related to other pictures.

While I am persuaded by the sharpness with which De Masi describes the pervert's world, I agree with Kernberg in believing that the perverse symptomatology acquires a different expressiveness related to the fact that it belongs to neurotic, borderline or psychotic pictures, with diverse consequences also from the point of view of psychotherapeutic treatment. The developing defences are increasingly diverse, but more importantly, it is possible to find in perversion (though on different levels) a capacity for representation which is reduced, yet still preserved, if only partially, while the features of sexual perversity are mainly the lack of capacity for thinking and symbolising. While in perversion object or non-object narcissism prevails, the perversity we find in antisocial personalities and in psychotics is characterised by the Self falling apart.

Looking at the defensive aspects of perversion, in its apparently more non-object forms, allows us to delve into the traumatic roots which nourish the perverse personality, the cumulative effect of repeated micro-traumas, pathogenic family communications, premature separations, abandonment. It also keeps at a distance the "innate" hypothesis according to which the human being would have some characteristics from birth—which would be likely to crystallise perversion as a pathology. This happened to some extent with Jasper, who considered the psychopathology of schizophrenia incomprehensible, and encouraged literary and contemplative attitudes which were not very therapeutic.

Notes

1. De Martis also includes paedophilia among the anomalies of object choice (1989).
2. Chasseguet-Smirgel (1985) reconsiders and assesses Freud's first contribution to regression. Due to an overwhelming castration anxiety, development towards a genital phallus relationship is blocked and is replaced by a level of sexuality dominated by the faecal phallus. This anal world lacks any gender diversities and any perception of generational diversities.
3. In 1994 a course on recovered memories was held at University College London. This was the first meeting between groups of psychologists, psychoanalysts, psychotherapists, counsellors, social workers, lawyers and parents who had been involved in accusations of abuse on the basis of memories recovered by their children. Sandler and Fonagy (1997) edited a volume that well describes the intense dramatic power of that course.

CHAPTER SEVEN

Contributions to the definition and typology of paedophilic personalities and behaviours through fiction

Paolo F. Peloso, Cosimo Schinaia and Giuseppina Tabò

> Hier, m'a dit Naïs, j'étais sur la place, quand une petite fille en loques rouges a passé, portant des roses, devant un groupe de jeunes gens. Et voici ce que j'ai entendu:
> Achetez-moi quelque chose.—Explique-toi, petite, car nous ne savons ce que tu vends: toi? tes roses? Our tout à la fois?—Si vous m'achetez toutes ces fleurs, vous aurez la mienne pour rien.
> Et combien veux-tu de tes roses?—Il faut six oboles à ma mère ou bien je serai battue comme une chienne.—Suis-nous. Tu auras une drachme.—Alors je vais chercher ma petite soeur?
> Et toutes deux ont suivi ces hommes. Elle n'avaient pas de seins, Bilitis. Elles ne savaient meme pas sourire. Elles trottaient comme des chevreaux qu'on emmène à la boucherie.
>
> —Pierre Louys[1]

Tales of abandoned and lost children, or of children taken away from their families to be ill-treated, fill the pages of a very extensive and terrifying literature of which Mark Twain's *Tom Sawyer* and Victor Hugo's *The Laughing Man* are just two unforgettable masterpieces. All these literary products, for instance stories of abduction such as Malot's *Nobody's Boy* or Stevenson's *Kidnapped*, derive from and are inspired by mythological and fairy tales and by paedophilic fantasies, which come more or less explicitly (through their expression or their repression) to belong to trans-generational relationships.

Although we believe that it is necessary to aim at detecting and re-knotting the *fil rouge* which links myth, fairy tale and fiction up to the present day, the archetypal primal plot which, with different and original narrative modalities related to diverse historical periods and diverse social contexts, still seems to re-present the same literary foundations, this chapter will tackle another problem. We shall look at how literature has described the diverse types of paedophile personalities and attitudes, which can assume universally paradigmatic features.

Though we are by no means attempting a comprehensive classification, we have taken the opportunity to distinguish diverse paedophile typologies. This leads us into an area where definition is confused, and encompasses relational modalities which are indeed extremely different from one another. Moreover, reasons of confidentiality make it difficult to provide extensive descriptions of diverse clinical cases, which could better represent the differences emerging from the universe of the paedophilic behaviours, the various dimensions that can stand out from the background and come to the fore. This difficulty can be reduced by the skill and psychological acuity with which some writers have been able to offer us a description of the diverse facets of this peculiar human behaviour. Our aim is therefore to go through a series of literary cases and create through them a versatile representation of a phenomenon which, alongside some common denominators, contains some elements of complexity.

"Polite" paedophilia: Aschenbach

Gustav Aschenbach, in Thomas Mann's *Death in Venice* (1912), is an intellectual in his fifties from Central Europe, tormented by a crisis of creativity and by his fear of ageing and physical decay, who goes on holiday to Venice. There he finds an atmosphere of cholera and death, as the novella increasingly reveals. Meanwhile, the intensity of his desire for Tadzio, a Polish ephebic adolescent who is staying in the same hotel, increases to the point where reality, dream and delirium become indistinguishable. Aschenbach, like Humbert Humbert (whom we will meet later), seeks noble roots for his desire, and his mind goes back to Socrates, to Greece, in the search for the historical and anthropological roots of the feelings by which he is overwhelmed and tormented.

Aschenbach clear-headedly perceives the two aspects of his paedophilic falling in love, one of Apollonian nostalgic and fantastic heaven, the other of Dionysian hell. The first aspect allows his unhappy heart to fully enjoy a holiday for the first time thanks to the object of his love, despite his distance: "Aschenbach did not enjoy enjoying himself … Only this place bewitched him, relaxed his will, gave him happiness" (p. 300). The second aspect, which indissolubly accompanies Aschenbach's paedophilic behaviour, is present, but remains constantly isolated and projected; for instance in the dream of the Sabbah in love, when

> Odours besieged the mind, the pungent reek of the goats, the scent of panting bodies and an exhalation as of staling waters, with another smell, too, that was familiar: that of wounds and wandering disease. His heart throbbed to the drumbeats, his brain whirled, a fury seized him, a blindness, a dizzying lust, and his soul craved to join the round-dance of the god. The obscene symbol, wooden and gigantic, was uncovered and raised aloft: and still more unbridled grew the howling of the rallying-cry. With foaming mouths they raged, they roused each other with lewd gestures and licentious hands, laughing and moaning they thrust the prods into each other's flesh and licked the blood from each other's limbs. But the dreamer now was with them and in them, he belonged to the stranger-god. Yes, they were himself as they flung themselves, tearing and slaying, on the animals and devoured steaming gobbets of flesh, they were himself as an orgy of limitless coupling, in homage to the god, began on the trampled, mossy ground. And his very soul savoured the lascivious delirium of annihilation. [pp. 334–335]

But this hellish atmosphere emerges also from the miasmas of the city, smelling of disease and impurity, which become increasingly unbearable. Lastly, we feel this atmosphere in the fight between

Jasciu and Tadzio, towards the end of the story, shortly before the boy reaches the open sea and Aschenbach joins him by sinking into death. In the condensation and confusion of identities, which perhaps represent the external projection of an internal conflict, he seems to experience himself as both an aggressor and defender of the boy: "Appalled, Aschenbach was about to spring to the rescue when the bully finally released his victim" (p. 342).

"Imperial" paedophilia: Hadrian

Memoirs of Hadrian (1951), the book in which Marguerite Yourcenar composes an extraordinarily poetic, magnificent historic fresco, contains the story of the Roman emperor's love for the youth Antinous. On page after page, keen to "do, from within, the same work of reconstruction which the nineteenth-century archaeologists have done from without" (p. 273), Yourcenar offers us the living and trembling image of a man who begins to "discern the profile of [his] death" (p. 269), and from this perspective turns his eyes onto his life, political activity, and human relationships. From this visual angle, suffused with desperate tenderness, Hadrian looks back over what in Yourcenar's book seems to be the most authentic and tortured of his love affairs.

At the age of forty-four, at the height of his consolidation of the Empire, during a literary meeting at the house of the procurator Attianus, Hadrian met Antinous. The son of a man who held a modest post in the administration of the vast imperial dominions, like many children in those days, he had been left to a grandfather's care at an early age and sent to study in Nicomedia. He lived there with a former guest of his parents, a local shipowner and builder. Hadrian was enchanted by the boy's beauty, noticing the thoughtful and distracted attention with which he listened to the difficult and complex verses which were being read out. The boy's absorbed expression evoked in his mind the image of "some shepherd, deep in the woods, vaguely aware of a strange bird's cry" (p. 135). Picking up on the boy's feelings of nostalgia and loss in an unfamiliar world, Hadrian kept him behind after the others had gone and supported him: "I had seen Claudiopolis, his native city, so I led him to speak of his home on the edge of the great pine forests which furnish masts for our ships" (*ibid*). An intimacy gradually developed, and Antinous became the Emperor's faithful life partner, who accompanied him on all his voyages, permanently detaching himself from his familiar world and offering the Emperor his entire childhood, vitality and needs.

> He had the infinite capacity of a young dog for play and for swift repose, and the same fierceness and trust. This graceful hound, avid both for caresses and commands, took his post at my feet. [p. 136]

The "fabulous years" began, a period which Hadrian would remember as a golden age. He seemed to be acquiring a fullness he had not tasted before and never for a moment thought he would have to renounce.

> Trouble was no more: past efforts were repaid by an ease which was almost divine. Travel was play … Work, though incessant, was only a form of delight. My life, where everything came late, power and happiness, too, now acquired the splendour of high noon, the luminous glow of siesta time when everything, the objects of the room and the figure lying beside one, bathes in golden shade. Passion satisfied has its innocence, almost as fragile as any other: the remainder of human beauty was relegated to the rank of mere spectacle, and ceased to be game for my pursuit. [p. 137]

That calm which was so propitious for him seemed to be one of the richest results of love:

> And it puzzles me that these joys, so precarious at best, and so rarely perfect in the course of human life, however we may have sought or received them, should be regarded with such mistrust by the so-called wise, who denounce the danger of habit and excess in sensuous delight, instead of fearing its absence or its loss; in tyrannizing over their senses they pass time which would be better occupied in putting their souls to rights, or embellishing them. [p. 143]

Antinous lived in the Emperor's world whilst losing his own. Hadrian built and fought for Rome, while Antinous followed him, unable to build and uninterested in building anything for himself, keen only on living for the Emperor.

> I marvelled at his gentleness, which had aspects of hardness, too, and the sombre devotion to which he gave his whole being. And yet this submission was not blind; those lids so often lowered in acquiescence or in dream were not always so; the most attentive eyes in the world would sometimes look at me straight in the face, and I felt myself judged. But I was judged as is a god by his adorer: my harshness and sudden suspicions (for I had them later on) were patiently and gravely accepted. I have been absolute master but once in my life, and over but one being. [p. 136]

As time went by, the boy grew up beside Hadrian:

> This tender body varied all the time ... The boy changed; he grew tall ... The boyish limbs lengthened out; the face lost its delicate childish round and hollowed slightly under the high cheekbones ... the brooding lips bespoke a bitter ardour, a sad satiety. In truth this visage changed as if I had moulded it night and day. [p. 137]

At some point the light changed: Hadrian's political activity proceeded and grew like a wonderful building; his success seemed to multiply its intoxicating effects. Anxiety and restlessness made their appearance. He did not love Antinous less—rather, he loved him more. But the weight of love, like that of an arm tenderly lying on the chest, was slowly becoming heavy.

Hadrian, who had got over his insatiability and anxiety to not rely exclusively on anyone, developed a passion for other bodies. He persuaded Antinous to have sex with a courtesan, in order to harm that touchy tenderness which risked becoming a hindrance in his life.

When Antinous committed suicide at the age of eighteen, Hadrian felt in his death the power of a revelation. The sacrificial aspect of it emerged like a propitiatory gift against the obscure foreboding of fate, and as the sign of absolute love:

> I myself felt a kind of terrible joy at the thought that the death was a gift. But I was the only one to measure how much bitter fermentation there is at the bottom of all sweetness, or what

degree of despair is hidden under abnegation, what hatred is mingled with love. A being deeply wounded had thrown this proof of devotion at my very face; a boy fearful of losing all had found this means of binding me to him forever. Had he hoped to protect me by such a sacrifice he must have deemed himself unloved indeed not to have realised that the worst of ills would be to lose him. [p. 172]

Hadrian was overwhelmed by sorrow and despair. Antinous's death taught him how painful life could be and how everything could assume a distorted aspect:

Death, in its aspect of weakness or decay, came to the surface everywhere: the bad spot on a fruit, some imperceptible rent at the edge of a hanging, a carrion body on the shore, the pustules of a face, the mark of scourges on a bargeman's back. My hands seemed always somewhat soiled. [p. 176]

Antinous was Hadrian's great love and great defeat. He was the cliff against which Hadrian was wrecked, because, as he told Marcus Aurelius, there was always wreckage—a bride, a son loved too much, one of those legitimate traps in which the most respectful and pure hearts remain caught, or simply ageing, illness, tiredness, disillusionment which warns us that if it is all futile, so is virtue.

There was much love in Hadrian, yet that love killed Antinous, overwhelmed him with an intensity that impaired his childhood and his need for development, created emptiness in the child's world by filling it with adult needs and thus estranged him from it. Hadrian approached Antinous as an Emperor and loved him as an Emperor, possessing and enjoying his beauty and the intense emotions he aroused in him, without ever putting himself in the child's position or asking himself what the child's real needs might be. He had no consideration for the real child, only for what he saw in him. Only after Antinous's death did Hadrian realise that he had been unable to understand his deepening melancholy:

Amid so many fantasies, and surrounded by such wonders, I sometimes forgot the purely human, the boy who vainly strove to learn Latin, who begged the engineer Decrianus for lessons in mathematics, then quickly gave up, and who at the slightest reproach used to take himself off to the prow of the ship to gaze broodingly at the sea. [p. 151]

"Child" paedophilia: Humbert Humbert

Humbert Humbert, in Vladimir Nabokov's novel *Lolita* (1955), is a divorced, quite lonely, melancholic university professor in his forties. He lives with a widow and her twelve-year-old daughter, by whom he is attracted and with whom, after a series of complex events, he runs away. The motive here is the exact opposite of violation—Humbert Humbert tries hard to show the cultural relativity of the conviction of paedophilia, citing Rahab in the Book of Joshua, who was apparently a harlot at the age of ten; the ten-year-old brides of the Classical world; the customs of the East Indies and the Lepchas; and Dante and Petrarch and their adolescent idealised amorous adventures. According to Humbert, paedophilia represents an attempt to re-live the first adolescent love now that it is no longer adolescent, the desire to go back to childhood, remembered as an idyllic world.

> What drives me insane is the twofold nature of this nymphet— of every nymphet, perhaps; this mixture in my Lolita of tender dreamy childishness and a kind of eerie vulgarity, stemming from the snub-nosed cuteness of ads and magazine pictures, from the blurry pinkness of adolescent maidservants in the Old Country (smelling of crushed daisies and sweat); and from very young harlots disguised as children in provincial brothels; and then again, all this gets mixed up with the exquisite stainless tenderness seeping through the musk and the mud, through the dirt and the death, oh God, oh God. And what is most singular is that she, *this* Lolita, *my* Lolita, has individualised the writer's ancient lust, so that above and over everything there is—Lolita. [pp. 44–45]

He defines the object of his love in the following terms:

> Between the age limits of nine and fourteen there occur maidens who, to certain bewitched travellers, twice or many times older than they, reveal their true nature which is not human, but nymphic (that is, demoniac); and these chosen creatures I propose to designate as "nymphets". [p. 16]

This element chimes with what Chabert (1993) wrote, referring to the story of Jupiter and Ganymede: the paedophile myth represents on the one hand the problem of narcissism, of eternal youth—a subject which is also highlighted by Callieri and Frighi (1999)—and on the other hand that of perversion through the denial of diversity and the abolition of castration anxiety.

Therefore the condition of nymphet represents for Humbert the magical balance between childhood and adulthood, and paedophilia represents the desire to magically make that fleeting moment everlasting. He therefore regrets that this is a transitional phase of these girls' lives, like the fleeting scent of spring, and that once they have grown up, they will only have a vague aroma. In contrast, for Hadrian in Yourcenar's novel, the beauty of love for an adolescent lies exactly in this sensation of vitality and time passing by.

Like Aschenbach, Humbert initially experiences paedophilia as a feeling in itself which involves the young girl only marginally. Humbert gets to a point where he is no longer rewarded by the relationship with the internal Lolita, but needs to open the way to the real Lolita. In fact, after taking the opportunity to touch her while playing, he says:

> What I had madly possessed was not she, but my own creation, another, fanciful Lolita—perhaps, more real than Lolita; overlapping, encasing her; floating between me and her, and having no will, no consciousness—indeed, no life of her own. The child knew nothing. I had done nothing to her. And nothing prevented me from repeating a performance that affected her as little as if she were a photographic image rippling upon a screen and I a humble hunchback abusing myself in the dark. [p. 62]

Humbert is indirectly responsible for the death of Lolita's mother, who represents Lolita's only bond with the world. This allows real Lolita to take her place inside dreamt Lolita, and the real child to be transformed into the object of Humbert's desire (as we shall see later, Stavrogin also takes advantage of Matryosha only when her mother is out). Humbert can now involve her in a mad dash across America, worried all the time that Lolita might find other possible connections with the world, or any anchorage, and could reveal or denounce their relationship.

Humbert gradually acknowledges the complex and muddled alternation of his roles as tutor and surrogate father—who offers sweets or money, or threatens, when Lolita flees this "fatherly love", to punish her or send her to reform school, and who paradoxically imposes himself as her protector "from all the horrors that happen to little girls in coal sheds and alley ways" (p. 147)—and as a lover of a tender love to be kept secret, since the world, the courts, couldn't really understand the magic.

For Humbert, therefore, the mere thought of Lolita being independent (and not matching his imagined Lolita) instantly becomes a source of sorrow and disillusion. He cannot accept that naïve Lolita has already discovered sex with her peers, is less green than he thinks she is on this subject, and has even already had a paedophile relationship. Likewise, as we shall see later, Stavrogin is frightened when it seems to be Matryosha who takes the initiative in their love gestures. He would like her to be the passive and amazed object of his gestures, like the passive object she was while being beaten by her mother before his complacent eyes.

Swinging between the adult's erotic dependence and the adolescent's wiliness, the novel keeps the role of victim equivocal between the protagonists (Centerwall, 1992). This concept of the child swinging between being seductive and being frightened in the relationship with the paedophile, between the roles of accomplice and of victim, has been explored by psychoanalysis. In this regard, Freud (1896b) argues that the adult in the paedophilic relationship on the one hand cannot escape the mutual dependence which any sexual relationship inevitably implies, and on the other hand has the authority and the right to punish, and alternates between these roles in order to satisfy his uncontrolled desires. We can see this role-swinging in *Lolita*: Nabokov describes in his afterword how one reader (perhaps searching for allegories suitable for giving the scandalous novel a sense more compatible with our culture) described Lolita as "Old Europe debauching young America", while another saw in it "Young America debauching old Europe" (p. 312).

"Hypocritical" paedophilia: Love

The gypsy girl Vesna is the main character in "Love", one of the stories in *For Solo Voice* by Susanna Tamaro (1991). Vesna was ten years old, the youngest of eleven siblings, and had a hare lip. Nobody believed that with her hare lip she would be able to find a husband. Her parents gave her to a trader in exchange for two snow-tyres. She was of no importance to her new parents, and was forced to beg. Their only interest was in seeing her pockets full of money when she came back in the evening. This condition of social decay, fear and resignation is much the same as that imagined by Pierre Louys in Mytilene thousands of years ago, in the epigram about the little rose seller with which this chapter began.

Deprived of any affection, one morning Vesna received money from a gentleman who stroked her hand. She was surprised that he had not laughed at her or walked away after one look at her lip, and held his hand tight in order to keep the warm touch of his fingers. All alone in the evening, after being beaten by her new father and deprived of supper, curled up on the floor, Vesna laid the hand that had been warmed by the stranger's touch on her cheek, and fell asleep protected by that warmth. Several days later the gentleman came back and took her to a flat where he bathed, fed and stroked her and told her that she was very beautiful. Vesna was not used to receiving so much without giving anything back. On her return home a few days later, she was raped by her new father, who seemed to be willing to assert his ownership of her.

Vesna waited a long time for the gentleman, letting the memory of him warm her, as she knew that he would come back. One day the gentleman returned and took her to his flat. In the warmth of the water, while he was bathing her, and while being caressed and caressing herself, Vesna felt a sensation of pleasure which merged with her infinite need to be loved. They spent four days together and told each other of their wish to have a child, a kitten to give milk to forever—Vesna thought—while the man, whom she called *Love*, was holding her. The following weeks, as hard days passed, Vesna still waited for him.

Caught in the act of stealing a wallet to buy a present for the gentleman, Vesna was taken to the police station and left in social care. A medical check detected that she was pregnant, and she was sent back to her parents. Vesna ran away again to see the gentleman in the flat, where she knew he was waiting for her. But nobody opened the door, while his voice resounded in the dark asking his wife and son to ignore the persistent ringing at the door.

The story deals with the subject of seduction, when the paedophile is not a brutal sex attacker, but plays the role of a heart-breaking rescuer. Vesna's need for affection, protection and reassurance after being humiliated and offended by her adopted family was balefully exploited for sexual advantage, which Love took in ways split from his ordinary existence. The paedophilic seduction could have no connection with his life. In fact, after enjoying some extravagant moments with the girl, Love returned to his family's shell, in which there was no room for Vesna, who kept ringing the doorbell in vain.

"Transgressive" paedophilia: Stavrogin

Child suffering is one of the central aspects of Dostoevsky's reflections. In his novel *Demons*, inspired by a terrorist act committed by the anarchist Sergei Nechaev and published in 1872, nearly a century before Nabokov's novel, a story of paedophilia and child abuse is central to the confession of the principal character, Stavrogin. The chapter containing this confession was censored when the novel was first published, due to its content of sadistic pleasure and transgression, and could only be included, as an appendix, in subsequent editions.

Stavrogin met Bishop Tikhon (an Orthodox theologian much admired by Dostoevsky), who was living in retirement in the monastery, and asked him to read the dramatic and desperate passages of his confession. He let Tikhon share in what he considered the central episode of his life.

Stavrogin rented a room from some Russians of the lower middle class, where he used to receive a certain lady who loved him. The landlords lived next door in another room. His room was tidied by their daughter, Matryosha, who was about fourteen and still no more than a child by the looks of her. Her mother loved her, but would often beat her and scream at her dreadfully. One day Stavrogin's penknife disappeared from the table. He told the landlady, not thinking for a moment that she would thrash her daughter in front of him. But she had just been screaming at the child because some rag had disappeared, and she suspected that the girl had swiped it, and even pulled her hair. The child had not taken the knife. When Stavrogin found it on his bed, where it had somehow fallen from the table, it immediately occurred to him not to say anything, so that the girl would be thrashed.

> The girl, after a good cry, became even more silent; but I am convinced that she harboured no angry feelings towards me. However, she most likely felt a certain shame for having been punished in such a manner in my presence. She hadn't screamed but only sobbed as she was being whipped, because, of course, I was standing there and could see everything. But being a child, she probably blamed only herself for her shame. [p. 765]

It was precisely then that Stavrogin was suffering from the disease of indifference and boredom. Only the possibility of experiencing unordinary sensations would have dissuaded him from killing himself due to boredom. He committed a theft in his lodgings, the only theft of his life, something incompatible with his aristocratic status. He used to pick fights, and married a crippled and feeble-minded woman for a bet. One day he saw Matryosha left alone at home.

> I quietly sat down on the floor next to her. She gave a start and at first was incredibly frightened and jumped up. I took her hand and kissed it gently, sat her back down on the bench, and began looking into her eyes. The fact that I had kissed her hand suddenly made her laugh, like a child, but only for a second, because she leaped up a second time, now so frightened that a spasm crossed her face. She looked at me, her eyes staring in terror, and her lips began to twitch, as if she were on the verge of tears, but nevertheless she didn't cry out. I began kissing her hands again, took her on to my knees and kissed her face and feet. When I kissed her feet, she drew away from me, and smiled as if from shame, but with a kind of crooked smile. Her whole face flushed in shame. I kept whispering something to her. Finally, something so strange occurred that I shall never forget it, something that astonished me: the girl threw her arms around my neck and suddenly began kissing me furiously. Her face wore an expression of utter rapture. This struck me as so unpleasant in such a tiny child that I almost got up and left out of pity. But I overcame my sudden feeling of fear and stayed.

> When it was all over, she was embarrassed. I didn't try to reassure her and I stopped caressing her. She looked at me, timidly smiling. Suddenly her face looked stupid to me. She was becoming more and more embarrassed with every passing moment. Finally, she covered her face with her hands and went to stand in the corner with her face to the wall, without moving. I was afraid she would become frightened again, as she had been earlier, and I left the house without saying a word. [p. 767]

He woke up in his own room the next morning. His first thought on awakening was whether she had told anyone or not; this was a moment when he felt genuine fear. A few days later Matryosha fell ill and, delirious, said she had committed an unspeakable crime and a mortal sin—that "she had killed God". Stavrogin went to visit her again:

> Her eyes had grown big and were staring at me with a kind of dull curiosity, or so it seemed to me at first. I was sitting in a corner of the sofa, looking at her and not moving. And then suddenly I felt hatred again. But I very quickly noticed that she had absolutely no fear of me, and perhaps was instead delirious. But she wasn't delirious either. She suddenly began shaking her head rapidly at me, as people do when they are reproaching you in earnest, and suddenly she raised her tiny fist at me and began to threaten me from where she was standing. At first this gesture seemed ridiculous to me, but then I couldn't bear it any longer: I stood up and moved towards her. There was such despair on her face, something unbearable to see on the face of a child. She kept waving her tiny fist at me in a threatening gesture, and kept shaking her head by way of reproach. [p. 770]

Stavrogin then had the thought that the girl had gone out to commit suicide, but did nothing to stop her. He knew that Matryosha, by hanging herself (as he would do at the end of the novel), would give up her relationship with reality in the external world, which she could have rebuilt by pressing charges against him, and would take their secret with her.

The episode of the sexual abuse and consequent suicide of a young girl also occurs in Luchino Visconti's film *La Caduta degli Dei*

(*The Damned*, 1969), which illustrates the vile and perverse immaturity of the scion of an important industrial dynasty, who became a Nazi.

The "ogre" paedophile: Justiniano Duarte da Rosa

Alongside the nineteenth-century intellectual Stavrogin, the early twentieth-century intellectual Aschenbach and the late twentieth-century intellectual Humbert, there is the character of Captain Justiniano Duarte da Rosa, portrayed by Jorge Amado in *Teresa Batista: Home from the Wars* (1972). With the mythical and exaggerated redundancies peculiar to the South American novel, he represents the modern version of the ogre in fairy tales. It is an ogre halfway between myth and reality, who takes his dreadful ringed necklace (each ring symbolising a virgin adolescent) everywhere with him, who looks after his business and travels in a lorry through the countryside looking for young victims.

Justiniano's main objective is to exercise full power over someone: to terrify, dominate and enslave her, to exploit her and then leave her to other men, and so begin to look for a new victim. Who better than a young girl to pursue these objectives?

Justiniano's character reveals a new aspect: there is not just the desire to contravene the fundamental social rules which enlivened Stavrogin (for Justiniano they were already broken *a priori*); nor is it the desire to be a child again (aroused by being with a child) which animated Humbert. In contrast, it is rather an exaggerated search for confirmation of the disproportion between two bodies—the asymmetrical relationship which is the true objective of the paedophile.

Among the innumerable young girls who animated Justiniano's furious night-time duels, only two seemed able to break his perpetual game, the desperate cycle of repetition: they were the two girls whom he accepted enough to drag from the closet of violence to the double bed, and with whom his relationship lasted longer. Only death would allow him to put an end to an endless game.

The first girl was the romantic and aristocratic Doris. She never felt frightened or subjugated by the captain as it had been all love, dream and illusion since she first met him. She was treated like a slave, but never felt that she was a slave, as only illusion and love made her choose her condition of slavery.

The second girl was the savage Teresa: terror and violence had made her a slave but not undermined her pride. With silent and powerless rage, Teresa yielded to Justiniano's threats, as she was aware that her strength was (temporarily) inferior to his, but would never spontaneously offer herself to please the captain. But when her young lover Dan cleverly dared to challenge and deceive Justiniano, he offered her the litmus test to reveal the captain's weakness and vulnerability, thus giving her the opportunity to escape his abuse of power and violence and free herself, her pride having remained uncontaminated, by killing her oppressor.

Doris's blind love and Teresa's hatred hotter than a fire or a whip are emotions which are far removed from fear and obedience; they are two different and opposite ways of reacting to violence and nevertheless reasserting their subjectivity. They represent the two obstacles in which the monotonous litanies of the captain's excessive power and the repeated confirmation of his victory become stuck, the second having fatal consequences.

Paedophilia as revenge: "Plenilunio"

In all the cases described so far, what is sought is the sexual act with a child, not murder. Although the sexual act can be followed for one reason or another by the death of the victim (as in the cases of Stavrogin and Justiniano), this does not represent the paedophile's objective. Things are different in the following cases: one in which the killing of the victim can still seem to be aimed mainly at eliminating the witness of a shameful act; and particularly in the second, where the sadistic aspects are even more evident, and rape and murder are really linked together indissolubly to meet one single objective, which is the satisfaction of Gilles de Rais.

Molina's novel *Plenilunio* (1997) begins with the murder of a seven-year-old child, whose body is found in a ditch, brutally marked by attempted sexual violence. The murder of the child represents the nucleus around which the stories of the police inspector and the murderer unfold. The two parallel stories are characterised by fairly different narrative styles, and drag the reader into the world of the leading characters, highlighting the contrast and almost a sense of irretrievable distance between them. Carrying the weight of a complex and painful personal and professional life within him, the inspector wanders the streets of the town devastated by Fatima's death, searching for the criminal, certain that he would recognise him by his eyes:

> Eyes, a face which should have been the mirror of a hidden soul, an empty mirror which reflected nothing, not even remorse or pity, perhaps not even fear of the police ... What drove him was an urge to repair and a passionate resentment which, though nobody could know it, was a clear desire for revenge. [p. 11]

Secret hatred and contempt seem to be the fundamental features of the world of the young murderer, who has never been able to have a sexual relationship with women because he is impotent. The concise and lashing narrative style reflects the rigid monotony of his thoughts: obsessively repetitive, lacking depth, conflict, complexity and sorrow. He felt contempt for his parents, their restricted world, and the poverty from which they had been unable to free themselves. He felt hatred for the hard work he did at the fish market, the strong smell of his hands with which he was obsessed, like a humiliation he was unable to get rid of. He hated his schoolmates who had mocked his small, floppy penis, and the women at whom he smiled and who appeared to stigmatise him for his impotence. Hatred alternated with violent arousal in his imagined aggressions when he met a young girl on the street and followed her into a doorway, lightly touching with his finger the cold blade of a knife. This induced in him a sense of triumphant strength, which weakened for a moment with the accelerating pulsing of a solitary excitation. Again, hatred led him to search for someone against whom he could relieve his need to emerge from impotence through violence and abuse, for the girls from whom he seemed willing to take something he felt he had been deprived of. Locked in his secret world of hostility, resentment and humiliation, and subjected to repetitive violence, unable to think, to feel pain or to hope, he remained caught in his impotence, which he tried to escape. And the inspector's last look at him is also without hope:

> The mediocre quality of the lie, the evidence of comedy filled him with indignation and despondency almost as much as the cold cruelty of the murder. Actually, it is possible he feels neither fear nor guilt, he thought, nor does he try hard to pretend. [p. 301]

Love and death in sadistic paedophilia: Gilles de Rais

Gilles de Rais, a Marshal of France, comrade-in-arms of Joan of Arc, a man with great power and influence, is the leading character in Michel Tournier's historical novel *Gilles et Jeanne* (1983). For him sexual attraction to children and destructive sadism aimed at total annihilation of the object were inseparable, and so the search for sexual satisfaction was inseparably linked with the other's death.

When Joan of Arc died, Gilles de Rais began to look for her face in all the children he came across, and, not finding her perfection in any of them, he impaled, burned and devoured them. According to Ernesto Ferrero (1998), Gilles represented the archetype of the myth of Bluebeard, killer of his wives: a myth moulded by people's attempt to mitigate the doubly disturbing aspect of the story by replacing the child with the young woman. This is also the myth of the "Monster of Düsseldorf", whose final confession seems to recall Gilles de Rais's late conversion during his trial a few days before his execution.

In Ferrero's reconstruction, this Bluebeard's victims were hundreds of young boys and girls he came across, most of them from poor social backgrounds. Attracted to power and wealth, they were abducted into his castles at a time when famine reigned supreme. The only exceptions were children who were suitable candidates for becoming little choristers: they escaped his violence because they were able to offer their lord enjoyment through singing.

As we mentioned earlier, in the early 1980s Michel Tournier attempted to revisit the character of Gilles de Rais. Tournier seems to link the beginning of Gilles's crimes to Joan of Arc's death at the stake, and thus alters the historical reality of the character by overestimating the importance of his encounter with Joan of Arc and of the nightmare represented by her martyrdom in Rouen. He repeatedly insists that Gilles is both child and adult: when he calls him a "giant with a child's heart", and when he assumes that between the moment of arrogance and that of regret during the trial, he went through a phase in which he was "at the same time brutal and childish, willing to clutch at anyone he considered able to help and rescue him".

Gilles is an example of paedophile perversity different from those considered earlier, as his disturbance consists not just of a deviation concerning the object of his sexual urge (diverted from the adult partner to the child), which characterises paedophile perversion.

What contributes to the disturbance are the ways in which the urge expresses itself, which belong to the diagnostic category of sadism. This is an association which is certainly not hard to find—and has recently recurred in the tragic news stories reported by Ponti and Fornari (1995) in a study presented to the press—but this must obviously be distinguished from paedophilia as it shows a different phenomenology.

The novel *Gilles et Jeanne* has become a sort of bible of paedophilia.

The "victim" paedophile: The Nightingale and Lucrecia

The Nightingale, by his real name Juan José Bernal, is the leading male character in "Wicked Child", one of the stories collected by Isabel Allende in *The Stories of Eva Luna* (1985). Incidentally, we note that Allende seems to allude to an episode from her childhood in which she was herself the victim of a paedophile; this is fully described in her subsequent book *Paula* (1996). We consider this story and the next one last because the cases of paedophilia presented in them represent a reversal of the preceding cases. The plot of "Wicked Child" has in its main structure some similarities with Nabokov's *Lolita*. Elena, a pre-pubescent girl, lived with her mother, who kept a boarding house. Juan José Bernal turned up at the boarding house and made himself out to be an artist, but would subsequently turn out to be an idler. In this case, though, it was the child who fell in love with an adult and mimicked her mother's behaviour to the point of trying to seduce him while he was asleep, after seeing him making love with her mother. The Nightingale woke up with a start after recognising the child. As a consequence of the scandal the child was sent away to college. The scene tormented Bernal for the rest of his life. He married Elena's mother, but thought about the child constantly, and began to be a fetishist and paedophile. One day, alone with his grown-up stepdaughter, he took the opportunity to confess his love for her. But as far as the grown-up Elena is concerned, Allende sharply notes,

> She had left her childhood far behind, and the pain of that first rejected love was locked in some sealed compartment of her memory. She did not remember any particular Thursday in her past. [p. 25]

Similar to the case of the Nightingale is that of Doña Lucrecia, the leading female character in Mario Vargas Llosa's novel *In Praise of the Stepmother* (1988), and the victim of seduction by her stepson Alfonso. For Elena the game of seducing the adult guest seems to be related to a desire to "act like an adult", to be a "young woman" and behave in the same way as her mother—something not dissimilar to imitating her in all the household and kitchen chores. On the other hand, for Alfonso to look at his stepmother through the bathroom door and then to seduce her with his kisses and accept the erotic games she begins to propose seems rather to be a more complex attempt to participate in the atmosphere of refined and complacent eroticism which characterises the relationship between Lucrecia and his father Rigoberto, and which Alfonso must have been able to perceive. The novel ends with Alfonso's full written confession to his father. As the author seems to make us understand, the confession is neither so innocent nor naïve, whatever the hidden intention: perhaps proudly showing off his success in having finally achieved a place in the erotic games from which he had been excluded by adults; perhaps regaining his father's exclusive care by causing his stepmother to leave; perhaps maintaining the presence of his mother's ghost, as the housemaid Justita assumes; or perhaps a mere desire for play, pique, or transgression, as the cheerful burst at the end of the novel could make us think.

Conclusions

Martorell and Coutanceau (1998b) have noted that as with sexuality between adults, paedophilia can give rise to a wide range of behaviours, from the most naïve *reverie* to the most cruel and vile acts up to and including rape, from homosexuality to bisexuality to exclusive heterosexuality. This brief review of paedophile behaviours described in fiction has shed light on this aspect. We make no claim to be exhaustive, but aim merely to provide examples of a sufficiently large and representative range of attitudes and behaviours.

Moving from shy Aschenbach to impetuous Gilles de Rais, we can see how through the literary sources to which we have referred, and which we have arbitrarily arranged along a sort of gradient suitable for our reading grid, paedophilic behaviour has shown significantly differing features and meanings, though love for a child remains the common defining quality. We shall try to consider these characteristics by referring to a grid represented by four categories, which we believe is necessary to explain how issues of paedophilia can be interpreted as being related to a greater or lesser degree to narcissism—conceived as hyper-valuation of one's own needs and desires, annihilation of the other, and inability to distinguish between his or her reality and our internal image of him or her. The four categories are: (a) paedophilia between desire and act; (b) the presence of the other as a subject of rights and emotions in the paedophilic scenario; (c) the peculiarity or serial nature of the paedophilic act; and (d) the degree of commixture of the paedophilic choice of object and the relational sadistic and destructive modalities which correspond to Bornemann's paedosadism.

In the case of Aschenbach, paedophilia is a feeling that is sufficiently gratified by the vision of the love object, whom he does not even dare to touch. The distinction between the self and the other is in this case clear and unquestioned, and contact is transposed through sublimation into the transitional area represented by dream and fantasy. Martorell and Coutanceau (1998b), referring to observations made by Krafft-Ebing, describe such individuals as inhibited paedophiles, ethical paedophiles, well socialised paedophiles: in other words, people who are able to adopt more appropriate and safe solutions in order to preserve both themselves and the victim. In *Death in Venice* there is a single love object, exclusively represented by Tadzio, and the inextricable relationship between paedophilia and violence and death is just foreshadowed in the image of Jasciu and Tadzio jerkily fighting at the end of the story. In this image we may suppose that we are seeing Aschenbach splitting and projecting the violent and destructive instincts indissolubly linked with his paedophilia onto Jasciu.

In all the subsequent cases the paedophile behaviour is put into action. Hadrian acts on his paedophile love: not only is he Emperor of the Romans, but he is also emperor of the relationship he has built with Antinous, the attractive greyhound whose desires and needs are annihilated in the relationship. However, for Hadrian Antinous is still an individual: their relationship does not contain sadistic and deliberately destructive aspects, like in the first case.

In Humbert we can see the paedophile's transition from an initial phase of love which we could describe as platonic to a second phase triggered by the loss of the third element—that of anchorage in reality—represented by the presence of the girl's mother. This is the phase of acted paedophilia, desperately guarded by avoiding the irruption of new third elements who could intervene and break the couple's fragile idyll. Humbert has only one object of acted love: Lolita, who seems to represent for him the archetype of all the nymphets he has dreamt of. When violence explodes between them, it is never an end in itself, but always aimed at maintaining the precarious balance of a relationship which is indeed felt as fragile and impossible, in other words at preventing the girl from running away or (even temporarily) distancing herself from him.

According to the classification of Groth and his collaborators (Groth & Burgess, 1977; Groth & Birnbaum, 1979; Groth, Hobson & Gary, 1982, cited in Martorell & Coutanceau, 1998a), we see in Humbert indecent exposure and not violent behaviour, for the means used are seduction and persuasion, whereas Justinian's acts, as we shall see, certainly belong to the second typology, as the child becomes the object of a desire for control and imposition.

Love's desire to preserve his life as a respectable person compels him to leave the little gypsy girl alone outside his door, not caring what will happen to her. In this case there is nothing to indicate that he is a serial paedophile. Most importantly, there are no links between paedophilia and sadism, not even in the relationship Love has with the child.

In the case of Stravogin, there is a single paedophile act, made possible (as with Humbert) by the temporary absence of the child's mother. The object of the paedophilic act is the child Matryosha, who, by becoming the subject of seduction, at least in the adult's imagination, becomes for him a cause of astonishment and disturbance. The child will later become no more than a sort of reliquary in which an embarrassing secret is kept, an element of encumbrance which he hopes will somehow spontaneously disappear.

The presence of sadistic elements is evident in Stravogin, though not because he lets Matryosha hang herself—this would correspond more to aspects of opportunism and hypocrisy which Dostoevsky leaves the reader to guess on many occasions—but rather because he enjoys seeing her being unfairly beaten by her mother. Another important element evident in the case of Stavrogin is that of social difference (already present in the cases of Hadrian and Love, but without the significance of the former) as a display of the social gap, of the disparity in strength and power that adds to the physical and mental age gap already present between an adult and a child. We shall see the same aspect in two of the following cases.

In the impetuous and arrogant Justiniano, desire and act coincide, and the scruples, moral harm and hypocrisy characterising the first three characters are totally absent. The other does not exist as a subject in his paedophile acts, except for Doris and Teresa, with whom the debasing and repetitive sequence of kidnapped, purchased and raped children somehow jams, as happens with Gilles and the child singers. Violence is no doubt an important component of Justiniano's paedophilia; yet not to the point of taking delight in eliminating the object through her death.

In *Plenilunio* the partner disappears as a subject and becomes merely the means by which a troubled man takes his revenge on fate. The paedophile act is recurrent, but the victim's murder would seem to be aimed rather at hiding the truth than at taking sadistic pleasure, as emerges from the killer's words during his trial.

On the other hand, sexuality and search for death are one and the same in Gilles de Rais, who particularly enjoys possessing his victims during their agony or when their bodies have just become motionless. This shows the greatest disparity in strength between paedophile and victim, and in this and other respects, Gilles shows characteristics similar to Amado's character Justiniano.

Groth and his collaborators distinguish, among paedophilic abusers, between an "angry" type, driven by the need to avenge an offence sustained (or supposed); a "powerful" type, who tends to use excessive and unnecessary violence in order to be absolutely certain of being the master of the situation; and a "sadist" type characterised by erotisation of anger and torture or power. On the basis of this classification we can note that the leading character of *Plenilunio* seems to belong to the first group, Justiniano to the second, and Gilles to the third.

The last two cases are to some extent different from the others in their initial phase, though not in their overall complexity. The adults Bernal and Doña Lucrecia are driven to paedophile behaviour through misunderstanding the meaning of two children's behaviour. The children attract them through a straightforward offer of a sexual relationship; but the real meaning of such a relationship is totally different from adult sexuality, both because it contains a particular element of a child's usual playing at "being an adult" (imitating adult activities and behaviours), and because it hides more complex aspects of secondary profit (such as competition with the widowed mother to gain a place beside the surrogate father, as with Elena and Lolita, or the objectives mentioned in the case of Alfonso).

The complex phenomenology of paedophile behaviours, apart from the lecturer Aschenbach's love at distance, shows us in each case the imposition, whether soft or violent, of adult sexuality on the child. The result, even when the child's response is apparently collusive or seductive, is the transformation of his or her need to be cared for and contained, which is unable to find an appropriate receptor. Sadistic escalation and death lie in wait permanently, even when there is no physical murder; the child's trust in adults is in any case undermined, and the damage to his or her whole emotional world is sometimes irreparable.

Note

1. "La Petite Marchande de Roses" in *Les Chansons de Bilitis*, at http://www.archive.org/stream/leschansonsdebi00lougoog/leschansonsdebi00lougoog_djvu.txt (an English translation by Alvah C. Bessie is at http://www.sacred-texts.com/cla/sob/sob134.htm). Interestingly, there is another version (e.g., at http://www.florilege.free.fr/recueil/louys-les_chansons_de_bilitis.html#130) in which the final section reads: "Cette enfant n'est pas courtisane, Bilitis, nul ne la connaît. Vraiment n'est-ce pas un scandale et tolérerons-nous que ces filles viennent salir dans la journée les lits qui nous attendent le soir?"

CHAPTER EIGHT

The paedophilic relationship

> Those who are violent and abuse their power are guilty not only of the evil they do to their victims but also of the evil induced in them as a consequence of the harm they have suffered.
>
> —Alessandro Manzoni

In "Dostoevsky and Parricide" (1928), Freud numbers the great writer among criminals and immoral people, and describes the perverse instinctual predisposition which must have made him inclined to sadomasochism. Among the reasons that led him to this diagnosis, which include the peculiar moral degradation of his characters and his gambling, Freud cites the probable sexual abuse he perpetrated against a pre-pubescent child (as Dostoevsky himself admitted). Freud reminds us that the issue of the sexual abuse of a young girl also appeared in Stavrogin's confessions in the novel *Demons* and in the incomplete work *The Life Story of a Great Sinner*. Freud sums up the main psychological peculiarities of the Russian writer:

> Dostoevsky's strong destructive instinct, which could easily have made him a criminal, was in his actual life directed

mainly against his own person (inward instead of outward) and thus found expression as masochism and a sense of guilt. Nevertheless, his personality retained sadistic traits in plenty, which show themselves in his irritability, his love of tormenting and his intolerance even towards people he loved, and which appear also in the way in which, as an author, he treats his readers. [p. 2]

The configuration of sadomasochistic perversion within the paedophile's personality is thus already present in Freud's works, although in other works he talks about this picture in different terms.

Far more than in other forms of perversion, we can detect in the paedophile a fundamentalist view of existence and relationships, with the consequent rigid and consistent application of the principles derived from his "ideological doctrine". The paedophile is dogmatically convinced of the rightness and lawfulness of his inclinations, desires and attitudes, and through systematic transgression of the rules, he opposes a society he judges unfair and ethically pervasive, a society which does not allow him to fully enjoy the child and does not allow the child to enjoy an adult's love (Schinaia, 2000).

> Paedophiles ... may feel that the world is a set of sexualised relations, that the children they desire are in turn full of sexual desires, and that it is impossible to forgo this unique source of pleasure. [De Masi, 1999, p. 85]

> The innovative seduction that should be based on qualities such as acknowledgement of the other and thus of gender and generational diversity, and on respect for such diversities, becomes instead fossilised as sexualised narcissistic seduction, which promotes incestuous, ambiguous and at the same time capturing and rejecting relationships. The drive for appropriation mentioned by Freud, which we could describe from a relational point of view as an imperative to possess the object, as appropriation and dominion, or as the imposition of a label, is the foundation of peremptory violence and pressing needs, and does not take into consideration the object as other, with his or her own diversities and particular needs. This violence is also the basis of physical and psychic mistreatment, sexual abuses, and perverse psychic functioning and acts. [Racalbuto, 1999, p. 49]

> One of the effects to which child sexuality is subjected is the paedophilic relationship, which offers the child an opportunity to fill the intolerable emptiness felt as a consequence of not having been "listened to" and not having had his or her pregenital sexual and emotional needs "contained". This relationship tends to be formed through quite precise rules of which secrecy and guilt are important mainstays. Such rules are easily introjected by the child, as they represent the rules shared by the primal reference models. [Lanotte, 1999, p. 74]

Bouchet-Kervella (1996) wonders whether the need to declare the irresistible erotic value a child has for an adult should be considered an attempt to deny and replace the unbearable reverse representation: that of the undesired and undesirable child who must be eliminated, according to a modality sometimes very close to a thinly veiled ghost of infanticide, which Raskovsky (1973) investigated.

Paedophilia implies the magical abolition of generational diversities and denies the value and even the existence of the parental role and function. It adheres totally to a sort of myth of eternal youth, so that the world of relationships is a nirvana of childhood in which the child's body and beauty are idealised and absolutised while adult bodies simply no longer exist either as desiring machines or as objects of desire. It is about a denial of origins, a ghost of self-procreation which leads to difficulty in the separation and differentiation of generations. Racamier (1992) talks about "Anti-Oedipus", meaning that mental configuration which is prior to Oedipus but also against Oedipus and which fights life's essential differences, such as generational and gender diversities (De Simone, 2002).

> The paedophile makes himself a child rather than expecting the child to suddenly become an adult, in order not to be a burden on him and relieve him of any responsibility. [Camarca & Parsi, 2000]

> The paedophile loves his two narcissistic sides and enjoys what he would have liked to be done to him. He is in the child's place, but also in the adult's place, often described as an authoritarian, strict, violent father, a caricature of the father of the primitive horde. He is a tyrannical and sadistic father, who abuses and dominates his children and demands total submission. Actually

the paedophile's father is more likely to be absent or deceased; in any case greatly devalued by the mother ... Identification with this sort of father implies a kind of inversion of values. The father of the horde, the paedophile father, becomes the ideal father. [Szwec, 1993, p. 592]

According to Devereux (cited in Gauthier-Hamon & Téboul, 1988, p. 226) paedophilia can be attributed to fathers' lack of interest in their children, who attempt to compensate for the "absence" of their father with other adult men.

The game of valuation and devaluation of the father in the paedophile's imaginary highlights the fact that actually nobody has taught him how to be a father. We can trace back to paternal absence various constructions on a false-self level of presumed paternal vocations, flaunted across the most varied professions implying stable contacts with children (teachers, educators, members of religious orders, etc). Glasser (1988) describes two cases of paedophilia in which the father's lack of empathy towards his son appears evident. Limentani (1991) also emphasises the centrality of deficiency in (and even absence of) the parental role to cases of paedophilia.

We can detect extreme narcissistic fragility alongside catastrophic anxiety, the shift from feelings of reparation and adoption to feelings of rejection of and disinterest in the child, a superficial compensation gained through resorting to an artificial personality corresponding to an ideal Ego, and constant threats of explosive violence whenever the consistency of the Ego is discussed. The specific imaginary can be formed according to the following characteristic modalities.

In the first scenario, the paedophile wants to be a boy among other boys in a world of games and fantasy: De Masi (1998) describes it as a world of boyishness. A tutor in his forties wrote about his dismissal from a boarding school due to "presumed" episodes of paedophilia: "I love my children and only want to help them express their best qualities ... we belong to the same world ... we are very close to each other. I have a document proving that I am a tutor and was born forty years ago, but I am actually one of them and belong to their world." His identification with the adolescent world does not appear to be weakened by any element of reality.

For the paedophile there is no development beyond adolescence, so that he loses interest in the love object at the moment when the object acquires adult somatic features. The idealised world of Peter Pan, in which children never grow up, seems to be a metaphor for the paedophile's ideal world. Peter Pan passionately explains that he doesn't want to become a man, he wants to remain a child forever and enjoy himself. So he runs away to Kensington Gardens and lives for a long time among the fairies (Barrie, 1906). Peter Pan is convinced that he is a self-made boy and his parental role is redeeming the lost children of humanity (Mancuso, 1997).

For the forty-year-old tutor, kindness and love could only be expressed in the encounter with the children's purity, while all evil was confined to the mean world of adults. This evil was represented by his mother in the past, and thus by the tutors at the boarding school where he was sent as a child and where he was subjected to sexual abuse, and finally by the analyst in the transference.

Thomä and Kächele (1988) describe a case of paedophilia in which it took nine months of meetings in which hypnosis alternated with the use of a recorder before psychoanalytic psychotherapy could begin properly to treat the manifested psychosexual disturbances that had become obsessive. At the beginning of the analysis, the authors explain, the patient was looking for himself in the children. It was a case of love by identification: children attracted him because, at least externally, they were the way he wanted to be as a child—independent, carefree, without bonds or fears (p. 257).

In the second place, we often note that paedophiles declare that they were intelligent, sensitive and privileged children; they enjoyed a wonderful childhood (which they idealise in their narrations), but emerged from it traumatically due to betrayal on the part of their parents or of people in whom they had placed their trust. This betrayal meant that they found it impossible to trust adults and needed to set up a new order by which to organise age, time and relationships. This avoidance of encountering the adult world and idealised escape into the world of childhood indicates the future paedophile's refusal to become the devalued and unconsciously hated adult (De Masi, 1998).

In actual fact, paedophiles were isolated children who felt that they were excluded by other children and envied the vitality of their peers. As adults they can attempt to possess and capture those children like prey, trying to obtain for themselves the vitality and energy which they admired and lacked. Such a vampiric tendency makes the paedophile's drive for children assume positive and ego-attuned characteristics; the paedophile needs the child's vital lymph to counteract "an underlying lethally depressive nucleus" (*ibid*, p. 24) that would drain him and lead to his death.

Principal features of the paedophilic relationship

The paedophilic relationship is asymmetrical. It is the adult who induces or compels the child to become an accomplice. The capacity to create the emotional atmosphere to solicit the child's voluntary participation is considered a real talent of the paedophile.

> Unsupervised by the conscience—because it is not in contact with the conscience—the look of desire is quick, agile and penetrating, ready to catch the nuances and allusions, the signs just mentioned. If this, the game of love, occurs on equal terms between consenting adults who want to discover each other's enigma and bewilderment inside themselves, it turns into tragedy when this dexterity of adult desire meets the undifferentiated desire of a child who only knows welcome and refusal. [Galimberti, 2000a, p. 17]

> The paedophile constructs his own pleasure, even asserts his right to do so, aggravating a hedonistic function which is vital for him, which he cannot give up because he would otherwise lose that "reparative possibility" (noumenon) and "cathartic opportunity" (phenomenal) which tragically mark his "being in the world". [Aguglia & Riolo, 1999, p. 11]

We are astounded by the facility with which a paedophile can access a child's world, his capacity to communicate with and meet, in the phenomenological sense, a non-adult world.

> In the paedophilic meeting an intimate emotional resonance seems to be aroused which is similar with regard to the need for love but fundamentally different with regard to the way of being in a love relationship: directed towards a child and driven by the paedophile's need for sexual satisfaction; directed towards an adult and driven by the child's need for gratification, protection and care. [Lanotte, 1999, p. 72]

The child's complicity following the allurement, which is noted sometimes in paedophilic relationships, must not be mistaken for reciprocity, but must be associated with phenomena of premature adult-like behaviour. These manifest themselves in a certain confusing promiscuity and an exhibited desire to seduce, and are clearly defences against the pain of abandonment and lack of care (De Masi, 1999). De Martis comments:

> In a mature sexual relationship, both in foreplay and in coitus all the aspects, even the most archaic (such as the aspiration for fusion and the cannibalistic elements), are put at the service of an authentic reciprocity, in which giving and receiving pleasure represent the goal of an affectively pacified relationship with the partner ... The opposite occurs in perversion: destructive sexuality is passed off as mystification of a burning pleasure. But the solution remains inevitably narcissistic, autoerotic, impulsive and acted. [1989, p. 283]

Through this perverse seductive game the paedophile catches and distorts the child's temptation to make his fantasies of a magic replacement for his parent come true, burning his developmental stages and making him accede without conflicts to the adult condition. He confirms the child's fantasies by falsifying and debasing them, and hampers the necessary confrontation and vital negotiation with the external world, reifying what is just a ghost. "True reciprocity is a relationship between subjects who inhabit the space of intersubjectivity, the space of encounter, in which the other always and in all circumstances remains other" (Fanali, 1998, p. 140).

The child with whom the paedophile comes into contact has no emotional consistency, which is indeed acknowledged and respected, but he is conceived and constructed as a *homunculus*, a sort of disharmonic miniature adult. The structure of the relational system is closed and self-referential, and within it the ritual of violence and tyranny is consummated, though disguised by seduction. To describe such a relational system Fanali refers to Pier Paolo Pasolini's film *Salò*, at the beginning of which the director

> ... introduces the scenario of the terrible and horrible violence committed by vile representatives of the fascist powers against

> defenceless adolescents. Pasolini frames an arch opposite the villas: it is the hedge surrounding the garden. The hedge represents the border beyond which there is life and this side of which is death ... The adolescents of Salò are tragically destined to die. They cannot get out. [*ibid.*, p. 143]

It is interesting to note that abusers generally choose the most forlorn, the most subdued children, not only because such children are easy to deceive but also because those are the very qualities they find attractive. "This corresponds to the fact that men have difficulties with their male identifications. So we can see ... why most studies show that the age at which children are most at risk is between nine and twelve years" (Balier, 1993, p. 576).

Moreover, we should add that the transition from the pre-pubertal stage to puberty does not necessary imply enough maturity to have a sexual relationship with an adult, especially in a historical context like the modern Western world. Here adolescents, particularly pre-adolescents, do not gain social functions which promote maturity, but stay in a condition of psychological minority sustained and facilitated by the social context. This pushes the point at which emancipation and maturity are achieved increasingly further into the future. We are therefore witnessing an asymmetry which overcomes the mere vital statistics and results in a relationship based always on psychological tyranny and devious seduction.

> Seen from this angle, violence, which clearly is still mainly a direct and brutal physical act, develops as a violation of shared interpersonal rules, as a constriction by the Ego of the *Alter*'s identity (or as a bi-directional constriction), as a disharmonic relationship, and as asymmetric and ineffective communication, often liable to hinder the communication itself, at least temporarily. [Moravia, 1998, p. 20]

The paedophilic relationship is repetitive and monotonous. The repetitiveness, in the absence of substantial symmetry, seems to guarantee the truthfulness of a relationship which would otherwise have no substance. It is not felt by the paedophile (who is the only one not to feel it) due to the excitement which accompanies the compulsion and which, like a drug, turns the same identical ritual into desirable novelty every time.

The predominant feelings aroused when reading the Marquis de Sade's contorted sadomasochistic features are boredom and annoyance rather than disgust, let alone feelings of excitement. Similar feelings are stirred when watching most pornographic films.

The paedophile, who usually manifests signs of hyper-normality and excessive conformism, feels the need to carry out the act as if it came from an urgent inner necessity which compels him to act with rigorous consistency. "His unwritten text consists of only one precept: the compulsion to enjoy. When he 'transgresses', as our common language would have it, he is actually just obeying. In other words, he is not a revolutionary but a model servant, a zealous executive" (André, 1999).

The characteristic of narrow-mindedness in mental cruelty goes hand in hand with the boring monotony of paedophilic behaviour, and also results from the extensive mental space given to perversion because of the extremely intense excitement it produces. This reduces the mental space available for other psychic operations. "In order to avoid conscious guilt, the perceptions of the mind are narrowed to give ostensible justification to the cruelty" (Brenman, 1988, p. 269).

The sexual encounter consists of the slavish repetition of what the paedophile has planned ahead in his mind. There is no room for improvisation or spontaneity, and each sequence of the encounter has to correspond geometrically to the imaginative film the paedophile has already made. The real presence of an Other and the introduction of his or her own needs would risk ruining the plan, which accepts no objection or variation; it would impair a plot already written, thereby compromising the possibility of orgasmic excitement. Like a character in Banana Yoshimoto's *NP* (1990), he is an individual able to start again from the beginning countless times without any fear of making a mistake. We are far from the child's omnipotence that according to Freud sustains the perverse fantasy. We are in the world of obligation and compulsion, one which lacks freedom and creativity.

These aspects of repetitiveness and monotony mean that relapse is always possible in sexual abusers' lives. For the psychologists of the Self, the paedophilic response represents a defensive attempt, always unsatisfactory and hence endlessly repeatable, to make massive use of sexuality to try and counteract the deficient cohesion of the Self.

While Balier (1996) sees in the repetition the search in the outside world of a failed internalisation of the phallus and the seal of the death instinct, Bonnet (1997) cites what Freud wrote in "Remembering, Repeating and Working Through": "We soon perceive that the transference is itself only a piece of repetition, and that the repetition is a transference of the forgotten past" (1914b, p. 151). Saying that the compulsion to repeat is also a piece of transference obviously has important therapeutic implications and reduces the sense of powerlessness that may pervade the analyst. Anna Freud (1964) has also distinguished compulsion to repeat from repetitive working through, a mechanism of the Ego which repeats an experience with variations useful for its assimilation, such as turning a passive experience into an active one.

Lichtenberg (2001) proposes the concept of *model scenes* to identify some interactive modalities that indicate kinds of relationships which are experienced repeatedly but hitherto never "thought about".

> This approach is based on the idea that an important part of our ways of being lacks a corresponding unconscious representation, for instance according to Klein's model of unconscious fantasy. Some ways of being are rooted instead in a sort of fundamental experience characterised by repetition, but this does not correspond to a recalling of interactive and relational modalities, of which the individual has never been aware. [Correale & Neri, 1999, p. 16]

According to the elected model, the repetition may represent the lethal or "not workable through" negative, or the basis of very difficult, yet possible therapeutic work.

As we have seen, even if single paedophilic attitudes or behaviours have nothing to do with sexual criminality, it is possible—in fact frequent—that the asymmetric dominator-dominated, adult-child relationship is subject to an extreme *escalation* and moves towards the ultimate perverse orgasm, which coincides with the pleasure deriving from the power of killing (De Masi, 1998). The escalation is related to addiction, which causes a rise in the threshold of pleasure (De Masi, 1999).

The persuasive and conciliatory modalities prevailing in the period which precedes violence are replaced by modalities of relationship in which psychological violence plays a central role, since the paedophile fears that the game unfolding in the half-light may be illuminated and appear on the surface, thus becoming reality. This is a cause of anxiety for the paedophile, who fears that reality may burst onto the scene built by his imaginary constructs (Aguglia & Riolo, 1999).

This perverse escalation, which from a situation in which an erotic game is apparently under control may lead right up to death, is described in Simona Vinci's novel *What We Don't Know About Children* (1997). Here the erotic games of a group of children, guided by a sadistic adolescent, end in the death of a young girl, after they have violently (though unaware of their violence) sodomised her with the handle of a tennis racket. The children find it difficult to get in touch with their anxieties; they also find it impossible to feel any sense of responsibility, and thus to become aware of their involvement in the development of the successive phases that determined the perverse escalation of the game. This is expressed in their automatic decision to bury the victim, thereby erasing and denying not only the murder but also all the steps that led to the child's death, as they are unable to elaborate them.

A piece of research using a sample of 91 individuals shows that eight percent of paedophiles kill or attempt to kill a child while or after physically abusing him or her (Aguglia & Riolo, 1999). The link between paedophilia and death, emphasising the complete power adults have over adolescents they consider beautiful and highly desirable (but inferior), is one of the fundamental topics in the Polish author Witold Gombrowicz's novel *Pornography* (1960):

> We, Frederick and I, two middle-aged gentlemen, see a young couple, a girl and a boy, who seem to be made for each other, welded to each other with a striking and reciprocal sex appeal. But as far as they are concerned, they might not even have noticed it: it is drowned, we might say, in their youthful incapacity for fulfilment (the inexperience peculiar to their age). We, the older ones, are excited by it; we would like the charm to take

shape. And, with due precautions, and keeping up appearances, we start to help them. But our efforts lead us nowhere, they founder in that sphere of pre-reality where they reside and which characterises them—in that antechamber of their existence. [p. ix]

Frederick and Witold seem to set up a theatre of intrigues as they are in love with the boy's youth.

The smoke that rises from this magic enclosure intoxicates us more and more and, exasperated by the indifference of the two children, it occurs to us that failing physical possession, sin, a common sin, can tie them together and—oh joy!—can tie *us* to *them*, like accomplices, despite the age difference ... We, the adults, weighed down by our awareness and our seriousness, know what death is. But someone light will accomplish it lightly—and we entrust this murder to the boy. In his hands it will become juvenile ... Frederick organises this youthful crime by drawing the girl into it. Thus it will become the common sin, mature and young, which will bind us together. [p. x]

The adults are intelligent, turbid, lascivious, and hold power; the adolescents represent innocence corrupted by seduction and swept along to the ultimate consequences. "It emerges indeed that neither the adults nor the children are dominators; it seems rather that slavery is reciprocal, even in the asymmetry" (Iaria, 1999). They are all in a state of excitement, whose highest expression is the pleasure of the murder, which represents the peak of the sadomasochistic relationship and desperately tries to keep the anxiety of death at bay.

The role of the eyes

As Fenichel reminds us (1945), Freud associated voyeuristic tendencies with a fixation on the primal scene, in which the child witnesses the parents' sexual relationship. This premature traumatic experience could stimulate castration anxiety and drive the child, when he reaches adulthood, to put the scene into practice repeatedly in an attempt to actively overcome a trauma he experienced passively.

We can imagine a muddle of desire for fusion, allurement and fear of destruction, which well justifies Bion's expression "unnamed terror". The different psychoanalytic schools essentially converge on the importance of these early events, whether a Kleinian or a Winnicottian, a Mahlerian or a Bionian perspective is privileged. Variously defined aspects are at play in the processes of separation-individuation and splitting-idealisation, in which the gender difference starts to be conceived. [De Martis, 1989, p. 273]

It is the imagination that accounts for the central role of the visual function in the construction of the perverse scene and for the importance of the aesthetic-voyeuristic component of the resulting pleasure. Looking as a way of capturing and incorporating the other, being looked at or wounding the other's look in exhibitionism, and the excited concentration on the sexual organs in pornography—all these form part of the imaginary scenery indispensable to perversion. [De Masi, 1999 pp. 78–79]

In all of Balthus's paintings we can read erotic allusions, see half-open eyes and swirling dresses on adolescents' radiant bodies—the greatest and sacral expressions of beauty. The painter, however, unashamedly denies that his works have any erotic content, even those in which the expression of paedophilic feelings is more evident and the representations of girls with prematurely hairless pubes, intent on listening to a sexual desire that they cannot control, are more morbid.

In Balthus's paintings we can see "glowering girls, the exaggerated exhibitionism of their genital parts and breasts, their sharp shoulders on bad terms with the world, their arms in perverse attitudes, a fearful loneliness, and the excessive separation of the childhood and adult world" (Almansi, 1990, p. 131). Balthus suggests a third way between being and nothing: the *possible*. A metaphysical anxiety emerges from his images of adolescents who are no longer children but not yet adults, "who dwell in that fragile space in which everything is at stake, and all of life's possibilities are still formulated in terms of desires, before blooming in pleasure and life itself" (Tasset, 1996, p. 17). The painting *Guitar Lesson* (1934) certainly has a meaning of turbid perversion. It is the representation of a teacher using her young girl pupil as an erotic object, though the painting is based on a figurative scheme on which the theme of the *Pietà* (the Madonna holding her dead son on her lap) also draws. Balthus "uses as a setting of psychological analysis the nymphets, the turbid ten- to twelve-year-old girls who are at once more provocative and less aware of what provocation means" (Almansi, 1990, p. 131).

The repeated presence of the theme of naïve and sensually blossoming adolescents in Balthus's paintings allows us to focus our attention on the accepted forms—being artistically significant—of an adult's narcissistically seductive eyes. Caravaggio also gave us a clear demonstration of the subliminal capacity of paedophilic eyes, transposing the sensuality of the adult eye's gaze into the provocative sensuality of his painted children's eyes and movements. In Caravaggio's paintings "the antithesis between tradition and revolution (rule and subversion) overcomes the hierarchy of the genres which is tied to contents and subjects (there is no genre painting in Caravaggio)" (Marini, 1981, p. 361).

Caravaggio chooses the social moment of the performance, also because of his requirements of sacred iconography. Between compliance and deviation, children's sensuality is highly eroticised and their scandalously seductive intentionality is evident on their faces, as we can see in the famous painting *The Musicians*, a juvenile work. According to Baglione (1642), a biographer of the painter, the figures are the portraits of naked young models. The art historian Czobor (1954) saw in the lute player the Maestro's idealised self-portrait.

"A ruling neo-feudal class locked in a strong ideological self-awareness and attentive to the cultural meaning of sacred and profane images would strictly have banned all Caravaggio's paintings. But instead the leading galleries like, appreciate and demand his paintings for their novelty and quality—of image, not of contemplated drawing up" (Conti, 1979, p. 222). The success enjoyed by Caravaggio's works, and nowadays by those of Balthus, can be understood not only in reference to their undeniable pictorial qualities, but also by acknowledging that their aesthetic transposition allows for the representation of feelings and desires which, though dwelling in the human mind, could not otherwise have been conveyed due to their ambiguous rarefaction and disturbing ineffability.

While paedophilia as an acted tendency is present in a significant and active "silent minority", paedophilia as a non-acted tendency is highly entangled with the dominant sexual imaginary which also contemplates the erotic appropriation of the infantile body, and certainly involves a larger proportion of the population (Foti & Roccia, 1994b). While an artistic representation of the perverse gaze makes also for unthinkable possibilities of identification and, by sounding out the depth of the human mind, avoids Manichean distinctions between normal and pathological, it cannot and should not become an instrument of propaganda for perversion, since it would probably betray the author's conscious and unconscious intention by ascribing connotations extraneous to him and arbitrarily assigning him to a "movement". According to Camarca, "there is no masterpiece able to equal the unique importance of a human life. There is no book, no sculpture, no scientific discovery which can be conceived in a child's viscera" (Camarca & Parsi, 2000, p. 40).

There often emerges from the stories of paedophiles a tendency to take and collect photographs of children, or to video them with very sophisticated technical equipment, not only in order to distribute pornographic images (which incidentally are highly sought after, including on the Internet), but as a way of adding to the paedophilic excitement.

> The paedophile gulps down as many photos as possible in a bulimic way. I am talking about individuals able to collect something like 100–150,000 images of brutalised children. These images are religiously placed in files scrupulously prepared, divided in alphabetical order and according to subject, place of origin, age and personal details of victims. [*ibid.*, p. 81]

It is the technical equipment itself that encourages voyeurism. Servadio reminds us that "staring at the object of the photograph, catching him or her in the best pose and at the best moment, incorporating the image inside the camera, and finally feeling that he or she is captured, imprisoned … all these feelings and acts are indisputably voyeuristic" (1967, p. 64).

Photography and children have long been technically incompatible due to the child's incapacity to stay still and maintain a pose. The surviving daguerreotypes of infants show us contracted, rigid, mummified young children probably told off, sometimes threatened in order to make them mild objects at the photographer's disposal.

The history of photography reveals that a child does not look right just as it is, according to Amodeo:

> A child needs to be disguised as a miniature adult with all the characteristics of elegance, either as Cupid or as a fairy. If one takes a picture of a child as it is, this is for other purposes: to convey one's social sensitivity (what is more shareable than a complaint about child abuse?) as in the case of Hine, or to stir up a debate through pictures of an unhappy childhood, as Riis did most rigorously, or ultimately to practise some cheap representation of reality using sketches, of which Cartier-Bresson has left the best examples. [1981]

Though in extremely provocative words, Amodeo expresses his concern that the photographed child is used and abused by the adult gaze. He stresses that innocence is absent from the history of the photographed child, and that educated photography is full of children who are all alien, foreign, masked, disguised and transfigured beings.

You only have to look at the apparently innocent photographs of Lewis Carroll (the pseudonym of the mathematician and writer Charles Dodgson, author of *Alice in Wonderland*) to realise that those images do not really belong to the young girls, but are both artistic and abusive voyeuristic transmutations of natural and spontaneous postures into seductive and knowing poses through an excited and perverse gaze.

The morbidity with which partly uncovered areas of the body are represented recalls Proust's perverse excitement when he describes, in a manner which is aesthetic and refined to the point of exhaustion, the sensuality of the ankles of Balbec's cyclists. Carroll fills countless plates with apparently acquiescent seduction, but it appears to be a falsification of reality, as he projects his sensual hyperaesthesia into the children (Gernsheim, 1949; Almansi, 1974; Cohen, 1979).

One of the early historical examples of pornographic photography is the nudes of Wilhelm von Gloeden (1856–1931) in Taormina. "In the Sicilian countryside, on the seashore, on terraces and courtyards, von Gloeden stages with the local children his dream of an ideal Homeric-Arcadian life" (von Taschizki, 1997). The adolescents posed in ancient Greek style (Falzone del Barbarò, Miroglia & Mussa, 1980) display facial expressions I would describe as "pre-Pasolinian", and their mask reveals a proletarian malice that hides fear and need. According to Hochkofler:

> When they look into the camera, they do it with an innocence not unaware of sensuality. The young people's innocence seems to be combined not with the experience of sin or guilt, which are alien to the author's eyes, but with the natural experience of sex. [2001, p. 13]

An analysis of these photographs which is based less on their artistic merit allows us to appreciate instead the heavy intervention of the photographer, who transforms the bodies into mannequins, the passive and interested condescendence into exhibitionist play, the ill-concealed shame of a condition so far removed from their cultural reality into the rarefied sharing of the paedophilic gaze. In the 1930s, after von Gloeden's death, most of his negatives on glass plates and his photos were destroyed by Fascists, who considered his nudes indecent. The re-evaluation of Wilhelm von Gloeden as one of the best nude photographers of the twentieth century dates back to the late 1960s (von Taschizki, 1997).

In Sally Mann's photographic volume *Immediate Family* (1992) we can encounter the paedophilic gaze of our own times: not the gaze described as pathological and morally censured on several levels, but the attractive, creative, and uninhibited gaze of a famous female photographer who photographs her own children, two girls and a boy, naked and in the most original and exciting poses. This book is intended to be an amusing game in which children are disguised as adults and assume the seductive poses we can see in advertisements or fashion magazines, in which the naked body is exhibited as a consumer object as well as a model of ideal beauty.

The outcome of this operation (artistic or commercial?) seems to be the creation of a perverse story in images in which the indecent display of the children's bodies and their improbable winking are clearly eroticised by the maternal gaze which seeks to conceal their poses with naïve sensuality; this is immediately felt by the reader to be inauthentic. If Sally Mann intended to play with her children's bodies, she was successful: she exposed their smooth delicacy, natural grimaces and immature intimacy to transformation and debasement into consumer objects, if only visual ones.

The difference between these images and the seductive poses portrayed in Greuze's paintings is enormous. Jean-Baptiste Greuze (1725–1805), an eighteenth-century French painter and a forerunner of Fragonard, produced genre paintings in which he depicted, with apparent innocence, scenes of everyday domestic life which seem to be snapshots of a family's real life, in a kind of realistic descriptivism. Whatever excuse the title expressed—innocence, malice, fidelity or, more openly, passion—he never missed an opportunity to display a round shoulder and often a breast through a shirt (Thuillier, 1964). In one of his most famous paintings, Greuze depicted the scene of a father reading from the Bible to his children, and highlighted the girl's malice through an uncovered breast—seductive nudity barely glimpsed—and her eyes turned to the sky, melancholically languid and unequivocally seductive.

While in Sally Mann's volume of photographs the communicative register is that of collusive pseudo-freedom, the complacent exhibitionism of her own perversions through the seductive display of her children's sensual nudity, in Greuze's painting there are more communicative registers, which refer to the complexity of relationships within the incestuous family. The painter's intentions—irritatingly and visibly judging and moralising (Thuillier, 1964)—are falsified by his young daughter's seductive winking, and the final outcome is not the evocation in the viewer of emotion and complacency regarding the religiosity which apparently pervades the family picture. In contrast, feelings of irritation are aroused by the inextricable co-presence of moving, didactic and seductive intentions.

While in Greuze's painting we can see behind the spectacles of the Bible reader the paedophile father whose gaze makes his daughter seductive, Sally Mann's photos nullify the complexity of the emotional and communicative movements that can come into play in the creation of the incestuous family, and make everything simple, evident and plain, without any *chiaroscuro*, just as sexuality seems to be advertised nowadays and, more importantly, just as it seems to occur in the paedophile's mind.

The relationship with the paedophile

It has been found that in the histories of paedophiles there are serious dysfunctions of the parental couple, family secrets censored to a greater or lesser extent, and disturbed early relationships. Paedophiles have often been subjected to traumas or child sexual abuse, and have become abusers in their turn.

Important roles are played in the trauma by the age of the child, the parameters of the abuse (frequency, duration, form of abuse), the psychobiological aspects of the personality (excitability, sensitivity to pleasure and pain), the quality of the external environment (for instance, whether it is possible to talk about it), and the modality of the aggression. A real trauma is one which cannot be turned into a psychic and symbolic experience, and for this reason it must be distinguished from traumatic situations that can be experienced later on in childhood and can be present in the patient's consciousness and autobiographical narration.

The essence of the trauma is the fact that the Ego is "put out of action": faced with an accumulation of both internal and external excitement, the Ego experiences a condition of powerlessness, becoming the central victim of the traumatic episode. If traumatic experiences have to be endured at a premature stage of the young child's life, his or her task of building up a barrier to stimuli and organised defences is made immeasurably more difficult, and maturation and development are likely to be distorted or even hindered, "just as the supporting walls of a house are more liable to damage during building operations than after completion" (A. Freud, 1964, p. 225).

Lopez (1997) states that in more than 50 per cent of cases the child victim in turn becomes an abuser; other statistics indicate approximately 80 per cent. In any case, most researchers have found that the abuser was himself a victim of abuse during his childhood (Stoller, 1975; Miller, 1979; Groth, 1979; de Young, 1982; Byng-Hall & Stevenson-Hinde, 1991; Dobash et al., 1993; Foti & Roccia, 1994b). By gaining access to the boy's sexual life, the abuser destroys the whole phantasmal process which, on the borderline between unconscious and preconscious, should have allowed the internal object to form during development (Balier, 1996), and deprives the boy of the psychic space within which the oedipal desires can be played out.

Gabbard (1997) points out that the most important technical problem arising during the analysis of patients bringing stories of child abuse is a lack of what Winnicott calls "potential space" and Ogden (1994) calls "analytical space" for reflection, and such a collapse fosters concreteness and a penchant for acting out. What Bollas (1989) described as the emotional nucleus of the incestuous trauma re-activates in analysis: beside her innocence, the young girl loses her capacity for imagination and her trust in the world. Abused patients reveal an excessive transferential concreteness and an incapacity to maintain a reflective psychoanalytic space, from which a penchant for enactment derives. This phenomenon indicates the traumatised patients' incapacity to think about themselves and about relationships in an articulate and reflective way, a feature that is also present in borderline patients.

> These patients lack the capacity to work through the trauma during the psychoanalytic treatment. They have a compulsion for repetitive acting but are unable to nourish representative and metaphorical thoughts about the traumatic event and situation, as the traumatic aspects can neither be reabsorbed by the psychic apparatus nor reformulated and given new meanings. [Zerbi Schwartz, 1998, p. 537]

The theory of the intergenerational transmission of child sexual abuse also receives significant contributions from attachment theory, which shows that maltreated children often manifest unusual attachment patterns, such as the "disorganised-disorientated" type D model which results from the experience of a relationship with a caregiver of a threatening and/or terrifying type (Simonelli & Petruccelli, 1999).

The abuse suffered by the child alters his internal operative models of relationships and corresponding internalisations so much that the regulation of emotions and behaviour is severely impaired, triggering off the intergenerational cycle of abuse. An inversion of roles occurs, in which the victim will turn into a torturer in order to feel less helpless in the face of the pain and passivity he experienced when he was abused, and to better tolerate the cognitive dissonance resulting from his inability to find adequate answers and causal attributions (Main & Goldwyn, 1984). The "disorganised-disorientated" behaviour is a sign of the collapse of behavioural and attentive strategies, and is linked to a major predisposition to dissociative disturbances, and to behaviours similar to the self-hypnosis induced by repeated exposure to the paradoxical situation that leads to states similar to trance (Main, 1987).

Obviously, while these remarks relate to most traumatised people, they cannot be generalised. In fact, attachment theorists, led by Fonagy (Fonagy, Steele, Moran & Higgit, 1991; Fonagy, 1993; Fonagy & Target, 1996; Fonagy, in Zerbi Schwartz, 2000), underline how even in cases of severe trauma in childhood the reflective and meta-cognition function can be preserved. This function is the individual's capacity to represent the nature of his or her own mental states and those of others (which in turn depends on the mother's capacity to represent her child's mental state) and to make sense of his or her own behaviour and that of others. A good use of the reflective function allows one to overcome the consequences of trauma, making sense of the abusive behaviour and so avoiding the reproduction of violent behaviours.

The importance of maintaining a good enough reflective function could explain why many patients who have been subjected to sexual abuse in their childhood do not in turn become abusers as adults, and are able to develop acceptable parental qualities. The experience of two minds working together in the psychoanalytic relationship may be able to provide the reflective function that has been actively damaged in order to enable the patient to handle the traumatic experience. These remarks on the analysis of people who were subjected to sexual abuse as children can also be applied (with the inclusion of a high degree of rigidity and fixity) to paedophiles in need of psychotherapeutic treatment.

We can note that the major emotional obtuseness present in sexual abusers is often linked to a complete absence of memory both of the trauma actively perpetrated in the recent past and of the trauma passively suffered in the remote past. The shadow of the trauma seems to enshroud not only the traumatised object but also the traumatising subject, in some sense recalling the historical trauma. In both cases, although the positions of the abused and the abuser remain non-superimposable, once the trauma has taken place, it induces a transformation which is very often irreparable. Acknowledging the importance of remote traumas—whether isolated or cumulative—and their close interrelation in the development of the paedophilic personality can allow us to create and maintain a setting in which patience and confidence in the importance of the containing experience can be a generator of desirable changes, rather than feeling defeated before even starting.

According to Camarca and Parsi (2000), sexual abuse suffered in childhood is "a fable, a lie used by paedophiles themselves as an alibi, a pathetic justification before the media and those who will judge them" (p. 28). By claiming that the paedophile was a victim in his childhood we run the risk of condemning the child victims beforehand for offences they will never commit. "So the paedophile wins twice. He rapes and then dirties them" (*ibid.*, p. 32). De Masi (1999) reminds us that the trauma is often untraceable, and when it is present, its direct connection with perversion is not directly provable.

I believe that instead of seeking the trauma—understood as an unexpected and occasional external event (whether directly violent or subtle) which is impossible to elaborate psychically and symbolically and interrupts the subject's existential storyline—we need to seek the traumatic micro-fractures, the events that day by day can lead to situations which are impossible to elaborate, and analyse the reciprocal internal and external influences of these phenomena.

Although I am aware that an extension of the concept of trauma may make the pathogenetic meaning of a traumatic situation imprecise and confusing, I believe that we should not stick to the old conceptual formulations. It is worth distinguishing severe trauma, which could cause anybody temporary or permanent traumatic consequences, from minor traumas (Semi, 1989). We need to think, however, of a balance between the subjective psychic experience, which determines the major or minor intensity of a trauma in relation to a certain event (Sandler, 1967), and the presence of detectable traumas whose traumatic consequences can be neither overcome nor ignored, as is the case with many minor traumas (Semi, 1989).

The apparent lack of connection between trauma and perversion can be explained by conceiving the traumatic macro-event as a modality to condense and make evident micro-traumas experienced in the earliest relationships, which would otherwise not be able to find a significant representation, internal or external. Studies in neuroscience also reveal the impact of a traumatic atmosphere and the consequences of early trauma on the behaviour and relationships of children and adults. According to Bessel van der Kolk,

The earliest and possibly most damaging psychological trauma is the loss of a secure base ... A rapidly expanding body of human research is showing that disturbances of childhood attachment bonds may have lifelong psychobiological consequences. There may be particularly vulnerable stages of development related to maturational processes in the central nervous system ... Children exposed to disruptions of attachment to their primary caregivers through separation, abuse or neglect often develop extreme reactivity to internal and external stimulation; that is, they overreact to subsequent situations and have trouble modulating anxiety and aggression, both against others and against themselves. [1987, pp. 32–33, 64]

Nemeroff (1999) sums up and comments on the importance of studies which record an increasing volume of data relating to the long-term neurological consequences of negative life events, such as child abuse or abandonment, or loss of parents. These alterations seem to increase the child's vulnerability to some serious psychiatric disturbances, such as affective and anxiety disorders. A case control study led by Agid and others provides further evidence of such correlations, thus supporting Freud's theories about the consequences of early trauma on health and mental disturbances (Laks Eizirik, 2000).

The enactments can be experienced and interpreted not just as attack, but in some cases as the only possible means of communication for patients who do not have the emotional and communicative resources to represent traumatic events that cannot be elaborated. When the analyst is led by the patient to the sites of the trauma through the language possible at that moment, he or she must not only respond to a request to share emotionally the experience of finding it impossible to think and represent—which is an absolutely necessary experience, indeed the *sine qua non* of the meeting—but, more importantly, he or she must confirm his or her own stable presence. The psychoanalytic experience can thereby become usefully vicarious and can actively supply psychic energy, associative richness, and a structuring experience.

In *Fear of Breakdown* (1974), Winnicott talked about the importance of being able to experience in the psychoanalytic relationship what could not be experienced when it happened. The analyst's refusal to revisit and retrace together with the patient the events of the violence suffered can obstruct the elaboration of feelings of punishment, anger and guilt linked to the trauma (Malacrea & Vassalli, 1990).

> The countertransference *enactments* are the ways in which the patient can create in the psychoanalytic relationship a scenario in which the analyst is led to play a role that is part of his internal world. If these countertransference *enactments* are an inevitable part of the psychoanalytic process with these patients, the evolutionary value of the analysis is not in the fact that the analyst comes to play this role (*enactment*), but in the observations and understanding following them. [Zerbi Schwartz, 2000]

An emotional attitude on the part of the analyst which tends to belittle the devastating sense of the trauma to which the patient has been subjected has to do with his or her difficulty in identifying with a changing individual, with an envious attitude and unconscious destructive rivalry prevailing, as the myths of Cronus and Laius seem to recall. We also need to consider the peculiar condition of vulnerability in which the patient finds himself at the moment when, setting off on a complex therapeutic journey, he comes to experience (though in a "protective" setting) conditions that take him back to those which triggered the traumatic experience, even at the risk of reproducing its effects.

The analyst is also a source of trauma, in that he makes himself available to assume those aspects of characters coming from the patient's internal world which have made the organisation of a pathological personality necessary (Mancuso, 1997). Moreover, if we do not distinguish the aspects of reality, and thus help the patient to distinguish them, we might determine an iatrogenic effect which fosters the conceptualisation of any aspect of reality as fantasy, thus inhibiting the process of knowledge (Laub & Auerhahn, 1993).

The difficulty of elaborating the trauma resides not only in the patient's emotional problems, but also in difficulties related to the analyst's unconscious fantasies. The analyst is involved in his patient's world, he breathes his ideologies and contradictions; for this reason he may not be able to provide the psychic distance and time necessary to recognise what is similar and what is different.

The analyst's identification with the paedophile's victim, which we shall describe later on, and his difficulty in establishing the minimum distance needed to develop a therapeutic relationship, can find a reasonable explanation in Puget and Wender's theory of "superimposed worlds" (1982). According to this theory, disturbance caused by the appearance of the expressed content of an event or situation connected with the analyst's everyday life, which belongs to the same world which fostered the traumatic situation, can give rise to real phenomena of observational and countertransference blindness.

Puget (1995) wonders whether the analyst can maintain a life independent of the fact that he lives in a social space. In this regard, I recall Helena Besserman Vianna's (1997) condemnation of the connivance between psychoanalysts and the military dictatorship in Brazil (in underestimating the responsibility of a student member of a Brazilian psychoanalytic society for episodes of torture), and of the subsequent silence of the whole psychoanalytic world.

Furthermore, there are several studies and pieces of research on the psychology of the torturer, such as Fanon's classical study (1961). This highlights not only stress phenomena but also major psychic problems resulting from the traumas suffered and the prolonged relationship with the suffering of others, such as auditory hallucinations projected into the external space and referred to the howls of tortured people. Primo Levi (1986, p. 29) also illuminated the topic of "the grey zone of collaboration by victims of the prison camps", reminding us that victims are ubiquitous. More recently, Françoise Sironi (1999) gave a detailed description of the strategies of violence which come into play in the torturer-victim relationship.

The analyst's involvement in the development of the therapeutic relationship, through the unconscious ethical evaluation of the traumatic event, involves difficult work on his own internal world, and thus on his countertransference, in part independently of his personal analysis. Access to the patient's "non-existent world" can be more or less "traumatic" for the analyst himself (Mancuso, 1997). In some cases the extreme conditions of the relationship with the paedophile can reactivate conflicts in the analyst that he believed had been fully elaborated, or can arouse conflicting situations that had not received the necessary prompting to be detected during his personal analysis.

It is absolutely vital for the analyst to use his self-analytical capacities as much as he can. If necessary, especially in cases of extreme suffering, he will need to return to the experience of a personal analysis; in any case, he will need to draw on the experience of supervision and exchange opinions with expert colleagues, possibly in groups for specific reflections.

All these complex operations could turn out to be useless if we came to create a situation similar to that in some American states, where specific laws require the analyst to breach professional confidentiality if paedophilic activity is discovered during treatment. "Only if the analyst does not feel that the ethical rigour of professional confidentiality is threatened can he make the choice between the need for support and the need for control, even in such peculiar cases" (Berti et al., 1999, p. 232). While juridical thinking in USA has already made analysts and psychoanalysts *New Informants*, in the dramatic words of Bollas and Sundelson (1995), we are also witnessing the first signs of change in the Italian juridical system. "We live in a more and more global (or globalised) society, which has long been following, with substantial consensus, a clearly Anglo-American inspired matrix" (Marzi, 2002).

The first phases of the therapeutic relationship are usually characterised by a high degree of wariness and distrust, something like the way drug addicts seek a kind of excited autarchy and avoid becoming dependent on a human being, although they try to find in the outside world a form of support which can ensure their existential continuity. Reticence and trivialisation or minimisation of paedophile behaviours are trademarks of the earliest communications, almost as if the patient were facing a police interrogation. The analyst is experienced as a figure to be feared, able to impose his own view of the world and thus to dissolve the interiority and principles on which the patient's behaviours are based. This recalls Peter Pan's words when he stresses that he does not want to go to school and learn solemn things, and nobody will take him and make him a man (Barrie, 1906).

The analyst is deprecated and accused of inability to understand. His sentences are demolished, his words isolated, and the sense of his speech is grossly distorted. The deprecation and mockery of the analyst are followed by the patient's attempt to destroy any interpretation, which he feels is intrusive and probably connects with his early experiences of intrusion. The patient may manifest scornfully transgressive behaviours, and the violence variously acted against the object he has systematically debased may take shape. The paedophile is transformed from a victim of misunderstanding into an obstinate critic of the analyst's mistakes.

The emotional and technical problems the analyst must immediately tackle are considerable. Already overloaded with his negative ethical and cultural attitude towards the paedophile, when he is attacked and feels that his capacity to think is at risk of being destroyed, he feels increasing irritation, distrust, powerlessness and, if the climate of the relationship becomes more agitated, even fear.

The risk in the early phases is that of returning the aggressiveness to the patient together with ill-concealed contempt, thus perpetuating the mutually aggressive communication and risking the intensification of the sadomasochistic vicious circle (De Masi, 1994). The analyst also runs the risk of assuming pseudo-consolatory attitudes which mystify the reality of the complex relationship and thus appear inauthentic and out of place, and lead to an increase rather than a reduction in the patient's capacity to act out. Even Winnicott, who was the first to draw attention to the centrality of the analyst's involvement in the patient's aggression and his capacity to cope with this aggression, was unable to put his recommendations into practice (Hoffman, 1998, quoted in Zerbi Schwartz, 2000).

Gabbard has highlighted some relational features of the paedophile patient during his hospitalisation. He states that the patient's denial of his perversion may lead staff members to collude with him by focusing on other problems.

> In general, patients with paraphilias will object to discussing their problems in group meetings or community meetings on an inpatient unit. However, when staff members comply with requests to avoid sexual issues in treatment meetings, they are colluding with the patient's tendency to go through an entire hospitalisation without dealing with the perversity that necessitated the hospitalisation ... Many paedophiles are extraordinarily smooth individuals who will charm other patients into avoiding confrontations ... Paedophiles on a hospital unit may

virtually paralyse the patient group from giving them the effective feedback it gives other patients. [1994, p. 345]

Gabbard underlines that paedophiles can deceive the staff members and actually turn group therapy into drama, and concludes that some paedophiles can be better treated in reform institutions through specialised programmes for sex offenders, which entail specific group confrontation approaches.

Ganzarain and Buchele (1990) have found that the exclusion of severely disturbed paedophiles—those suffering from organic cerebral syndromes, psychosis, substance abuse, sociopathy and pure perversions—can foster the identification of a subgroup of paedophiles who will respond effectively to group psychoanalytic psychotherapy. As a result, despite enormous defences in the early stages (determined also by the fact that the treatment is generally imposed), this subgroup is likely to benefit from an enhanced sense of guilt and shame and an improvement in their capacity for object relations. Another important aspect of group psychotherapy is the possibility of weakening the attitude of denial that paedophiles persist in assuming even though there is evidence of their abuse (O'Donohue & Letourneau, 1993).

The conflict between the need to guarantee the utmost confidentiality of the psychoanalytic relationship and the need to contribute, by communicating one's own experience, to the scientific development of psychoanalysis has been analysed by several authors, such as Klumpner and Frank (1991), Goldberg (1995), Tuckett (2000) and Gabbard (2000). Gabbard highlights the analyst's need to navigate his way through the possibility of substantially disguising all the elements that can facilitate identification of the clinical case and bring the intimacy and confidentiality of the psychoanalytic meeting into question, the ethical duty to request informed consent for publication of the clinical material, and the composition of a model clinical case based on fragments of different cases which have relevant aspects in common. No precise strategy is recommended, but options are proposed which can be variously combined according to the specific clinical material intended for presentation and publication.

Cases of paedophilia in which the patient gives his consent to the scientific communication of clinical material regarding his sessions are very rare, and when it does happen, the patient requests total anonymity and absolute unrecognisability. The usual reasons of confidentiality which generally make it difficult to present the available clinical material are even more emphatic in cases of paedophilia. These cases are usually concerned with very secret and personal situations, and those directly involved do not want any kind of publicity, often demanding a confidentiality which comes close to the secrecy of the paedophilic relationships they sought.

Although these requests have been completely met in the preparation and publication of the clinical material presented here, the outcome is completely paradoxical. The harder I tried to disguise the clinical cases in writing them up, paradoxically the more recognisable they became. The tendency for similar behaviours to be repeated in different clinical situations and the superimposability of some anamnesic and relational data in the paedophiles' accounts resulted in different patients being able to recognise themselves to a greater or lesser extent in the material presented. "You are talking about me," asserted a patient receiving therapy due to paedophilic behaviours when I invited him to read some clinical cases. A similar phenomenon occurs when medical students, like one of Jerome K. Jerome's *Three Men in a Boat* (1889), believe they are catching all the diseases as they study them. When I explained to the patient that it was not him or his account, but literary situations which, like a collage, combine feelings, affects and experiences relating to different cases, he was astounded. He was also incredulous at the superimposability—if not the reproducibility—of his own experience, which he had hitherto considered absolutely unique.

These elements, arising from my choice to think about a publication on paedophilia, reinforce my decision to highlight repetitiveness, monotony and lack of imagination as the main features of a paedophile's life. I believe that for this reason the material offered in this book can be paradigmatic of paedophilic behaviours, and therefore particularly useful in deciphering specific states of mind and very significant in describing relationships with people who present this kind of pathology.

In the following chapters we shall describe two clinical stories which, both arbitrarily and after due consideration, were created in order not to violate the privacy of our patients, and include episodes deriving from different clinical cases we have followed. The two cases presented describe the relational vicissitudes occurring in the encounter with the paedophile and the peculiarities intrinsic to a picture of paedophilic perversion and a picture of perverse paedophilia.

CHAPTER NINE

A case of paedophilic perversion

A man's most open actions have a secret side to them.

—Joseph Conrad

G is a well-known *maître d'hotel*, who has been convicted and jailed for having lasciviously touched an eight-year-old child's genitals in a park, after having lured her with some presents and told her several nice stories, ensnaring her kindness with his warm and persuasive voice.

When he first meets the analyst his face looks tired, prematurely aged. He appears not to care much about his appearance, and as he constantly looks down, the analyst has the feeling that he is trying to magically camouflage himself, as children do when they cover their eyes with their hands, thinking that will make them invisible. He seems to be making an enormous effort when he looks up to meet the analyst's eyes; their eyes meet just for a moment, then G instantly resumes his usual posture and talks while staring at the floor relentlessly. They have take a brief sidelong look at each other, making momentary eye contact somehow secretly—not even real eye contact. Later, as has been described in another case

(Pandolfi, 2000), G avoids the analyst's eyes in order to defend himself against the dread of his venomousness, but also from the fact that he has formed an image of the analyst as absolutely narcissistic, and this image must not be disturbed by the presence of the real analyst.

The analyst assumes that since the patient has been caught and convicted for his paedophilic behaviour, this might have triggered shame mechanisms due to the consequent social disapproval, and feels that the significance of his looking down is to protect himself from a situation he feels is entirely uncontrollable. The discomfort the analyst has also felt at other moments is related to the discrepancy between the seriousness of the acts for which the patient is responsible and an apparently peaceful, calm, balanced attitude, which is even able to understand other people's reasons. Only later will he manifest vengeful aspects, manic claims for damages, excessively aggressive defence of his own reasons, and denial of his responsibilities.

G's personal story is scarred by a traumatic event which dramatically affected his childhood. When he was six years old, his father—described quite vaguely as a big, authoritarian, yet jovial man—died as a result of an accident at the port where he worked. G was an only child, and his mother, a dressmaker in an important dressmaker's shop, sent him to live with his grandparents in the countryside. He talks about his childhood with misery, since his grandparents lived in a remote house and he had no opportunity to establish significant relationships with his peers; in addition, his school was a long way from home. His very young mother—she had become pregnant at the age of seventeen—would initially visit him every weekend, then less often, so that over time G came to regard his grandmother as his real mother and himself as the little man in the house. Some years later, his mother married again and had two daughters, but G refused to see or contact his stepfather and two half-sisters.

G recalls having been brutally and unexpectedly raped at the age of eleven by the farm manager's son, who was six years older, and whom he had chosen as his only friend and reference point. It was not one of those more or less consensual sexual games in which curiosity is mixed up with excitement aroused by the pleasure of prohibited things, but real aggression from behind, with the threat of fierce retaliation if he revealed what he had experienced to adults.

We often hear about stories of sexual games between children or between children and adolescents. Their predominant feeling is increasingly of clandestine collusion and excited and scared complicity in keeping a secret, shame of their family's possible reprehension, or enjoyable and curious involvement in a childhood phase in which transgression is experienced as a challenge without any particularly relevant significance, even if it is very important in strengthening their sense of identity. In G's case, the unexpected and uncontrolled violence had probably fostered those aspects of passivity and compliance which the analyst thought he had detected in G's behaviours from their first meeting. But it had probably also fostered excessive self-control and control over others, and a paranoid attitude towards others which was to become increasingly evident.

G went to a hotel management school and soon showed undoubted cooking skills. In a short time he became popular for some dishes he had "created", and thus had no difficulty in getting a job as a restaurant chef after graduating. Thanks to his acknowledged hard work and undeniable reliability, his career rapidly took off, and at a very young age he became *maître d'hotel* in a renowned and fashionable hotel. He described himself as a painstaking, punctual, consistent person and showed evident signs of excessive conformism. These characteristics have been described by Ferenczi (1933) in the *wise baby*, the baby who, after "losing" his love object, is compelled to "lose" aspects of his self, of his child being. They were later reconsidered by Winnicott and described as fundamental for the formation of the *false Self*.

While G showed curiosity and versatility in learning to cook, prepare and display dishes, he showed little interest in human beings. He had no friends, only occasionally visited his grandparents in the countryside, and even more rarely saw his mother, showing no interest in her new family. While at work he was immaculate and elegant, when he was not in his work uniform he looked extremely scruffy. While he demanded tidiness, cleanliness and decency from the hotel staff, his house was dirty and untidy. To cap it all, he said he preferred to eat pre-packed food, especially tinned food, despite his well-known and admired capacity to cook tasty and delicious dishes for other people.

G's only sexual relationships were mercenary. He used to have sex with prostitutes, whom he described as belonging to the "lowest category"; and for some time he went out with transvestites and transsexuals, as he took intense pleasure in sodomising them. It seems clear that using transvestites and transsexuals for sexual performances and taking pleasure in active sodomy is related to the violence to which G was subjected, which is acted out through sexually transgressive (though on the whole socially accepted) modalities against individuals felt as ambiguously subdued to his desires. This is also linked with the shabbiness of his non-working life and a tendency to self-debasement, which is an expression of guilt and shame as well as of not having been loved and thus of being pitiful and unworthy.

G's first experience of paedophile love went back to some years earlier and was with an adolescent who was helping as a baker's boy in the restaurant in which he was working. He had decided to teach the boy how to become a cook, pass on to him all the secrets of cooking, and invent innovative recipes for him. Although the boy showed perplexity and disinterest in the culinary arts, G did not want to give up and persisted with his Pygmalion interests. As the boy did not respond to his stimulation, G decided to offer him some money. This little bribe soon proved to be effective, as the baker's boy more and more frequently attended the restaurant kitchen and listened to real lessons in high culinary technique.

Increasingly in love with his pupil, G began to invite the boy to his home and doubled the amount of money he offered. At the same time his demands began to increase. He not only demanded total attention to his culinary lessons, but also asked the boy to take all his clothes off and practise in the kitchen naked. G loved sitting in an armchair while talking amusingly about cooking, whereas the boy had to turn his naked back to him while cooking and put the lessons received into practice.

G began to stroke the boy's buttocks and then masturbate him, still remaining behind him, as if he were masturbating an extension of himself with a boy's penis, and looking down whenever his eyes by chance met those of the boy. He told the boy he didn't want to hurt him, just stroke him. He tells the analyst that at some point he made a more abrupt gesture and stroked him a little more firmly. After that the boy never came back, and G tried in vain to persuade him to change his mind.

Back to his loneliness and, more importantly, deprived of the excitement he felt while touching the boy who turned his back while cooking, G felt increasingly depressed and even thought of suicide. He tells the analyst that from then he no longer felt sexual attraction for a child, until he met an eight-year-old girl in a park, who aroused feelings of fatherly tenderness in him. From the first enticements, he understood that the girl was unhappy and lonely, and he was going to take care of her problems and solve them. He went to the park many times, and was able to win the trust of the child and her mother with his very refined and kind manners.

G often played with the girl in the park, and told her several fanciful tales which he carefully prepared in advance at home for each subsequent meeting. He regularly gave her sweets, dolls, books and cartoon video tapes as presents. He often chatted with her mother and (in the mother's absence) with her nanny, and assumed a view about the most important media stories that was somewhere between responsible and conservative. In so doing he began to create for them a respectable and trustworthy image of himself.

One day when he was on his own with the child, not too far from the nanny, and looking through a book with her, he began to stroke her legs, then to put his hands under her briefs and thus touch her vagina. G recalls: "The child looked at me in astonishment, yet didn't rebel; if anything, she seemed not to dislike it, as she continued to flip through the book as if nothing had happened. I must have pressed harder on her vagina, as suddenly the scene changed: the child began to cry out and shout at the top of her voice as if I was slitting her throat, inducing her nanny to intervene immediately and call the park keeper."

By way of explanation, G continues: "It was not my intention to harm her, and to be quite honest, I don't remember the sequence of events as it was reconstructed during the trial. I only know that I was very attached to that child. I am not a paedophile monster; I was even writing a fairy tale for her." As for the baker's boy, G describes the sudden change from the gentle seduction of a stroke to a more violent approach which abruptly interrupted the seductive act, causing the victim's bewilderment and fear.

On the basis of G's behaviours we can infer that he seems to assume a fatherly identity that proves to be superficial and false. The absence of his father, who is nearly a stranger to him, and G's later idealisation of him through the absolutisation of qualities such as kindness and authoritarianism have fostered the formation of a false Self. Consequently, authoritativeness is replaced by mere conformism, and the capacity to protect is replaced by adult seductiveness which uses presents and fairy tales as a passport to gaining the trust of a girl who wants nothing but to trust.

The seductive attitude which he also assumed towards the child's mother and the nanny, his behaving as a respectable, kind and well-educated person, and his attempts to impress them through completely conformist views on the news stories reported in the media make us think of the frequency with which this kind of disturbance can be seen in anonymous personalities: lacking a strong personality, superficially conforming to the most traditional models of social behaviour, and stirring feelings of mediocrity and two-dimensionality in the interlocutor. Moreover, as Hannah Arendt warns, any attempt to detect the roots of evil, to understand the personal and deep-seated motives that have led to it, is doomed to failure, since it is impossible to find in violent behaviours (such as the Nazi atrocities) anything at all. Rather than their monstrosity, Arendt highlights in the murderers their mediocrity, their lack of vitality, their passivity in the execution of orders, and their lack of an independent outlook on life. This lack of thinking, which makes it impossible to give one's actions a meaning related to a personal and autonomous choice, is at the root of behaviours aimed at mere survival, in which one commits acts that do not need be understood. Any unpredictability and spontaneity of actions, which reveal the identity of any individual subject and are the foundations of relationships between human beings and of their way of expressing themselves freely, are not only not sought, but represent an obstacle and pose a threat to the system (D'Agostino Trevi, 2000). An absolutely ordinary, normal person can be unable to distinguish between good and evil. Eichmann represented such absolute mediocrity (Arendt, 1963).

Ernesto Sabato writes in his memoir: "the triviality with which the most noble feelings can deteriorate makes a human being degenerate into a pathetic caricature, into a being who is unrecognisable in his or her own humanity" (1998, p. 154). We notice a similar attitude, as Berti (1999) reminds us, in Petronius's *Satyricon*; this shows that certain behaviours or attitudes are immutable despite the passage of two thousand years. Petronius describes how Eumolpus, an old and corrupt poet and "guest of a family from Pergamon, became infatuated with the landlord's young son and, after gaining the family's trust with arguments based on extreme morality, won the child's trust with two pigeons" (p. 106). Eumolpus recounts how he gained the family's trust, and goes on to describe how he seduced the young boy:

> Whenever we were at the table and the practice of ephebic love came up in conversation, I flew into a rage with such indignation, and with such grave contempt did I try not to become upset at hearing that obscene kind of talk, that I was considered—especially by his mother—to be one of the great philosophers. By then it was I who began to take the ephebe to the gymnasium, to plan his education, and to give him lessons, in order to prevent anybody from having access to the house and offending his sense of decency. [pp. 343–345]
>
> As I noticed that his father was snoring I began to plead with the boy to make up—which meant to allow me to give him pleasure—telling him, besides, whatever is suggested by sexual arousal. But the boy, quite annoyed, did nothing and said: "If you don't go to sleep I will wake my father now." But there is nothing so unacceptable that impudence cannot extort. And while he was saying "I will wake my father now", I slipped in beside him anyway and stole the supreme joy from my rival, who was defending himself, but without much conviction. [pp. 347–349]

G's mother was too young for both motherhood and widowhood, and unable to look after her son—who was brought up by his grandparents living in the countryside—rather than the phallic mother often described in cases of paedophilia. Nor were his grandparents able to become significant reference figures. G grew up as a lonely child, and it was this feeling of emotional deprivation which nourished the pseudo-intimacy and generated the violent abuse to which he had been subjected by his best friend, and therefore the consequent disillusion and suffering caused by the abuse he felt to be incomprehensible. The sexual trauma is described in harsh terms, not only for its violence but also (and mainly) for its betrayal. The sodomisation occurred while the boy was trustingly turning his back, without consensus or any attempt to get involved.

When fathers die, mothers run away and friends become untrustworthy, there can be no compromise with the adult world. When G cooked for others, he did not do it with loving care; he did it just with extreme precision and detachment. He could feed others, but he did not want or need to be fed by anybody. The meaning of his choice to eat mainly tinned food is to deny dependence on others and to satisfy his needs with the nutrients of food preserved in a tin, which obviously does not provide the organoleptic characteristics of just-cooked, piping hot food.

G's work experience, first as a chef and later as a *maître d'hotel*, evolved according to the child's omnipotent narcissism, dominated by the fantasy that it is the child who nourishes him- or herself as well as adults, whereas adults neglect and betray the child. His first paedophile experience was also moulded by a narcissistic investment. As in the medieval workshops, the master taught his arts but demanded absolute devotion. Cynically, G exchanged his experience and creativity for the excitement the boy's immature body could arouse in him. He did not rape the boy violently, as he himself had been raped as a child, but by lewd stroking and clandestine masturbation. He used to ask the boy to walk around his house naked, and looked at his buttocks, never at his face.

It seems that the scenario of the abuse to which G was subjected as a child was reconstructed through modalities of perverse excitement which made it possible for him to re-experience the trauma, yet without the original characteristics of violent annihilation. He is the child who learns the art of cuisine and the child who is sexually stroked and masturbated, but he is also the abuser who acts from behind, the vile and violent betrayer. Once again the paedophile identifies himself with both the child and the abuser.

G has never had an emotionally involving relationship. His mercenary relationships are meant to exchange sexual pleasure for money. The exchange is immediate, as he cannot tolerate any situation which implies dependence.

When G has to pay for his first session, he gives the analyst twice the fee, saying that he is paying for next session as well. The analyst's refusal to accept money for a service that he has not yet offered, and his re-consideration in the following session of the defensive meaning of the manoeuvres used by G to deny dependence on the other, do not result in an increase in G's capacity to reflect upon himself. On the contrary, this stirs in G feelings of annoyance and rejection of rules he feels are excessively rigid and inappropriate for understanding his kind of behaviour. His payment irregularities occur frequently and consist of delays and fee calculation errors. This aspect further illuminates G's difficulty in establishing bonds of dependency, which characterise a stable relationship, by acknowledging the help he has received.

At the end of the first session, when the analyst is just about to say good-bye to him, G stops by the door, opens his bag and takes out a picture of a statue. He says: "Seeing the picture of *La Città Ideale* displayed in the waiting room inspired me to give you a little sample of my artistic taste, so that you will know me better." With a sense of irritation for what he perceives as a little ambush, the analyst looks at the picture of the sculpture, which comes from a contemporary art museum. It is a pile of mangled metallic wreckage, which makes one think of a wrecked old car after it has been compressed—like the ones that can be seen in the car cemeteries on the outskirts of towns—rather than a work of art.

The extension of the meeting beyond the fixed hour, G's showing the picture of the sculpture which contrasts with the figurative perfection of *La Città Ideale*, and the sense of discomfort, irritation and intrusion felt by the analyst give an idea of the complexity of the emotions involved. G wants to show the harsh and lethal parts of himself (wants the analyst to know him), but can only do this in underhand and intrusive ways. The session time is spent highlighting his capacity to be patient and disciplined, and to understand others. He has to blandish the analyst to keep rage and persecutory anxiety at bay. It is only by taking extra time and extraterritorial space from the setting that he can exhibit his separation anxiety and make his most destructive aspects visible, perhaps unconsciously fearing that talking about them might disturb or even destroy the analyst.

Showing the pile of mangled metallic wreckage as a work of art gives a clear idea of an increase in aesthetic value, a transformation of the perverse pathology into something aesthetic, captivating and seductive, according to the idealised destructive narcissism.

G's aggressive aspects are not criticised but transformed and sublimated by displaying the work of art. While during the session he tries to show a warmly complaisant behaviour which can even be submissive, outside that setting he can show the metallic coolness he doesn't know how to get rid of.

The episode of the allurement and abuse of the girl is described in a later session as the result of a misunderstanding of the events, which, once clarified, will reveal his good intentions. G claims to dabble, in his free time, in writing children's stories, and offers to let me read some, so that I will understand his constant efforts to understand children's needs and interpret their world.

The young girl appeared to him so lonely, helpless, and in need of affection that he could not control his need to stroke her. He knows what feeling lonely means and how much children need to receive love, and that adults are often unable to meet children's needs. He wanted to stroke her entire body, make her feel his protective, warm hands on her defenceless little body; he certainly didn't want to sexually abuse her. He stresses that he is not a paedophile—if being a paedophile means doing dirty things with children—but simply a man able to appreciate a child's purity and beauty, and able immediately to understand children's needs, which are so often neglected by adults. The analyst has a feeling of repulsion, which he can hardly control, when G smilingly reminds him that the etymology of the word paedophilia is love for children.

G recalls the girl's smile, her joy at seeing the presents, her acceptance of his caresses, and then he says he remembers nothing else and there is absolute darkness in his mind. He says: "If the girl says that I hurt her while pressing my hand on her little vagina, and that consequently she began to cry and scream, I can only believe her, as I know that such a pure child cannot lie. I trust her and believe what she says. But at the same time I can claim that it was not my intention to abuse her. I am fond of her, and my sexual inclinations are normally towards adults." He continues, with a poor sense of self-criticism: "The girl misinterpreted my good intentions and got a fright, and by crying and screaming she alarmed the nanny, who knows me well and can give evidence that I am a refined and respectable person."

There seems to be a link between the trauma suffered by the child and the transition from an erotised seduction to something more violent. Just as G is unable to elaborate his childhood trauma, to talk about his abuser, to describe his features, but can only remember the subsequent sensation of brutality and dirtiness, so he glosses over the transition to abuse in the traumas in which he plays an active role. His reflective blindness and incapacity to elaborate seem to have the same original roots as the narcissistic elation and sadistic destructiveness. It seems that the borderline represented by tolerance and compassion no longer exists, and an inextricable tangle of destructive and sexual instincts has formed.

Meanwhile G had gone back to work. His acknowledged culinary qualities allowed him to be employed in a renowned hotel, which was a source of enormous satisfaction: he had begun to try to convince others of his good intentions. All his communications seem to be aimed at modifying positively his public (and legal) image. An educated and well-mannered person, a hard worker whose skills are universally acknowledged, he had begun to break off all his sexual relationships, including the mercenary ones. Although he shows great respect for the victim's and her parents' version, he is eager to declare the true facts, firmly defending his probity and incapacity to be violent.

The therapeutic relationship in this phase is imbued with G's need to show that he is patient, obedient and submissive, unable to be argumentative, punctual at meetings, able to treasure what he has learned and to re-elaborate in rational terms the events which have led him to turn to an analyst.

Certainly due to an intensely persecutory emotional atmosphere, G is not receptive to the analyst's attempts to highlight that his need to convince himself and the analyst of his commitment and self-denial in the re-construction of himself and his social relationships is felt as a way of not facing up to his most secret feelings, and avoiding anxiety which he felt was unbearable. Undeterred, G lists all his faults and the mistakes he made in the past, including falling in love with the boy, but this seems to be the ritualised practice of the sacrament of confession, which some Catholics perform just to salve their conscience, without true suffering or any real mature power of self-criticism.

The formal decency of G's attitude annoys the analyst, who feels its coolness and lack of authenticity, although he knows that the journey to facing true and painful feelings will be long and beset with difficulties. On the other hand, when G seems to let himself go, when his control over his emotions weakens, the communication shifts to a tune of intrusion and insinuating collusion. There seems to be no possibility of integration between the two communicative poles.

G reports a recurring dream. He dreams of being a Templar, a crusader, a knight kitted out in his best clothes and protected by indestructible armour. While he describes the knight with whom he identifies himself, he smiles at the idea of the association between what the analyst has made him note about his armour and his difficulty in feeling or making others feel the authenticity of his emotions. The analyst underlines that the crusaders fought to defend the Holy Sepulchre, but they were willing to wage war and kill for their ideals, therefore he points out the grandiosity of idealisation and G's destructive violence, and his tendency to experience human relationships as devastating wars.

"Let's leave the ideals to one side!" says G. "The Templars, crusader knights, were few in number, and so were their friends, the Assassins, Arab knights from whose name the term 'assassin' comes. They were an extremist and terrorist Muslim sect with whom the crusaders came into contact in Syria in 12th and 13th centuries. They grew rich through the wars, while the poor devils were sent to die. You can't imagine how much wealth the Templars accumulated during the wars. Nowadays they could be described as a mafia organisation."

While on the one hand the dream illuminates the idealisation of violence and its use as a defence against the attacks of external enemies, on the other hand it highlights the mystifying aspect of the Crusades, holy wars described as historical falsifications, convenient arrangements passed off as good, whose main objective was to enrich the Templars, being in the service of their greed and willingness to overpower. The idealisation of G's aggressiveness (which is acted through the sexualisation of the relationship with children) begins to show signs of weakness, and in this dream the secondary profit represented by the pleasure felt in being violent begins to appear. The knights' idealised armour contrasts with their greed. The knights' religious kindness, their greed and their terrible violence have the same origin in a confused world where good and evil are indistinguishable—a sort of native melting pot from which everything comes undifferentiated and is interchangeable.

A fairy tale G wrote and read to the little girl can help us better understand the paedophile's world. A young boy runs away from home using an aerostatic balloon he has built out of sight of his parents. After an exciting journey in a blue sky full of multicoloured birds, he lands on an apparently deserted island. However, the island turns out to be inhabited by a monster which is apparently scary, but actually kind and friendly towards children. The monster is injured and the boy nurses him, as he is not afraid of him. The boy spends wonderful days on the island, playing, singing, and eating very sweet fruit. After saying good-bye to the monster, who in the meantime has recovered, the child and the balloon take off, but he is attacked by a prehistoric bird. He defends himself from the bird by catching it in a big cage, which he will open to let it go only when he lands on the terrace of his house.

G underlines that the big rapacious bird is not nasty, but has the characteristics Mother Nature has given it, and has been designed in that way in order to guarantee the survival of its species. He goes on to say, catching the analyst off guard, that he is not the island monster, nor the big rapacious bird, nor the adventurous child; he is the aerostatic balloon which contains and protects the child, and guides him safely to his destination.

The innocent child who can meet the monster without fear and heal his injuries seems to well represent the paedophile world, in which there is no space to meet adults. It illustrates the difficulty in giving up a miraculous medicine, a sort of elixir of eternal youth which consists of the child's closeness to him, of being in the child's world, and of being the child. Rapacity is not a decisive element in the relationship, but a normal corollary in the service of survival, while the essence of the relationship is in its capacity to contain the child's needs and sustain, like the aerostatic balloon, the fantastic flight. The erotic exaltation, the various teachings, the moral support and the extraordinary dreams are all elements depicting a fetishistic relationship which goes beyond the level of the merely erotic (Camassa, 1988).

G's narcissistic idealisation of his fatherly qualities, in a sort of maniacal crush, adds to the idealisation of his qualities as a writer, so that as soon as he can, he will write a book of fairy tales and donate the profits to a charity for poor children. Then he begins to come into open conflict with the analyst.

G reveals that he has written a gastronomic recipe book with lots of psychological implications, in that all the recipes have been created according to the widest variety of personality characteristics. If the book was published, G could become an honorary member of the same institute of psychoanalysis to which he thinks the analyst belongs. The modest attitude manifested during the earliest sessions is replaced with euphoric grandiosity, which drives him to compete awkwardly with the analyst, but prevents him from coming into contact—and maintaining contact—with the infantile areas of need and dependence.

This excessive maniacal removal of inhibition can be interpreted as an attempt to divert the sense of guilt from inside to outside. The guilt is denied, and through a mechanism of reversal, the reprehensible act is transformed into a meritorious act. The monster and the rapacious bird of the fairy tale are kind, and violence has been banished. Children don't need to defend themselves because monsters aren't violent—and if they are, it's only because they have been designed that way.

G says: "My interest in children is linked with a pedagogic motivation—I only want to help them and do them a world of good." Guilt is a persecutory judgement that is projected onto the object. When G says that he stroked the boy's buttocks and the girl's pubis, he turns to the analyst and says: "You are a puritan. I am sure you judge what I did to be an act as serious as a murder."

The identification with an aggressor who attacks and rapes determines the internalisation of the guilt, which is then projected onto the persecutory analyst. This overturning is very common, and is the foundation of a vast, explicit, propagandistic literature defending paedophiles which, in the search for new followers, seems to guarantee relief from guilt on the basis of the principle that "a trouble shared is a trouble halved".

The analyst has accepted for a long phase of the analysis that he is felt as the persecutory object in the relationship with the patient, trying to contain him despite the emotional difficulties, the projective barrages he unleashes. However, this dramatic work, of which containment and firmness are fundamental constituents, in which there seem to be no immediately appreciable results, and which at some moments comes close to the limits of tolerability (Green [1975] talks about *le temps mort* in the analysis), has created the possibility of talking about the violence to which G has been subjected, not so much in anamnestic terms—which have already been accurately defined—but in emotional terms.

G has begun to externalise, though haltingly, emotions such as disbelief, pain, fear, shame, disillusion, and lack of self-esteem due to the harm he suffered when he was raped by his friend. Distrust and fear of betrayal have emerged in the relationship with the analyst, but G also feels sorry for the girl, who until now has been felt and described in collusively excited terms. Primal antinomies between subject and object, between good and evil have come to light, and the narcissistic glue which has until now guaranteed the sense of identity has begun to melt (De Martis, 1989). The dynamics of the relational field are back and forth, totally unstable, so we cannot talk yet of reparative hints, even if we can note feelings of sorrow and concern, which then tend to dissolve in the magma of persecution.

Cognitivists underline how important it is for a paedophile to realise the psychological damage his behaviour has caused to his victim. For instance, showing him videos about the visible physical and psychic consequences of the violence committed gives him a realistic image of the child which is the opposite of his false image based on the belief that a child likes what an adult proposes for him or her sexually.

The psychoanalytic work makes it possible, though with enormous difficulties, to access the paedophile's child world, his infantile anxieties, the sexual trauma to which he was subjected and which he has never elaborated, and his unspeakable feelings. By doing so, and by triggering processes of identification with the victim, who is no longer experienced as a consenting partner in an exchange of sexual games but as a traumatised and suffering person, psychoanalysis allows for the constitution of hints of depression which can contribute to the prevention of possible relapses.

CHAPTER TEN

A case of paedophilic perversity

Luisella Peretti and Cosimo Schinaia

> Our Lady of Sorrows—she invoked humbly—Mother of all those who have been killed, will You hear my prayer? … I too have the right to pray to you. Can I pray for my poor soon who is a murderer?
>
> —Maria Teresa Di Lascia

P is a middle-aged man who used to work as an educator in a private school and is now an office worker. The first time he meets the analyst, he is very well groomed, wearing a conservative suit and a tie, but with some fashionable features, such as the design and colour of his outfit. His lined face displays changeable expressions, now participating and seductive, now cool and unobservant, and is framed by a well-trimmed beard.

P walks slowly into the room, looking around suspiciously, as if he had to capture in a short time as many details as possible about the arrangement of the objects in the room. When he sits down and begins to describe himself, he does not take his aloofly inquisitive eyes off the analyst for one moment. The analyst has the feeling that P has put out a challenge straight away in an attempt to control the situation. In order to prevent P from feeling that he has responded to it, he avoids sustaining his direct and sharp gaze. The signs of challenge and provocation thus soon emerge as a kind of business card which the patient offers through his eyes.

P describes his parents as originally a wonderful, young and close-knit couple, who lived a life with their children which was on the whole peaceful and untroubled. When his father lost his job, this was a real trauma that totally devastated the family picture he had so tenderly described. His mother, who until then had lovingly looked after her children, was forced to work and became unable to look after her family full-time. His father, who until then had been felt as the mainstay of the family's economy, began to lose solidity, and thus value, in the son's imaginative world. He began to get up late in the morning, lazily stay in his pyjamas, and wander around the house doing nothing. He often got drunk, and increasingly often threw violent jealous fits against his wife, accusing her of loving to go out and accepting the advances of other men.

P's accounts switch without interruption from descriptions of the Eden of an idealised family picture to those of a relational hell, of which P is a silent and powerless witness. His parents soon separated and the children were sent to a boarding school. While his younger brothers were later sent back home to stay with their mother since they could not cope with the hardness of the school, P stayed, and in fact changed schools several times due to his excessively quarrelsome and rebellious attitude.

In one of the boarding schools in which he was obliged to stay, he was probably subjected to sexual abuse. He has often revealed, in several sessions, his worry about not being able to say whether it happened in real life or whether it was a fantasy which over time has acquired enough consistency to give him the feeling of a real event. P expresses his difficulty in stating exactly when he received the sexual abuse, saying that he has "major difficulty in remembering" remote life events.

The analyst sees this area of uncertainly as an expression of his inability to distinguish between fantasy and reality, but also as his need to reconstruct his life history in a way which gives space to aspects of compensation for damage and altruistic requests. However, for the first time the analyst detects in P's words a difficulty in reconstructing his past, which he interprets as a wedge that fits the patient's armoured assertiveness and perfect systematisation of his past, in which everything always seems to have a place and a clearly defined explanation.

P's difficulty in registering whether the sexual abuse to which he was subjected is real or a product of fantasy may be also seen as an expression of his need to know what really happened to him. Once enabled to talk about it with someone, he needs to reconstruct his childhood trauma in depth without relying on a false memory, and to continue the journey towards self-knowledge with more open modalities, not by repeatedly putting forward preconceived ideas.

Although P was described as a naughty and hyperactive boy, for some years he had pleasing marks at school, but in the last years of high school he achieved very poor results, so that he obtained his diploma with a considerable delay. When P finished school, he took to living on his own in a little flat in a suburb, and got a job as an educator in a private institute. Not long afterwards he married an attractive woman the same age as himself, with whom his relationship soon became noticeably conflictual.

P describes his wife as a quite egocentric woman, mainly concerned about being attractive and elegant, who often went out with her girl friends and was neglectful of P and the child who had meanwhile been born of their marriage. P's description of his wife makes it noticeable that there is a confused superimposition of the images of his wife and his mother. In this case we can also see the change from the initial depiction of an angelic woman to that of a superficial woman totally neglectful of children's needs and rights. The switch from one image to the other is abrupt, without a gradual transition.

P and his wife separated when their child was still very young. His wife soon started going out with another man, and took the child with her. P continued to see his child, but less and less frequently, as he could not bear to be close to a "child without a father". The elements of identification with a fragile and needy child who has been deprived of his father's protection begin to peep out, but are immediately rejected because they are intolerable.

P seemed to offset the loneliness permeating his existence against an increased work commitment and a particular dedication to needy children whose parents did not visit them, so they had to spend their holidays in an institute. P used to organise highly appreciated cultural and school programme-revision meetings, sporting activities and trips, spending more time with children than the institute expected of him.

P and the children experienced moments of increasing intimacy, of physical and emotional liberation, which he describes as similar to those experienced by the teacher and his students in the film *Dead Poets Society*. They went as far as masturbating together, first each on his own and then mutually. They played with their urine, trying to wet each other by directing the jet at each other. P took pictures of the naked children in the most varied stances and then, amused and excited, showed the pictures to them. The epilogue of the sexual games was reached when P began to have a full sexual relationship with one of them, the most rebellious and "crooked" of the group. This is the boy who revealed his relationship with the educator to his parents after P had refused to be blackmailed into covering up a serious infringement of the institute's rules by the boy.

P could not accept having been betrayed by a "snotty kid" who had been granted his love and trust. In an outburst of rage, and with tears in his eyes, he tried to strangle the boy. The terrified boy managed to run away from P, who chased him for a while, declaring the intensity of his feelings at the top of his voice, but then, exhausted, gave up his pursuit. Once he was caught, he was finally sacked, and later he was reported to the judicial authorities and put on trial. Incredibly, he was acquitted, thanks to a very talented lawyer—but also, as he claims, thank to his "mimetic skills". P got a clerical job, and at the same time met a simple woman of humble origins, who, although aware of his ups and downs, agreed to live with him and later gave him a son.

It was during the course of the prosecution, and at the suggestion of his assessor, that P contacted a psychoanalyst, who agreed to help him. In P's reconstructed history we can highlight the following aspects:

1. P's idealisation of the first part of his life, which is not concretely confirmed from the events he has described, and is extremely lacking in details. The emotional perfection characterising his family's relationships clearly reflects the absence of good parental functions. The idealisation of his parents as a wonderful couple, which governs his memory of them, is also present in the wonderful couple that P and his first wife were, in the sculptural beauty

of the children's bodies which he photographed, and ultimately in the intense passion bonding him to the selected boy.
2. The split we can see in the significant difference between his two wives. The first one is beautiful, egocentric, neglectful of his needs, and therefore more similar to his mother. His second wife is submissive and less ostentatious, but has more mothering abilities, though these are basically depreciated by P. The choice of a woman antithetic to the first one makes us think that rather than acknowledging his needs and consequently reorganising his narcissistic investment, P devalues the object's qualities: she is only described negatively because of her deficient qualities and P's relating back to his previous idealised experience. This seems to result in a lack of integration, in that the image of his first wife, a simulacrum of beauty and passion, remains split from the second one, who represents mothering and satisfaction of needs.
3. The sadomasochistic relational modalities characterising both marriage relationships are also present in the paedophilic relationship with the selected boy. The boy, initially submissive and acquiescent, later turns into a blackmailer and a spy; and P, from being a director and *master* of the perverse relationship, becomes a disillusioned victim at the mercy of the boy's accusations. The *escalation* of passion, which leads P very close to murder, is reorganised not only in its intensity, but also in the significance of its effects. The fact that P has been acquitted of both paedophilia and attempted murder strengthens his feeling of his behaviour being socially irreproachable and of a substantial omnipotent immunity.
4. The precarious balance achieved in his working and social life is compensated in a paranoid way. His mother, his first wife and then the analyst become intolerable persecutors according to his modalities of idealisation of the absent figure: the absent person is imagined as present, very demanding, nasty and accusatorial. The commixture of terror and states of paedophilic excitement seems to refer to paranoid anxieties as a degenerative basis of perversion. The transformation of fear into a sexualised aggressive state allows for the changeover from the terrifying experience to which P was subjected to the elation implied in the sexual pleasure.

5. P's identification with more lonely and unfortunate children highlights how his attempt at repairing manifests itself initially with a certain authenticity as he looks after them, but then leads to sexual contact, which is governed by intrusive identification, predatory appropriation of adolescent characteristics and the narcissistic use of them. The aspects of abuse and asymmetry are then trivialised, minimised and abusively transformed into the children's adherence to his ideals and their complete deliberate involvement in the sexual pleasure.

P's intolerance of dependence has manifested itself from the first sessions, to which he arrives late, feigning that he had to meet some of the more important commitments with which his days are fully occupied, while he considers the meeting with the analyst of little importance or value. At the same time P tries to keep the situation under control, so that he has quickly read some psychiatric and psychoanalytic books and is eager to stress that he is not unprepared but knows the territory in which the other moves.

P is scornful of the attachment he could form with the analyst, and considers it a product of the analyst's narcissistic fantasy, something common to all analysts, whom he depicts as odd characters convinced that their patients could not survive without their help. P speaks in a sarcastic and mocking tone which alternates with language that at times moves from vulgar eroticism to real obscenity. In an interview with Zerbi Schwartz (2000, p. 26), Gabbard explains that "the patient seeks a 'bad enough' object and will do what is necessary to transform the analyst into the abusive figure of his past. At the same time the patient hopes to find an idealised omnipotent rescuer, who will turn his childhood negative experiences into present positive experiences".

The use of erotised language which often lapses into foul language makes one think of seductiveness and aggressiveness having a common area of mental origin, as Freud had already pointed out (1940a). These are two defensive modalities whose borderlines are unclear; one changes into the other without an appropriate capacity for regulation. There is no transitional intermediate space, so that there is either a terrifying hand to hand or a sidereal distance. While P dramatically expresses his need to be treated, at the same time he tends to destroy the tie of dependency that could take shape in his relationship with the analyst.

P sarcastically asks: "How should the therapeutic alliance between you and me be formed? Should it arise from love at first sight? Look, I don't have time for a load of rubbish like the transference. I know you need that, I know your work relies on the patient's anxiety, on his upheaval and desire to see only the analyst, but I have too many fucking things in my head and can't think about this bullshit." His mind is crowded with faecal phalluses which penetrate, soil and destroy the mental and relational environment, but there is no space for falling in love or for emotions in general. The degraded sexuality used in compulsive terms comes into the session and causes the analyst, who feels that he is no more than a receptacle for the patient's evacuations, bewilderment and uneasiness.

Once he has recovered from an initial and unpleasant feeling of fear and depreciation, and from the general feeling that he will cease to exist if he does not behave in a way that will satisfy the patient's projective identifications (Turillazzi Manfredi, 1994), the analyst begins to perceive P as a scared child who needs to make his screams louder in order to alarm his mother and so attract her attention. He then tells P that he does not need to *escalate* his verbal provocations in order to make himself heard and give foundations to his accounts; he (the analyst) is there just to listen.

P's need to show his availability and understanding is defensive, and on this occasion cheats the anxieties and fears of the analyst, who shows himself to be complaisant. P does not have a containing mother inside him, able to listen to him and make her child's worries her own, so that the interpretation of his aggressiveness as a request to be heard results in a harsh response, since it is perceived as out of place and intrusive; in other words, it is a countertransference *enactment*. At the end of his verbal barrage P, as though seized by a state of mental excitement which thrives on extreme hostility to relationships, brings the provocation to its peak, rolling a joint with theatrical sluggishness.

This gesture can be traditionally interpreted as an *enactment*, an attack on the setting of rules, with added aggressiveness (given the limited social tolerance of hashish); in other words, as an attempt to scuttle a possible good relationship with the analyst. I believe, though, that it is more appropriate to regard P's gesture as a response that short-circuits the analyst's misunderstanding. The analyst should probably have felt and tolerated the evacuative meaning of the message without resorting to a defensively complaisant interpretation.

Smoking hashish induces a light dizziness that weakens the initial aggressiveness, and paradoxically has an alleviating and compensating effect on the isolation in which P has felt confined and the estrangement to which he has been forced while he was being verbally offered understanding. So this is an event conjunctively created, implying identification with the patient's Self-object representations, which act with the Self-object representations pre-existing in the analyst (Gabbard, in Zerbi Schwartz, 2000).

P fears dependence, since he does not want to be at the mercy of anybody, of an object perceived as unstable, changeable, and thus unreliable. Moreover, he feels the same contempt for being in need as he perceived in his mother (rightly or wrongly), with whom he tends to identify in other aspects. When his mother went to work, she mocked her husband, who was afraid that she was going out to meet young lovers. Initially tender and in contact with her child, soon afterwards she was able to leave him alone, neglecting his emotions.

Although P denies any physical and behavioural resemblance to his mother, he likes to look well groomed and elegant like his mother, and seeks the company of adolescents, as his mother used to do in his father's imagination, which he has made his own. By behaving in the way he thinks she did, trying to be like her, P denies the experience of separation and abandonment he has experienced. Therefore, the traumatic area resides in P's relationship with his mother, an area that in the course of the therapy has long been glimpsed and perceived (though marginally); P has accepted it as being unsolvable, and has encapsulated it in order to be able to differentiate himself from it to some degree. (Pandolfi, 2000).

The process of P's identification with his mother is favoured by the weakness of his father figure, whose fragility means that he cannot become a valuable and stable identification object. We can suppose there has been an inversion in the identification process. The absent and valueless father generates a violent and paedophilic father, who seduces and terrifies his son and becomes a reference figure for his paedophilic relationships, as emerges from the transference.

P says: "When I was at the boarding school my Mum used to call me often but never came to see me, and I was afraid of everything, even myself. I was afraid that my fear would be noticed, that I would be unable to keep it inside; I felt as if I were about to vomit and trying hard to get to the toilet in time. But where was my toilet? Where was my mother? Then I remembered the arguments between my mother and my father, the way he chased her around the house in agitation while she was getting dressed to go out. She laughed at him and mocked him, while I was playing on the cold floor with the toy soldiers and made them all die. Women have always made me suffer. My mother used to hug me and then go away from me so quickly that I got the feeling that she had never truly hugged me or even been there, and that I had only dreamt of her. My mother was very childlike, with a child's head and an adult's beautiful body—the exact opposite of you, doctor, whose head is that of an adult and whose body seems too young to do this job and understand me."

The inconsistent and superficial attitude of P's mother and the disillusioned resentment the child feels against her shape a monstrous image of the reference maternal figure, in which there is no balance between the various parts, as there are always dissimilarities and deformities.

The cold and uncomfortable floor and the dead toy soldiers highlight the correlation between the emotional cold and the consequent death, which the child feels, but experiences in terms of captive helplessness. Nevertheless, we cannot rule out that P's furious attacks on his mother and then on the analyst represent an attempt to appease the suffering caused by his absent mother, in accordance with the principle that if the object becomes nasty, it is easier to stay away from it. Therefore, these attacks can be considered the crystallisation of a desperate subterfuge to enable P to tolerate the solitude into which he feels he has been forced.

Although P feels a cold inside coming from far away, he prefers a relationship with an inanimate object containing some of the characteristics he seeks in the animate object on whom he feels he cannot depend. These characteristics are isolated and vampirically extracted, and this operation allows him to avoid a relationship with a person in her or his wholeness, a person for whom he nevertheless still feels furiously nostalgic. The outcome of P's mental processes consists of de-animating and depersonalising the object-analyst, who ceases to have his own original qualities and assumes only those ascribed by P.

With regard to the room in which his sessions take place, P says: "I have always felt cold in here, although the room isn't cold thanks to this big stove." Then he adds defiantly: "I don't think it is due to your merit, doctor, just to the big stove, that I can warm myself." The relationship is therefore deprived of qualities such as the warm human contact the analyst offers. Instead of the man there is a metallic stove, a source of heat which is not only inanimate but (more importantly) controllable, and whose heat supply itself is adjustable, in the same way that P regulates the temperature of his paedophilic relationships.

The solution *par excellence* that P seems to find in order to face the difficulties of being dependent is the denial of adults, of his parents. All individuals are equal in a world of children, who are able to fend for themselves and do not need adults. Real children do not exist; their authentic needs are neglected. We can see P's narcissistic projections when he states: "They are desperate boys who have to do everything for themselves, from washing their socks to swallowing the tears caused by the pain of being far from home and abandoned. They are all the same (apart from physically), they all want me as one of them, as a big boy."

The only kind of diversity that can be accepted consists of a finer and stronger physique put at the service of children's weakness, as little children dream with the plastic reproductions of very muscular superheroes (such as Big Jim dolls), or when they see cartoon characters with hyperbolic physical strength. P is convinced that adults can no longer be trusted. At the very most one can rely on a child with an adult's body, which is what he feels he is.

The accounts through which P theatrically expresses his emotions and talks about his ghosts, mingling rage, aggressiveness and devaluation with ambiguously seductive tones, arouse contradictory and contrasting feelings in the analyst. The analyst feels that P is attacking him, provoking him and making fun of him. With his mind impoverished, robbed by P's aggressiveness, he feels held back from an emphatic and self-evocative availability (Pandolfi, 2000); sometimes he can even feel seduced like one of the children, and would sum up his mental state in a discussion group by describing himself as "subjected to a hail of fire". The analyst feels inside him an increasing sense of alarm and worry about the children involved, and wonders whether the necessary steps have been taken to protect potential victims. He can feel driven to take concrete action to stop P, to report him, as if the worry about and responsibility for the object, which P does not keep inside him (if anything, they have probably never been formed in order to be felt), have been violently projected inside the analyst—to put it better, are intensively felt and lived by the analyst instead of P, who lacks the capacity to feel them as they are absent.

A feature we can generally find in all paedophiles is avoidance of a sense of guilt, perceived as responsibility for and concern about the children involved in the sexual relationships. Whereas in the case of paedophilic perversion we can talk about deflection of the sense of guilt, which does seem to be felt intensely but is hushed up through the most varied defensive modalities (Speziale-Bagliacca, 1997), in the case of paedophilic perversity we have to talk about evanescence of the sense of guilt, since the introjective identification with the aggressor has led to his introjecting not only the aggressiveness but also the sense of guilt and the hatred present in adults. In this case the paedophile is almost impudent in his refusal to acknowledge his responsibilities, and like the "exceptions" Freud mentioned (1916, p. 630), he seems to feel justified in being spared any further calls to account for his actions because he has already suffered.

The patient's defences are so powerful and primitive that he is unable to atone for the sense of guilt; in this situation some incorrectly talk about the sense of guilt being absent because it has failed to form. Brenman comments:

> When love and hate crash, either we feel guilt and make reparation, or we are persecuted by guilt. To avoid either consequence, we can pervert the truth, draw strength from a good object and feel free to practise cruelty in the name of goodness. It is as though we omnipotently hijack human righteousness and conduct cruelty in the name of justice. [1988, p. 257]

Dubret explains: "When sexual perversity and perversion rejoin, they produce clinical pictures in which guilt seems to be absent, systematically evacuated through multiple rationalisations" (1996, p. 144).

When the sense of guilt has not developed, no specific anxiety is perceivable: it is in this case that the analyst may experience a sense of guilt in the patient's place and rely on the possibility of introjection from the beginning, determined by the therapeutic relationship; this also functions as ethical orthopaedics, though it shuns any moralistic aim.

Fear, irritation, disdain, and tiredness caused by the feeling of not being able to relax, are almost constantly present during the session, and make it difficult to value the patient's rare moments of letting go and insight, facilitating instead falsely consolatory answers which basically increase the distance between the patient and the analyst. The patient's rancorous aggressiveness, which tends to undermine first and foremost the analyst's human competence, is at some moments perceived with such intensity that the analyst fantasises about possible concrete acts of aggression against him and his children.

It is possible to identify in these fantasies (and in those of filing a charge against the paedophile) the precursors of a sense of guilt sustaining an intoxicated temptation to retaliate. Once the sense of guilt is formed and weighed, as time passes it can be re-proposed to the patient; and when the analyst re-thinks the session after it has ended, it can enable the countertransferential fear and rage to be replaced by a feeble feeling of compassion, which is less likely to surface when he feels immediately threatened by the patient. In an interview with Zerbi Schwartz (2000), Fonagy explains that people cannot remember, only "be", and when they cannot be, they have to make others play this role. Then he says that the transference of abused patients, at least in the initial phase, consists of the exteriorisation of parts of self-representations.

The analyst feels shaken and possessed by ambivalent feelings: he is attracted by this patient, whom he perceives in any case as being in great need of treatment; and at the same time he is rejected by the aggressive tones and the ambiguously seductive manners the patient uses (and which can also be found in the anamnestic reality of his history). These complex and tortured relational dynamics explain how difficult it is to find the right distance and the appropriate timing, and make us think that the set of internal object relations cannot easily be changed.

> On the other hand, when the patient's capacity to reflect and mentally represent have improved, he can develop the capacity to observe, think about his repeated patterns, and so create a sense of self-mastery and control. In other words, these patients can become able to understand when they repeat modalities of pathological and malfunctioning relationships, so that they can modify the influence of the past abusive relationships on the present relationships in their life. [Gabbard, in Zerbi Schwartz, 2000, p. 30]

Acknowledging the power of the evacuative introjective identifications and elaborating the heavy drives to action which such a patient can arouse, containing as they do very intense and ambivalent emotions (sometimes antithetic, confused, mingled with different qualities), represents an extremely complex and delicate process of containment and elaboration in the relationship with a patient who falls within the group of paedophilic perversity. Noting that it is nearly impossible to treat such disturbed and disturbing patients imposes as a *conditio sine qua non* the presence of a supervisor and the protection of a reflective group to use as a reference.

CHAPTER ELEVEN

The working group

Luisella Peretti and Cosimo Schinaia

> Men are not ashamed to think something dirty, but they are ashamed when they imagine that others might believe them capable of these dirty thoughts.
>
> —Friedrich Nietzsche

The working group whose ups and downs will be described in this chapter is made up of psychoanalysts, psychiatrists, and psychoanalytically trained psychologists, who use various modalities in relating with paedophile patients: psychoanalytically oriented psychotherapy carried out privately or institutionally, psychiatric examinations in mental health centres or in prisons, and psychiatric examinations for assessment purposes. The drive to form a working group for paedophilia was generated by the desire to reflect upon the emotional difficulties encountered in the clinical relationship with paedophile patients, and to better understand the phenomenon of paedophilia, which has for some years been forcefully brought to the collective attention by news stories in the mass media, generally presented in witch-hunting tones. Our goal was to study paedophilia, looking at it from different angles and using the psychoanalytic perception as the main reading instrument (Speziale-Bagliacca, 1980), since it constitutes the most familiar way for the group participants to face and understand the clinical reality.

The emotional and relational developments of this working group seemed to be closely linked with the specific subject we dealt with, with the fantasies related to it, and with the emotional ups and downs of our relationships with our paedophile patients. Our ups and downs were reflected in this working group; or, to be more precise, they penetrated it, giving particular colouring to the group members' personal experiences and to their relationships with one another. It seemed to us that this penetration presented the characteristics of *commuting*, a phenomenon described by Neri as "fluctuations from the individual to the group dimension, with the switching of a topic, affect or fantasy from the group to the individual and vice versa" (1996, p. 153). We therefore have to assume that a specific surge progressed from the dual relationship into the working group, as a prerequisite for the transformation of the material in the clinical elaboration. This transfer has a communicative meaning which is more difficult to detect the more serious the patients' clinical picture is, especially if psychotic nuclei are present. Therefore, our emotional "adventures" in the group seemed in some ways paradigmatic, and we hope they will be useful to those who seek possible solutions to the problem of therapy for paedophiles.

As in all ventures considered pioneering, the working group and study group participants were initially pervaded by feelings of braveness and exceptionality, linked to a driving and involving messianic idea and slightly appeased by the rational certainty of the complexity of the task, as one could infer from the frequent situations of relational impasse which each member could describe in regard to their experiences of treating paedophiles. The group was characterised by idealisation of the task and our capacities, which was probably a reaction to the experiences of frustration aroused in our individual work with paedophiles. Hurt in our individual therapeutic narcissism, we were seeking compensation in a group narcissism. However, our initial enthusiasm and illusion about our possibilities were also instrumental in creating the group and making it work. As always, the group illusion has more sides. It is a reaction to total anxiety and dismay, but also a condition of birth and development (Anzieu, 1975).

We started off by deciding to analyse the clinical material and at the same time to investigate the paedophile aspects of many branches of knowledge, from painting to photography, from myth to fairy tale, from fiction to cinema. In our meetings we alternated discussion of clinical material with cultural material, broadly speaking.

From the very first stages it was possible to detect different behaviours on the part of the group members. Some were very active and propositional, bringing an abundance of stimuli for reflection: new bibliographic sources, the latest films or novels for discussion; others, on the other hand, appeared passive, excessively compliant, silent, often absent, despite repeatedly stating their real interest in the subject we were tackling and in the group's progress. We often ended up giving priority to the bibliographic part and the exchange of information and comments on the collected material, leaving little space for the presentation of clinical cases.

The splitting of the group into an active and a passive part, the predominance of the time spent on the cultural aspects in general—though we had agreed to alternate work on the two aspects and give priority to our specific area, namely the clinic—and the difficulty of organising the abundant collected material at some point seemed to us to be clear signs of an impasse. We spent some time reflecting on this, and realised that our situation was like the dual psychoanalytic relationship in which intellectualisation and rationalisation act as persistent defences against the intensity of emotional involvement, and restrict any opportunity for novelty and originality in order to allow one to escape into the already known and into prejudice. Similarly, by over-investing in our research into various fields of knowledge, our group was likely to propose a massive manoeuvre to avoid or anaesthetise an impact on our emotions which was hard to cope with, without paying the duty of relational involvement.

The group leader, who also worked shoulder to shoulder with the other members and contributed with his own thinking, on the one hand had to slow down excessively fast and shattering processes which could have generated too much suffering; and on the other hand he had to promote and sustain the collective capacity to metabolise anxiety and anguish, keeping early depressive collapses at bay.

We needed to acknowledge that the behaviours manifesting in our group also and mostly had to do with the specific object of our meetings, and the only guarantee against dispersing our research into thousands of trickles and against losing sight of our sense of the group was to remain faithful to the clinical material: in other words, to cling to the substance of our relationships with paedophiles, with all the load of anxiety and anguish that this implied. Moreover, we had to recognise that the feelings of discomfort and repulsion towards paedophilia, which we had noticed and criticised not only in the general public but also in professionals, were also present within us, and we had to reckon with them. We could not talk about the paedophile without first meeting him within the group and within us. Nor could we be spared the general need to distance ourselves from bewildering and ambivalent emotions and personal experiences. On the one hand we were willing to understand the motivations of those who have unacceptable feelings and manifest unacceptable behaviours, and understood that the abuser is himself a victim and, more importantly, isolated and rejected. On the other hand, however, the simple fact of our strong identification with the reasons of the child who is the abuser's victim, and, more importantly, the unacceptability of the fact that adults' feelings towards children are ambivalent, full of *chiaroscuro* and contradictions, pushed us to a phobic avoidance of real contact with the problem.

Our analysis and attempt to understand the early phases of the group's development allowed us to better and more deeply tolerate paedophiles, as emerged from our group discussions. As also happens with patients who have committed any sort of crime, contact with their suffering and misery, and telling their stories and the stories of our meetings with them, had an initial organising function and enabled us to cautiously acknowledge an *other* emotional world, however coerced and darkened by unacceptable desires it may be.

The belief that seemed to sustain the group was that we were experiencing what had happened in our meetings with severely psychotic patients, whose feelings of extraneousness, fear and embarrassment had over time been replaced by a fragile feeling of familiarity which had softened their rigid and frightened initial feelings and made them more malleable. We saw the same process in our meetings with paedophiles, who, once rid of their aura of unacceptability, could give space to fears, weakness and relational incapacity, and these anxieties could create initial hints of identifications in the analysts, whose feelings of sharing their patients' emergent suffering would then prevail over their feelings of rejecting and stigmatising them.

As often happens, when a more stable group structure started to take shape, we began to go through a series of emotional ups and downs whose intensity and turbulence had until then been unimaginable. The first case presented in the group discussion had features of paedophilic perversity, with all the severe symptomatology that this clinical situation brings. The analyst who was brave enough to try his hand at dealing with a severe patient, who had sexually abused children several times and showed a clearly paranoid symptomatology, soon found himself in extreme difficulty when he began to explain his problems to the group. Rather than feeling helped and supported in this difficult task, he felt criticised and attacked by the group. He felt endangered by the threats of his patient, and appeared several times to believe that he was not understood or given enough support by the group. He thought they were unable to believe him and understand the concreteness of the risk he was running, and therefore unable to make him feel more protected. He was experiencing feelings of exploitation, as his case offered the group "very interesting, even burning" material, and believed that the group was more interested in using the material for research purposes than in acknowledging and containing his needs and difficulties. The abused child's experience took dramatised tones and was faced through the paedophile-analyst relationship and then through the analyst-working group relationship.

As emerged from a subsequent collective reflection, it would probably have been better for the group to refrain from any interpretation, as the patient had created an impossible situation within the analyst: it was impossible for him to be understood because of the absence from the outset of a mother capable of understanding. In fact, any attempt on the part of the analyst to understand the emotional reasons for the patient's suffering was not appreciated by him; instead, the patient distorted its meaning and criticised it as the result of intellectualised trivialisation, and accused the analyst of devaluing the objective difficulties in favour of excessive psychologism. More respectful silence towards the difficulties faced by the analyst in the relationship with his patient would perhaps have had those containing potentialities which the several verbal interventions failed to have, and would perhaps have allowed the analyst to overcome the turbulent early months of the group experience and thus to be surrounded by a more relaxed and collaborative atmosphere.

The group felt in turn that its existence and clinical research project was threatened by a restless attitude considered unproductive. A field was formed in which emotions tended not to meet; everybody spoke their own dialect, producing a chaos of languages, each with some meaning, yet indecipherable and unable to convey the need for a common communicative territory. This field was made up of the patient, unable to think of a consensual space within which understanding would be possible; the analyst, who perceived himself as a guinea pig whose difficulties and emotional peculiarities were sacrificed on the altar for cold and impersonal research purposes rather than being acknowledged; and the group, who felt threatened and accused of being a cold laboratory by the frightened analyst despite their containing and hermeneutic efforts.

The analyst requested that the clinical material he had brought into the group meetings should not be published, and desperately argued that making it anonymous would not be enough. His patient, an inveterate reader of any published material on paedophilia, would find the published paper and identify his story and analyst, and might even avenge the breach of confidentiality.

It was no use the group or its leader guaranteeing anonymity and non-identification of the material, or stressing the importance of sharing his fears, which were justified on the levels of both emotion and reality. In any case, it was pointed out that since the patient sought out any text dealing with paedophilia, he would inevitably have identified the clinical material that had been proposed in a specific clinical vignette, and this process would have been facilitated by his analyst's name appearing among the authors of the publication.

In short, we could have talked about paedophilia softly, just in secret and not in public, in order to prevent the patient as well as the analyst from feeling shameful and fearful of the disclosure of the secret. It is obvious that when we propose such a publication, respect for privacy represents one of the central aspects, also because of the profound and severe social implications that a possible identification of the person concerned would involve. But our feeling was that there was more at stake. The analyst's obstinate and worried reference to the right to privacy, as a consequence also of the patient's possible reprisals, evoked the ambiguous secrecy in which the paedophile-child relationship unfolds.

The shadow of moral guilt concerns both poles of the paedophilic relationship. The need for secrecy passes over from the patient to the analyst, as it passed over from the paedophile to the child, often subjected to blackmail and threats of retaliation as well as seductive calls to become an accomplice. The analyst's fear of being identified and caught, and so of finding himself in a dangerous situation, can give an idea of the intensity of the patient's fear of being caught, of his intimate feeling of social disapproval, but also of the intimidating strength he can exert over his little victims by all means, licit or illicit, to make sure that they keep it secret.

Rather than witnessing forms of projective identification with some communicative value, we seemed to be seeing a kind of evacuative outpouring of the patient's feelings into the analyst, which in turn passed into the group without any function of mediation. Neri describes an unintentional and unconscious *commuting* modality between individual and group as "trans-temporal propagation".

> The trans-temporal diffusion does not refer to transport or passage, but to a silent occupation of the group field, like the diffusion of a gas, which is not halted by the barriers represented by the group and the individuals' "psychic skin". The term *trans-temporal* means that this diffusion occurs between individuals and groups who are distant in time and space. What is transmitted is a modality of being together, a certain way of perceiving themselves ... The elements which are diffused in a trans-temporal way often have viral characteristics, in that they use the energies of the host, in this case the group, thus distorting the communication. [1996, pp. 160, 163]

Any attempt at reconciling the need to protect the therapeutic experience with the need to propose a theoretical and clinical reflection upon the subject of paedophilia seemed to be obstructed by misunderstanding and polemics.

The analyst stated his intention to stop participating in the group. In support of this he stressed that it was impossible for him to be understood by anyone who had not experienced the intensity and dangerousness of his relational experience, and underlined the objective and particular gravity of his patient's clinical picture.

The sadomasochistic aspect of the paedophile-child relationship arose again in the group through demands which were intense enough to undermine the group's constitutive aim. If the child victim reveals the abuses to which he or she has been subjected, he or she becomes a traitor, since (just as in the Mafia) the only governing codes are a conspiracy of silence and total adhesion to the paedophile's (family's) ideology, unless we also consider possible secondary benefits (little gifts, seductive kindness or avoidance of violence), the difficulty of pseudo-understanding (the paedophile claims to understand the child, whereas other adults are unable to understand the relationship as they are unable to understand the child's emotional needs), and the extension of shame (the paedophile declares that the child is also responsible due to his or her alleged seductive capacity, and the child subsequently suffers social reprehension and pillorying due to a shared behaviour which is judged shameful and morally unacceptable).

The analyst's feeling of not being understood by the group, which at some moments assumed a persecutory aura, led him to plan to leave the group, making any subsequent elaboration of the stalemate impossible. The extremely intense emotions unfolding between the patient and the analyst, the sadomasochistic issues and the paranoid anxieties present in the patient, had been reflected and acted into the group like *enactment*, a non-verbal communication secretly transmitted, breaking the evolution of group discourse through an increased anxiety within the group, which prevented its members from listening to and reflecting upon the reported material (Tylim, 1999).

> If shame represents the external manifestation of a feeling of contempt for infantile parts of the self, no doubt these can only be contained in the group and transformation processes can only be triggered through communication. If talking in a group assumes the meaning of a public confession, it is evident that the emotional field is dominated by a fantasy of persecutory guilt, which is more likely to lead to sanction and prescription of certain behaviours than to their transformation. [Contardi & Vender, 1993, p. 38]

We came to learn later that the analyst's interruption of his participation in the group had been followed by a unilateral and sudden interruption of the therapy by his patient, who was in turn quite critical of his analyst, though unaware of the analyst's emotional turmoil within the paedophilia study group.

The group spent a long time wondering about the sense of such a painful experience, the incurable fracture that had formed despite several attempts to repair it, the group's probable inability to contain, and the possible prevalence of the narcissistic and exhibitionistic aspects implied in the intention to publish a book on painstaking underground work, not to show off but as an extension of the group's elaboration of the clinical material. However, the group also had to realise, both depressively and realistically, that the potentiality to "absorb parts of emotions violently expelled and placed in the group's emotional area is not infinite, but limited by the group's emotional saturation level itself" (*ibid*).

If *commuting* and *enactment* can sometimes represent communicative possibilities (Neri, 1996; Steiner, 2000), in this case the severity of the clinical picture was nevertheless so intense, and the strength of the projective identifications played out in the relationship and then in the group so violent, that only afterwards could a thorough understanding and analysis of what had happened become possible. There are levels of psychopathological severity which can deeply and permanently disconnect a therapeutic relationship to the point of making its relational field impossible. As we were able to see, they can undermine the very foundations of the process by which a working and clinical reflection group is formed, independently of its members' goodwill and availability to put themselves forward as therapists and participants. When the member who is presenting to the group manifests excessive difficulty in representing a favourable evolution of the therapeutic relationship, so that he perceives any optimistic view as consolatory or as denying the real difficulties and not as an expression of a continuous tension in the search for meaning, and when it does not seem possible to give oneself time for elaboration, construction, collaboration and trust, the group as an entity tends to collapse and no longer be a working group.

Despite the group's intention to stop meeting after the analyst left, the collective will to continue the clinical research work prevailed, and the analyst was replaced by an equally motivated and experienced colleague. New clinical cases were presented, less psychopathologically severe than the first, though also quite difficult. These operations allowed the group, after a painful period of elaboration of loss, to continue its experience of clinical reflection and search for a more relaxed atmosphere, less loaded with tension, alongside a meaningful experience of the limit of their containing capacities and the impossibility of being therapeutic in any case and all the time.

The clinical illustrations are presented in another part of this book, but the descriptions of the emotional experiences, of the shockwaves to which the group was subject, are intended to illuminate how the problem to tackle is not just the paedophilic behaviour or the symptomatology of seduction or abuse. We must also deal with the quality of the psychopathological disturbances which are at the base of a perverse behaviour, the different defensive modalities and the different transference-countertransference relationships resulting from them, and the different relational and group fields which are established.

The emotional turbulences governing the first part of the working group's life are closely linked to the disintegrating aspects, inability to think, intense dissolution and annihilation anxieties present in the patient who is the subject of reflection and supervision. These turbulences did not gain equal consistency in the second part of the group's work, in which, despite the difficult behaviours and attitudes to be integrated with the group members' emotional world, the passionate and differentiated discussion could proceed without the previous serious hitches.

The group's experiences reported here refer to their discussion of a case of paedophilic perversion, and we draw the reader's attention to them, as they seem to us illustrative of the working group's developments in the light of a less serious clinical picture than the first one. The material presented was characterised by two opposite polarities: on the one hand by bright representations (dreams, fairy tales, film or book themes) and on the other hand by repetitive moments in which the same concepts and relational modalities were highlighted and explained in a poor and trivial way.

In the working group attention, interest and free associations alternated with aloofness and boredom, as if everything had already been heard and was not worth discussing again. Boredom was caused by the concreteness and schematic nature of the relationships described and re-proposed in the patient-analyst relationship, but also by the odd incomprehensibility of some reported sequences of events. The narrative incomprehensibility and poverty corresponded to caesuras, gaps relating to aggressive and needy parts which were being hidden and therefore altered the picture of the various factors involved. The schematic nature of some of the relationships described corresponded to poor mental representations, lacking nuances, which manifested themselves through the slowness and boredom experienced by the group. These mental representations are very probably the result of the trauma and subsequent microtraumas experienced by the patient, which have blocked his development in certain relational areas, whereas other areas have been able to evolve and become structured. Such uneven development can explain the superimposition of contrasting feelings experienced and represented by the group.

"The individual alternating movements, first centripetal, then centrifugal, towards the group seem to have emotional qualities similar to the regressive and progressive movements leading an individual now towards a tendency to fuse with the primal love object, now towards moments of differentiation" (Gaburri, 1993, p. 17). In this case, a peculiarity of the regressive and progressive emotional movements was their contemporaneity, which wrong-footed the group members and resulted in their finding them difficult to understand.

In addition to reasons intrinsic to the lesser severity of the clinical case and to the group's acquired experience, there is one more element to be taken into consideration which brought increased group harmony: effective narration.

> Narrating effectively does not mean describing and representing thoughts and states of mind, but making it possible for them to interact directly with the people who are listening and the elements present in the field. The language of effectiveness, as Bion states (1965), is not a substitute for action, but has the same immediacy and strength as action. [Neri, 1993, p. 81]

Effective narration has to contain and express—in addition to the personal experience—also the emotions and fantasies present in the group in that moment (Neri, 1993). "The capacity to describe one's own present feelings coincides with the re-positioning of the object in its prospective loftiness, so with an improved descriptive capacity" (Boccanegra, 1997, p. 196).

A virtuous circle is formed, so that effective narration is followed by an improved emotional climate in the group, which can in turn improve the descriptions, which become more detailed and a more accurate reflection of the climate of the reported therapeutic relationship. The outline of an idea, a cognitive-affective and sensorial conglomerate not yet expressible and organisable, can find in the facilitating temporary personification with a colleague—for assonance, for contrast, or in any case for the complex journeys of fantasy—an incentive to further representative elaboration. This displays itself through the balanced overcoming of an initial confused experience, yet does not excessively exceed it, making the initial emotional trace last alongside its transformation (Boccanegra et al., 2000). Rinaldi comments:

> A continuous attention to the quality of one's own communications is fundamental in order to avoid destructive transformations of the group's functioning potentialities. Therefore, it is necessary to estimate to what extent these communications are used for connecting, in other words looking for "connections", for creating a network of affective relationships, sharing, a more expanded identity, and to what extent they are used for separating the narrators from one another. We have to take into consideration that sometimes the latter function should also prevail, in order to prevent one from resorting to the mass anonymity of the group, and to combat the difficulties of seeing oneself as an individual within the group with personal responsibilities. [1997, p. 292]

The effective narration proposed by Neri seems therefore to be based on the capacity to navigate one's way between the poles of sharing and individuation, in other words on the capacity to be together and to be on one's own in Winnicott's sense. In the group words come to life through a shared sensory and bodily experience, nourished by contradictions, made prismatic by the facets of the group itself. Words become familiar and renewed, rehabilitated to try to reach the other (Boccanegra et al., 2000).

We shall bring as an example a meaningful dream reported by the patient, which seems to shed light on the characteristics of his internal world and his relational attitudes. The patient describes dreaming of a fossil print left by a spider trampled by a tennis shoe. There is a strange temporal contradiction in this representation: the fossil print is dated back thousands of years to the remotest past, while the tennis shoe is an everyday object, a product of our times. The patient represents his story effectively: a remote story which he re-lives in a present which has features of the past. As he felt trampled in the remote time of his childhood, so today he feels trampled in his relationships with others, in particular his relationship with the analyst. Moreover, different developmental phases co-exist within him, so that (for example) technical and relational competences on a professional level alternate with poverty and concreteness in several of his interpersonal relationships.

Similarly, some members of the group became bored while examining the material and were unable to produce original reflections, while others remained lively and active; or those group members who felt bored and detached later suddenly rediscovered their capacity to imagine and think. Observing the group and the developments in our reactions made us realise that the patient's mental contents and the characteristics of his relationships were reflected into the group.

The patient clearly had difficulty in remembering the traumatic event he had suffered. While he carefully described his affective capacity and his professional success, he was unable to explain to himself and to others the reasons which had led him to attempt child abuse.

When the analyst brought to the group his ambivalent feelings about the contents of the patient's communication, which were out of tune with his countertransference experiences indicating a suggestive seductiveness, two parties formed. The first argued that the patient was "beating about the bush", that is to say he was trying by any means to divert the analyst's attention from the traumatic event, so that all the rest—his past, emotions, feelings, conflicting areas—overflowed in a collusive way onto the therapeutic relationship, whereas the event and its related emotions had to be kept clandestine and inaccessible to the therapeutic work. The second party sided with the psychoanalytic work on the patient's good elements, which by expanding over time would have made it possible to access the traumatic area which the patient was unable to access.

The first patient, cunning and seductive, clashed with the second patient, confused and doleful, but also traumatised by an event that he could not acknowledge as his. However, in the discussion of the clinical material the group offered a reflective space (Hinshelwood, 1994) in which the patient's splitting parts found a sense and were put together again. This patient's different levels of mental and emotional development did not have the devastating effect on the group that the first case of paedophilic perversity had. Moreover, it was possible to keep inside both images, without feeling compelled to prematurely expel one of them, in an attempt to nourish a new representation of the patient which took into consideration the complexity and contemporaneity of his experiences, as the dream of the tennis shoe and the fossil print had tried to reveal.

> Both the effect of the individual's self-focused attention and being close to others entail on the one hand an experience of unity with the group participants, and on the other hand a crisis in the individual, his or her history and identity. This phenomenon of homogenisation, that is to say of depersonalisation, certainly induces a personal crisis, triggered by powerful emotions present in the group field, and becomes the premise of a potentially therapeutic change. Each behaviour and speech in the new group experience loses its ordinary sense and meaning. Such a destabilising effect, alongside the adjoining disorganising homogenising process, must be attentively evaluated in order to prevent the participants' escape or expulsion, which can represent a thermometer of the emotional climate of the group and hence of its tolerance to change. [Contardi & Vender, 1993, p. 37]

These annotations seem to us particularly explicative of the two different experiences in the same group. In the first case the drive for disorganisation and depersonalisation had been very intense in the patient-analyst relationship, and had been accompanied by that physiological amount of homogenisation which any group experience entails in its initial phases. The result was the traumatic interruption of the group experience. In the second case the depersonalisation experiences of the patient (and hence of the analyst) were less intense, at any rate more accessible, and therefore more containable by the working group. The group was able to provide the analyst with the energy necessary to transform his meetings with the patient, which acquired three-dimensional and authentic qualities. "In the face of the experience of loss of sense, of chaos and depersonalisation, the group language, a depository of cultural shareable experiences, alleviates the fragmentation and dispersion by producing narrations, which by giving a limit to emotions, offer a sense to affections" (*ibid.*, p. 38). It is a process of sensory regeneration, which through social life, for a few moments and short epiphanies, makes it possible to see with new eyes, or to hear with new ears, what is living (Boccanegra et al., 2000).

Probably due to the lesser severity of the clinical picture presented by the patient, perhaps related to the fact that it had been warned by its previous experience, the group was able to tolerate its own emotions and understand their sense, at least partially. In this way the group was able to carry out its work, offering help also to the analyst and the patient, who were able to benefit from a group climate that was, on the whole, understanding and containing.

The group experience we have undergone and described seems to evidence the different levels of psychic falling apart that can be present in a patient with a paedophilic symptomatology. The differentiation between paedophilic perversion and paedophilic perversity has to do with diverse psychopathological pictures in which the transference, countertransference, relationship and relating group field must be weighed up and elaborated by absolutely different modalities, in order not to risk inducing transferential and countertransferential reactions of varying levels and severity, which are on the agenda in these patients, as we have been able to see. Furthermore, alongside the specificity represented by the individual subjectivities and by the specific group subjectivity, the differing assessment of paedophilic disturbances can explain why in some cases, even when acted responses occur, it is possible to maintain a reflective space which the same group is unable to guarantee when dealing with cases involving a higher level of psychic falling apart and fragmentation. In any case, resorting to a discussion group is necessary in order to face anxieties that would otherwise be unbearable.

BIBLIOGRAPHY

Abraham, K. (1907). The Experiencing of Sexual Trauma as a Form of Sexual Activity. In: *Selected Papers on Psychoanalysis*. London: Karnac, 1988.

Accerboni, A.M. et al. (1987). *La Cultura Psicoanalitica: Atti del Convegno, Trieste 5–8 dicembre 1985*. Pordenone: Tesi.

Agid, O. et al. (1999). Environment and Vulnerability to Major Psychiatric Illness: A Case Control Study of Early Parental Loss in Major Depression, Bipolar Disorder and Schizophrenia., *Molecular Psychiatry* 4: 163–172.

Aguglia, E. & Riolo, A. (1999). *La Pedofilia nell'Ottica Psichiatrica*. Rome: Il Pens. Scient.

Allende, I. (1985). *The Stories of Eva Luna*. London: Penguin, 1991.

Allende, I. (1995). *Paula*. London: Harper Perennial, 2005.

Almansi, G. (1974). *Le Bambine di Carroll*. Parma: F.M. Ricci.

Almansi, G. (1990). Il Grande Gatto Guarda Ancora. *Panorama*, 14 October: 130–131.

Amado, J. (1972). *Tereza Batista Cansada de Guerra*. São Paulo: Martins. English translation: *Tereza Batista: Home from the Wars*. New York: Avon, 1988.

American Psychiatric Association (1980). *Diagnostic and Statistical Manual of Mental Disorders. Third Edition* (DSM-III). Cambridge University Press.
American Psychiatric Association (1987). *Diagnostic and Statistical Manual of Mental Disorders. Third Edition Revised* (DSM-III-R) American Association Press.
American Psychiatric Association (1994). *Diagnostic and Statistical Manual of Mental Disorders. Fourth Edition* (DSM-IV). American Psychiatric Press.
Ames, M.A. & Houston, D.A. (1990). Legal, Social and Biological Definitions of Pedophilia. *Arch Sex. Behav.* 19: 333–342.
Amodeo, F. (1981). Innocenti Senza Innocenza. I Bambini e i Grandi Fotografi. *Phototeca 2*: 88–99.
Andersen, H.C. (1936–7). Andersen's Fairy Tales. Ware, Herts: Wordsworth Editions, 1993.
Anderson, C.A. & Bushman, B.J. (2002). The Effects of Media Violence on Society. *Science, 295*: 2377–2379.
André, S. (1999). La Signification de la Pédophilie. Conference presentation. http://www.oedipe.org/fr/actualites/pedophilie
Anzieu, D. (1975). *The Group and the Unconscious.* London: Routledge 1984.
Appleyard, B. (2000). What are we Doing to our Children? *The New Statesman Essay*, 21 August.
Arendt, H. (1951). *The Origins of Totalitarianism.* New York: Harcourt, 1973.
Arendt, H. (1963). *Eichmann in Jerusalem: A Report on the Banality of Evil.* London: Penguin, 2006.
Arfouilloux, J.C. (1993). Laïos Cannibale. *Rev. Franç. Psychanal.* 2: 495–505.
Ariès, P. (1960). *Centuries of Childhood: A Social History of Family Life.* New York: Random House, 1988.
Arieti, S. (1959–1966). *American Handbook of Psychiatry.* New York: Basic Books.
Arveiller, J. (1998). Pédophilie et Psychiatrie: Repères Historiques. *Évol. Psychiat.* 63: 11–34.
Aulagnier, P. (1975). *The Violence of Interpretation: From Pictogram to Statement.* Hove: Routledge, 2001.
Bachschmidt, C. et al. (1997). *Il Bambino e la Violenza Sessuale. Atti del Convegno, Genova, 1996.* Genoa: Coedital.
Baglione, G. (1642). *Le Vite de' Pittori, Scultori, Architetti, ed Intagliatori dal Pontificato di Gregorio XII del 1572 fino a'Ttempi de Papa Urbano VIII.*

nel 1642 [Lives of the painters, sculptors, architects, and engravers during the papacies of Gregory XII in 1572 to Urban VIII in 1642].
Baldaro Verde, J. (1997). Violenza Sessuale e Prostituzione Minorile. In: *Il Bambino e la Violenza Sessuale. Atti del Convegno, Genova, 1996.* Genoa: Coedital.
Bales, K. (1999). *Disposable People: New Slavery in the Global Economy.* Berkeley: University of California Press.
Balier, C. (1993). Pédophilie et Violence: L'Eclairage apporté par un Approche Criminologique. *Rev. Franç. Psychanal.* 57: 573–589.
Balier, C. (1996). *Psychanalyse des Comportements Sexuels Violents.* Paris: PUF.
Balint, M. (1969). Trauma and Object Relationship. *Int. J. Psychoanal.* 50: 429–436.
Bambino, A.M. (1995). *La Pedofilia: Considerazioni Storico-Sociologiche.* Rome: Centro Studi e Ricerche in Psichiatria e Scienze Umane "S. Maria della Pietà".
Barale, F. (1999). Preface. In: F. De Masi, *The Sadomasochistic Perversion: The Entities and the Theories.* London: Karnac, 2003.
Barale, F. (2001). Prefazione. In: C. Schinaia, *Pedofilia Pedofilie* (pp. 13–20). Turin: Bollati Boringhieri.
Barale, F. & Ferruta, A. (1997). But is Paris Really Burning? Uncertainty Anxieties and the Normal Chaos of Love. *Int. J. Psychoanal.* 78: 373–378.
Baranger, M., Baranger, W. & Mom, J. (1988). The Infantile Psychic Trauma from Us to Freud: Pure Trauma, Retroactivity and Reconstruction. *Int. J. Psychoanal.* 69: 113–128.
Barrie, J.M. (1906). Peter Pan in Kensington Gardens. In: *Peter Pan.* London: Penguin, 2004.
Baruk, H. (1959). *Traité de Psychiatrie.* Paris: Masson.
Becchi, E. (1994). *I Bambini nella Storia.* Bari: Laterza.
Bergeret, J. (1987). *Le Petit Hans et la Réalité.* Paris: Payot.
Bergeret, J. (1998). La Violenza Quotidiana. Riflessioni di uno Psicoanalista. *Psiche 6*: 87–93.
Bergler, E. (1938). Preliminary Phases of the Masculine Beating Fantasy. *Psychoanal. Q.* 7: 514–536.
Bergler, E. (1949). *The Basic Neurosis: Oral Regression and Psychic Masochism.* New York: Grune & Stratton.
Bergler, E. (1958). *Counterfeit Sex.* New York: Grune & Stratton.

Berti, A. (1999). La Perizia Psichiatrica del Pedofilo. In: M. Acconci & A. Berti (Eds.), *Grandi Reati, Piccole Vittime*. Genoa: Erga.
Berti, A. et al (1999). Proposte di Trattamento degli Abusatori Sessuali. In: M. Acconci & A. Berti (Eds.), *Grandi Reati, Piccole Vittime*. Genoa: Erga.
Berti, A. et al (1999). – Conseguenze Psicopatologiche dell'Abuso Sessuale. In: M. Acconci & A. Berti (Eds.), *Grandi Reati, Piccole Vittime*. Genoa: Erga.
Berti Ceroni, G. & Correale, A. (1999). *Psicoanalisi e Psichiatria*. Milan: Cortina.
Besserman Vianna, H. (1997). *Politique de la Psychanalyse face à la Dictature et à la Torture. N'en Parlez a Personne*. Paris: L'Harmattan.
Bettelheim, B. (1975). *The Uses of Enchantment: The Meaning and Importance of Fairy Tales*. London: Penguin, 1991.
Bianchi, L. (1924). *Trattato di Psichiatria*. Naples: Idelson.
Bini, L. & Bazzi, T. (1954). *Psicologia Medica*. Milan: Vallardi.
Bini, L. & Bazzi, T. (1967). *Trattato di Psichiatria*. Milan: Vallardi, 1972.
Bion, W.R. (1965). *Transformations*. London: Karnac.
Bion, W.R. (1966). Catastrophic Change. *Bulletic of the British Psychoanalytical Society 5*.
Bion, W.R. (1977). *Two Papers: The Grid and The Caesura*. London: Karnac, 1989.
Biondetti, L. (1997). *Dizionario di Mitologia Classica*. Milan: Baldini & Castoldi.
Biondi, G. (1950). *Manuale di Psichiatria*. Milan: Vallardi.
Blass, R. & Simon, B. (1994). The Value of the Historical Perspective to Contemporary Psychoanalysis: Freud's "Seduction Hypothesis". *Int. J. Psychoanal*. 75: 677–694.
Bléandonu, G. (1990). *Wilfred R. Bion: His Life and Works 1897–1979*. London: Free Association Books, 1994.
Bleuler, E. (1916). *Textbook of Psychiatry*. New York: Dover, 1952.
Blissett, L. (1997). *Lasciate che i Bimbi. Pedofilia: un Pretesto per la Caccia alle Streghe*. Rome: Castelvecchi.
Boccanegra, L. (1997). La "Poltrona Vuota": L'elaborazione Controtransferale Attraverso il Gruppo dei Colleghi. In: E. Gaburri (Ed.), *Emozione e Interpretazione* (pp. 193–202). Turin: Bollati Boringhieri.
Boccanegra, L. et al. (2000). *Autocredibilità Insatura: l'Apporto del Gruppo di Colleghi all'Elaborazione Controtransferale dell'Analista Impegnato con Pazienti Psicotici*. Unpublished.
Bollas, C. (1989). *Forces of Destiny: Psychoanalysis and Human Idiom*. London: Free Association Books.

Bollas, C. & Sundelson, D. (1995). *The New Informants.* London: Karnac.
Bonafiglia, L. (1999). Rassegna Bibliografica sulle Possibili Strategie Terapeutiche Impiegate con Pazienti Pedofili. In: B. Callieri & L. Frighi (Eds.), *La Problematica Attuale delle Condotte Pedofile* (pp. 289–302). Rome: EUR.
Boncinelli, E. (2000). *Le Forme della Vita. L'Evoluzione e l'Origine dell'Uomo.* Turin: Einaudi.
Bonfiglio, B. (1996). Il Trauma tra Freud e Ferenczi *Riv. di Psicoanal. 42*: 629–647.
Bonfiglio, B. (1997). Evoluzione del Concetto di Trauma e sua Utilità nella Clinica. *Riv. di Psicoanal. 43*: 583–606.
Bonnet, G. (1997). A Propos de "Psychanalyse des Comportments Sexuels Violents". *L'Évol. Psychiat. 62*: 565–573.
Bonnetaud, J.P. (1998). Critique de l'Argumentation Pédophilique. *Évol. Psychiat. 63*: 83–102.
Borgogno, F. (1999). *Psychoanalysis as a Journey.* London: Open Gate Press, 2007.
Bouchet-Kervella, D. (1996). Pour une Differenciation des Conduites Pédophiliques. *Évol. Psychiat. 61*: 55–73.
Bowlby, J. (1988). *A Secure Base: Clinical Applications of Attachment Theory.* London: Routledge.
Brandi, G. (1998). Pedofilia: un'Amicizia Ostile. *Il Reo e il Folle 2*: 109–120.
Brenman, E. (1985). Hysteria. *Int. J. Psychoanal. 66*: 423–432.
Brenman, E. (1988). Cruelty and Narrowmindedness. In: E. Bott Spillius (Ed.), *Melanie Klein Today. Development in Theory and Practice, Vol. 1: Mainly Theory.* London: Routledge.
Breuer, J. & Freud, S. (1893–95). Studies on Hysteria. *SE 2.*
Bumke, O. (1929). *Lehrbuch der Geisteskrankheiten.* Munich: Bergmann.
Burke, P. (1979). L'Artista: Momenti e Aspetti. In *L'Artista e il Pubblico, Storia dell'Arte Italiana, Vol. 2* (pp. 85–113). Turin: Einaudi.
Busi, A. (1997). Scusi, mi dà una caramella? In: Luther Blissett, *Lasciate che i Bimbi. Pedofilia: un Pretesto per la Caccia alle Streghe* (pp. 111–119). Bologna: Castevecchi.
Byng-Hall, J. & Stevenson-Hinde, J. (1991). Attachment Relationships Within a Family System. *Infant Mental Health Journ. 12*: 187–200.
Calandra, C., Monteleone, F. & Di Rosa, C. (1998). Il Maltrattamento ai Bambini. Ricerca attraverso la Cronaca. *Minerva Psichiatrica 39*: 147–153.
Calasso, R. (1988). *The Marriage of Cadmus and Harmony.* Colchester: Vintage, 1994.

Callieri, B. & Frighi, L. (1999). Aspetti Psicologici e Psicopatologici delle Pedofilie. In: B. Callieri & L. Frighi (Eds.), *La Problematica Attuale delle Condotte Pedofile* (pp. 39–50). Rome: EUR.
Calvino, I. (1973). La Tradizione Popolare nella Fiaba. In: R. Romano & C. Vivaldi (Eds.), *Storia d'Italia, Vol. V pt. II* (pp. 1253–1264). Turin: Einaudi.
Calvino, I. (1988). *Sulla Fiaba*. Turin: Einaudi.
Camarca, C. (1998). *I Santi Innocenti*. Milan: Baldini & Castoldi.
Camarca, C. & Parsi, M.R. (2000). *SOS Pedofilia. Parole per Uccidere l'Orco*. Milan: Baldini Castoldi Dalai.
Camassa, P. (1988). Alcune Considerazioni in un Caso di Pedofilia. In: L. Russo & M. Vigneri (Eds.), *Del Genere Sessuale*. Rome: Borla.
Campailla, G. (1975). *Manuale di Psichiatria*. Turin: Minerva Medica.
Campbell, D. (2008). The Shame Shield in Child Sexual Abuse. In: C. Pajaczkowska & I. Ward (Eds.), *Shame and Sexuality* (pp. 75–91). London: Routledge.
Camus, A. (1942). *The Myth of Sisyphus*. London: Penguin, 2000.
Cantarella, E. (1995). *Secondo Natura. La Bisessualità nel Mondo Antico*. Milan: Rizzoli.
Caper, R. (1998). Psychopathology of Primitive Mental States. *Int. J. Psychoanal. 79*: 539–549.
Capri, L. (1999). La Pedofilia: Difficoltà e Complessità di Interpretazione. In: B. Callieri & L. Frighi (Eds.), *La Problematica Attuale delle Condotte Pedofile* (pp. 15–37). Edizioni Univ. Romane.
Carloni, G. (1987a). Mistero, Magia e Meraviglia (Fiaba, Cinema e Psicoanalisi). In: *La Cultura Psicoanalitica*. Pordenone: Studio Tesi.
Carloni, G. (1987b). La Fiaba nella Psicoanalisi e la Psicoanalisi nella Fiaba. In: E. Morpurgo & V. Egidi (Eds.), *Psicoanalisi e Narrazione*. Ancona: Il Lavoro Editoriale.
Carotenuto, A. (1992). *Trattato di Psicologia Analitica*. Turin: UTET.
Carrasco, R. (1989). Le Châtiment de la Sodomie sous l'Inquisition. In: A. Corbin, *Violences Sexuelles*. Paris: Imago.
Casilli, R. (1998). Monopolio Sociale sulla Produzione dei Corpi. *Derive Approdi 16*: 36–38.
Cassity, J.H. (1927). Psychological Considerations of Pedophilia. *Psychoanal. Rev. 14*: 189–209.
Centerwall, B.S. (1992). Vladimir Nabokov: A Case Study in Paedophilia. *Psychoan. and Contemporary Thought 15*: 199–240.
Chabert, C. (1993). Mon Père Préfère les Blonds. *Rev. Franç. Psychanal. 57*: 329–341.

Chasseguet-Smirgel, J. (1985). *Creativity and Perversion*. London: Free Association Books.
Chervet, B. (1993). Des Amours d'Enfants. Mithe, "Médusage" et Différenciation Primordiale. *Rev. Franç. Psychanal. 57*: 535–549.
Citati, P. (2002). Piccoli Schiavi della TV. *La Repubblica*, 25 March.
Cohen, M.N. (1978). *Lewis Carroll, Photographer of Children: Four Nude Studies*. New York: Clarkson Potter.
Colli, G. (1977). *La Sapienza Greca, Vol. I*. Milan: Adelphi.
Collodi, C. (1883). *Pinocchio: The Tale of a Puppet*. London: Penguin, 2002.
Conrad, J. (1911). Under Western Eyes. New York: Dover, 2003.
Contardi, R. & Vender, S. (1993). Le Sorgenti del Nilo: Dall'Impersonale al Soggetto Gruppale. In: R. Contardi, E. Gaburri & S. Vender, *Fattori Terapeutici nei Gruppi e nelle Istituzioni* (pp. 23–40). Rome: Borla.
Conti, A. (1979). L'Evoluzione dell'Artista. In: *L'Artista e il Pubblico: Storia dell'Arte Italiana, Vol. 2* (pp. 117–263). Turin: Einaudi.
Cooper, A.M. (1986). Toward a Limited Definition of Psychic Trauma. In: A. Rothstein (Ed.), *The Reconstruction of Trauma*. Madison, CT: International Universities Press.
Corbin, A. (1989). *Violences Sexuelles*. Paris: Imago.
Corno, D. (1979). Voce: Fiaba. In: *Enciclopedia, Vol. VI* (pp. 116–134). Turin: Einaudi.
Correale, A. & Neri, C. (1999). Psicoanalisi e Gruppo. In: G. Berti Ceroni & A. Correale, *Psicoanalisi e Psichiatria* (pp. 11–18). Milan: Cortina.
Czobor, A. (1954). Autoritratti del Giovane Caravaggio. *Acta Hist. Art Acad. Sci. Hung. 2*: 201–213.
D'Agostino Trevi, E. (2000). Hanna Arendt: Il Male "Banale". In: F.P. Pieri (Ed.), *Il Male* (pp. 25–41). Milan: Cortina.
Dalla Volta, A. (1974). *Dizionario di Psicologia*. Florence: Giunti Barbèra.
Dante Alighieri (1321). *The Divine Comedy*. London: Penguin, 2006.
D'Avanzo, G. (2000). La Caccia al Pirata Albanese. *La Repubblica*, 6 December.
Davies, J.M. & Frawley, M.G. (1994). *Treating the Adult Survivor of Childhood Sexual Abuse*. New York: Basic Books.
De Martis, D. (1989). La Perversione. In: A.A. Semi (Ed.), *Trattato di Psicoanalisi*, Vol. II (pp. 255–370). Milan: Cortina.
De Masi, F. (1994). Note su un Trattamento Analitico di un Caso di Perversione Pedofila. Paper read to the Centro Milanese di Psicoanalisi.

De Masi, F. (1998). Il Mondo del Pedofilo. *Famiglia Oggi 12*: 20–27.
De Masi, F. (1999). *The Sadomasochistic Perversion: The Entities and the Theories*. London: Karnac, 2003.
De Masi, F. (2000). Il Fascino del Male nella Mente: Dal Male alla Malattia. In: CIPA, *Il Male* (pp. 141–153). Milan: Cortina.
De Masi, F. (2007). The Paedophile and his Inner World: Theoretical and Clinical Considerations on the Analysis of a Patient. *Int. J. Psychoanal. 88*: 147–165.
DeMause, L. (1974). *The History of Childhood*. New York: Aronson, 1995.
DeMause, L. (2000). La Historia del Ultraje Infantil. *Rev. de Psicoanalisis, Número Especial Internacional "Violencia y perversidad" 7*: 103–133.
Denis, P. (1993). Fantasmes Originaires et Fantasme de la Pédophilie Paternelle. *Rev. Franç. Psychanal. 57*: 607–612.
Denis, P. & Ribas, D. (1993). Argument. *Rev. Franç. Psychanal. 57*: 325–326.
De Paoli, G. (1878). *Note sul Tatuaggio nel Manicomio di Genova*. Gazz. Osp.
De Simone, G. (2002). *Le Famiglie di Edipo*. Rome: Borla.
Detienne, M. (1980). Voce: Mito/Rito. In: *Enciclopedia, Vol. 9*. Turin: Einaudi.
Detienne, M. (1981). *The Creation of Mythology*. Chicago: University of Chicago Press, 1986.
Dettore, D. (1999a). Il Pedofilo: Miti e Realtà. In: D. Dettore & C. Fuligni (Eds.), *L'Abuso Sessuale sui Minori. Valutazione e Terapia delle Vittime e dei Responsabili* (pp. 283–315). Milan: McGraw-Hill.
Dettore, D. (1999b). L'Intervento sui Responsabili di Reati Sessuali e la Relapse Prevention. In: D. Dettore & C. Fuligni (Eds.), *L'Abuso Sessuale sui Minori. Valutazione e Terapia delle Vittime e dei Responsabili* (pp. 317–353). Milan: McGraw-Hill.
Devereux, G. (1953). Why Oedipus Killed Laius: A Note on the Complementary Oedipus Complex in Greek Drama. *I. J. Psychoanal. 34*: 132–141.
Devereux, G. (1966). The Cannibalistic Impulses of Parents. In: *Basic Problems of Ethnopsychiatry*. Chicago: University of Chicago Press, 1980.
De Young, M. (1982). *The Sexual Victimization of Children*. London: McFarland.
De Zulueta, F. (1993). *From Pain to Violence: The Traumatic Roots of Destructiveness*. London: Whurr.

Dhawan, S. & Marshall, W.L. (1996). Sexual Abuse Histories of Sexual Offenders. *Sexual Abuse: A Journal of Research and Treatment, 8*: 7–15.
Di Chiara, G. (1999). *Sindromi Psicosociali. La Psicoanalisi e le Patologie Sociali.* Milan: Cortina.
Di Lascia, M.T. (1998). Veglia. *Nessuno Tocchi Caino 5*: 76–77.
Disertori, B. & Piazza, M. (1970). *Trattato di Psichiatria e Sociopsichiatria.* Padua: Liviana.
Dobash, R.P. et al. (1993). Child Sexual Abusers. Recognition and Response. In: L. Waterhouse (Ed.), *Child Abuse and Child Abusers* (pp. 113–135). London: Jessica Kinglsley.
Dogliani, M. (1997). Introduction. In: Thomas Mann, *La Legge.* Milan: Baldini & Castoldi.
Doni, E. & Valentini, C. (1993). *L'Arma dello Stupro: Voci di Donne della Bosnia.* Palermo: La Luna.
Dorr, D. (1998). Psychopathy in the Pedophile. In: T. Millon et al., *Psychopathy: Antisocial, Criminal and Violent Behavior* (pp. 304–320). New York: Guilford.
Dostoevsky, F. (1863). *Winter Notes on Summer Impressions.* London: Oneworld Classics, 2008.
Dostoevsky, F. (1872). *Demons.* London: Penguin, 2008.
Dubret, G. (1996). Pervers, Perversions, Perversité: Continuum ou Alterité. *Évol. Psychiat. 61*: 137–145.
Dumont, V. (1997). *J'ai Peur du Monsieur.* Arles: Actes Sud.
Durieux, M.C. (1993). Le Complexe de Laïos selon John Murder Ross. *Rev. Franç. Psychanal. 58*: 551–559.
Eagle, H. (1992). La Natura del Cambiamento Teorico in Psicoanalisi. *Psicoter. e Scienze Umane 3*: 5–42.
Eidelberg, L. (1968). *Encyclopedia of Psychoanalysis.* New York: Free Press.
Erikson, E. (1950). *Childhood and Society.* St Albans: Triad/Paladin, 1977.
Ey, H. (1950). Perversité et Perversions. In: *Études Psychiatriques 2* (pp. 233–340). Paris: Disclée de Brouwer.
Ey, H., Bernard, P. & Brisset, C. (1967). *Manuel de Psychiatrie.* Paris: Masson.
Falzone del Barbarò, M., Miraglia, M. & Mussa, I. (1980). *Le Fotografie di Wilhelm von Gloeden.* Milan: Longanesi.
Fanali, A. (1998). Pedofilia: Riflessioni sugli Aspetti Relazionali. In: C. Bogliolo, *Bambini e Violenza* (pp. 139–146). Tirrenia: Del Cerro.
Fanon, F. (1961). *The Wretched of the Earth.* London: Penguin, 2001.
Fenichel, O. (1945). *The Psychoanalytic Theory of Neurosis.* New York: Norton.

Ferenczi, S. (1930). The Principle of Relaxation and Neocatharsis. In: *Final Contribution to the Problems and Methods of Psychoanalysis* (pp. 108–125). London: Hogarth, 1955.
Ferenczi, S. (1933). Confusion of Tongues between Adults and the Child. In: *Final Contributions to the Problems and Methods of Psychoanalysis* (pp. 156–167). London: Hogarth, 1955.
Ferrante Capetti, L. (1910). *Reati e Psicopatie Sessuali.* Turin: Bocca.
Ferrari, A. (1999). *Dizionario di Mitologia Greca e Latina.* Turin: UTET.
Ferrero, E. (1998). *Barbablù: Gilles de Rais e il Tramonto del Medioevo.* Piemme: Casale Monferrato.
Ferriani, L. (1902). *I Drammi del Fanciullo. Studio di Psicologia Sociale e Criminale.* Como: Tipografia Omarini.
Ferro, A. (1985). Psicoanalisi e Favole. *Riv. di Psicoan. 31*: 216–230.
Finkelor, D. (1984). *Child Sexual Abuse: New Theory and Research.* New York: Free Press.
Fonagy, P. (1993). Psychoanalytic and Empirical Approaches to Developmental Psychopathology: An Object Relations Perspective. *J. Am. Psychoanal. Ass. 41S*: 245–260.
Fonagy, P., Steele, M., Moran, G. & Higgitt, A.C. (1991). The Capacity for Understanding Mental States: The Reflective Self in Parent and Child and its Significance for Security of Attachment. *Inf. Ment. Health. J. 13*: 201–218.
Fonagy, P. & Target, M. (1996). Playing with Reality: I. Theory of Mind and the Normal Development of Psychic Reality. *Int. J. Psychoan 77*: 217–233.
Forel, A. (1905). *The Sexual Question: A Scientific, Psychological, Hygienic and Sociological Study for the Cultured Classes.* New York: Rebman, 1908.
Fornari, U. (1999). Il Comportamento Pedofilo e le sue Implicazioni Medico-Legali. In: B. Callieri & L. Frighi (Eds.), *La Problematica Attuale delle Condotte Pedofile* (pp. 149–158). Rome: EUR.
Foti, C. (1998). Dare Voce al Disagio. *Famiglia Oggi 12*: 12–19.
Foti, C. & Roccia, C. (1994a). La Sessualità dei Minori tra Educazione e Abuso. In: C. Roccia & C. Foti (Eds.), *L'Abuso Sessuale sui Minori. Educazione Sessuale, Prevenzione, Trattamento* (pp. 11–54). Milan: Unicopli.
Foti, C. & Roccia, C. (1994b). La Fiaba: un'Occasione per Parlare di Violenza Sessuale ai Bambini. In: C. Roccia & C. Foti (Eds.), *L'Abuso Sessuale sui Minori. Educazione Sessuale, Prevenzione, Trattamento* (pp. 127–138). Milan: Unicopli.

Foucault, M. (1978). *The History of Sexuality. Vol. 1: The Will to Knowledge.* London: Penguin, 1998.
Foucault, M. (1979). Sexual Morality and the Law [originally published as "La Loi de la Pudeur"]. In: *Politics, Philosophy, Culture: Interviews and Other Writings 1977–1984.* London: Routledge, 1990.
Foucault, M. (1984). *The History of Sexuality. Vol. 2: The Use of Pleasure.* London: Penguin, 1998.
Frances, A., First, M.B. & Pincus, H.A. (1995). *DSM IV Guidebook.* American Psychiatric Press.
Franz, M.-L. von. (1970). *Interpretation of Fairytales.* Boston, Mass: Shambhala, 1996.
Frawley-O'Dea, M.G. & Goldner, V. (2007). *Predatory Priests, Silenced Victims: The Sexual Abuse Crisis and the Catholic Church.* London: Routledge.
Freud, A. (1964). Comments on Psychic Trauma. In: *The Writings of Anna Freud, Vol. 5.* New York: International Universities Press.
Freud, S. (1890). Psychical (or Mental) Treatment. *SE 7.*
Freud, S. (1893–95). Studies on Hysteria. *SE 2.*
Freud, S. (1895). Project for a Scientific Psychology. *SE 1.*
Freud, S. (1896a). Draft K. The Neuroses of Defence: A Christmas Fairy Tale. *SE 1.*
Freud, S. (1896b). The Aetiology of Hysteria. *SE 3.*
Freud, S. (1900). The Interpretation of Dreams. *SE 4.*
Freud, S. (1901). On Dreams. *SE 5.*
Freud, S. (1905). Three Essays on the Theory of Sexuality. *SE 7.*
Freud, S. (1906). Delusions and Dreams in Jensen's "Gradiva". *SE 9.*
Freud, S. (1908). Creative Writers and Day-Dreaming. *SE 9.*
Freud, S. (1909). Notes on a Case of Obsessional Neurosis. *SE 10.*
Freud, S. (1912–13). Totem and Taboo. *SE 13.*
Freud, S. (1913). The Claims of Psychoanalysis to Scientific Interest. *SE 13.*
Freud, S. (1914a). On Narcissism: An introduction. *SE 14.*
Freud. S. (1914b). Remembering, Repeating and Working Through. *SE 12.*
Freud, S. (1915–17). Introductory Lectures on Psychoanalysis. *SE 16.*
Freud, S. (1916). Criminals from a Sense of Guilt. *SE 14.*
Freud, S. (1918). From the History of an Infantile Neurosis [the "Wolf Man"]. *SE 17.*
Freud, S. (1919a). A Child is Being Beaten. *SE 17.*
Freud, S. (1919b). The Uncanny. *SE 17.*
Freud, S. (1920). Beyond the Pleasure Principle. *SE 18.*

Freud, S. (1921). Group Psychology and the Analysis of the Ego. *SE 18.*
Freud, S. (1926). Inhibitions, Symptoms and Anxiety. *SE 20.*
Freud, S. (1928). Dostoevsky and Parricide. *SE 21.*
Freud, S. (1930). Civilization and its Discontents. *SE 21.*
Freud, S. (1931). Female Sexuality. *SE 21.*
Freud, S. (1932–36). New Introductory Lectures on Psychoanalysis. *SE 22.*
Freud, S. (1932). The Acquisition and Control of Fire. *SE 22.*
Freud, S. (1933). New Introductory Lectures on Psychoanalysis. *SE 22.*
Freud, S. (1937). Analysis Terminable and Interminable. *SE 23.*
Freud, S. (1940a). An Outline of Psychoanalysis. *SE 23.*
Freud, S. (1940b). Splitting of the Ego in the Process of Defence. *SE 23.*
Fritzlaer, J.K.E. von (1969). *Summa Sexualis.* Turin: Dellavalle.
Gabbard, G.O. (1994). *Psychodynamic Psychiatry in Clinical Practice.* Arlington, VA: American Psychiatric Publishing, 2005.
Gabbard, G.O. (1997). Challenges in the Analysis of Adult Patients with Histories of Childhood Sexual Abuse. *Canadian J. Psychoanal.* 5: 1–25.
Gabbard, G.O. (2000). Disguise or Consent: Problems and Recommendations Concerning the Publication and Presentation of Clinical Material. *Int. J. Psychoanal. 81*: 1071–1086.
Gaburri, E. (1993). Introduction. In: R. Contardi, E. Gaburri & S. Vender, *Fattori Terapeutici nei Gruppi e nelle Istituzioni* (pp. 13–19). Rome: Borla.
Galimberti, U. (1992). *Dizionario di Psicologia.* Turin: UTET.
Galimberti, U. (2000a). Quando i Bambini sono Merce. *La Repubblica,* 28 September.
Galimberti, U. (2000b). La Violenza sui Bambini e il Pericolo del Silenzio. *La Repubblica,* 30 September.
Galimberti, U. (2001). Il Baratro della Pedofilia. Quel Buco Dentro di Noi. *La Repubblica,* 22 April.
Ganzarain R. & Buchele, B.J. (1990). Incest Perpetrators in Group Therapy. *Bulletin of the Menninger Clinic 54*: 295–310.
Gargani, A.G. (1995). La Figura del Maestro. Esemplarità, Autenticità e Inautenticità. In: G. Vattimo (Ed.), *Filosofia '94.* Bari: Laterza.
Gauthier-Hamon, C. & Téboul, R. (1988). *Entre Père et Fils: La Prostitution Homosexuelle des Garcons.* Paris: Presses Universitaires de France.
Geissmann, C. & Geissmann, P. (1997). *A History of Child Psychoanalysis.* London: Routledge.
Gernsheim, H. (1949). *Lewis Carroll, Photographer.* New York: Dover, 1970.
Giallongo, A. (1990). *Il Bambino Medioevale.* Bari: Dedalo.

Giberti, F. & Rossi, R. (1996). *Trattato di Psichiatria*. Padua: Piccin & Vallardi.
Gide, A. (1924). *Corydon*. New York: Farrar, Strauss & Giroux, 2001.
Gilman, S.I. (1993). *Difference and Pathology. Stereotypes of Sexuality, Race and Madness*. Baltimore, MD: Cornell University Press.
Glasser, M. (1988). Psychodinamic Aspects of Paedophilia. *Year Book Psychoanal. Psychother. 3*: 121–135.
Glasser, M. (1992). Problems in the Psychoanalysis of Certain Narcissistic Disorders. *Int. J. Psychoanal. 73*: 493–503.
Glover, E. (1933). The Relation of Perversion Formation to the Development of Reality Sense. *Int. J. Psychoanal. 14*: 486–504.
Glover, E. (1955). *The Technique of Psychoanalysis*. London: Bailliere Tindall & Cox.
Glover, E. (1964). Aggression and Sadomasochism. In: *The Pathology and Treatment of Sexual Deviations*. London: Oxford University Press.
Glueck, B.C. Jr. (1956). Psychodynamic Patterns in the Homosexual Sex Offender. *Am. J. Psychiat. 112*: 584–590.
Goethe, J.W. *Selected Poetry*. London: Penguin, 2005.
Goldberg, A. (1995). *The Problem of Perversion: The View from Self Psychology*. New Haven, CT: Yale University Press.
Gombrowicz, W. (1960). *Pornografia*. London: Marion Boyars, 1994.
Goodrich, M. (1976). Sodomy in Medieval Secular Law. *J. Homosex. 1*: 295–302.
Goretti, G. (1997). Le Menti Violate: Pensieri su Dora, Schreber, Paul ed Altri. *Riv. di Psicoanal. 44*: 635–657.
Gozzano, M. (1970). *Compendio di Psichiatria*. Turin: Rosemberg & Sellier.
Grant, M. & Hazel, J. (1973). *Who's Who in Classical Mythology*. Abingdon: Routledge, 2002.
Graves, R. (1955). *The Greek Myths*. London: Penguin.
Green, A. (1975). Le Temps Mort. *Nouv. Rev. Psychanal. 11*: 103–109.
Green, A. (1990). *On Private Madness*. London: Karnac, 1997.
Green, A. (1992). *La Deliaison. Revelations de l'Inachevement. A Propos du Carton de Londres de Leonard da Vinci*. Paris: Flammarion.
Green, A. (1997). Note on Paedophilia. In: *The Chains of Eros: The Actuality of the Sexual in Psychoanalysis*. London: Karnac, 2001.
Grimal, P. (1951). *Dictionnaire de la Mythologie Grecque et Romaine*. Paris: PUF, 1999. [English edition: *Dictionary of Classical Mythology*. Oxford: Blackwell, 1996.]
Grimm, J. & Grimm, W. *Complete Fairy Tales*. London: Routledge, 2002.

Grinberg, L. (1981). The Oedipus as a Resistance against the Oedipus in Psychoanalytical Practice. In: *The Goals of Psychoanalysis: Identification, Identity, and Supervision*. London: Karnac, 1990.
Groth, A.N. & Burgess, A.W. (1977). Motivational Intent in the Sexual Assault of Children. *Criminal Justice and Behavior* 4: 253–264.
Groth, A.N & Birnbaum, H.J. (1979). *Men Who Rape: The Psychology of the Offender*. New York: Plenum.
Groth, A.N., Hobson, W.F. & Gary, T.S. (1982). The Child Molester: Clinical Observations. *Journal of Social Work and Human Sexuality* 1: 129–144.
Guasto, G. (2001). Abuso e Mondo Interno: Trauma, Difese, Devastazione, Mentalizzazione. In: C. Roccia (Ed.), *Riconoscere e Ascoltare il Trauma. Maltrattamento e Abuso Sessuale sui Minori: Prevenzione e Terapia*. Milan: Franco Angeli.
Hanus, M. & Le Guillou-Eliet, C. (1971). *Psychiatrie Integrée de l'Etudiant*. Paris: Maloine.
Hasler, E. (1997). *Die Vogelmacherin*. Zurich: Nagel & Kimhe.
Henderson, D. & Gillespie, R.D. (1927). *A Textbook of Psychiatry for Students and Practitioners*. London: Oxford University Press.
Herdt, G. (1981). *Guardians of the Flutes*. New York: McGraw-Hill.
Hinshelwood, R. (1994). Group Mentality and "Having a Mind". Attacks on the Reflective Space. In: V.L. Shermer & M. Pines (Eds.), *Ring of Fire: Primitive Affects and Object Relations in Group Psychotherapy*. London: Routledge.
Hinsie, L. & Campbell, R. (1970). *Psychiatric Dictionary*. London: Oxford University Press.
Hochkofler, M. (2001). I Carusi di Taormina. *Il Manifesto* (11 January).
Hoffman, L. (1998). Presentation at the symposium "The Seduction Hypothesis One Hundred Years Later: Trauma, Fantasy, and Reality Today", New York.
Huesmann, L.R. et al. (2003). Longitudinal Relations between Children's Exposure to TV Violence and their Aggressive and Violent Behavior in Young Adulthood: 1977–1992. *Developmental Psychology*. 39: 201–221.
Iaria, A. (1999). Lo Psichiatra di Fronte al Problema della Pedofilia. In: B. Callieri & L. Frighi (Eds.), *La Problematica Attuale delle Condotte Pedofile* (pp. 51–64). Rome: EUR.
Iaria, A. et al. (1996). La Pedofilia. Comunicazione e Contesto Sociale nell'Ambito dei Reati Sessuali sui Minori. *Attualità in Psicologia 11*: 209.

Imbasciati, A. (1994). *Fondamenti Psicoanalitici della Psicologia Clinica*. Turin: UTET.
James, H. (1898). *The Turn of the Screw*. London: Penguin, 2007.
Jerome, J.K. (1889). *Three Men in a Boat*. London: Penguin, 2007.
Jervis, G. (1975). *Manuale Critico di Psichiatria*. Milan: Feltrinelli.
Johnson, J.G., Cohen, P., Smailes, E.M., Kasen, S. & Brook, J.S. (2002). Television Viewing and Aggressive Behavior During Adolescence and Adulthood. *Science, 295*: 2468–2471.
Jolles, A. (1930). *Einfache Formen*. Tübingen: Max Niemeyer, 1999.
Jones, G.P. (1990). The Study of Intergenerational Intimacy in North America: Beyond Politics and Pedophilia. *J. Homosex. 20*: 275–295.
Joseph, B. (1971). A Clinical Contribution to the Analysis of a Perversion. In: *Psychic Equilibrium and Psychic Change*. Hove: Routledge, 1989.
Joseph, B. (1982). Addiction to Near-Death. In: *Psychic Equilibrium and Psychic Change*. Hove: Routledge, 1989.
Joseph, B. (1989). Psychic Change and the Psychoanalytic Process. In: *Psychic Equilibrium and Psychic Change*. Hove: Routledge, 1989.
Jung, C.G. & Kerényi, K. (1940). *Introduction to a Science of Mythology: The Myth of the Divine Child and the Mysteries of Eleusis*. London: Routledge, 1951.
Kaplan, H.I. Sadock, B.J. (1989). *Comprehensive Textbook of Psychiatry IV*. Baltimore, MD: Williams & Wilkins.
Karpman, B. (1950). A Case of Pedophilia (Legally Rape) Cured by Psychoanalysis. *Psychoanal. Rev. 37*: 235–276.
Kerényi, C. (1951). *The Gods of the Greeks*. London: Thames & Hudson, 1976.
Kernberg, O.F. (1992). *Aggression in Personality Disorders and Perversions*. New Haven, CT: Yale University Press.
Khan, M.M.R. (1979). *Alienation in Perversions*. London: Karnac, 1987.
Kirk, G. (1974). *The Nature of Greek Myths*. London: Penguin, 1990.
Klumpner, G.H. & Frank, A. (1991). On Methods of Reporting Clinical Material. *J. Am. Psychoanal. Ass. 39*: 537–551.
Kluzer, G. (1996). Nuove Ipotesi Interpretative sul Concetto di Trauma. *Riv. di Psicoanal. 42*: 405–423.
Kochansky, G.E. & Cohen, M. (2007). Priests who Sexualize Minors: Psychodynamic, Characterological and Clerical Considerations. In: M.G. Frawley-O'Dea & V. Goldner (Eds.), *Predatory Priests, Silenced Victims: The Sexual Abuse Crisis and the Catholic Church* (p. 35). London: Routledge.

Kraepelin, E. (1902). *Clinical Psychiatry*. Whitefish, MT: Kessinger Publishing, 2007.
Krafft-Ebing, R. (1886). *Psychopathia Sexualis*. London: Velvet Publications, 1997. [16th German edition edited and re-elaborated by A. Moll (1923); Italian translation by P. Giolla, Milan: Manfredi, 1952].
Kramer, S. & Akhtar, S. (1991). *The Trauma of Transgression*. New York: Aronson.
Krystal, H. (1978). Trauma and Affects. *Psychoanal. Study Child 33*: 81–116.
Laks Eizirik, C. (2000). Salute Mentale e Psicoanalisi: Sfide Attuali. *Riv. di Psicoanal. 46*: 753–762.
Lampignano, A. (2000). A Proposito del Rapporto tra Maestro e Allievo. *Riv. It. Gruppoanal. 14*: 37–50.
Lang, A. (1888). Introduction. In: *Perrault's Popular Tales*. Oxford: Clarendon.
Lanotte, A. (1999). La Relazione Pedofila. In: B. Callieri & L. Frighi (Eds.), *La Problematica Attuale delle Condotte Pedofile* (pp. 65–76). Rome: EUR.
Lantéri-Laura, G. (1966). Réflexions Historiques sur Certaines Questions Relatives aux Singularités des Conduites Sexuelles. *L'Évol. psychiat. 61*: 17–25.
Laplanche, J. & Pontalis, J.P. (1967). *The Language of Psychoanalysis*. London: Karnac, 1988.
La Rochefoucauld, F. de (1665). *Maxims*. London: Penguin, 1959.
Laub, D. & Auerhahn, N.C. (1993). Knowing and Not Knowing Massive Psychic Trauma: Forms of Traumatic Memory. *Int. J. Psychoanal. 74*: 287–302.
Leach, E.R. (1954). *Political Systems of Highland Burma*. London: Berg, 2004.
Lebrun, J.P. (1997). *Un Monde sans Limite. Essai pour une Clinique Psychanalytique du Social*. Toulouse: Érès.
Leguay, J.-P. (1989). Un Cas de Force au Moyen Age: Le Viol de Margot Simmonet. In: A. Corbin, *Violences Sexuelles*. Paris: Imago.
LeRoy, J.T. (2000) *Sarah*. London: Bloomsbury.
Le Roy Ladurie, E. (1975). *Montaillou: The Promised Land of Error*. London:
Vintage, 1979.
Levi, P. (1986). *The Drowned and the Saved*. London: Abacus, 1989.
Lévi-Strauss, C. (1958). *Structural Anthropology*. New York: Basic Books, 1963.

Lévi-Strauss, C. (1960). Structure and Form: Reflections on a Work by Vladimir Propp. In: V. Propp, Theory and History of Folklore (p. 167). Minneapolis: University of Minnesota Press, 1984. [Chapter 5 of this book is Propp's response to Lévi-Strauss.]
Lichtenberg, J.D. (2001). Motivational Systems and Model Scenes with Special References to Bodily Experiences. *Psychoanalitic Inquiry* 21: 430.
Limentani, A. (1991). Neglected Fathers. Aetiology and Treatment of Sexual Deviations. *I.J. Psychoanal.* 72: 573–584.
Lingiardi, V. (2001). La Fabbrica dei Traumi. *Diario VI*, supplement to no. 4: 99–105.
Lombroso, C. (1884). Pazzo Morale e Delinquente Nato. In: D. Frigessi, F. Giacanelli & L. Mangoni (Eds.), *Delitto, Genio e Follia. Scritti Scelti* (pp. 545–559). Turin: Bollati Boringhieri, 2000.
Lopez, D. (1985a). Dialogo con Lopez a Proposito di Masson. Edited by A. Todisco. *Gli Argonauti 25*: 83–90.
Lopez, D. (1985b). L'Aletheia del Sacro nell'Oresteia. *Gli Argonauti 26*: 161–172.
Lopez, G. (1997). *Les Violences Sexuelles sur les Enfants*. Paris: PUF.
Lugaro, E. (1906). *I Problemi Odierni della Psichiatria*. Milan: Sandron.
Lüthi, M. (1947). *The European Folktale: Form and Nature*. Bloomington: Indiana University Press, 1986.
Machado, L.M. (1996). Transferencia e Controtransferencia Erotica na Analise de Crianças e Adolescentes. *Rev. Brasileira de Psicanalise 30*: 1157–1172.
Mafai, M. (2000). Il Teorema di un Procuratore. *La Repubblica*, 22 December.
Maffeo, R. (1994). Il Lupo, il Re e l'Orco: Tre Casi di Abuso Sessuale. In: C. Roccia & C. Foti (Eds.), *L'Abuso Sessuale sui Minori. Educazione Sessuale, Prevenzione, Trattamento* (pp. 117–125). Milan: Unicopli.
Magli, I. (1984). L'Antica Violenza contro i Bambini. *La Repubblica*, 22 September.
Magris, C. (1999). *Utopia e Disincanto. Storie, Speranze, Illusioni del Moderno*. Milan: Garzanti.
Main, M.B. (1987). Parents' Representations of Attachments which Correlate with Attachment Behaviour of their Children: A Potential Meeting Point between Research and Psychotherapy. London: Tavistock Clinic (sound recording).
Main, M. & Goldwyn, R. (1984). Predicting Rejection of her Infant from Mother's Representation of her own Experience: Implications for the

Abused-Abusing Intergenerational Cycle. *Child Abuse and Neglect 8*: 203–217.
Malacrea, M. & Vassalli, A. (1990). *Segreti di Famiglia*. Milan: Cortina.
Malaparte. C. (1949). *The Skin*. Evanston, IL: Northwestern University Press, 1997.
Mancuso, F. (1997). Peter Pan e il Mondo-che-non-c'è. Ipotesi Psicoanalitiche su una Particolare Risposta a Traumi Precoci. *Riv. di Psicoanal. 43*: 559–581.
Mann, S. (1992). *Immediate Family*. London: Phaidon.
Mann, T. (1912). *Death in Venice*. London: Penguin Classics, 1999.
Mann, T. (1956). Freud and the Future. *Int. J. Psychoanal. 37*: 106–115.
Manzoni, A. (1827). *The Betrothed*. London: Penguin, 1972.
Marchesini, R. (2001). *Bioetica e Scienze Veterinarie*. Naples: Edizioni Scientifiche Italiane.
Marchesini, R. (2002). *Post-Human: Verso Nuovi Modelli di Esistenza*. Turin: Bollati Boringhieri.
Marchiori, E., Simioni, A. & Colombo, G. (2000). Violenza Sessuale e Stampa Italiana. Indagine su Quotidiani negli anni 1977, 1987, 1997. *Minerva Psichiatrica. 41*: 189–201.
Marcuse, H. (1963). *The Obsolescence of Psychoanalysis*. Chicago: Black Swan, 1969.
Marini, M. (1981). Caravaggio e il Naturalismo Internazionale. In: *Cinquecento e Seicento: Storia dell'Arte Italiana 6** (pp. 347–445). Turin: Einaudi.
Martin-Cabré, L.J. (1997). Freud-Ferenczi: Controversy Terminable and Interminable. *Int. J. Psychoanal 78*: 105–114.
Martorell, A. & Coutanceau, R. (1998a). Inceste Pédofilique? Ou Abus Sexuel Incesteux sur Enfant(s). *Évol. Psychiat. 63*: 117–132.
Martorell, A. & Coutanceau, R. (1998b). Des Conduites Pédofiliques. Considerations Cliniques et Sociales. *L'Évol. Psyichiat. 63*: 35–67.
Marzi, A. (2002). Confidentiality and the Psychoanalytic Setting in Italy: Some Problematic Issues. Read at the EPF Congress, Prague.
Masson, J.M. (1984). *The Assault on Truth*. London: Faber & Faber.
Masson, J.M. (1985). *The Complete Letters of Sigmund Freud to Wilhelm Fliess, 1887–1904*. Cambridge, MA: Belknap.
Maura, E. & Peloso, P.F. (1999). *Lo Splendore della Ragione. Storia della Psichiatria Ligure nell'Epoca del Positivismo*. Genoa: La Clessidra.
Mayer-Gross, N., Slater, R. & Roth, M. (1954). *Clinical Psychiatry*. London: Cassell.

McDougall, J. (1982). Alexithymia, Psychosomatics, and Psychosis. *Int. J. Psychoanal. 9*: 379–388.
McDougall, J. (1986). *Theatres of the Mind. Illusion and Truth on the Psychoanalytic Stage.* London: Free Association Books.
McDougall, J. (1990). *Plea for a Measure of Abnormality.* London: Free Association Books.
McDougall, J. (1993). L'Addiction à l'Autre: Réflexions sur les Néosexualités et la Sexualité Addictive. In: A. Fine, A. Le Guen & A. Oppenheimer (Eds.), *Les Troubles de la Sexualité.* Paris: PUF.
Meltzer, D. (1973). *Sexual States of Mind.* StrathTay: Clunie Press.
Milella, M. (2001). *Pedofilia, Pedofilie:* Qualche Riflessione. Unpublished.
Miller, A. (1979). *The Drama of Being a Child.* London: Virago, 1997.
Miller, A. (1988). *Banished Knowledge.* New York: Anchor Press, 1991.
Moglie, G. (1940). *Manuale di Psichiatria.* Rome: Pozzi.
Molina, A. (1997). *Plenilunio.* Madrid: Punto de Lectura, 2008.
Mollon, P. (1998). *Remembering Trauma.* Chichester: Wiley.
Montherlant, H. de (1951). *La Ville dont le Prince est un Enfant.* Paris: Gallimard, 1967.
Moravia, S. (1998). La Violenza come Linguaggio della Vita Offesa. In: C. Bogliolo (Ed.), *Bambini e Violenza: Dalle Dinamiche Familiari all'Evento Sociale.* Florence: Del Cerro.
Morin, E. (1999). *La Tête Bien Faite.* Paris: Seuil.
Morselli, A. (1915). *Manuale di Psichiatria.* Naples: Idelson.
Mosse, G.L. (1985). *Nationalism and Sexuality.* New York: Howard Fertig.
Musatti, C. (1949). *Trattato di Psicoanalisi.* Turin: Boringhieri, 1977.
Musatti, C. (1987). Scienza e Mito: Un'inversione di Tendenza. In: *Chi ha Paura del Lupo Cattivo?* Rome: Editori Riuniti.
Nabokov, V. (1955). *Lolita.* London: Penguin, 1997.
Nemeroff, C.B. (1999). The Preeminent Role of Early Untoward Experience on Vulnerability to Major Psychiatric Disorders: The Nature-Nurture Controversy Revisited and Soon to be Resolved. *Mol. Psychiatry 4*: 106–108.
Neri, C. (1993). Commuting. In: R. Contardi, E. Gaburri & S. Vender, *Fattori Terapeutici nei Gruppi e nelle Istituzioni* (pp. 79–88). Rome: Borla.
Neri, C. (1996). *Gruppo.* Rome: Borla.
Neumann, E. (1949). *Origins and History of Consciousness.* London: Routledge, 1954.

Niccoli, O. (1995). *Il Seme della Violenza. Putti, Fanciulli e Mammoli nell'Italia tra Cinque e Seicento*. Bari: Laterza.
Nicolaïdis, G. & Nicolaïdis, N. (1993). Incorporation, Pédophilie, Inceste. *Rev. Franç. Psychanal. 57*: 507–514.
Nietzsche, F. (1878). *Human, All Too Human: A Book for Free Spirits*. Cambridge University Press, 1996.
Oberti, J. (1999). "Please Believe Me": Essere Presenti in una Guerra Etnica. *Riv. Psicoanal. 45*: 817–827.
O'Donohue, W. & Letourneau, E. (1993). A Brief Group Treatment for the Modification of Denial in Child Sexual Abusers: Outcome and Follow-up. *Child Abuse Negl. 17*: 299–304.
Ogden, T. (1982). *Projective Identification and Psychotherapeutic Technique*. New York: Aronson.
Ogden, T. (1994). *Subjects of Analysis*. London: Karnac.
Oliverio Ferraris, A. & Graziosi, B. (2001). *Pedofilia. Per Saperne di Più*. Bari: Laterza.
Pancheri, P. & Cassano, G. (1999). *Trattato Italiano di Psichiatria* (2nd ed). Milan: Masson.
Pandolfi, A.M. (2000). *Lo Sguardo Negato. Un Caso Clinico: Il Trattamento Psicoterapeutico*. Presentation to the conference "Il Contributo della Psicoanalisi alla Cura delle Psicosi", Bologna, 28–29 October.
Perrault, C. (1697). *Perrault's Fairy Tales* (trans. A.E. Johnson). Ware, Herts: Wordsworth Editions, 2004.
Person, E.S. (1985). Paraphilias and Gender Identity Disorders. In: J.O. Cavenar (Ed.), *Psychiatry, Vol. I* (pp. 447–465). Philadelphia: Lippincott.
Petrella, F. (1981). Ritorno del Rimosso nel Rimovente: dalla Definizione Metapsicologica alla Narrazione. *Gli Argonauti 11*: 265–278.
Petrella, F. (1997). Pedofilia. *Avvenimenti*, 9 July.
Petronius. *The Satyricon* (trans. P.G. Walsh). Oxford University Press, 2009.
Picard, C. (1951). Préface. In: P. Grimal, *Dictionnaire de la Mythologie Grecque et Romaine*. Paris: PUF, 1999.
Piccione, R. (1995). *Manuale di Psichiatria*. Rome: Bulzoni.
Pindar. *The Odes of Pindar* (trans. C.M. Bowra). London: Penguin, 1969.
Plato. *The Symposium* (trans. C. Gill). London: Penguin, 1999.
Ponti, G.L. & Fornari, U. (1995). *Il Fascino del Male. Crimini e Responsabilità nella Storia di Vita di Tre Serial Killer*. Milan: Cortina.
Popper, K.R. & Condry, J. (1994). *Cattiva Maestra Televisione*. Venice: Marsilio, 2002.

Porot, A. (1960). *Manuel Alphabétique de Psychiatrie et Therapeutique*. Paris: PUF.
Propp, V.J. (1928). *Morphology of the Folktale*. Austin: University of Texas Press, 1968.
Proust, M. (1919). *In the Shadow of Young Girls in Flower: In Search of Lost Time, Volume II*. London: Penguin, 2003.
Puget, J. (1995). Psychic Reality or Various Realities. *Int. J. Psychoanal.* 76: 29–34.
Puget, J. & Wender, L. (1982). Analista y Paciente en Mundos Superpuestos. *Psicoanálisis 4*: 503–536.
Racalbuto, A. (1999). Il Potere della Seduzione tra Libertà e Possesso. *Psiche 7*: 43–52.
Racamier, P.C. (1992). *Le Génie des Origines. Psychanayse et Psychoses*. Paris: Payot.
Rank, O. (1909). *The Myth of the Birth of the Hero*. Baltimore: Johns Hopkins University Press, 2004.
Raskovsky, A. (1973). *El Filicidio*. Buenos Aires: Orion.
Reda, G. (1982). *Trattato di Psichiatria*. Florence: USES.
Reiche, R. (1968). *Sexuality and Class Struggle*. London: New Left Books, 1970.
Reik, T. (1925). *The Compulsion to Confess: On the Psychoanalysis of Crime and Punishment*. New York: Farrar, Straus & Cudahy, 1959.
Resta, E. (1999). Preface. In: G. De Leo & I. Petruccelli (Eds.), *L'Abuso Sessuale Infantile e la Pedofilia* (pp. 9–11). Milan: Franco Angeli.
Rinaldi, L. (1997). Problemi e Prospettive del Lavoro in Équipe. In: A. Correale & L. Rinaldi, *Quale Psicoanalisi per le Psicosi?* (pp. 281–305). Milan: Cortina.
Roccato, P. (1998). Dal Paziente Freudiano al Paziente Catodico. *Micromega 3*: 218–229.
Roccia, C. & Foti, C. (1994). Pedofilia: Dal Bambino Abusato all'Adulto Perverso. In: C. Roccia & C. Foti (Eds.), *L'Abuso Sessuale sui Minori. Educazione Sessuale, Prevenzione, Trattamento* (pp. 185–202). Milan: Unicopli.
Róheim, G. (1945). *The Eternal Ones of the Dream*. New York: International Universities Press.
Rosenfeld, H. (1987). *Impasse and Interpretation: Therapeutic and Anti-Therapeutic Factors in the Psychoanalytic Treatment of Psychotic, Borderline and Neurotic Patients*. London: Tavistock.
Rossini, R. (1971). *Trattato di Psichiatria*. Bologna: Cappelli.
Rousseau, J.-J. (1762). *Emile*. New York: Basic Books, 1979.

Rycroft, C. (1968). *A Critical Dictionary of Psychoanalysis*. London: Penguin, 2005.
Sabato, E. (1998). *Antes del Fin: Memorias*. Buenos Aires: Seix Barral.
Sandler, J. (1967). Trauma, Strain and Development. In: S. Furst (Ed.), *Psychic Trauma* (pp. 154–174). New York: Basic Books.
Sandler, J. (2000). *Clinical and Observational Psychoanalytic Research: Roots of a Controversy*. London: Karnac.
Sandler, J. & Fonagy, P. (1997). *Recovered Memories of Abuse: True or False?* London: Karnac.
Sapir, M. (1997). Quelques Réflexions sur le Trauma. *Champ Psychosomatique 38*: 11–22.
Sarteschi, P. & Maggini, C. (1982). *Manuale di Psichiatria*. Noceto (Parma): SBM.
Scaraffia, G. (1987). *Infanzia*. Palermo: Sellerio.
Scardaccione, G. & Baldry, A. (1997). Tipologia dell'Abuso Sessuale e Intervento Giudiziario. *Rass. It. Criminol. 8*: 127–150.
Scarry, E. (1985). *The Body in Pain: The Making and Unmaking of the World*. Oxford: Oxford University Press.
Schermer, V.L. & Pines, M. (1994). *Ring of Fire. Primitive Affects and Object Relations in Group Psychotherapy*. London: Routledge.
Schinaia, C. (1999). Chi ha Paura del Lupo Cattivo? Appunti e Divagazioni su Stupratori e Pedofili. *La Via del Sale 3*: 55–65.
Schinaia, C. (2000). Pedofilia, Pedofilias. *Rev. de Psicoanalisis*, *Número Especial Internacional "Violencia y perversidad" 7*: 79–101.
Scoppa, A. (1972). *Trattato di Psichiatria Clinica Moderna*. Rome: SEU.
Segal, H. (1957). Notes on Symbol Formation. *Int. J. Psychoanal. 38*: 391–397.
Semi, A.A. (1989). Psiconevrosi e Trauma. In: *Trattato di Psicoanalisi*, *Vol. 2*. Milan: Cortina.
Sergent, B. (1986). *Homosexuality in Greek Myth*. Boston: Beacon Press.
Servadio, E. (1967). Psicologia e Psicopatologia del Fotografare. *Ulisse 20*: 63–67.
Shafer, R. (1983). *The Analytic Attitude*. New York: Basic Books.
Simon, R.J. (1999). *Bad Men Do What Good Men Dream*. Arlington, VA: American Psychiatric Publishing, 2008.
Simonelli, C. & Petruccelli, I. (1999). L'Autore e il Contesto Socioculturale. In: G. De Leo & I. Petruccelli (Eds.), *L'Abuso Sessuale Infantile e la Pedofilia* (pp. 29–42). Milan: Franco Angeli.

Singer, I.B. (1998). *Shadows on the Hudson*. New York: Farrar Straus & Giroux, 2008.
Sironi, F. (1999). *Bourreaux et Victimes: Psychologie de la Torture*. Paris: Odile Jacob.
Socarides, C.W. (1959). Meaning and Content of a Paedophilic Perversion. *J. Amer. Psychoanal. Assn. 7*: 84–87.
Socarides, C.W. (1988). *The Preoedipal Origin and Psychoanalytic Therapy of Sexual Perversions*. Madison, CT: International Universities Press.
Socarides, C.W. & Loeb, L.R. (2004). *The Mind of the Paedophile: Psychoanalytic Perspectives*. London: Karnac.
Sohn, A-M. (1989). Les Attentats à la Pudeur sur les Fillettes en France (1870–1939) et la Sexualité Quotidienne. In: A. Corbin (Ed.), *Violences Sexuelles*. Paris: Imago.
Spence, P.D. (1982). *Narrative Truth and Historical Truth*. London: Norton.
Speziale-Bagliacca, R. (1980). *Formazione e Percezione Psicoanalitica*. Milan: Feltrinelli.
Speziale-Bagliacca, R. (1997). *Guilt: Revenge, Remorse and Responsibility after Freud*. London: Routledge, 2004.
Steiner, J. (1993). *Psychic Retreats. Pathological Organizations in Psychotic, Neurotic and Borderline Patients*. London: Routledge.
Steiner, J. (2000). Containement, Enactment and Communication. *Int. J. Psychoanal. 81*: 245–255.
Stoller, R.J. (1975). *Perversion: The Erotic Form of Hatred*. London: Karnac, 1986.
Stoller, R.J. (1985). *Observing the Erotic Imagination*. New Haven, CT: Yale University Press.
Sulloway, F.J. (1979). *Freud, Biologist of the Mind: Beyond the Psychoanalytic Legend*. New York: Basic Books.
Süskind, P. (1985). *Perfume*. London: Penguin, 2007.
Svevo, I. (1923). *Zeno's Conscience*. London: Penguin, 2002.
Székács, J. (1987). Le Favole come Fonte di Interpretazione. In: A.M. Accerboni et al, *La Cultura Psicoanalitica: Atti del Convegno, Trieste 5–8 dicembre 1985*. Pordenone: Tesi.
Szwec, G. (1993). Faudra Mieux Surveiller les Petits! *Rev. Franç. Psychan. 57*: 591–603.
Tamaro, S. (1991). Love. In: *For Solo Voice*. London: Vintage, 1997.
Tanzi, E. (1905). *Malattie Mentali*. Milan: Società Editrice Libraria.

Tanzi, E. & Lugaro, E. (1916). *Malattie Mentali*. Milan: Società Editrice Libraria.
Taschizki, T. von (1997). Wilhelm von Gloeden. In: *Fotografia del XX Secolo, Museum Ludwig, Köln*. Cologne: Taschen.
Tasset, J.M. (1996). Risveglio, Vita e Silenzio. In: *Omaggio a Balthus* (pp. 17–21). Milan: Skira.
Thomä, H. & Kächele, H. (1988). *Lehrbuch der Psychoanalytischen Therapie*, Vol. 2: *Praxis*. Berlin: Springer.
Thorstad, D. (1990). Man/Boy Love and the American Gay Movement. *J. Homosex. 20*: 251–274.
Thuiller, J. (1964). Greuze and Genre Painting. In: J. Thuillier & A. Chatelet, *French Painting from Le Nain to Fragonard*. Geneva: Skira.
Todisco, A. (1985). Dialogo con Lopez a Proposito di Masson. *Gli Argonauti 25*: 83–90.
Torre, M. (1969). *Psichiatria*. Turin: UTET.
Tournier, M. (1970). *The Erl-King*. London: Fontana, 1974.
Tournier, M. (1975). *Gemini* [*Les Météores*]. Baltimore, MA: John Hopkins University Press, 1998.
Tournier, M. (1977). *The Wind Spirit*. London: Methuen, 1991.
Tournier, M. (1983). Gilles and Jeanne. New York: French & European Publications, 1985.
Tuckett, D. (2000). Reporting Clinical Events in the "Journal": Towards the Construction of a Special Case. *Int. J. Psychoanal. 81*: 1065–1069.
Turillazzi Manfredi, S. (1994). *Le Certezze Perdute della Psicoanalisi Clinica*. Milan: Cortina.
Tylim, I. (1999). Group Supervision and Psychoanalytic Process. *Int. J. Group Psychother. 49*: 181–195.
Unità di Crisi "Luciana Nissim" (2000). Appunti da una Guerra Etnica. *La Via del Sale 3*: 51–54.
Van der Kolk, B.A. (1987). *Psychological Trauma*. Washington DC: American Psychiatric Press.
Vargas Llosa, M. (1988). *In Praise of the Stepmother*. London: Penguin, 1991.
Vassalli, A. (1994). Preface. In: C. Roccia & C. Foti (Eds.), *L'Abuso Sessuale sui Minori: Educazione Sessuale, Prevenzione, Trattamento*. Milan: Unicopli.
Vattimo, G. (1995). Introduction. In: Filosofia '94. Bari: Laterza.
Vinci, S. (1997). *What We Don't Know About Children*. New York: Knopf, 2000.

Weininger, O. (1903). *Sex and Character*. Bloomington, IN: Indiana University Press, 2005.
Weitbrecht, H.J. (1963). *Psychiatrie im Grundriss*. Springer, Berlin.
Williams, G. (1997). *Internal Landscapes and Foreign Bodies: Eating Disorders and Other Pathologies*. London: Duckworth.
Winnicott, D.W. (1974). Fear of Breakdown. *Int. R. Psychoanal. 1*: 103–107.
World Health Organisation (1992). *Classification of Mental and Behavioural Disorders* (ICD-10). Geneva: WHO.
Yoshimoto, B. (1990). *NP*. London: Faber & Faber, 2001.
Yourcenar, M. (1951). *Memoirs of Hadrian*. London: Penguin, 2000.
Zerbi Schwartz, L. (1998). Trauma nella Sessualità: Il Trattamento Analitico dell'Abuso Incestuoso Infantile. *Riv. di Psicoanal. 44*: 529–547.
Zerbi Schwartz, L. (2000). I Traumi Abusivi Incestuosi: Una Discussione con Jody Davies, Peter Fonagy, Glen Gabbard e Leonard Shengold su Alcuni Problemi Teorici. *Gli Argonauti 84*: 17–36.

INDEX

Aberrant inquisitorial mechanism 105
Adult sexuality 188
Adult's defensive apparatus 104
Adult-child relationship 103
Adultification 17
The Aetiology of Hysteria 147
Agamemnon 43
Aitkenhead, Decca
  The Guardian 23
Albert, Laura 113
Alexandre Bjerre de Boismont 119
Alexithymia 5
Allende, Isabel, *The Stories of Eva Luna* 183
Amado, Jorge 179
American forensic psychiatrist 7
American Psychiatric Association 131
  Diagnostic and Statistical Manual of Mental Disorders (DSM) 131
Amphisexuality 128
Andersen, Hans Christian 66
  Picture Book Without Pictures 64
Androgenic hormones 135
Antagonism 63
Anthropophagy 49–56
Anti-androgen drugs 135
Antisocial personality 140
Apollo's duplicity 43
Apollonian nostalgic and fantastic heaven 167
Appleyard, Bryan 23
Arfouilloux 36
Ariès 103
Arieti's *American Handbook of Psychiatry* 130
Aristophanes cites Falete 44
Arrogant aggressiveness 155
Aschenbach, Gustav 166, 185
Athenian law 92
Augustan Age 96

Bacchus 44
Baglione, painter 202
Bales, Kevin 26
Barale 140
Baruk's *Traité de Psychiatrie* 130
Bazzi's *Psicologia Medica* 130
Behavioural psychologists 138
Bergler theory 141
Bernal, Juan José 183
Bertolucci's film *Novecento* 138
Bettelheim 71
    Little Red Riding Hood 84
Bianchi, Leonardo, *Trattato di psichiatria* 126
Bilderbuch ohne Bilder 88
Bion 111
    concept of maternal 111
Black-and-white moralistic message 78
Bleuler, *Textbook of Psychiatry* 126
Blissett, Luther 14, 17
    Lasciate che i Bimbi 17
Bonaparte, Marie 81
Bonnetaud 12–13
    repercussions for the child 13
Bouchet-Kervella 140, 191
Brachycephalic 28
Brazilian psychoanalytic society 213
Brisset's *Manuel de Psychiatrie* 130
Brouardel, Paul 147
Brutality 119

Calvino, Italo 61
    co-operation 62
    Tales of Mother Goose 63
Camarca, Claudio
    I Santi Innocenti 25
Campailla's *Manuale di Psichiatria* 130
Campbell's *Psychiatric Dictionary* 130
Cannibalism 81

Capetti, Ferrante 122
Caravaggio's paintings 202
Carmina Burana 102
Carrasco 105
Carroll, Lewis 204
Castration anxiety 156
Cattiva Maestra Televisione 6
Cerebral-organic disease 129
Chabert's myths constitute 35
Chasseguet-Smirgel 158, 163
Chemical castration 135
Child photography 108
Childolatry 27
Children's Newspaper 87
Child sexual abuse 101, 104, 112
    intergenerational transmission of 208
Christian Emperor Justinian 96
Christianity, central issue 102
Chrysippus 45, 47–49
Church council 102
Cithaeron, Mount 42
Clergyman 105
Cognitive distortions 133
Cognitive-behavioural
    techniques 137
    therapy 136
Coherent sadistic and masochistic behavioural model 158
Collective pseudonym 14
Colli 43
Collodi 63
Collusive pseudo-freedom 206
Comic-like technological abstraction 4
Communication 2–5
    value 3
The Compulsion to Confess 10
Compulsory therapies 10
Constitutional neurasthenia 117
Conviviality, pleasure of 3
Co-operation 62, 67

INDEX   293

Cooper, Merian Creelman
 King Kong 18
Countertransference
 enactments 212
Cruel and aberrant inquisitorial
 mechanism 105
Cultural transmission 27

Dalai Lama, Nobel Peace Prize 7
Danet, Jean 12
Darbieto, Jehannico 100
De Martis 163
De Zulueta 142
Dead Poets Society 238
De-animation of human beings 5
Deconstructability 5
Degenerationism 119, 125
Dehumanisation 9
Delusions and Dreams 6
De Masi 162
 sexualisation 159
 theories 139, 154
DeMause 102
 central mechanism 103
 child sexual abuse 104
 psycho-historical ideas of 103
 psychological mechanism 104
Demeter 46
Depression 2
Destructive sadism 78
De-symbolisation of events 5
Dettore 132
Devereux 47, 53
*Diagnostic and Statistical Manual
 of Mental Disorders* (DSM) 131
Die Vogelmacherin 105
Dionysus 42–43
Disorganised-disorientated
 behaviour 208
Diverse and complex
 mechanisms 142
Dodgson, Charles 204
Dogliani 11

Dolichocephalic 28
Dora's treatment 110
Dostoevsky 116
Dream-symbolism 33
DSM-IV 132
Dumont, Virginie
 J'ai Peur du Monsieur 20

Ego development 155
Egoistical attitude 1
Egyptian fairy story 74,
 78–79
Eisenstein, Sergei 3
Eromenoi 93
Eromenos 91
Eros
 Socrates and Plato description 91
 Eros paidagogos 91
Eurydice, death of 44

False Memory Syndrome
 Foundation 151
Fascism 28
Fenichel 143
Ferriani, Lino 116
 Nuova Antologia 116
Ferrus, Guillaume 119
Finkelor 133
Forel, August 120
Foucault, Michel
 comment on the case 12
 vindication 12
Foville, Achille 119
Frankfurt School 18
Franz, Marie-Louise von
 Jungian psychologist 61
Freud, Anna 3, 6–7, 13
 A Child is Being Beaten 156
 Beyond the Pleasure
  Principle 28
 Civilization and its
  Discontents 111
 concomitant self-analysis 110

Criminals from a Sense
of Guilt 10
early formulations 112
Introductory Lectures on
Psychoanalysis 110, 144
The Life Story of a Great Sinner 189
myth of Oedipus 37
mythopoetic effects 32
On Narcissism 143
socialisation 27
theories of early trauma
on health and mental
disturbances 211
theories 109
thinking 144
Freudian child 109

Gabbard 207
relational features of
paedophile patient 215
Ganymede 43–44, 53
Gardens, Kensington 193
Gargani
teacher-pupil relationship 98
Gide, André, *Corydon* 12
paedophilia 12
Gilles de Rais 182
Gillespie's *Texbook of Psychiatry for
Students and Practitioners* 130
Giolla, Pietro 138
Girard's theory of sacrificial
victim 24
Glover theory 141, 155
Glueck 140
G, *maître d'hotel* 219–233
aggressive aspects 228
aggressiveness 230
attitude annoys 229
behaviours 221, 223
capacity 227
case 221
destructive violence 230
difficulty 227

feelings of annoyance 227
first experience of paedophile
love 222
La Città Ideale 227
mother 225
personal story 220
pseudo-intimacy 225
sexual relationships 221
work experience 226
Gombrowicz, Witold
Pornography 199
Gothic period 102
Gozzano's *Compendio di
Psichiatria* 130
Gratuitousness 1
Graves, Ancient Greek mythology
mirrors 35–36
Green
myth functions as
representation 35
paedophilia 142–143
reverie 112
Greuze, Jean-Baptiste 206
Grien, Hans Baldung 103
Grimm, Brothers 63, 75
Allerleirauh 74
Complete Fairy Tales 79
Donkey Skin 75, 79, 83
fairy story 83
fireside 63
Guasto 112
Guilty child 106–113
Augustine's and Martin
Luther's thinking 106
Christian doctrine 106
Gulf war 4

Hadrian 168–172
great love and great defeat 171
Hansel and Gretel 63, 83
Hanus and Le Guillou-Eliet's
*Psychiatrie Intégrée
de l'Etudiant* 130

Harpalyce 52
Hasler, Eveline 105
Henry, Iron 62
Heracles 43
Heterosexual relationships 97
Hocquenghem, Guy 12
Homeric-Arcadian life 204
Homicidal extreme 161
Homophilia 100
Homosexuality 94, 96, 116, 121
Hugo, Victor
  The Laughing Man 165
Humbert Humbert 172
Hyacinthus 43
Hyperbolic masks 5
Hypnosis 3
Hypnotic effect 3

Infantile sexuality 12
Innocent child 106–113
  integrity and relational
    capacity 111
  libidinal potential 112
  natural integrity 112
  Oedipus attitude 110
  projections 112
  sexuality 109
  vital lymph to counteract 194
Instinctive cunning 61
Integrated defence 4
Intergenerational cycle of abuse 208
Intergenerational intimacy 14
Intrapsychic mediation 152
Italian national dailies 21

Japanese animated cartoons 3
Jolles 72
Jones 14
Joseph, Betty 156
Judaeo-Christian tradition 97
Jung
  mythological theme 34
Jungian concepts 34

Justiniano Duarte da Rosa 179
  paedophilia 187

Karpman 155
Kerényi 34
  compares mythology 34
Kernberg 140
Khan, Masud 112, 152, 159
  theory 142
Kidnapping 55
Klein, Melanie 68, 111
  projective identification 105
Knossos 50
Kraepelin, *Clinical Psychiatry* 126
Krafft-Ebing 116–117, 119–120, 147
  diversity of paedophilic
    behaviours 122
  Friedrich's Blätter 118
  masturbation 124
  Psychopathia Sexualis 138
  thought 119

Lacanian 112
Ladurie, Le Roy 100
Laius 45, 47–49
Lang, Fritz
  The Monster of Düsseldorf 22
Lantéri-Laura 115
Leguay, Jean-Pierre 100
Levi, Primo 213
LHRH agonists 135
Libidinal frustrations 155
Libidinal-emotional conflicts 36
Lichtenberg, concept of *model
    scenes* 198
Literary criticism 63
Little Red Riding Hood 82–85
Llosa, Mario Vargas 184
Logography, legal 94
Lolita 174
Lombroso, Cesare 108
Lopez
  grand themes of myth 36

Lucrecia, Doña 184
Lüthi 58, 63
Lycaon 49
Lydia 45

Maggini's *Manuale di Psichiatria* 130
Magnan, Victor 119
Magris 5
   teacher-pupil relationship 98
Malaparte, Curzio
   The Skin 116
Malignant narcissism 140
Malot's *Nobody's Boy* 166
Manichean character 22
Mann, Sally, *Immediate Family* 205
Mann, Thomas 33
   Das Gesetz 11
   Death in Venice 166
   parallels between myth and psychology 33
Marcuse, Herbert 18
   repressive desublimation 108
Marcusian allusions 28
Martin-Cabré, Analysis Terminable and Interminable 150
Masochism 190
Materialisation of childhood 27
Mayer-Gross, *Clinical Psychiatry* 130
McDougall, Joyce 5
Meltzer 110, 157
Memoirs of Hadrian 168
Mental sexuality 145
Metapsychological model 81
Microphysics of power 12
Micro-social
   groups 1
   interests 1
Miller, Alice 20, 154
Molina's novel *Plenilunio* 180
Moll, Albert 138
Moralisation 107
Mother Earth 41

Musatti, Cesare 8
Myth
   child in 42–43
   Greek 35, 49
   of Uranus 41
   paedophilia in 43
Mythology 32–35
   Arfouilloux points 37
   Brenman's view 37
   Chabert's view 35
   classical 41
   Davide Lopez's view 41
   Franz's view 39
   Graves 35
   Green view 35
   Lopez's opinion 41
   olympic 41
   origin 40–42
   Roman mythology the divinity 37

Nabokov, Vladimir 172
   Lolita 183
Narcissism
   destructive 161
   malignant 161
   sense of 8
Narcissistic
   exaltation 78
   fragility 192
   seduction 15
   sexuality 140
   personality disorder 161
Nazi
   atrocities 224
   regime 87
Nazism 28
Nechaev, Sergei 176
Nemeroff 211
Neolithic Europe 40
Neo-Platonists 32
Neosexual plot 153

Neo-sexuality 158
Neumann 36
Neurosis 111
Nicolaïdis and Nicolaïdis 81
Nicomedia 168
Nightingale and Lucrecia 183
Nili, Caput 147
No entry syndrome 113
Nomos 91
Non-sexual destructive element 110

Oedipal hate 36
Oedipus cursed lines, genealogy of 37
Oligophrenics, sexually abnormal behaviour 126
Olympian
   equilibrium 36
   scene 55
Olympic mythology 41
Omega function 112
On Dreams 33
Oral-incorporative paedophilic fantasies 81–87

Paedophile-child relationship 255
Paedophiles 107, 120
   analyst 9
   attitudes 23
   child world 233
   consciousness of being ill 10
   criminalisation 14
   diverse behaviours 128
   ethno-historical relativity 14
   heterosexual 128
   histories of 206
   homosexual 128
   ideology 256
   imaginary highlights 192
   imagination 16
   myth and 31
   paradise 85
   personality 190
   pleasure 16
   presumption of 107
   relationship with 206–217
   Sidney Cooke 23
   source of gratification 15
   transition 185
   victim 183–184
Paedophilia 1, 18, 107, 127, 141
   anthropophagy 49–56
   as revenge 180–181
   child 172–174
   co-determinism of 135
   Diagnostic and Statistical Manual of Mental Disorders (DSM) 131
   dogmas of 91
   erotic 121
   function of resolving internal conflicts 137
   Gilles et Jeanne 138
   hypocritical 174–176
   imperial 168–172
   in Bianchi, Leonardo, *Trattato di psichiatria* 126
   in medical and psychiatric thought 115–137
   in middle ages 97–106
   in myths 43–44
   Judaeo-Christian tradition 97
   love and death in sadistic 182–183
   non-acted tendency 202
   notes on history 89–113
   ogre 179–180
   polite 166–168
   positivism 122
   problems of 120
   psychoanalysis 139–162
   sexual freedom and social acceptance of 94
   social corruption 94

social organisation of 29
transgressive 176–179
Paedophilic
    collector syndrome 86
    homosexual 100
    instincts 107
    personality 83
    perversion, case of 219–233, 245
    perversity, case of 235–247
    promises 77
Paedophilic behaviour 101, 105
    Gabbard's view 161
    polymorphism of 141
    social and cultural aspects 1
Paedophilic fantasies, fairy tales 57–87
    Bettelheim's view 67
    Fireside Fairy Tales 63
    migration 62
    optimism and pessimism in 60
    oral-incorporative 81–87
    supernatural intervention 61
    theories of fairy tale 58–64
Paedophilic personalities and behaviours
    definition and typology 165–188
Paedophilic relationship 189–217
    asymmetrical 194
    principal features of 194–200
    repetitive and monotonous 196–197
Pan, Peter 193
Pasolini, Pier Paolo 195
Pathological
    personality 212
    sexuality 131
Pathos and cynicism 4
Patient's infantile anxieties 9
Pausanias 92
Pedagogic system 94
Pederasty 96

Augustan Age 96
Pelops story 45–47
Peloso, Paolo F. 115, 165
Peretti, Luisella 235, 249
Perrault
    Little Red Riding Hood 82
    Sleeping Beauty 83
Personality organisation 140
Perverse
    child 111
    escalation 199
    mechanism 1
    organisation 159
    pathology 227
    sexuality 110
Perversion 11, 140, 142, 159–162
    castration anxiety in 155
    criminal 157–158
    drug addictive 157
    habitual 157–158
    perversity 159–162
    sadomasochistic 190
    sexual 140
Perversity 159–162
Pessimism and aggressiveness 22
Petronius's *Satyricon* 224
Pezzoni, Franca 57
Philammon 43
Phrenological abnormality 120
Piazza's *Trattato di Psichiatria e Sociopsichiatria* 130
Piccione's *Manuale di Psichiatria* 131
Picture Book Without Pictures 87
Pinocchio 85, 88
Pitto, Clara 31
Plenilunio 180–181
Pluto 45
P, middle-aged man 235
    aggressiveness 244
    description of his wife 237
    fears dependence 242
    furious attacks 243

gesture 242
idealisation of first part of his life 238
intolerance of dependence 240
mental processes 243
narcissistic projections 244
sadomasochistic relational modalities 239
school programme-revision meetings 237
seductiveness and aggressiveness 240
self-evocative availability 244
self-object representations 242
Political asceticism 18
Political-religious resentment 105
Polymorphism 110
Popper, Karl 6
Pornography 24
Porot's, *Manuel Alphabetique de Psychiatrie* 128
Poseidon 46
Post-Kleinian psychoanalysts 37
Postmodernity 5
Premature sexual experience 83
Pre-oedipal and oedipal conflicts 140
Pre-Olympian
  conception 53
  Greek mythology anthropophagy 52
Priggish catholic mentality 130
Propp, Vladimir
  functions 59
  Morphology of the Folktale 58
Provisional identities 5
Pseudo-modern stance 6
Psychiatric and Neurological Society of Vienna 147
Psychiatrist 29
Psychic
  complexity 132
  nuclei, multiplicity of 5
  skin 255
Psychoanalysis 151
  fairy tale 64–69
  Lingiardi's view 151
  therapeutic objectives of 8
Psychoanalysis and mythology 32
  parallels between 33
Psychoanalysis and paedophilia 139–162
Psychoanalytical
  standpoint 2
  treatment 4, 24
Psychoanalytic journey 149
  Masson's view 150
Psychoanalytic psychotherapy 193
Psychodynamic understanding 140
Psycho-emotional development 11, 153
Psychogenesis 103
Psycho-historical theories 104
Psychological
  homeostasis 104
  mechanism 104
  striptease acts 3
Psychopathic personalities 125
Psychopathological
  disturbances 133
  severity 257
Psychopathology 132
Psychosexual
  development 5
  disturbances 193
Psychosis 140
Psychotic
  behaviour 140
  personality 38
  picture 139
Puget, theory of "superimposed worlds" 213
Pygmalion interests 222
Pythagoreans and Stoics 32

Raskovsky 191
Recognizable 'nucleus' 5
Reda's *Trattato di Psichiatria* 130
Reiche, Reimut 18
   repressive desublimation 108
Reik, Theodor 10
Relapse prevention 137
Religious obscurantism 105
Repressive desublimation 18
Róheim, Géza 67
Roman culture 96
Roman mythology the divinity 37
Rops, Félicien 6
   etching 7
Rossellini, Roberto
   Germany Year Zero 28–29
Rossi's *Trattato di Psichiatria* 131
Rousseau's theories 106

Sabato, Ernesto 224
Sadock's *Comprehensive Textbook of Psychiatry* 131
Sambia people of New Guinea 14
Sapir 17
Satyriasis 120
Scheherazade 62
Schinaia, Cosimo 31, 57, 115, 165, 235, 249
Schizophrenic disturbance 140
Schoedsack, Ernest Beaumont 18
Schwarz, Zerbi 152, 240, 246
Scoppa's *Trattato di Psichiatria Clinica Moderna* 130
Second World War 116, 128
Secular dreams, of youthful humanity 33
Segal, Hanna 6
Self-regulation processes 136
Senile dementia 120
Serbia war 4
Sergent 44
Sex-murderer 149

Sex-phobic
   morality 18
   visions 20
Sexual
   abusers 197
   activity 131
   appetite 120
   appropriation 29
   deviation 131
   friendship 127
   games 221
   identity 15
   intercourse 148
   inversion 127
   offences 107
   paedophilic fantasies 70–81
   perversions 115, 160
   perversity 159, 161
   polymorphism 11
   pseudo-liberty 18
   psychopathy, Krafft-Ebing's monograph on 115
   relationships 156
   satisfaction 194
   traumas 145, 148, 225
   violence 21, 28
Sexual abuse 14, 136
   of children 20, 146, 149
Sexualisation 156, 158–159
Sexually abnormal behaviour, oligophrenics 126
Sexually abusive behaviours 89
Sexuology, modern 138
Shame mechanisms 220
Sifneos, Peter 5
Simmonet, Jehan 100
Simon, Robert J. 7
Sironi, Françoise 213
Socarides 156
Social corruption 94
Social hypocrisy 11
Socio-cultural background 145

Socio-economic reality 101
Sodomy 90
Sohn, Anne-Marie 106
Soleil, Roi 87
Spartan society 113
Spasmodic attention 21
Speziale-Bagliacca 5
Stavrogin's confession 189, 176
Stevenson's *Kidnapped* 166
Stymphalus 46
Superego 65, 111
    deteriorate 140
Supreme Inquisition 105
Süskind's *Perfume* 117
Swabia, Upper 105

Tabò, Giuseppina 165
Tamaro, Susanna, *For Solo Voice* 174
Tantalus 46
Tardieu, Ambroise 119
Teacher-pupil relationship 91,
    98–99
        Gargani 98–99
        Magris 98–99
Thamyris 43
Thyestes 46
Tikhon, Bishop 176
Titanic to Olympian mythology 51
Torre's *Psichiatria* 130
Torturer-victim
    relationship 213
Totem and Taboo 67
Tournier, Michel 28, 153, 182
    The Erl-King 85
    Gilles et Jeanne 80
Toyland children 85
Transference-countertransference
    relationship 38, 258
Trans-temporal diffusion 255

Trans-temporal propagation 255
Trauma-perversion sequence 154

Uncritical idealisation 99
Urania, Aphrodite 44

Vattimo, Gianni 5
Vianna, Helena Besserman 213
Vinci, Simona 17
    What We Don't Know About
        Children 199
Visconti, Luchino
    The Damned 28, 178
von Gloeden, Wilhelm 205
Voyeuristic transmutations 204

Weininger, *Sex and Character* 127
Weitbrecht, *Psychiatrie im*
    Grundriss 129
Wender theory of "superimposed
    worlds" 213
What We Don't Know About
    Children 17
Wicked Child 183
Williams, *eating disorders* 112
Winnicott 111
    Fear of Breakdown 211
    sense 260
Winter Notes on Summer
    Impressions 116
World Health Organisation's
    ICD-10 132

Yoshimoto, Banana, *NP* 197
Yourcenar, Marguerite 168
Youthophilia 28

Zagreus 50
Zeus 42–45, 49